P9-DFV-431

How to Prepare for the

MAT

Miller Analogies Test

Sixth Edition

ROBERT J. STERNBERG

IBM Professor of
Psychology and Education
at Yale University

All inquiries should be addressed to:
Barron's Educational Series, Inc.
250 Wireless Boulevard
Hauppauge, New York 11788

Library of Congress Catalog Card No. 93-43357
International Standard Book No. 0-8120-1776-5

Library of Congress Cataloging-in-Publication Data

Sternberg, Robert J.
Barron's how to prepare for the MAT Miller analogies test / Robert J. Sternberg—6th ed.
p. cm.
Includes bibliographical references.
ISBN 0-8120-1776-5
1. Miller analogies test—Study guides. I. How to prepare for the MAT Miller analogies test. II. Title.
LB2367.6.S74 1994
378.1' 664—dc20

93-43357
CIP

Printed in the United States of America

4567 100 98765432

Contents

Part Three

Part Four

Introduction

What This Book Can Do for You

The most this book can do for you is to help bring you to the point where your performance on the *Miller Analogies Test (MAT)* is the best of which you are capable. If the book succeeds in doing so, it has succeeded admirably, and so have you.

Many individuals do not reveal their true abilities on the *MAT* and other standardized tests. There are several reasons why this is so:

1. *The mystique of standardized tests.* One reason for underperformance stems from the aura of mystery that surrounds standardized tests. The mystique of standardized tests evolves from three common misconceptions. The first misconception is that the tests evaluate the whole person. In fact, the tests evaluate just a small segment of the person's behavior, and their evaluation of this small segment of behavior is, as we shall soon see, highly fallible. A second misconception is that there is nothing one can do to improve one's test performance, since the tests measure something that is innate rather than something that is learned. In fact, there is a great deal you can do to improve your test score, and in reading this book and in working on the practice tests, you are already doing it. The third misconception is an emotional one—it is the feeling of awe that people often have when faced with something they don't understand. By the time you are done with this book, however, you will understand the *Miller Analogies Test* very well, and what once seemed mysterious to you will be quite familiar.

   There are certain basic facts about the *MAT* that anyone who is to take the test ought to know. Some of these facts are readily available to the public through various pamphlets provided by the test publisher, but others are not. Many of the most important facts are among the least well known. Parts Two and Six of this book contain the basic facts that you ought to know about the *MAT*.

2. *Unfamiliarity with test-taking strategies and skills.* Many individuals never acquire the test-taking strategies and skills that would enable them to optimize their performance on the *MAT*. As a result, they make blunders that reflect their deficiencies in test-taking rather than in intellectual ability. Part Three of this book shows you just what an analogy is, the types of analogies that appear on the *MAT*, and the strategies you can employ to systematically approach *MAT* problems. Included are helpful hints that will prove useful to you in preparing for and then taking the actual test.

   Part Five will help you in learning the words commonly used on the *MAT* and in reviewing some of the basic facts from the content areas used in the test. As you will see, the number of questions from each content area is small, and an extensive review of all possible areas is simply unfeasible.

3. *Lack of practice in taking MAT-type tests.* It is one thing to have developed a repertoire of test-taking strategies and skills, but it is another to readily apply them. Part Four of this book contains ten practice tests that are similar in difficulty, content, and form to the actual *MAT*. Like the actual test, each practice test has 100 items, is timed for 50 minutes, and requires a multiple-choice answer selection process from among four possible alternatives. As in the real test, answers are recorded on a separate answer sheet. By taking these tests, you will have an opportunity to utilize the test-taking strategies that you will acquire. You will build up a facility with *MAT*-type questions so that when you take the actual test, you will not have to waste time and points warming up to the types of questions that appear.

   Before reading about the *MAT* and how to improve your performance on it, take the pretest in Part One to give yourself a sense of what the *MAT* is like. You will then stand to profit more from the suggestions that follow.

4. *Misconception about the nature of intelligence.* Frequently, we make the mistake of believing that there is nothing more to intelligence than what tests such as the *MAT* measure. Nothing could be further from the truth, as you will discover in Part Seven of this book.

Part One Pretest

DIRECTIONS: In each of the following questions, you will find three initial terms and, in parentheses, four designated answer options *a*, *b*, *c*, and *d*. You are to select from the four answer options the one that best completes the analogy with the three initial terms. To record your answers, use the answer sheet at the back of the book.

TIME: *50 minutes*

1. GRAY : ELEPHANT :: (*a.* white, *b.* brown, *c.* green, *d.* gray) : GRIZZLY BEAR
2. (*a.* ratatouille, *b.* vermouth, *c.* lemonade, *d.* gin) : EAT :: MANHATTAN : DRINK
3. MOON : PLANET :: (*a.* asteroid, *b.* sun, *c.* planet, *d.* Orion) : STAR
4. JOHN : (*a.* Jackson, *b.* Adams, *c.* Pierce, *d.* Garfield) :: ANDREW : JOHNSON
5. 1 + 2 : MARCH :: 12 – 3 : (*a.* September, *b.* October, *c.* November, *d.* December)
6. CANNON : CANNON :: STIMULI : (*a.* stimulation, *b.* stimuluses, *c.* stimulate, *d.* stimulus)
7. GRAPES : WINE :: (*a.* alcohol, *b.* hops, *c.* alfalfa, *d.* kemp) : BEER
8. SCROOGE : GREEDY :: (*a.* Antony, *b.* Portia, *c.* Cassius, *d.* Macduff) : TREACHEROUS
9. (*a.* hurricane, *b.* hail, *c.* sleet, *d.* thunder) : RAIN :: BLIZZARD : SNOW
10. BLANC : ALPS :: EVEREST : (*a.* Andes, *b.* Himalayas, *c.* Jungfrau, *d.* Caucasus)
11. i : e :: (*a.* $-\infty$, *b.* π, *c.* 1, *d.* $\sqrt{-1}$) : 2.71828
12. (*a.* Na, *b.* Al, *c.* O_2 *d.* N) : SALT :: H : HYDROCHLORIC ACID

13. UROLOGIST : (*a.* bladder, *b.* urine, *c.* heart, *d.* ears) :: OPHTHALMOLOGIST : EYES

14. A : C :: ALPHA : (*a.* lambda, *b.* kappa, *c.* omicron, *d.* gamma)

15. (a. coin, *b.* bullion, *c.* currency, *d.* check) : CASH :: PROBABLE : CERTAIN

16. SKINNER : ENVIRONMENT :: (*a.* Galton, *b.* Locke, *c.* Watson, *d.* Spence) : HEREDITY

17. DOG : NOUN :: (*a.* newspaper, *b.* at, *c.* the, *d.* is) : ARTICLE

18. IRISH : (*a.* setter, *b.* Guernsey, *c.* mutt, *d.* St. Bernard) :: LABRADOR : RETRIEVER

19. PERSHING : (*a.* French, *b.* U.S., *c.* English, *d.* Canadian) :: WELLINGTON : ENGLISH

20. MORNING STAR : EVENING STAR :: VENUS : (*a.* Mercury, *b.* Mars, *c.* Jupiter, *d.* Venus)

21. HYPERBOLE : HYPERBOLA :: STATEMENT : (*a.* statements, *b.* curve, *c.* exaggeration, *d.* ellipse)

22. $\overline{X}$: SAMPLE :: (*a.* μ, *b.* σ, *c.* λ, *d.* ρ) : POPULATION

23. METHYL : ETHYL :: GRAIN : (*a.* turpentine, *b.* alcohol, *c.* rain, *d.* wood)

24. SHORTEST : (*a.* February, *b.* August, *c.* April, *d.* December) :: LONGEST : JUNE

25. (*a.* nadir, *b.* zenith, *c.* summit, *d.* hilt) : BOTTOM :: APEX : TOP

26. PERCENT : 100 :: PROPORTION: (*a.* 0, *b.* 1, *c.* 0.1, *d.* 0.01)

27. RATIONAL : $\sqrt{100}$ :: IRRATIONAL : (*a.* $\sqrt{1}$, *b.* $\sqrt{-4}$, *c.* $\sqrt{50}$, *d.* $\sqrt{0}$)

28. ENORMITY : (*a.* great wickedness, *b.* great largess, *c.* great size, *d.* great passion) :: VILIFICATION : SLANDER

29. VANILLA : TEA :: (*a.* stem, *b.* root, *c.* flower, *d.* bean) : LEAF

30. NOON : EVE :: 12:21 : (*a.* 8:34, *b.* 10:01, *c.* 7:54, *d.* 11:29)

31. (*a.* soap, *b.* aspirin, *c.* base, *d.* litmus) : ACID :: LYE : ALKALINE

32. SAM : AIR :: ABM : (*a.* sea, *b.* land, *c.* ballistic, *d.* missile)

33. STEP : STAIRCASE :: (*a.* notch, *b.* support, *c.* poles, *d.* rung) : LADDER

34. OCHER : (*a.* yellow, *b.* green, *c.* blue, *d.* gray) :: LAVENDER : PURPLE

35. MARE : EWE :: HORSE : (*a*. goat, *b*. sheep, *c*. pig, *d*. deer)

36. RAVIOLI : (*a*. spaghetti, *b*. linguine, *c*. cannelloni, *d*. enchilada) :: MANICOTTI : TORTELLINI

37. (*a*. bacteria, *b*. viruses, *c*. fungi, *d*. rickettsiae) : TYPHUS :: BACTERIA : TUBERCULOSIS

38. ONE : IMPEACH :: (*a*. zero, *b*. one, *c*. three, *d*. four) : CONVICT

39. 0 PROOF : 0% :: 50 PROOF : (*a*. 10%, *b*. 25%, *c*. 75%, *d*. 100%)

40. BENEDICT : ALFREDO :: EGGS : (*a*. oeufs, *b*. clams, *c*. ziti, *d*. fettuccini)

41. INDUCE : INDUCT :: (*a*. adduce, *b*. reason, *c*. persuade, *d*. deduct) : INSTALL

42. (*a*. maroon, *b*. crimson, *c*. pink, *d*. scarlet) : RED :: GRAY : BLACK

43. STOP : POT :: STOOL : (*a*. feces, *b*. toilet, *c*. chair, *d*. loot)

44. PICASSO : (*a*. Bosch, *b*. Daumier, *c*. Tintoretto, *d*. Dali) :: GUERNICA : GARDEN OF EARTHLY DELIGHTS

45. $3x^2$: $6x$ :: $5y$: (*a*. 5, *b*. 10, *c*. $5y^{1/2}$, *d*. $10y^{1/2}$)

46. UNICORN : (*a*. mythical beast, *b*. duet, *c*. zebra, *d*. union) :: SINGLETON : BICYCLE

47. (*a*. Holland, *b*. Yugoslavia, *c*. Denmark, *d*. Switzerland) : ALPINE :: GREECE : MEDITERRANEAN

48. M.D. : EARNED :: (*a*. D.D., *b*. Ph.D., *c*. D.D.S., *d*. O.D.) : HONORARY

49. (*a*. Don Juan, *b*. Pablo, *c*. Sancho, *d*. Dulcinea) : DON QUIXOTE :: WATSON : HOLMES

50. SONATA : (*a*. movement, *b*. sonatina, *c*. coda, *d*. solo) :: NOVEL : NOVELLA

51. NOVICE : EXPERT :: (*a*. teacher, *b*. apprentice, *c*. journeyman, *d*. layman) : MASTER

52. CLUB : (*a*. diamond, *b*. heart, *c*. spade, *d*. ace) :: LOWEST : HIGHEST

53. GOSLING : GOOSE :: SHOAT : (*a*. goat, *b*. sheep, *c*. horse, *d*. hog)

54. C : LEMON :: A : (*a*. liver, *b*. lettuce, *c*. orange, *d*. cake)

55. PACIFIC : OCEAN :: (*a*. Mercury, *b*. Jupiter, *c*. Uranus, *d*. Neptune) : PLANET

56. ICHTHYOLOGIST : (*a.* sentences, *b.* algae, *c.* insects, *d.* fish) :: ZOOLOGIST : ANIMALS

57. ELECT : SELECT :: TIE : (*a.* lose, *b.* win, *c.* sty, *d.* rope)

58. MALLET : (*a.* hunting, *b.* rugby, *c.* cricket, *d.* croquet) :: BAT : BASEBALL

59. BAROMETER : AIR PRESSURE :: TACHOMETER : (*a.* speed of descent, *b.* speed of rotation, *c.* acceleration, *d.* inertia)

60. EMERALD : GRUE :: (*a.* ruby, *b.* sapphire, *c.* amethyst, *d.* diamond) : BLEEN

61. MARTIN : DAVID :: (*a.* Dombey, *b.* Micawber, *c.* Magoun, *d.* Chuzzlewit) : COPPERFIELD

62. (*a.* 2:00, *b.* 3:00, *c.* 5:00, *d.* 6:00) : SEATTLE :: 4:00 : CHICAGO

63. VENUS : (*a.* Uranus, *b.* Mars, *c.* Saturn, *d.* Pluto) :: LOVE : THE DEAD

64. SUBORN : (*a.* give birth to, *b.* prove, *c.* bribe, *d.* demand) :: SUBORDINATE : INFERIOR

65. A : O :: (*a.* E, *b.* OA, *c.* B, *d.* RH) : AB

66. (*a.* coal, *b.* petroleum, *c.* black opal, *d.* uranium) : BLACK GOLD :: PYRITE : FOOL'S GOLD

67. MALACHITE : GREEN :: LAPIS LAZULI : (*a.* blue, *b.* red, *c.* yellow, *d.* amber)

68. LONGITUDE : LATITUDE :: (*a.* 110°, *b.* 90°, *c.* 70°, *d.* 50°) : 20°

69. VALENTINE : SECOND :: NICHOLAS : (*a.* first, *b.* sixth, *c.* tenth, *d.* twelfth)

70. MARK : (*a.* Munich, *b.* Berlin, *c.* Zurich, *d.* Basel) :: FRANC : PARIS

71. (*a.* biology, *b.* chemistry, *c.* physics, *d.* astronomy) : HERSCHEL :: SURGERY : LISTER

72. METER : KILOMETER :: LOG 10 : (*a.* e, *b.* 10, *c.* 10^3, *d.* $\sqrt{10{,}000}$)

73. (*a.* Ash Wednesday, *b.* St. Bartholomew's Day, *c.* Maundy Thursday, *d.* All Saints' Day) : EASTER :: FIRST : LAST

74. GHOST : SPIRIT :: GHOUL : (*a.* body, *b.* vampire, *c.* nightmare, *d.* grave robber)

75. GERUND : (*a.* adverb, *b.* pronoun, *c.* conjunction, *d.* noun) :: PARTICIPLE : ADJECTIVE

76. N.Y. : N.J. :: N.H. : (*a.* N.D., *b.* N.C., *c.* N.M., *d.* N.W.)

77. (*a.* Abelard, *b.* Aquinas, *c.* Erasmus, *d.* Eusebius) : HELOÏSE :: TRISTAN : ISOLDE

78. GOBI : (*a.* Africa, *b.* Asia, *c.* South America, *d.* Central America) :: SAHARA : AFRICA

79. X : X^2 :: STANDARD DEVIATION : (*a.* mode, *b.* median, *c.* variance, *d.* chi square)

80. LEONINE : (*a.* vulpine, *b.* porcine, *c.* supine, *d.* bovine) :: LION : FOX

81. AUGUST 8 : LEO :: (*a.* January 8, *b.* April 8, *c.* October 8, *d.* December 8) : SAGITTARIUS

82. CHESS : CHESSMEN :: GO : (*a.* cards, *b.* stones, *c.* pegs, *d.* balls)

83. CIPHER : NAUGHT :: (*a.* zero, *b.* all, *c.* most, *d.* one) : NONE

84. SEVENTH-DAY ADVENTIST : (*a.* Friday, *b.* Saturday, *c.* Sunday, *d.* Monday) :: MUSLIM : FRIDAY

85. (*a.* 10, *b.* 11, *c.* 12, *d.* 13) : DUODECIMAL :: 13 : DECIMAL

86. (*a.* shawl, *b.* belt, *c.* cloak, *d.* sash) : BURNOOSE :: CAP : BUSBY

87. LEGHORN : (*a.* cattle, *b.* goat, *c.* sheep, *d.* fowl) :: ANGORA : GOAT

88. LISZT : HUNGARY :: MENOTTI : (*a.* U.S.A., *b.* Greece, *c.* Spain, *d.* England)

89. MELODY : (*a.* immediate, *b.* successive, *c.* retrogressive, *d.* momentary) :: HARMONY : SIMULTANEOUS

90. SINUSITIS : SINUS :: MENINGITIS : (*a.* liver, *b.* heart, *c.* artery, *d.* membrane)

91. APPROXIMATE : EXACT :: (*a.* analog, *b.* analogous, *c.* analogical, *d.* analogy) : DIGITAL

92. (*a.* is as, *b.* is almost, *c.* is virtually, *d.* is) : IS LIKE :: METAPHOR : SIMILE

93. CONGRESS : U.S.A. :: DIET : (*a.* Hungary, *b.* Turkey, *c.* Japan, *d.* China)

94. MAYOR : (*a.* Montevideo, *b.* Sussex, *c.* Casterbridge, *d.* Marseilles) :: HUNCHBACK : NOTRE DAME

95. INDUCTION : DEDUCTION :: HUME : (*a.* Locke, *b.* Leibniz, *c.* Berkeley, *d.* Mill)

96. STOP : (*a.* h, *b.* j, *c.* t, *d.* v) :: FRICATIVE : F

97. (*a.* $\frac{1}{2}gt^2$, *b.* ra, *c.* $\frac{1}{4}g^2k$, *d.* pc) : D :: MA : F

98. FIDELIO : BORIS GODUNOV :: BEETHOVEN : (*a.* Rimski-Korsakov, *b.* Shostakovich, *c.* Prokofiev, *d.* Mussorgsky)

99. MISER : AVARICIOUS :: SYCOPHANT : (*a.* plutonic, *b.* veracious, *c.* unctuous, *d.* sybaritic)

100. (*a.* genitive, *b.* dative, *c.* ablative, *d.* vocative) : ACCUSATIVE :: INDIRECT : DIRECT

Answer Key for the Pretest

1. *b*	11. *d*	21. *b*	31. *b*	41. *c*	51. *b*	61. *d*	71. *d*	81. *d*	91. *a*
2. *a*	12. *a*	22. *a*	32. *c*	42. *c*	52. *c*	62. *a*	72. *c*	82. *b*	92. *d*
3. *c*	13. *a*	23. *c*	33. *d*	43. *d*	53. *d*	63. *d*	73. *a*	83. *a*	93. *c*
4. *b*	14. *d*	24. *d*	34. *a*	44. *a*	54. *a*	64. *c*	74. *d*	84. *b*	94. *c*
5. *a*	15. *d*	25. *a*	35. *b*	45. *a*	55. *b*	65. *c*	75. *d*	85. *b*	95. *b*
6. *d*	16. *a*	26. *b*	36. *c*	46. *b*	56. *d*	66. *b*	76. *c*	86. *c*	96. *c*
7. *b*	17. *c*	27. *c*	37. *d*	47. *d*	57. *c*	67. *a*	77. *a*	87. *d*	97. *a*
8. *c*	18. *a*	28. *a*	38. *a*	48. *a*	58. *d*	68. *a*	78. *b*	88. *a*	98. *d*
9. *a*	19. *b*	29. *d*	39. *b*	49. *c*	59. *b*	69. *d*	79. *c*	89. *b*	99. *c*
10. *b*	20. *d*	30. *b*	40. *d*	50. *b*	60. *b*	70. *b*	80. *a*	90. *d*	100. *b*

Explanation of Answers for the Pretest

1. GRAY : ELEPHANT :: (*a.* white, ***b.* brown**, *c.* green, *d.* gray) : GRIZZLY BEAR

   (b) An elephant is gray; a grizzly bear is brown.
   General Information—Description

2. (***a.* ratatouille**, *b.* vermouth, *c.* lemonade, *d.* gin) : EAT :: MANHATTAN : DRINK

   (a) Ratatouille is something one eats; a Manhattan is something one drinks.
   General Information—Description

3. MOON : PLANET :: (*a.* asteroid, *b.* sun, ***c.* planet**, *d.* Orion) : STAR

   (c) A moon revolves around a planet; a planet revolves around a star.
   Natural Science—Description

4. JOHN : (*a.* Jackson, ***b.* Adams**, *c.* Pierce, *d.* Garfield) :: ANDREW : JOHNSON

   (b) John Adams and Andrew Johnson were both U.S. presidents.
   Humanities—Completion

5. 1 + 2 : MARCH :: 12 – 3 : (***a.* September**, *b.* October, *c.* November, *d.* December)

   (a) March is the third (1 + 2) month of the year; September is the ninth (12 – 3) month.
   General Information—Description

6. CANNON : CANNON :: STIMULI : (*a.* stimulation, *b.* stimuluses, *c.* stimulate, ***d.* stimulus**)

   (d) *Cannon* is the plural form of *cannon*. *Stimuli* is the plural form of *stimulus*.
   General Information—Class

7. GRAPES : WINE :: (*a.* alcohol, ***b.* hops**, *c.* alfalfa, *d.* kemp) : BEER

   (b) Wine is made from grapes; beer is made from hops.
   General Information—Description

8. SCROOGE : GREEDY :: (*a.* Antony, *b.* Portia, ***c.* Cassius**, *d.* Macduff) : TREACHEROUS

   (c) Scrooge (in *A Christmas Carol*) was greedy; Cassius (in *Julius Caesar*) was treacherous.
   Humanities—Description

9. (***a.* hurricane**, *b.* hail, *c.* sleet, *d.* thunder) : RAIN :: BLIZZARD : SNOW

   (a) A hurricane is characterized by strong wind and heavy rain; a blizzard is characterized by strong wind and heavy snow.
   General Information—Description

10. BLANC : ALPS :: EVEREST : (*a.* Andes, ***b.* Himalayas**, *c.* Jungfrau, *d.* Caucasus)

    (b) Mont Blanc is the highest mountain peak in the Alps; Mount Everest is the highest mountain peak in the Himalayas.
    General Information—Description

11. i : e :: (*a.* $-\infty$, *b.* π, *c.* 1, ***d.*** $\mathbf{\sqrt{-1}}$) : 2.71828

    (d) The quantity *i* is equal to $\sqrt{-1}$; the quantity *e* is (approximately) equal to 2.71828.
    Mathematics—Equality/Negation

12. (***a.* Na**, *b.* Al, *c.* O_2, *d.* N) : SALT :: H : HYDROCHLORIC ACID

    (a) Salt is a compound containing sodium (Na); hydrochloric acid is a compound containing hydrogen (H).
    Natural Science—Part/Whole

13. UROLOGIST : (***a.* bladder**, b. urine, *c.* heart, *d.* ears) :: OPHTHALMOLOGIST : EYES

    (a) A urologist treats the bladder; an ophthalmologist treats the eyes.
    General Information—Description

14. A : C :: ALPHA : (*a.* lambda, *b.* kappa, *c.* omicron, ***d.* gamma**)

    (d) *A* is the first letter and *c* is the third letter of the Roman alphabet; alpha is the first letter and gamma is the third letter of the Greek alphabet.
    Humanities—Class

15. (*a.* coin, *b.* bullion, *c.* currency, ***d.* check**) : CASH :: PROBABLE : CERTAIN

    (d) A check has probable value in a financial transaction (it is not certain to clear). Cash has certain value.
    General Information—Description

16. SKINNER : ENVIRONMENT :: (***a.* Galton**, *b.* Locke, *c.* Watson, *d.* Spence) : HEREDITY

    (a) Skinner is known for his belief that environment largely shapes behavior; Galton believed that heredity largely shapes behavior.
    Social Science—Description

17. DOG : NOUN :: (*a.* newspaper, *b.* at, ***c.* the**, *d.* is) : ARTICLE

    (c) *Dog* is a noun; *the* is an article.
    Humanities—Description

18. IRISH : (***a.* setter**, *b.* Guernsey, *c.* mutt, *d.* St. Bernard) : : LABRADOR : RETRIEVER

    (a) An Irish setter and a Labrador retriever are both kinds of dogs.
    General Information—Completion

19. PERSHING : (*a.* French, ***b.* U.S.**, *c.* English, *d.* Canadian) :: WELLINGTON : ENGLISH

    (b) Pershing was a U.S. general; Wellington was an English general.
    Humanities—Description

20. MORNING STAR : EVENING STAR :: VENUS : (*a.* Mercury, *b.* Mars, *c.* Jupiter, ***d.* Venus**)

    (d) Venus is known both as the morning star and as the evening star.
    General Information—Similarity/Contrast

21. HYPERBOLE : HYPERBOLA :: STATEMENT : (*a.* statements, ***b.* curve**, *c.* exaggeration, *d.* ellipse)

    (b) A hyperbole is a type of statement; a hyperbola is a type of curve.
    Mathematics—Description

22. $\overline{X}$: SAMPLE :: (***a.*** μ, *b.* σ, *c.* λ, *d.* ρ) : POPULATION

    (a) $\overline{X}$ is a symbol for a sample mean; μ is a symbol for a population mean.
    Mathematics—Description

23. METHYL : ETHYL :: GRAIN : (*a.* turpentine, *b.* alcohol, ***c.* rain**, *d.* wood)

    (c) *Ethyl* is *methyl* without the initial *m*; *rain* is *grain* without the initial *g*.
    Nonsemantic

24. SHORTEST : (*a.* February, *b.* August, *c.* April, ***d.* December**) :: LONGEST : JUNE

    (d) The shortest day of the year occurs in December. The longest day of the year occurs in June.
    General Information—Description

25. (***a.* nadir**, *b.* zenith, *c.* summit, *d.* hilt) : BOTTOM :: APEX : TOP

    (a) The nadir is the lowest point, or bottom of something; the apex is the highest point, or top.
    Vocabulary—Similarity/Contrast

26. PERCENT : 100 :: PROPORTION : (*a.* 0, ***b.* 1**, *c.* 0.1, *d.* 0.01)

    (b) The highest possible percent is 100; the highest possible proportion is 1.
    Mathematics—Description

27. RATIONAL : $\sqrt{100}$ :: IRRATIONAL : (*a.* $\sqrt{1}$, *b.* $\sqrt{-4}$, ***c.*** $\sqrt{\mathbf{50}}$, *d.* $\sqrt{0}$)

    (c) $\sqrt{100}$ is a rational number; $\sqrt{50}$ is an irrational number.
    Mathematics—Description

28. ENORMITY : (***a.* great wickedness**, *b.* great largess, *c.* great size, *d.* great passion) :: VILIFICATION : SLANDER

    (a) Enormity is great wickedness; vilification is slander.
    Vocabulary—Similarity/Contrast

29. VANILLA : TEA :: (*a.* stem, *b.* root, *c.* flower, ***d.* bean**) : LEAF

    (d) Vanilla is from a bean, tea from a leaf.
    General Information—Description

30. NOON : EVE :: 12:21 : (*a.* 8:34, ***b.* 10:01**, *c.* 7:54, *d.* 11:29)

    (b) *Noon* and *eve* are both palindromes (they read the same spelled backward and forward), as are 12:21 and 10:01.
    Nonsemantic

31. (*a.* soap, ***b.* aspirin**, *c.* base, *d.* litmus) : ACID :: LYE : ALKALINE

    (b) Aspirin is acid; lye is alkaline.
    General Information—Description

32. SAM : AIR :: ABM : (*a.* sea, *b.* land, ***c.* ballistic**, *d.* missile)

    (c) The second letter in the acronym *SAM* (surface-to-air missile) stands for air; the second letter in the *ABM* (anti-ballistic missile) stands for ballistic.
    General Information—Part/Whole

33. STEP : STAIRCASE :: (*a.* notch, *b.* support, *c.* poles, ***d.* rung**) : LADDER

    (d) A staircase has steps; a ladder has rungs.
    General Information—Part/Whole

34. OCHER : (***a.* yellow**, *b.* green, *c.* blue, *d.* gray) :: LAVENDER : PURPLE

    (a) Ocher is a shade of yellow; lavender is a shade of purple.
    Vocabulary—Description

35. MARE : EWE :: HORSE : (*a.* goat, ***b.* sheep**, *c.* pig, *d.* deer)

    (b) A mare is a female horse; a ewe is a female sheep.
    Vocabulary—Description

36. RAVIOLI : (*a.* spaghetti, *b.* linguine, ***c.* cannelloni**, *d.* enchilada) :: MANICOTTI : TORTELLINI

    (c) Ravioli, cannelloni, manicotti, and tortellini are all stuffed pasta dishes.
    General Information—Class

37. (*a.* bacteria, *b.* viruses, *c.* fungi, ***d.* rickettsiae**) : TYPHUS :: BACTERIA : TUBERCULOSIS

    (d) Typhus is caused by rickettsiae, tuberculosis by bacteria.
    Natural Science—Description

38. ONE : IMPEACH :: (***a.* zero**, *b.* one, *c.* three, *d.* four) : CONVICT

    (a) One president of the United States has been impeached; no president has been convicted.
    Humanities—Description

39. 0 PROOF : 0% :: 50 PROOF : (*a.* 10%, ***b.* 25%**, *c.* 75%, *d.* 100%)

(b) Something that is 0 proof has a 0% concentration of alcohol; something that is 50 proof has a 25% concentration of alcohol.
General Information—Description

40. BENEDICT : ALFREDO :: EGGS : (*a.* oeufs, *b.* clams, *c.* ziti, ***d.* fettuccini)**

(d) Eggs Benedict and fettuccini Alfredo are both food dishes.
General Information—Completion

41. INDUCE : INDUCT :: (*a.* adduce, *b.* reason, ***c.* persuade**, *d.* deduct) : INSTALL

(c) To induce is to persuade; to induct is to install.
Vocabulary—Similarity/Contrast

42. (*a.* maroon, *b.* crimson, ***c.* pink**, *d.* scarlet) : RED :: GRAY : BLACK

(c) Pink is red mixed with white; gray is black mixed with white.
General Information—Description

43. STOP : POT :: STOOL : (*a.* feces, *b.* toilet, *c.* chair, ***d.* loot)**

(d) *Pot* is all but the first letter of *stop* reversed; *loot* is all but the first letter of *stool* reversed.
Nonsemantic

44. PICASSO : (***a.* Bosch**, *b.* Daumier, *c.* Tintoretto, *d.* Dali) :: GUERNICA : GARDEN OF EARTHLY DELIGHTS

(a) Picasso painted *Guernica*. Bosch painted *The Garden of Earthly Delights.*
Humanities—Description

45. $3x^2$: 6x :: 5y: (***a.* 5**, *b.* 10, *c.* $5y^{1/2}$, *d.* $10y^{1/2}$)

(a) The expression $6x$ is the first derivative of $3x^2$; 5 is the first derivative of $5y$.
Mathematics—Description

46. UNICORN : (*a.* mythical beast, ***b.* duet**, *c.* zebra, *d.* union) :: SINGLETON : BICYCLE

(b) A unicorn and a singleton both refer to one of something; a duet and a bicycle both refer to two of something.
General Information—Equality/Negation

47. (*a.* Holland, *b.* Yugoslavia, *c.* Denmark, ***d.* Switzerland**) : ALPINE :: GREECE : MEDITERRANEAN

(d) Switzerland is an Alpine country; Greece is a Mediterranean country.
General Information—Description

48. M.D. : EARNED :: (***a.* D.D.**, *b.* Ph.D., *c.* D.D.S., *d.* O.D.) : HONORARY

(a) An M.D. (Doctor of Medicine) degree is earned; a D.D. (Doctor of Divinity) degree is honorary.
General Information—Description

49. (*a.* Don Juan, *b.* Pablo, ***c.* Sancho**, *d.* Dulcinea) : DON QUIXOTE :: WATSON : HOLMES

(c) Sancho was the sidekick of Don Quixote; Watson was the sidekick of Holmes.
Humanities—Description

50. SONATA : (*a.* movement, ***b.* sonatina**, *c.* coda, *d.* solo) :: NOVEL : NOVELLA

(b) A sonatina is a short sonata; a novella is a short novel.
Humanities—Description

51. NOVICE : EXPERT :: (*a.* teacher, ***b.* apprentice**, *c.* journeyman, *d.* layman) : MASTER

(b) An apprentice is a novice; a master is an expert.
Vocabulary—Similarity/Contrast

52. CLUB : (*a.* diamond, *b.* heart, ***c.* spade**, *d.* ace) :: LOWEST : HIGHEST

(c) In bridge, the club represents the lowest suit and the spade represents the highest suit.
General Information—Description

53. GOSLING : GOOSE :: SHOAT : (*a.* goat, *b.* sheep, *c.* horse, ***d.* hog**)

(d) A gosling is a young goose; a shoat is a young hog.
Vocabulary—Description

54. C : LEMON :: A : (***a.* liver**, *b.* lettuce, *c.* orange, *d.* cake)

(a) A lemon is a very good source of vitamin C; liver is a very good source of vitamin A.
General Information—Description

55. PACIFIC : OCEAN :: (*a.* Mercury, ***b.* Jupiter**, *c.* Uranus, *d.* Neptune) : PLANET

(b) The Pacific Ocean is the largest of the oceans; Jupiter is the largest of the planets.
General Information—Description

56. ICHTHYOLOGIST : (*a.* sentences, *b.* algae, *c.* insects, ***d.* fish**) :: ZOOLOGIST : ANIMALS

(d) An ichthyologist studies fish; a zoologist studies animals of all types.
Natural Science—Description

57. ELECT : SELECT :: TIE : (*a.* lose, *b.* win, ***c.* sty**, *d.* rope)

(c) *Elect* is pronounced like *select,* minus the initial *s* consonant sound; *tie* is pronounced like *sty*, minus the initial *s* consonant sound.
Nonsemantic

58. MALLET : (*a.* hunting, *b.* rugby, *c.* cricket, ***d.* croquet**) :: BAT : BASEBALL

(d) Croquet is played with a mallet, baseball with a bat.
General Information—Description

59. BAROMETER : AIR PRESSURE :: TACHOMETER : (*a.* speed of descent, ***b.* speed of rotation**, *c.* acceleration, *d.* inertia)

(b) A barometer measures air pressure; a tachometer measures speed of rotation.
General Information—Description

60. EMERALD : GRUE :: (*a.* ruby, ***b.* sapphire**, *c.* amethyst, *d.* diamond) : BLEEN

(b) In Nelson Goodman's famous paradox, an emerald can now be construed as grue (green until the year 2000 and blue thereafter), whereas a sapphire can be construed as bleen (blue until the year 2000 and green thereafter).
Humanities—Description

61. MARTIN : DAVID :: (*a.* Dombey, *b.* Micawber, *c.* Magoun, ***d.* Chuzzlewit**) : COPPERFIELD

(d) *Martin Chuzzlewit* and *David Copperfield* are both titles of novels by Charles Dickens.
Humanities—Completion

62. (***a.* 2:00**, *b.* 3:00, *c.* 5:00, *d.* 6:00) : SEATTLE :: 4:00 : CHICAGO

(a) When it is 2:00 in Seattle, it is 4:00 in Chicago.
General Information—Description

63. VENUS : (*a.* Uranus, *b.* Mars, *c.* Saturn, ***d.* Pluto**) :: LOVE : THE DEAD

(d) In Roman mythology, Venus was the goddess of love; Pluto was alleged to be the god of the dead.
Humanities—Description

64. SUBORN : (*a.* give birth to, *b.* prove, ***c.* bribe**, *d.* demand) :: SUBORDINATE : INFERIOR

(c) *Suborn* and *bribe* are synonyms, as are *subordinate* and *inferior.*
Vocabulary—Similarity/Contrast

65. A : O :: (*a.* E, *b.* OA, ***c.* B**, *d.* RH) : AB

(c) A, O, B, and AB are all blood types.
Natural Science—Class

66. (*a.* coal, ***b.* petroleum**, *c.* black opal, *d.* uranium) : BLACK GOLD :: PYRITE : FOOL'S GOLD

    (**b**) Petroleum is black gold; pyrite fool's gold.
    General Information—Similarity/Contrast

67. MALACHITE : GREEN :: LAPIS LAZULI : (***a.* blue**, *b.* red, *c.* yellow, *d.* amber)

    (**a**) Malachite is green in color; lapis lazuli is blue.
    General Information—Description

68. LONGITUDE : LATITUDE :: (***a.* 110°**, *b.* 90°, *c.* 70°, *d.* 50°) : 20°

    (**a**) Lines of longitude and latitude are at right (90°) angles to each other, as are lines at 110° and 20°.
    Mathematics—Description

69. VALENTINE : SECOND :: NICHOLAS : (*a.* first, *b.* sixth, *c.* tenth, ***d.* twelfth**)

    (**d**) St. Valentine's Day occurs during the second month of the year; St. Nicholas Day occurs during the twelfth month.
    General Information—Description

70. MARK : (*a.* Munich, ***b.* Berlin**, *c.* Zurich, *d.* Basel) :: FRANC : PARIS

    (**b**) The mark is the unit of currency in Germany, of which Berlin is the capital; the franc is the unit of currency in France, of which Paris is the capital.
    General Information—Description

71. (*a.* biology, *b.* chemistry, *c.* physics, ***d.* astronomy**) : HERSCHEL :: SURGERY : LISTER

    (**d**) Herschel is famous in the field of astronomy; Lister is famous in the field of surgery.
    Natural Science—Description

72. METER : KILOMETER :: LOG 10 : (*a.* e, *b.* 10, ***c.* 10^3**, *d.* $\sqrt{10{,}000}$)

    (**c**) A kilometer is 1000 meters; 10^3 is 1000 times log 10.
    Mathematics—Equality/Negation

73. (***a.* Ash Wednesday**, *b.* St. Bartholomew's Day, *c.* Maundy Thursday, *d.* All Saints' Day) : EASTER :: FIRST : LAST

    (**a**) Ash Wednesday is the first day of Lent; Easter is the last day.
    General Information—Description

74. GHOST : SPIRIT :: GHOUL : (*a.* body, *b.* vampire, *c.* nightmare, ***d.* grave robber**)

    (**d**) A ghost is a spirit; a ghoul is a grave robber.
    Vocabulary—Similarity/Contrast

75. GERUND : (*a.* adverb, *b.* pronoun, *c.* conjunction, ***d.* noun**) :: PARTICIPLE : ADJECTIVE

(**d**) A gerund is a verb form that can act like a noun; a participle is a verb form that can act like an adjective.
General Information—Description

76. N.Y. : N.J. :: N.H. : (*a.* N.D., *b.* N.C., ***c.* N.M.**, *d.* N.W.)

(**c**) N.Y., N.J., N.H., and N.M. are all abbreviations for two-word states of which the first word is *New.*
General Information—Class

77. (***a.* Abelard**, *b.* Aquinas, *c.* Erasmus, *d.* Eusebius) : HELOÏSE :: TRISTAN : ISOLDE

(**a**) Abelard and Heloïse were lovers, as were Tristan and Isolde.
Humanities—Class

78. GOBI : (*a.* Africa, ***b.* Asia**, *c.* South America, *d.* Central America) :: SAHARA : AFRICA

(**b**) The Gobi Desert is in Asia; the Sahara Desert is in Africa.
General Information—Description

79. X : X^2 :: STANDARD DEVIATION : (*a.* mode, *b.* median, ***c.* variance**, *d.* chi square)

(**c**) A variance is a standard deviation squared.
Mathematics—Description

80. LEONINE : (***a.* vulpine**, *b.* porcine, *c.* supine, *d.* bovine) :: LION : FOX

(**a**) *Leonine* means *like a lion*; *vulpine* means *like a fox.*
Vocabulary—Description

81. AUGUST 8 : LEO :: (*a.* January 8, *b.* April 8, *c.* October 8, ***d.* December 8**) : SAGITTARIUS

(**d**) Someone born on August 8 is born under the sign of Leo; someone born on December 8 is born under the sign of Sagittarius.
General Information—Description

82. CHESS : CHESSMEN :: GO : (*a.* cards, ***b.* stones**, *c.* pegs, *d.* balls)

(**b**) The game of chess is played with chessmen; the game of go is played with stones.
General Information—Description

83. CIPHER : NAUGHT :: (***a.* zero**, *b.* all, *c.* most, *d.* one) : NONE

(**a**) *Cipher, naught, zero,* and *none* all refer to nullity.
Vocabulary—Class

84. SEVENTH-DAY ADVENTIST : (*a.* Friday, ***b.* Saturday**, *c.* Sunday, *d.* Monday) : MUSLIM :: FRIDAY

(b) Sabbath occurs on Saturday for a Seventh-Day Adventist, and on Friday for a Muslim.
General Information—Description

85. (*a.* 10, ***b.* 11**, *c.* 12, *d.* 13) : DUODECIMAL :: 13 : DECIMAL

(b) The number 11 in duodecimal (base 12) notation equals the number 13 in decimal (base 10) notation.
Mathematics—Equality/Negation

86. (*a.* shawl, *b.* belt, ***c.* cloak**, *d.* sash) : BURNOOSE :: CAP : BUSBY

(c) A burnoose is a type of cloak; a busby is a type of cap.
General Information—Description

87. LEGHORN : (*a.* cattle, *b.* goat, *c.* sheep, ***d.* fowl**) :: ANGORA : GOAT

(d) A leghorn is a type of fowl; an angora is a type of goat.
General Information—Description

88. LISZT : HUNGARY :: MENOTTI : (***a.* U.S.A.**, *b.* Greece, *c.* Spain, *d.* England)

(a) Liszt was a noted composer from Hungary; Menotti is a noted composer from the United States.
Humanities —Description

89. MELODY : (*a.* immediate, ***b.* successive**, *c.* retrogressive, *d.* momentary) :: HARMONY : SIMULTANEOUS

(b) Melody is successive; harmony, simultaneous.
Humanities—Description

90. SINUSITIS : SINUS :: MENINGITIS : (*a.* liver, *b.* heart, *c.* artery, ***d.* membrane**)

(d) Sinusitis is an inflammation of the sinus; meningitis is an inflammation of a membrane.
Natural Science—Description

91. APPROXIMATE : EXACT :: (***a.* analog**, *b.* analogous, *c.* analogical, *d.* analogy) : DIGITAL

(a) An analog computer yields approximate results; a digital computer yields exact results.
Natural Science—Description

92. (*a.* is as, *b.* is almost, *c.* is virtually, ***d.* is**) : IS LIKE :: METAPHOR : SIMILE

(d) A metaphor often uses the linking verb *is*; a simile links two concepts by *is like*.
Humanities—Description

93. CONGRESS : U.S.A. :: DIET : (*a.* Hungary, *b.* Turkey, ***c.* Japan**, *d.* China)

(c) The main legislative body of the United States is the Congress; the main legislative body of Japan is the Diet.
General Information—Description

94. MAYOR : (*a.* Montevideo, *b.* Sussex, ***c.*** **Casterbridge**, *d.* Marseilles) :: HUNCHBACK : NOTRE DAME

(c) *The Mayor of Casterbridge* and *The Hunchback of Notre Dame* are both titles of books.
Humanities—Completion

95. INDUCTION : DEDUCTION :: HUME : (*a.* Locke, ***b.*** **Leibniz**, *c.* Berkeley, *d.* Mill)

(b) Hume, an empiricist, used induction as his major mode of reasoning. Leibniz, a rationalist, used deduction as his major mode of reasoning.
Humanities—Description

96. STOP : (*a.* h, *b.* j, ***c.*** **t**, *d.* v) :: FRICATIVE : F

(c) The sound of *t* is a stop; the source of *f* is a fricative.
Social Science—Description

97. (***a.*** **$\frac{1}{2}$ gt^2**, *b.* ra, *c.* $\frac{1}{4}g^2k$, *d.* pc) : D :: MA : F

(a) Distance fallen by an object equals one-half the force of gravity times the amount of time squared; force equals mass times acceleration.
Natural Science—Equality/Negation

98. FIDELIO : BORIS GODUNOV :: BEETHOVEN : (*a.* Rimski-Korsakov, *b.* Shostakovich, *c.* Prokofiev, ***d.*** **Mussorgsky**)

(d) *Fidelio* is an opera by Beethoven; *Boris Godunov* is an opera by Mussorgsky.
Humanities—Description

99. MISER : AVARICIOUS :: SYCOPHANT : (*a.* plutonic, *b.* veracious, ***c.*** **unctuous**, *d.* sybaritic)

(c) A miser is avaricious; a sycophant is unctuous.
Vocabulary—Description

100. (*a.* genitive, ***b.*** **dative**, *c.* ablative, *d.* vocative) : ACCUSATIVE :: INDIRECT : DIRECT

(b) In Latin, the dative case is used for indirect objects; the accusative case is used for direct objects.
Humanities—Description

Item Classification Chart

Pretest	RELATIONSHIP						
CONTENT	Similarity/ Contrast	Description	Class	Completion	Part/ Whole	Equality/ Negation	Nonsemantic
Vocabulary	25, 28, 41, 51, 64, 74	34, 35, 53, 99, 80	83				
General Information	20, 66	1, 2, 5, 7, 9, 10, 13, 15, 24, 29, 39, 42, 47, 48, 52, 54, 55, 58, 59, 62, 67, 69, 70, 73, 75, 78, 81, 82, 84, 86, 87, 93	6, 36, 76	18, 40	32, 33	46	
Humanities		8, 17, 19, 38, 44, 49, 50, 60, 63, 88, 89, 92, 95, 98, 100	14, 77	4, 61, 94			
Social Science		16, 96					
Natural Science		3, 37, 56, 71, 89, 90, 91	65		12	97	
Mathematics		21, 22, 26, 27, 45, 68, 79				11, 72, 85	
Nonsemantic							23, 30, 43, 57

Achieving Success on the *Miller Analogies Test*

Facts about the *MAT*

Description of the Test

The *MAT* is a 100-item, 50-minute verbal analogies test. All the questions are of the form A : B :: C : D (A is to B as C is to D), with one of the four terms missing. Four possible options are given for the missing term.

Your task is to select the option that best completes the analogy. Answers are recorded on a separate answer sheet. You are not allowed to make any marks in the test booklet. The answer sheet is later scored either by hand or by machine.

Reasons for Taking the *MAT*

Most people who take the *MAT* do so for one of four reasons:

1. Graduate Study—The most common reason for taking the *MAT* is to support an application for admission to a graduate level academic program, at either the masters' or the doctoral level.

2. Scholarship Aid—A second common reason for taking the *MAT* is to support an application for financial aid in pursuing a graduate program.

3. Business—A third use of the *MAT* is as a selection or placement device in a business firm or agency. For example, an industrial organization may require the test of applicants to their management traineeship program.

4. Guidance—A fourth use of the *MAT* is for personal guidance by a college adviser or placement office.

No matter what the reason for taking the test, it is usually not taken before the senior year in college unless it is administered through a special program that has received explicit authorization from The Psychological Corporation, publishers of the test.

Testing Centers

At present, there are more than 600 testing centers in 50 states and in several foreign countries. Special arrangements can be made in foreign countries where there are no regular centers, but you should allow at least a month for arrangements of this kind to be made. If you reside more than 100 miles from a test center, or if you will not be able to reach such a center within a month, special arrangements may also be made, but again you should allow ample time for these to be completed.

A complete list of testing centers may be obtained by writing to the CTC Administrator, The Psychological Corporation, 555 Academic Court, San Antonio, TX 78204. You should also write to The Psychological Corporation if you have made arrangements to take the *MAT* but have not received the bulletin of information regarding the test.

Test Dates The *MAT* is administered throughout the year by appointment. Since testing dates and times vary from one center to another, you will have to consult a local center for this information.

Test Fees The test fee also varies from center to center, so you should consult your local center for this information. At the present time, the fee is generally around $35.

Score Reports When you report for the test, you will be given an *Examinee's Report* to address to yourself. It will be returned to you with your score recorded on it a few days after you take the test.

At the time of testing, you may also list up to three addresses to which you want official score reports sent. It is essential that you know at this time the correct and complete address of any institution to which you want the score sent. You cannot expect the testing center to supply this information. The charge for reporting scores at the time of testing to as many as three institutions is included in the test fee.

Should you later decide that you wish additional score reports sent out, you will have to mail a request to The Psychological Corporation. Your request should include the following information:

1. The location of the testing center and the approximate date of testing.
2. Your name (clearly printed).
3. Your date of birth.
4. Your signature.
5. The complete address(es) to which you want the report(s) sent.

The fee is $15 for each report. Requests should be addressed to The Psychological Corporation, Controlled Testing Center, 555 Academic Court, San Antonio, TX 78204.

Scores of tests taken more than 5 years ago will not be reported, since these scores may not be accurate reflections of current ability. You must therefore take the test again if you need a score reported but have not taken the test during the preceding 5 years. If you took the test more than 2 years, but less than 5 years, ago, the old score will be reported, but you are strongly urged to retake the test nevertheless. If you take the test twice within 2 years, both scores will be reported.

Information Regarding Retesting Individuals who have taken the *MAT* previously are expected to indicate this at the time of testing, and to specify their reasons for desiring to be retested. In no case should you take the same form of the test twice. To do so will result in the invalidation of your more recent score. You are not expected to remember the form designation of the test you took previously; your indication to the examiner that you are retaking the test should result in your being given an appropriate form. If you begin the test but then clearly recognize the form as one you took previously, you should tell the examiner.

Information for the Handicapped

Nonstandard administrations can be arranged for the handicapped, but the testing center must be notified well in advance so that appropriate preparations can be made. Both Braille and enlarged-print editions of the *MAT* are available. If you are unable to mark your answer sheet yourself, you may make oral responses to an examiner, who will then mark the answer sheet for you. Oral administration of the *MAT* by a reader provided by the Testing Center is permitted.

Information for Those Who Speak English as a Second Language

You will not be permitted to use a dictionary or any other aids while taking the *MAT*. Although scores obtained by individuals for whom English is not a first language are always difficult to interpret, these scores would be completely uninterpretable if test-takers were allowed to use English-language aids. If your command of the English language does not reflect your true verbal abilities, you will obviously be at a competitive disadvantage in taking the test, although, as the *Bulletin of Information* points out, you will very likely find yourself at a similar disadvantage when entering the academic or employment situation for which the *MAT* is required.

Since there are no foreign-language editions of the *MAT*, you must take the test in English. However, any competent test user aware of your linguistic background will take into account in interpreting your score the fact that English is not your native language. It would probably be to your advantage to make this fact known to the appropriate official at any institution to which your score is sent.

What to Bring to the Test Center

1. Bring all necessary forms and identification.
You will receive the necessary forms in the mail. Don't forget to bring them to the test, as well as other informaton you may want to supply, such as addresses of the universities to which you want the scores to be sent. Do not bring notes, dictionaries, or the like; they are not permitted.

2. Bring a watch.
There may not be a clock in the room, or it may not be easily visible. Having your own watch ensures that you will be able to check the time easily. A watch will also help you to pace yourself as you work on the test and will enable you to fill in any unanswered questions before the end of the testing period.

3. Bring two or three pencils with good erasers.
Be prepared for the unexpected (a broken pencil point). Bring extra, sharpened pencils with good erasers so you won't have to waste time sharpening a pencil or trying to find another one.

How to Solve Analogies

What Is an Analogy?

An analogy is a problem of the form A is to B as C is to D. For notational convenience, the problem is often written as

A : B :: C : D.

This is the way problems are presented on the *MAT*.

Four Ways of Presenting Analogies

On *MAT* analogies, one of the four terms, A, B, C, or D, will be missing. In its place will be four options. Your task will be to select the option that best fits the analogy. For example, the following analogy might be presented in any of four ways.

EXAMPLE

BLACK : WHITE :: DARK : LIGHT

1. BLACK : WHITE :: DARK : (*a.* gray, *b.* shaded, *c.* light, *d.* heavy)
2. BLACK : WHITE :: (*a.* somber, *b.* blue, *c.* gray, *d.* dark) : LIGHT
3. BLACK : (*a.* color, *b.* white, *c.* gray, *d.* coal) :: DARK : LIGHT
4. (*a.* gray, *b.* black, *c.* heavy, *d.* somber) : WHITE :: DARK : LIGHT

The correct options, of course, are *c, d, b,* and *b,* respectively.

Ways of Perceiving Relationships

You may conceive of the relationship between the terms of the above analogy in two ways. First, you may say to yourself something like "White is the opposite of black, and light is the opposite of dark." Instead, you may say "Black is dark and white is light." Either way you will arrive at the same answer.

The first way looks at the two terms on the left (A : B) as one unit and the two terms on the right as a unit (C : D). The second way looks at the first and third terms as a unit (A : C) and the second and fourth terms as another unit (B : D). The important thing is to discover a relationship that is the same between the two terms in each unit.

Sometimes it is more convenient to solve an analogy in one way, and sometimes in the other.

EXAMPLE

1. DOCTOR : PATIENT :: LAWYER : (*a.* judge, *b.* jury, *c.* district attorney, *d.* client)

In solving this analogy, it is most convenient to look at the first and second terms as one unit (DOCTOR : PATIENT) and the third and fourth terms as one unit (LAWYER : CLIENT). A person who seeks the professional services of a doctor is called a patient, while one who seeks the professional services of a lawyer is termed a client.

EXAMPLE

2. DOCTOR : LAWYER :: PATIENT : (*a.* judge, *b.* jury, *c.* district attorney, *d.* client)

If the analogy is presented in this form, it is easier to consider the first and third terms as one unit, and the second and fourth terms as another.

A Common Mistake

A common mistake made by those who are relatively unfamiliar with analogies is to try to find a relationship between the first and fourth or the second and third terms. Don't do this. Often an incorrect answer option is waiting to be picked by those who use this kind of faulty reasoning.

In solving analogies, keep the following diagram in mind:

A : B :: C : D	This is OK.
A : B :: C : D	This is OK.
~~A : B :: C : D~~	This is NOT OK!

The analogy DOCTOR : PATIENT :: LAWYER : CLIENT is acceptable. The analogy DOCTOR : LAWYER :: PATIENT : CLIENT is acceptable. The analogy DOCTOR : PATIENT :: CLIENT : LAWYER is *not* acceptable. The third and fourth terms of an analogy may not be reversed, nor may the first and second terms.

Errors Stemming from Reversals

Errors stemming from reversals are frequent.

EXAMPLE

BIRD : SPARROW :: (*a.* boy, *b.* species, *c.* mammal, *d.* phylum) : HUMAN BEING

The relationship is that a sparrow is a type of bird, and a human being is a type of mammal.

Someone might carelessly interpret the analogy as requiring him or her to infer that a sparrow is a type of bird and a boy is a type of human being. This relationship is correct, but it is not the one posed by the analogy.

What Makes an Analogy Difficult?

Miller analogies differ widely in difficulty. In general, one analogy may be more or less difficult than another analogy for any one or more of five reasons.*

1. Difficulty of Words—You may simply be unfamiliar with the meanings of some or all of the words in the analogy. In this case, you may be stumped by vocabulary limitations before you even begin to figure out relationships. For example, the analogy IDOLATRY : IDOLS :: OPHIOLATRY : (*a.* icons, *b.* fire, *c.* serpents, *d.* darkness) would be easy for most people to solve if they knew that *ophiolatry* is serpent worship. The difficulty of the analogy resides in the unfamiliarity of a single word.
2. Difficulty of Relation between A and B—You may know the meanings of the A and B (first two) terms of the analogy, but be unable to figure out the relationship between them. Consider, for example, the analogy TRAP : PART :: TEN : (*a.* net, *b.* twenty, *c.* whole, *d.* lost). The terms are all easily recognizable. The difficulty of the analogy is in recognizing that the relationship between the first two terms is that the second is the first spelled backward.
3. Difficulty of Relation between A and C—An analogy may be difficult because it is not immediately obvious how the A and C (first and third) terms match up. Consider, for example, the analogy GARMENT : WEAR :: POTION : (*a.* clothing, *b.* liquid, *c.* drink, *d.* magic). The terms *garment* and *potion* have little in common. Recognizing that one wears a garment does not immediately help you to decide what to do with *potion*. You must

---

*Sternberg, R.J. Component processes in analogical reasoning. *Psychological Review,* 1977, 8 353–378.

Sternberg, R.J. *Intelligence, Information Processing, and Analogical Reasoning: Th Componential Analysis of Human Abilities.* Hillsdale, N.J.: Lawrence Erlbaum Associate 1977.

recognize that the rule that relates the first half of the analogy to the second half is that *"B* is what one does with *A."* One wears a garment, and drinks a potion.

4. Difficulty of Relation between C and D—Sometimes you may be able to infer the relation between *A* and *B*, but have difficulty applying the analogous relation from C to D. Consider, for example, the analogy GOVERNOR : PRESIDENT :: LEGISLATURE : (*a.* Capitol, *b.* Congress, *c.* House, *d.* Speaker). The terms of the analogy are all familiar ones, and the relations between A and B and between A and C are straightforward. The difficulty of this analogy is in applying the analogy rule from *legislature* to the best answer. Options *a, b,* and *c* are all fairly plausible, but reflection will reveal that *b* is the best answer. Option *a, Capitol,* refers to a specific building; option *c, House,* refers to only one of two congressional bodies. *Congress* (option *b*) is the national legislative body, however, and a legislature is a state legislative body.

5. Difficulty of Relation between D and Ideal Answer—Occasionally, you may come upon an analogy that for one reason or another seems to have no "perfect" answer. Consider, for example, the analogy MINUTE : HOUR :: FOOT : (*a.* yard, *b.* day, *c.* inch, *d.* length). The best answer is option *a*, although one could argue that this answer is far from perfect, since there are 60 minutes in an hour, but 3 feet in a yard. When none of the answer options seems quite right, you must either reconsider the way you have interpreted the analogy or else simply pick the answer that seems closest to the ideal one.

How to Select the Correct Answer

1. Read all the options.
You must choose the best of the four alternative options presented. Keep in mind that item-writers make a deliberate (and usually successful) effort to make the incorrect options as plausible as possible. This fact has an important implication: *Read all the possible answer choices before selecting one.* Ace and Dawis (1973) found that analogies in which the last option is the correct one tend to be most difficult. A likely reason is that people sometimes don't bother to read through all the answers; they pick a plausible but incorrect option before they ever get to the last and correct option.

2. Check the parts of speech.
In selecting an option, be systematic. When you don't know what all the terms mean, or when the relationship between them is not obvious to you, try to use context cues to figure things out. Remember that while not all terms of the analogy have to be of the same part of speech, they can be of no more than two parts of speech (except for nonsemantic analogies). Therefore, if an option you are considering introduces a third part of speech, it is probably incorrect.

3. Infer the type of analogy.

EXAMPLE

THRIFTY : (*a.* wasteful, *b.* economical, *c.* cheerful, *d.* wealthy) ::
SLATTERNLY : UNTIDY

Suppose that you don't know what the word *slatternly* means. You need not give up on the analogy either by skipping it or by answering randomly. The first inference you can make is that it is probably a Vocabulary item (see Content Category I, page 40). As you will soon learn by taking the practice tests, Vocabulary items frequently turn out to be Similarity or Contrast items (see Relationship Categories I-1 and I-2, page 46), and they are more likely to be items of the former kind (synonyms) than of the latter kind (antonyms). So a reasonable inference to make would be that *slatternly* means untidy, and that therefore option *b* is the correct answer, since *thrifty* means economical. Of course, you might not want to rule out the possibility of an antonym.

4. Consider the sounds of words.
One thing you can do (and this really works on many occasions) is simply to look at the word *slatternly* and decide whether it *sounds* more like a word meaning tidy or one meaning untidy. Most people will choose *untidy,* and they will be correct. The answer to this problem is option *b.*

5. Guess intelligently.
Suppose the item had been presented in this form:

> THRIFTY : ECONOMICAL :: SLATTERNLY : (*a.* cheerful, *b.* quickly, *c.* circular, *d.* untidy).

The problem is now more difficult, with fewer context cues available. However, you can still approach the item systematically. First, you can reasonably eliminate option *b*. You know that *thrifty* and *economical* are adjectives, and three of the four answer options are also adjectives. *Quickly,* however, is an adverb, probably included as an incorrect option because it ends in *-ly,* as does *slatternly.* Next, you can reasonably eliminate option *c*. Although it is an *adjective,* it describes a property of an object, whereas *thrifty* almost always describes a characteristic of a person. You are now left with two options and have to make a choice, based on your past experience with words. When you finally choose an answer, you will still be guessing, but you will be guessing intelligently rather than blindly. Guessing can improve your score if you do it intelligently.

6. Use word association.
You will probably encounter some analogies on the *MAT* in which you find yourself simply unable to infer the relationship between the given terms. When all else fails, a strategy that is slightly better than wild guessing is to try word association. In using this strategy, you attempt to select the option that seems most closely related (in whatever way) to the given terms of the analogy.

The psychologist A. Willner had individuals take a form of the *MAT* as a word association test. Rather than try to solve the analogies, subjects were instructed to pick the answer option that seemed most highly associated to the given element. Willner found that on one of every four items, the correct answer (as keyed for the analogies test) was picked with greater than chance frequency. The indication is that, at least on some items, the word association technique will help you to do better than would random guessing. It is by no means a powerful strategy, however, and should be used only when your attempts to discover any kind of relationship have failed.

For example, consider the very first item of the Pretest. Suppose you were not sure of the exact relation being sought. If you selected option *b* because the color brown has the highest association with bears, in general, or grizzly bears, in particular, you would get the item correct, as brown is the color of the grizzly bear as well as being more highly associated with bears than are the other colors.

Practice in Analogical Thinking

Directions: In each of the following, the first two terms are related, sometimes in multiple ways. The third term is like the first two terms in some one way but different from them in another. See how the third term is (a) like the first two terms and (b) different from them.

1. LEMON : TANGERINE :: PEACH
2. JUICE : MILK :: PANCAKES
3. DANCE : LEAP :: TURNED
4. PLANETS : ASTEROIDS :: SUN
5. ¾ : 0.75 :: 0.25
6. CENTIMETER : MILLIMETER :: INCH
7. DEGAS : MONET :: COURBET
8. SATURN : MERCURY :: PLANETS
9. BRASS : TUBA :: PERCUSSION
10. MISSISSIPPI : HUDSON :: HURON
11. MORGAN : MUSTANG :: MALTESE
12. WHELK : LIMPET :: KELP
13. STAMP : PHILATELIST :: NUMISMATIST
14. PURPLE : GREEN :: RED
15. DISCOVERY : ATLANTIS :: VIKING
16. CALDECOTT : ART :: NEWBERY
17. LIMESTONE : SANDSTONE :: MARBLE
18. PHALANGES : METATARSALS :: FEMUR
19. MILK : CHEESE :: WHEAT
20. VITAMIN A : VITAMIN B :: VITAMIN C

21. ARTERIOSCLEROSIS : MYOCARDIAL INFARCTION :: CARDIOVASCULAR DISEASE

22. CARBON MONOXIDE : NITROGEN OXIDE :: ASBESTOS

23. MONOPHONIC : HOMOPHONIC :: DUPLE METER

24. INCUS : STAPES :: PINA

25. PRESIDENT'S DAY : VALENTINE'S DAY :: MARTIN LUTHER KING, JR., DAY

26. WOOD-CARVED RELIEF : CORK INLAY :: TEXTURE DRAWING

27. WATERCOLOR : TEMPERA :: CHARCOAL

28. EQUILATERAL TRIANGLE : SQUARE :: RHOMBUS

29. SPAN : CUBIT :: STONE

30. PHAEDO : REPUBLIC :: POETICS

31. SOPHOCLES : ARISTOPHANES :: HIPPOCRATES

32. TUNDRA : TAIGA :: TROPICAL RAIN FOREST

33. DONATELLO : MASACCIO :: RAPHAEL

34. DADA : SURREALISM :: SOCIAL REALISM

35. LYMPHOCYTES : MONOCYTES :: ERYTHROCYTES

36. SPRUCE : PONDEROSA :: HICKORY

37. PECK : BUSHEL :: FLUIDRAM

38. TROPIC OF CANCER : ARCTIC CIRCLE :: INTERNATIONAL DATE LINE

39. STARS AND STRIPES : OLD GLORY :: STARS AND BARS

40. FLINT : MATCHES :: LIGHTNING

41. DOMINICAN REPUBLIC : CUBA :: CHAD

42. OFFSIDE : CLIPPING :: GOALTENDING

43. KENYA : BRAZIL :: AUSTRALIA

44. FILMORE : VAN BUREN :: MARSHALL

45. TALLAHASSEE : COLUMBUS :: HOUSTON

46. IONESCO : BECKETT :: IBSEN

47. STIGMA : STYLE :: ANTHERS

48. CIRRUS : CIRROCUMULUS :: NIMBOSTRATUS

49. ORTHOCLASE : QUARTZ :: CALCITE

50. ST. PETER'S : SISTINE CHAPEL :: SANTA MARIA DELLA SALUTE

Answer Key with Explanations

1. A lemon, tangerine, and peach are fruits. Lemons and tangerines are citrus fruits, but peaches are not.

2. Juice, milk, and pancakes are foods. Juice and milk are liquid; pancakes are solid.

3. *Dance*, *leap*, and *turned* are verbs. *Dance* and *leap* are present tense; *turned* is past tense.

4. Planets, asteroids, and the sun are heavenly bodies. Planets and asteroids revolve around a star (the sun), whereas the sun is a star.

5. $\frac{3}{4}$, 0.75, and 0.25 are numbers less than 1. $\frac{3}{4}$ equals 0.75, whereas 0.25 does not.

6. Centimeter, millimeter, and inch are units of measure. Centimeter and millimeter are units in the metric system; inch is a unit in the English system.

7. Degas, Monet, and Courbet were painters. Degas and Monet are considered impressionists; Courbet, a realist.

8. Saturn and Mercury are planets; planet is the superordinate category.

9. A tuba is an instrument in the superordinate category "brass." Percussion is a different category of musical instruments.

10. The Mississippi, Hudson, and Huron are all bodies of water. The Mississippi and Hudson are rivers; Huron is a lake.

11. Morgan, Mustang, and Maltese are all breeds. Morgan and Mustang are breeds of horses. Maltese is a breed of dog or cat.

12. Whelk, limpet, and kelp are found in the ocean. Whelk and limpet are shells. Kelp is seaweed.

13. A philatelist and a numismatist are collectors. A philatelist collects or studies stamps; a numismatist, coins.

14. Purple, green, and red are colors. Purple and green are secondary colors; red is primary.

15. Discovery, Atlantis, and Viking are space vehicles. Discovery and Atlantis are space shuttles; Viking is a planetary probe.

16. The Caldecott and Newbery are awards given to children's books. The Caldecott is awarded for artwork; the Newbery, for literature.

17. Limestone, sandstone, and marble are rocks. Limestone and sandstone are sedimentary rocks; marble is a metamorphic rock.

18. The phalanges, metatarsals, and femur are bones. The phalanges and metatarsals are bones in the foot; the femur is a bone in the leg.

19. Milk, cheese, and wheat are foods. Milk and cheese are members of the dairy nutritional group; wheat is not.

20. A, D, and C are vitamins. Vitamins A and D are fat-soluble; C is a water-soluble vitamin.

21. Arteriosclerosis and myocardial infarction are examples of the superordinate category "cardiovascular disease"—a disease of the heart and blood vessels.

22. Carbon monoxide, nitrogen oxide, and asbestos are air pollutants. Carbon monoxide and nitrogen oxide are gases that contribute to outdoor air pollution. Asbestos is usually an indoor air pollutant; also, asbestos is not a gas.

23. Monophonic, homophonic, and duple meter are examples of basic musical elements. Monophonic and homophonic are examples of musical texture; duple meter is an example of musical rhythm.

24. The incus, stapes, and pina are parts of the ear. The incus and stapes are parts of the inner ear; the pina is part of the outer ear.

25. President's Day, Valentine's Day, and Martin Luther King, Jr., Day are observed as special days in the United States. President's Day and Valentine's Day are in February; Martin Luther King, Jr., Day is in January.

26. Wood-carved relief, cork inlay, and texture drawing are art techniques. Wood-carved relief and cork inlay are three-dimensional; a texture drawing is two-dimensional.

27. Watercolor, tempera, and charcoal are media of artwork. Watercolor and tempera are types of paints, but charcoal is not.

28. An equilateral triangle, a square, and a rhombus are polygons. An equilateral triangle and a square are regular polygons; a rhombus is not a regular polygon because its angles do not have the same number of degrees.

29. Span, cubit, and stone have been used as units of measure. Span and cubit are measures of length; stone is a measure of weight.

30. The *Phaedo*, the *Republic*, and the *Poetics* are literary works associated with Greek philosophy. The *Phaedo* and the *Republic* are Platonic dialogues, whereas the *Poetics* was written by Aristotle.

31. Sophocles, Aristophanes, and Hippocrates were Greek. Sophocles and Aristophanes were masters of dramatic art; Hippocrates is identified with science and medicine.

32. Tundra, taiga, and tropical rain forest are examples of biomes. Tundra and taiga are cold-climate biomes; tropical rain forests are warm-climate biomes.

33. Donatello, Masaccio, and Raphael were Italian painters. Donatello and Masaccio are associated with 15th century Italian art and are considered painters of the "Proto-Renaissance." Raphael's work is classified as 16th century, High Renaissance.

34. Dada, surrealism, and social realism are 20th century art movements. Dada art is against everything organized. Some dada artists and surrealists felt art had no meaning. Social realists, however, used art as a form of social commentary; to a social realist, art has a social purpose and meaning.

35. Lymphocytes, monocytes, and erythrocytes are blood cells. Lymphocytes and monocytes are white blood cells; erythrocytes are red blood cells.

36. Spruce, ponderosa, and hickory are trees. Spruce and ponderosa are pines; hickory is a broad-leaf tree.

37. Peck, bushel, and fluidram are all units of measure. Peck and bushel are units of capacity (dry measure); fluidram is a unit of liquid measure.

38. The Tropic of Cancer, the Arctic Circle, and the International Date Line are divisions of the earth. The Tropic of Cancer and the Arctic Circle divide the earth horizontally; the International Date Line divides the earth vertically.

39. Stars and Stripes, Old Glory, and Stars and Bars are names given to American flags. Stars and Stripes and Old Glory denote the flag; Stars and Bars was a name for the Confederate flag.

40. Flint, matches, and lightning can start fires. Flint and matches are human means of starting a fire; lightning is a natural means.

41. The Dominican Republic, Cuba, and Chad are countries. The Dominican Republic and Cuba are in the Western Hemisphere; Chad is in Africa.

42. Offside, clipping, and goaltending are penalties imposed in sports. Offside and clipping are used in football; goaltending, in basketball.

43. Kenya, Brazil, and Australia are countries. Kenya and Brazil are located on the equator. Australia is in the Southern Hemisphere.

44. Filmore, Van Buren, and Marshall have served as high officials of the U.S. government. Filmore and Van Buren were presidents. Marshall was a Supreme Court judge.

45. Tallahassee, Columbus, and Houston are cities in the United States. Tallahassee and Columbus are capital cities; Houston is not.

46. Ionesco, Beckett, and Ibsen are playwrights. Ionesco and Beckett are considered modern playwrights (1944–1975). Ibsen preceded Ionesco and

Becket but is considered the "father of modern drama" because he introduced social problems into his plays.

47. Stigma, style, and anthers are all parts of a flower. Stigma and style are considered parts of the "female" flower (carpel); the "male" plant structure (stamen) is tipped with anthers that produce pollen.

48. Cirrus, cirrocumulus, and nimbostratus are clouds. Cirrus and cirrocumulus are high-altitude clouds; nimbostratus clouds often occur at low altitude.

49. Orthoclase, quartz, and calcite are minerals. Orthoclase and quartz are silicate minerals; calcite is a carbonate mineral.

50. St. Peter's, the Sistine Chapel, and Santa Maria Della Salute are cathedrals. St. Peter's and the Sistine Chapel are in Rome; Santa Maria Della Salute is in Venice.

Twenty Helpful Hints

HINT 1. *Don't wait until the last minute to prepare for the test.*
Research shows that you will do better if you spread your studying a little at a time over a longer period, rather than cramming all your study into a shorter time right before the test.

HINT 2. *When preparing for the test, take the practice tests under real, test-taking conditions.*
The practice tests will be of greatest use if you strictly observe the time limits, don't allow distractions (such as phone calls or errands), and otherwise simulate as closely as possible the actual conditions under which you will take the test.

HINT 3. *Be self-confident.*
Even if you're a notoriously poor test-taker, after working through this book you will have done pretty much all you can do to ensure that you will perform up to your full potential. That's the most you can ask of yourself. Try techniques to manage anxiety and stress, such as relaxation exercises. Being well prepared and rested should also give you self-confidence.

HINT 4. *Read every question carefully.*
Read all the answer options presented for each question. Don't confuse words that look alike, such as *ingenious* and *ingenuous,* or *forward* and *froward.* (If you don't know what these words mean, now is the time to look them up.)

HINT 5. *Remember that the test questions are arranged in order of difficulty.*
If a question early in the test seems hard, you may be complicating a relatively easy question. On the other hand, if a test question late in the test seems easy, you may be overlooking a point that makes the question difficult.

HINT 6. *Don't avoid questions that initially look difficult.*
Sometimes, a question that looks difficult when you first glance at it proves not to be very hard at all. Therefore, before deciding to skip a question and come back to it, make sure that the question actually is difficult.

HINT 7. *Watch out for reversals.*
Remember that the direction of the relationship between terms must be the same on both sides of the analogy.

HINT 8. *Try out different relationships.*
Remember that you can look for relationships either between the first and the second and then the third and fourth terms, or between the first and third and then second and fourth terms.

HINT 9. *Analyze item content.*
Remember that not all terms of the analogy have to be from the same content area.

HINT 10. *Examine parts of speech.*
Check that parts of speech match properly. Be aware that some words may function as nouns or verbs, or as adjectives or adverbs.

HINT 11. *Look for different meanings of a word.*
Many words have multiple meanings, depending on their use in a sentence. For example, *saw* may be a tool (a noun) or the past tense of *see* (a verb). Look for alternative meanings or uses of a word if your first attempt to find a relationship fails.

HINT 12. *Be systematic.*
Try to be systematic in selecting the correct option. Use word association only if all else fails. Use a process of elimination to increase your chances of guessing correctly.

HINT 13. *Don't rely on tricks.*
Tricks, such as counting the number of questions in a row that have the same letter answer, are not reliable as a means for choosing an answer. Such tricks are based on probabilities: the probability is very low that more than four questions in a row will have the same answer option. A better strategy is to eliminate wrong answer options and then to choose between two remaining choices. This strategy increases your chances of guessing correctly, in contrast to guessing among all four options or using tricks.

HINT 14. *Pace yourself.*
Since you will have 50 minutes to answer 100 items, you should average no more than 30 seconds per analogy. Some items will take more time, some less. But don't get bogged down on a few difficult items; this can be a tremendous waste of time. If an answer just doesn't come to you, leave the question and go back to it when (or if) you have time.

HINT 15. *Answer every question.*
If you have only a couple of minutes left, and have not reached questions near the end, fill in answers to these items anyway. There is no penalty for incorrect answers, and by leaving questions

unanswered you are wasting possible points. Remember that to fill in these answers a minute or two before time is up is called test-wiseness, but to do so at any later time is called *cheating*. Therefore, make sure you're test-wise.

HINT 16. *Use all the time you are allotted.*
Never hand in your test booklet early. If you have time at the end of the test, review your answers, particularly to questions that you found difficult.

HINT 17. *Forget about other problems in your life.*
If you start thinking about anything but the test (e.g., a misunderstanding with a friend, or a money problem), STOP! You can think about these other things later. Give the test 100% concentration.

HINT 18. *Don't panic.*
If you find you don't know the answer to the first question or to the second or third, don't worry. Although items are arranged in order of difficulty, this ordering represents average difficulty. What is difficult for one person may be easy for another, and vice versa. The test is tough to begin with, so you can expect to find questions you can't answer scattered throughout. Skip questions that at first seem too difficult (mark your answer sheet in some way), and come back to them later if you have time.

HINT 19. *Remember that the test score is only one factor that is considered in admissions and financial-aid decisions.*
Decisions about admissions and financial aid are almost always based on many factors. Thus, you should not believe that your whole future will hinge on how you do on the *MAT*. After making your best effort, keep in mind that in most cases the test score is not a decisive factor in admissions and financial-aid outcomes.

HINT 20. *Remember that the MAT measures only a very limited aspect of your abilities.*
No matter how well or poorly you did, remember that the *MAT* measures only a few of your abilities. The test does not measure creative capacity or mechanical skills, for example. Thus, keep the test score in perspective, remembering that it is not all important!

Advice on Preparing for the *MAT*

That the *MAT* is not just a test of your reasoning abilities is probably evident to you from doing the pretest in this book. The *MAT* also assesses your vocabulary and your store of general information, as well as specific information in diverse areas. A person whose native language is not English and whose culture is not mainstream will find the *MAT* extremely difficult, even if the aid of a dictionary were allowed. The level of vocabulary on the test is high; in addition, the definition used for a particular word is not always the most salient or obvious.

In using this book, you are strongly advised to keep a notebook of words you don't know along with their definitions. Use a dictionary to look up words you're not sure of. Study these words regularly, and use them as much as possible, in order to add them to your vocabulary. Also study the vocabulary given in this book as well as the words in the practice tests. The vocabulary on pages 252–274 contains words often used in graduate-level tests and, in addition, provides you with useful synonyms and antonyms.

Five other techniques are also useful in learning new words:

1. Use mnemonics as much as possible, visualizing the words and their meanings as vividly as you can.
2. Group together similar words to study. Also, put together words with similar roots and related meanings.
3. Make flashcards with words on one side, definitions on the other. Study the cards during any free time you have.
4. Whenever possible, study the words with their antonyms and synonyms.
5. Read a good newspaper regularly, such as the *The New York Times* or *The Wall Street Journal,* to reinforce the vocabulary you have learned.

Not all these techniques work for everyone; some are better than others for different people. But the benefits of increasing your vocabulary are enormous—you will raise not only your *MAT* scores but other test scores as well.

Improving Your Intellectual Skills

Recommended Reading

Most people read this book in order to attain as high a score as possible on the *Miller Analogies Test.* Many readers are also interested in improving the general level of their intellectual skills. Whereas the material in this book is aimed primarily at raising your score on the *MAT*, and only secondarily at improving your general intellectual skills, other books with the primary aim of improving your general intellectual skills are available. Although such books are not intended to improve your score on any one particular test, sharpening your intellectual skills can be expected to help you on a large variety of tests, including the *MAT*.

Should you wish to read other books that may help you on the *MAT*, the following books are recommended.

1. Intelligence Can Be Taught

By Arthur Whimbey with Linda Shaw Whimbey, published as a paperback by Bantam, 1976. This thoughtful, highly readable book is an excellent place to start for anyone seriously interested in improving his or her intellectual skills. The book reviews the concept of the IQ, discusses some of its inadequacies, suggests ways to improve cognitive processing, and discusses issues such as the genetics of intelligence. The book's greatest strength is in its intelligent overview of the field of training intelligence as a whole. Its weakness is its relative lack of specific exercises for self-improvement.

2. Conceptual Blockbusting
By James L. Adams, published as a paperback by the Stanford University Alumni Association, 1974. This book reviews the kinds of blocks that get in the way of problem solving, including perceptual, cultural-environmental, emotional, and intellectual-expressive ones. It also suggests ways to go about conscious and unconscious blockbusting. The book is highly readable, entertaining, and immediately useful in improving one's thinking abilities.

3. Reasoning
By Michael Scriven, published as a paperback by the McGraw-Hill Book Company, 1976. This highly practical book has as its self-stated aims the improvement of the reader's skills in analyzing and evaluating arguments; skill in presenting arguments, reports, and instructions clearly and precisely; critical instincts; and knowledge about the facts and arguments relevant to contemporary issues of various kinds. The author is a noted philosopher-educator who specializes in practical reasoning. The book is highly readable and practical, and should be of great use to readers in sharpening their critical abilities.

4. Problem Solving and Comprehension: A Short Course in Analytical Reasoning
By Arthur Whimbey and Jack Lochhead, published as a paperback by the Franklin Institute Press, 1978. This book provides a nice complement to Whimbey's *Intelligence Can Be Taught*, because the emphasis here is on putting into practice much of what Whimbey talks about in the earlier book. This book contains problems of a variety of types, and suggests general methods that can be useful in solving these and other problems.

5. How to Solve Problems
By Wayne Wickelgren, published as a paperback by W. H. Freeman, 1974. This book, which has been quite influential in the psychological study of problem solving, reviews what psychologists have learned about problem-solving techniques and gives examples of how the various techniques can be applied to problems of different types. The book's greatest strengths are its breadth in covering a great deal of what we know about problem solving, and its close ties to psychological theory. The book's greatest weakness, from the standpoint of many readers, will be its rather technical nature and its occasional use of what to many is unfamiliar jargon.

6. Up the IQ!
By Paul I. Jacobs, published as a hardcover by Wyden Books (and distributed by Simon & Schuster), 1977. This book opens with a review of the nature of intelligence and intelligence tests and proceeds to what the author calls the "twelve basic rules of intelligence tests." The book will very likely be useful in improving the reader's ability to solve one particular kind of intelligence-test item, the matrix problem, in which a two-dimensional array of geometric figures with one or more blank entries is presented. The individual has to fill in the blank entry or entries. The book will probably be much less useful in training for other kinds of performances.

7. The IDEAL Problem Solver, 2nd edition
By John Bransford and Barry Stein, published as a paperback by W. H. Freeman, 1993. This book describes five steps for solving a wide variety of problems: Identifying the problem, Defining and representing the problem, Exploring pos-

sible strategies, Acting on the strategies, Looking back and evaluating the effects of one's activities. (IDEAL is an acronym for the five steps.) The book is lucid, is easy to read, and contains many practical problems utilizing a variety of intellectual skills, including reasoning, memory, and creative problem solving. The book is suitable for anyone at the high school level and beyond, and can be read through quickly.

8. Intelligence Applied
By Robert J. Sternberg, published as a paperback by Harcourt, Brace, Jovanovich, 1986. This book is the most wide-ranging of all, and is based on Sternberg's "triarchic" theory of intelligence. It contains extensive text and problems for developing learning, reasoning, and problem-solving skills, especially as they involve coping with novel kinds of situations. Problems range from the academic to the everyday. A whole chapter discusses emotional and motivational blocks to the full utilization of one's intelligence.

9. The Triarchic Mind
By Robert J. Sternberg, published as a paperback by Penguin, 1988. This book contains further exercises for mind improvement based on the author's triarchic theory of human intelligence.

Other Test Preparation Books

Numerous other books containing problems of various kinds, including other test preparation books, can be quite helpful in improving general thinking skills. Thus, for the person whose goal is general improvement in thinking, Barron's other test preparation books, such as *How to Prepare for the Graduate Record Examination,* are recommended as supplements to the more theoretically based books just described.

Part Three Kinds of Analogies Found on the *Miller Analogies Test*

Content of *MAT* Analogies

Success on the *MAT* requires familiarity with a broad range of subjects. There are different ways of classifying the subject areas. The following list of the general content areas covered by the *MAT* shows just one way to group these areas conveniently.

I Vocabulary

II General Information

III Humanities
A. History
B. Literature
C. Mythology
D. Philosophy
E. Religion
F. Art
G. Music
H. Grammar

IV Social Sciences
A. Psychology
B. Sociology
C. Economics
D. Linguistics
E. Anthropology
F. Political Science

V Natural Sciences
A. Biology
B. Physics
C. Chemistry

VI Mathematics

VII Nonsemantic

The following examples will give you an idea of what each area covers:

1. *Vocabulary:*

STRIDENT : (*a.* wide, *b.* shrill, *c.* confident, *d.* rigid) :: TURBULENT : AGITATED
Answer: (**b**). This analogy deals with similarities in meaning. *Strident* and *shrill* are synonyms, as are *turbulent* and *agitated.*

2. *General Information:*

JAPAN : ORIENT :: FRANCE : (*a.* Europe, *b.* Continent, *c.* Paris, *d.* Occident)
Answer: (**d**). This analogy concerns locations of countries. Japan is a country in the Orient. France is a country in the Occident.

3. *History:*

(*a.* T. Roosevelt, *b.* F. Roosevelt, *c.* Wilson, *d.* Eisenhower) : SQUARE DEAL :: TRUMAN : FAIR DEAL
Answer: (**a**). This analogy involves presidential programs. T. Roosevelt introduced what he called the Square Deal. Truman introduced what he called the Fair Deal.

4. *Literature:*

NAPOLEON : FRENCH ARMY :: MAJOR BARBARA : (*a.* Salvation Army, *b.* English Army, *c.* American Army, *d.* Children's Army)
Answer: (**a**). This analogy is about army affiliations of officers. Napoleon was an officer in the French Army. Major Barbara, in Shaw's play by the same name, was an officer in the Salvation Army.

5. *Mythology:*

ZEUS : HERA :: JUPITER : (*a.* Venus, *b.* Minerva, *c.* Juno, *d.* Diana)
Answer: (**c**). This analogy requires recognition of two different names for the same god. Zeus was the Greek name and Jupiter the Roman name for the king of the gods. Hera was the Greek name and Juno the Roman name for his wife.

6. *Philosophy:*

LOCKE : INDUCTION :: (*a.* Berkeley, *b.* Bentham, *c.* Hume, *d.* Spinoza) : DEDUCTION
Answer: (**d**). This analogy deals with methodologies used by major philosophers. Locke was an empiricist philosopher and hence his mode of reasoning was primarily inductive. Spinoza, a rationalist philosopher, relied primarily upon deductive reasoning in order to draw conclusions.

7. *Religion:*

ADAM : (*a.* Eve, *b.* Eden, *c.* Heaven, *d.* Israel) :: OEDIPUS : THEBES
Answer: (**b**). This analogy concerns places from which people were expelled. Adam was expelled from Eden. Oedipus was expelled from Thebes.

8. Art:

RENOIR : IMPRESSIONIST :: (*a.* Monet, *b.* Bosch, *c.* Van Gogh, *d.* Munch) : EXPRESSIONIST
Answer: (**d**). This analogy involves schools of famous painters. Renoir was an impressionist painter. Munch was an expressionist painter.

9. Music:

(*a.* coda, *b.* aria, *c.* overture, *d.* coloratura) : OPERA :: PREFACE : BOOK
Answer: (**c**). This analogy is about introductions to works of art. An overture introduces an opera. A preface introduces a book.

10. Social Sciences:

FREUD : OEDIPUS COMPLEX :: (*a.* Jung, *b.* Horney, *c.* Adler, *d.* Allport) : INFERIORITY COMPLEX
Answer: (**c**). This analogy requires recognition of originators of terms describing psychological complexes. Freud coined the expression *Oedipus complex*; Adler coined the expression *inferiority complex*.

11. Biology:

(*a.* stomach, *b.* throat, *c.* lung, *d.* gullet) : PHARYNX :: WINDPIPE : TRACHEA
Answer: (**b**). This analogy deals with organs in the body. The pharynx is the throat. The trachea is the windpipe.

12. Physics:

MECHANICAL ADVANTAGE : RESISTANCE :: (*a.* distance, *b.* rate, *c.* effort, *d.* seconds) : TIME
Answer: (**a**). This analogy concerns variation between physical concepts. Mechanical advantage varies directly with resistance (when effort is held constant). Distance varies directly with time (when rate is held constant).

13. Chemistry:

HCl : hydrochloric :: H_2SO_4 : (*a.* hydrofluoric, *b.* hydrocyanic, *c.* sulfuric, *d.* nitric)
Answer: (**c**). This analogy involves chemical symbols for acids. HCl is the chemical formula for hydrochloric acid. H_2SO_4 is the chemical formula for sulfuric acid.

14. Mathematics:

$2^1 : 2^3 :: 1^2$: (*a.* 0, *b.* 1, *c.* 2, *d.* 4)
Answer: (**d**). This analogy is about equivalent ratios. 2 is to 8 as 1 is to 4.

15. Nonsemantic:

DEER : DEER :: OX : (*a.* oxen, *b.* oxes, *c.* oxae, *d.* oxena)
Answer: (**a**). This analogy requires recognition of plurals of words. The plural of deer is deer. The plural of ox is oxen.

NOTE: One thing to keep in mind while solving analogies is that the two relationships that comprise the analogy need not come from the same content domain. In the analogy presented as an example of literary content, NAPOLEON : FRENCH ARMY :: MAJOR BARBARA : SALVATION ARMY, the left side of the analogy is taken from the content domain of history, while the right side, the one requiring selection of a correct answer, comes from the content category of literature.

Practice in Recognizing Content Areas

DIRECTIONS: The following quiz consists of 30 pairs of words. Your task is to write next to each pair of words the relationship between the words and then to classify the pair of words in terms of the 15 content categories just described. The purpose of the quiz is to get you thinking actively about the different content areas from which *MAT* items are drawn. There are two examples of each content area. An answer key is given at the end of the quiz.

Word Pair	*Relationship*	*Content Area*
1. PIAGET : STAGE THEORY	______	______
2. NEON : INERT	______	______
3. MARS : WAR	______	______
4. DESCARTES: RATIONALIST	______	______
5. ANDES : SOUTH AMERICA	______	______
6. RESISTANCE : OHMS	______	______
7. SKIN : ORGAN	______	______
8. MITIGATE : ASSUAGE	______	______
9. EROICA : BEETHOVEN	______	______
10. SAWYER : FINN	______	______
11. PETER : THE GREAT	______	______
12. KORAN : ISLAM	______	______
13. IMAGINARY : COMPLEX	______	______

Word Pair	*Relationship*	*Content Area*
14. PERSONA : PERSONAE	______	______
15. MUNCH : EXPRESSIONIST	______	______
16. LINCOLN : REPUBLICAN	______	______
17. STEP : PETS	______	______
18. PATON : SOUTH AFRICA	______	______
19. DURKHEIM : SUICIDE	______	______
20. TRENCHANT : INCISIVE	______	______
21. AORTA : ARTERY	______	______
22. MICHELANGELO : DAVID	______	______
23. TREBLE : BASS	______	______
24. BASE : EXPONENT	______	______
25. HOLLANDAISE : CHEESE	______	______
26. MONK : MONASTERY	______	______
27. CAMUS : EXISTENTIALIST	______	______
28. FORCE : MASS × ACCELERATION	______	______
29. PLUTO : HADES	______	______
30. WATER : HYDROGEN	______	______

Answer Key with Explanations*

	Relationship	Content Area
1.	Piaget's theory of intellectual development is a stage theory.	SOCIAL SCIENCES (10)
2.	Neon is an inert gas.	CHEMISTRY (13)
3.	Mars was the god of war in Roman mythology.	MYTHOLOGY (5)
4.	Descartes was a rationalist philosopher.	PHILOSOPHY (6)
5.	The Andes Mountains are in South America.	GENERAL INFORMATION (2)
6.	Resistance is measured in ohms.	PHYSICS (12)
7.	The skin is an organ.	BIOLOGY (11)
8.	*Mitigate* and *assuage* are synonyms (meaning "to make less severe or to improve").	VOCABULARY (1)
9.	Beethoven wrote the Eroica Symphony.	MUSIC (9)
10.	Tom Sawyer and Huck Finn are characters in novels by Mark Twain (named after these characters).	LITERATURE (4)
11.	Peter the Great was a Russian czar.	HISTORY (3)
12.	The Koran is the holy book of Islam.	RELIGION (7)
13.	*Imaginary* and *complex* are two kinds of numbers.	MATHEMATICS (14)
14.	*Personae* is the plural form of *persona*.	NONSEMANTIC (15)
15.	Munch was an expressionist painter.	ART (8)
16.	President Lincoln was a member of the Republican Party.	HISTORY (3)
17.	*Pets* is *Step* spelled backwards.	NONSEMANTIC (15)

*In some cases, more than one content area could be justified. For example, Camus was also an existentialist writer, and hence item 27 could have been classified under LITERATURE. Also, multiple relationships are sometimes possible, meaning that you may have discovered a relationship other than or in addition to the one mentioned in each item.

Relationship	*Content Area*
18. Paton is a famous South African author.	LITERATURE (4)
19. Durkheim is the author of *Suicide*.	SOCIAL SCIENCES (10)
20. *Trenchant* and *incisive*, both of which mean "penetrating," are synonyms.	VOCABULARY (1)
21. The aorta is an artery in the body.	BIOLOGY (11)
22. Michelangelo was the sculptor of *David*. (Alternatively, David was an artist, as was Michelangelo.)	ART (8)
23. Treble and bass are musical clefs.	MUSIC (9)
24. In the numerical expression x^y, x is the base and y the exponent.	MATHEMATICS (14)
25. Hollandaise is a cheese-based sauce.	GENERAL INFORMATION (2)
26. A monk lives in a monastery.	RELIGION (7)
27. Camus was an existentialist philosopher.	PHILOSOPHY (6)
28. In physics, force = mass × acceleration.	PHYSICS (12)
29. Pluto (the Roman name) and Hades (the Greek name) were the god of the underworld.	MYTHOLOGY (5)
30. Water is composed in part of hydrogen gas.	CHEMISTRY (13)

Relationships Used in *MAT* Analogies

Analogical reasoning requires you to recognize many possible relationships between pairs of concepts. Unfortunately, classification of relationships is not nearly so straightforward as classification of content areas. There have been numerous attempts to classify the possible ways in which words can be related, but none of the systems is completely successful. To quote George Miller, "Words are related to one another in an amazing number of ways."

The classification system outlined on pages 46–48, similar to one proposed by George Miller, comprises 14 specific categories, which are organized into 7 general groups. Such a scheme, which makes use of a relatively small number of categories, strikes a balance between being too general and being too particular in describing a relationship.

I Similarity/Contrast
1. Similarity
2. Contrast

II Description
3. Predication

III Class
4. Subordination
5. Coordination
6. Superordination

IV Completion
7. Completion

V Part/Whole
8. Part-Whole
9. Whole-Part

VI Equality/Negation
10. Equality (equivalence)
11. Negation

VII Nonsemantic
12. Sound Relationships
13. Letter Relationships
14. Word Relationships

The following examples will give you an idea of what each relationship means.

1. Similarity
Relationships are between synonyms or words that are nearly the same in meaning.

HAPPY : GLAD :: DULL : (*a.* razor, *b.* blunt, *c.* sharp, *d.* bright)
Answer: (**b**). This analogy deals with similarities in meaning. *Happy* and *glad* are synonyms, as are *dull* and *blunt*.

2. Contrast
Relationships are between antonyms or words that are nearly the opposite in meaning.

WET : (*a.* dry, *b.* moist, *c.* towel, *d.* water) :: STOP : GO
Answer: (**a**). This analogy concerns contrasts in meaning. *Wet* and *dry* are opposites, as are *stop* and *go*.

3. Predication
Terms of the analogy are related by a verb or verb relationship. One term *describes* something about the other term. Most analogies fall in this category. Some of the variations are as follows: A is caused by B; A makes B; A rides on B; A eats B; A is a source of B; A induces B; A studies B; A is made of B; A uses B.

AUTOMOBILE : ROAD :: TRAIN : (*a.* conductor, *b.* track, *c.* engine, *d.* ticket)
Answer (**b**). This analogy involves surfaces on which vehicles travel. An automobile travels on a road, and a train travels on a track. The implicit verb is *travels.*

DOG : BARK :: (*a.* cat, *b.* giraffe, *c.* frog, *d.* rabbit) : MEOW
Answer: (**a**). This analogy involves sounds made by animals. A dog barks. A cat meows.

4. Subordination
Relationships are those in which an object A is a type of B.

(*a.* lizard, *b.* toad, *c.* sponge, *d.* trout) : FISH :: FROG : AMPHIBIAN
Answer: (**d**). This analogy is about types of animals. A trout is a type of fish and a frog is a type of amphibian.

5. Coordination
The first two terms are one type of thing and the last two are another.

LETTUCE : CABBAGE :: PEAR : (*a.* fruit, *b.* peach, *c.* radish, *d.* carrot)
Answer: (**b**). This analogy requires recognition of members of classes. Lettuce and cabbage are both types of vegetables, while a pear and a peach are both types of fruit.

6. Superordination
Relationships are those in which A is a category into which B falls.

BIRD : ROBIN :: MOLLUSK : (*a.* fish, *b.* water, *c.* sponge, *d.* snail)
Answer: (**d**). This analogy deals with category membership. Bird is a category that includes the robin; mollusk is a category that includes the snail.

7. Completion
Each term of this kind of analogy is part of a complete expression.

SAN : FRANCISCO :: (*a.* San, *b.* Santa, *c.* La, *d.* Los) : ANGELES
Answer: (**d**). This analogy concerns full names of cities. *San* and *Los* complete the names of two cities, San Francisco and Los Angeles, respectively.

8. Part-Whole
Relationships are those in which A is a part of B.

DAY : WEEK :: MONTH : (*a.* hour, *b.* minute, *c.* year, *d.* time)
Answer: (**c**). This analogy involves parts of larger amounts of time. A day is part of a week, and a month is part of a year.

9. Whole-Part
Relationships are those in which B is a part of A.

(*a.* hour, *b.* minute, *c.* year, *d.* time) : MONTH :: WEEK : DAY
Answer: (**c**). This analogy is about parts of amounts of time. A month is part of a year. A day is part of a week.

10. Equality

Relationships involve mathematical or logical equivalence.

$1/2 : 1/4$ :: 0.26 : (*a.* 0.52, *b.* 0.18, *c.* 0.13, *d.* 0.11)
Answer: **(c)**. This analogy requires recognition of mathematical equalities. Whereas $1/4$ is equal to one-half of $1/2$, 0.13 is equal to one-half of 0.26.

11. Negation

Relationships involve logical or mathematical negation.

EQUAL : UNEQUAL :: GREATER THAN : (*a.* less than, *b.* equal to, *c.* greater than or equal to, *d.* less than or equal to)
Answer: **(d)**. This analogy deals with possible relationships between pairs of numbers. Any number is either ***equal*** to or ***unequal*** to another number. Any number is either ***greater than*** or ***less than*** or ***equal to*** another number.

12. Sound Relationships

Two words are related because they sound similar in some way. The relationship is nonsemantic in that it has nothing to do with the meanings of the words.

TOE : ROW :: LO : (*a.* now, *b.* crow, *c.* boy, *d.* you)
Answer: **(b)**. This analogy concerns vowel sounds in words. All the terms have a long $\bar{o}$ vowel sound.

13. Letter Relationships

The letters of one term are permuted or in some other way transformed to form the letters of another term.

PAT : TAP :: RAT : (*a.* trap, *b.* skunk, *c.* tar, *d.* eat)
Answer: **(c)**. This analogy involves backward spelling of words. *Tap* is obtained by spelling *pat* backwards, *tar*, by spelling *rat* backwards.

14. Word Relationships

These usually express grammatical relationships between words.

EAT : ATE :: MEET : (*a.* meat, *b.* meet, *c.* met, *d.* meets)
Answer: **(c)**. This analogy involves past tenses of verbs. *Ate* is the past tense of *eat* and *met* is the past tense of *meet.*

NOTE: You will need to recognize much more specific relationships than those described above. However, if you understand the preceding relationships, you will have a general framework into which you can fit specific relationships.

Practice in Using and Recognizing Relationships

DIRECTIONS: The following quiz consists of 28 pairs of words. Your task is to write next to each pair of words the relationship between the words and then to classify the pair of words in terms of the 14 relationship categories just described. The purpose of the quiz is to get you thinking actively about the different ways in which pairs of words on the *MAT* can be related. There are two examples of each relationship. An answer key is given at the end of the quiz.

Word Pair	*Relationship*	*Classification*
1. COVER : BOOK	______________	______________
2. RUE : CHEW	______________	______________
3. AIRPLANE : FLIES	______________	______________
4. DAFFODIL : LILAC	______________	______________
5. EMPTY SET : NULL SET	______________	______________
6. CLUE : HINT	______________	______________
7. LAID : DIAL	______________	______________
8. EARLY : LATE	______________	______________
9. LADDER : RUNG	______________	______________
10. NEGATIVE : NONNEGATIVE	______________	______________
11. BETTER : BEST	______________	______________
12. HUMAN : MAMMAL	______________	______________
13. NEW : ORLEANS	______________	______________
14. STAR : DWARF	______________	______________
15. CARPENTER : HAMMER	______________	______________
16. X or Y : Not X and Not Y	______________	______________
17. CIRCLE : SEMICIRCLE	______________	______________
18. CRATE : FREIGHT	______________	______________
19. FURNITURE : CHAIR	______________	______________

Word Pair	Relationship	Classification
20. MELIORATE : IMPROVE	________	________
21. STICK : STUCK	________	________
22. HEAVENLY : HELLISH	________	________
23. FINGER : HAND	________	________
24. TAP : PAT	________	________
25. ABRAHAM : LINCOLN	________	________
26. $\sqrt{64} : 2^3$	________	________
27. CLUB : WEAPON	________	________
28. POLLACK : COD	________	________

Answer Key with Explanations*

Relationship	Classification
1. A cover is a part of a book.	PART-WHOLE (8)
2. *Rue* and *chew* rhyme.	SOUND (12)
3. An airplane flies for its locomotion.	PREDICATION (3)
4. A daffodil and a lilac are both kinds of flowers.	COORDINATION (5)
5. The empty set and the null set are mathematically equivalent.	EQUALITY (10)
6. *Clue* and *hint* are synonymous.	SIMILARITY (1)
7. *Dial* is *laid* spelled backwards.	LETTER (13)
8. *Early* and *late* are antonyms.	CONTRAST (2)

*In some cases, more than one classification can be justified. For example, an empty set and a null set (item 5) can be viewed as synonymous, and hence as related via category 1 (Similarity). Also, multiple relationships are possible in some cases, meaning that you may have discovered a relationship other than the one mentioned in the explanation.

	Relationship	*Classification*
9.	A ladder is composed in part of rungs.	WHOLE-PART (9)
10.	All real numbers that are not negative are nonnegative.	NEGATION (11)
11.	*Better* is the comparative form and *best* the superlative form of *good*.	WORD (14)
12.	A human is a kind of mammal.	SUBORDINATION (4)
13.	New Orleans is a city.	COMPLETION (7)
14.	A dwarf is a kind of star.	SUPERORDINATION (6)
15.	A carpenter uses a hammer.	PREDICATION (3)
16.	The logical negation of "X or Y" is "Not X and Not Y."	NEGATION (11)
17.	A circle can be divided into two semicircles.	WHOLE-PART (9)
18.	*Crate* and *freight* rhyme.	SOUND (12)
19.	One kind of furniture is a chair.	SUPERORDINATION (6)
20.	*Meliorate* and *improve* are synonyms.	SIMILARITY (1)
21.	*Stuck* is the past tense of *stick*.	WORD (14)
22.	*Heavenly* and *hellish* are antonyms.	CONTRAST (2)
23.	A finger is part of a hand.	PART-WHOLE (8)
24.	*Pat* is *tap* spelled backward.	LETTER (13)
25.	Abraham Lincoln was a president of the United States.	COMPLETION (7)
26.	$\sqrt{64}$ and 2^3 both equal 8.	EQUALITY (10)
27.	A club is a kind of weapon.	SUBORDINATION (4)
28.	Pollack and cod are both kinds of fish.	COORDINATION (5)

Distribution of Categories

All *MAT* items are classified both by content and relationship. The items on the *MAT* practice tests in this book are also classified in this way. A content/relationship item categorization is included in the explanatory answer for each question. Following each practice test is an Item Classification Chart that shows the breakdown of item categories.

Each content/relationship item categorization grid consists of a matrix of the 7 major content areas and 7 major relationship categories described in the preceding sections. Because there are 7 content areas and 7 relationship areas, there are 49 cells in the overall matrix. However, you will notice that some cells in the charts are empty, while others contain many entries. This occurs because content and relationship areas are not "independent." Certain types of item content and relationship never go together, and hence no items fall in the corresponding cells. Other types of item content and relationship are frequently associated, and hence the corresponding cells are filled with entries. For example, Mathematics items frequently fall into the Equality/Negation relationship category, but never into the Sound/Letter/Word category.

As a rule, more items fall into the General Information content category than into any other content category. With respect to content, General Information and Humanities (including history, literature, mythology, philosophy, religion, art, and music) are usually the largest categories, and Nonsemantic is the smallest. On the most recent forms of the *MAT*, there are no Nonsemantic items at all. However, older forms of the *MAT* are still in use, and hence such items are included in the practice tests. With respect to relationship, Description is usually the largest category and Sound/Letter/Word the smallest. Again, the latter category does not appear on the most recent forms of the *MAT.*

For several reasons, there is always a certain amount of ambiguity in the assignment of items to categories. One reason is that different individuals may arrive at the correct answer to a given item via alternative routes, and thus use different relationships to reach the same conclusion. A second reason for the ambiguity is that there is not always a clear line of demarcation between different categories. What is General Information to one person may appear to be Humanities, for example, to another. Hence, item classification is a useful tool in understanding the "anatomy" of an item, but only up to a certain point.

It is not recommended that you make extensive use of the Item Classification Charts during your preparation for the *MAT*. The primary purpose of these charts is to give you an idea of the breakdown of items on typical forms of the *MAT*, not to assist you in pinpointing your strengths and weaknesses. There are two reasons why you should not use the charts for diagnostic purposes. First, on the *MAT* (and on the practice tests) items within the various categories are not of equal difficulty, so that part scores on various categories are not directly comparable. For example, Mathematics items tend to be the most difficult ones, and hence more errors are to be expected on them. Second, it would not be worth your time to study a textbook or other aid in an area in which, if you used the charts diagnostically, you perceived yourself as weak. On a typical form of the *MAT*, there will be only a few items from any one specific content area, and so the probability of your learning from a textbook skimmed a few days before the test exactly what is covered on the particular form of the *MAT* you will take is exceedingly small.

The best way to prepare for the various types of content and relationship that will appear on the *MAT* is to take as many of the practice tests as you have time for, preferably all of them, and to make sure that you understand each error you have made. The Explanation of Answers following each Answer Key will help you to understand your errors. Once you have taken the tests and studied the kinds of items that give you difficulty, you can be confident that you will do your best on the *MAT*.

Part Four 10 Complete Analogy Tests for *MAT* Practice

Miller Analogies Test PRACTICE TEST 1

DIRECTIONS: In each of the following questions, you will find three initial terms and, in parentheses, four answer options designated *a*, *b*, *c*, and *d*. You are to select from the four answer options the one that best completes the analogy with the three initial terms. To record your answers, use the answer sheet at the back of the book.

TIME: *50 minutes*

1. CANARY : (*a.* red, *b.* blue, *c.* brown, *d.* yellow) :: POLAR BEAR : WHITE
2. SHIRT : WEAR :: BLOODY MARY : (*a.* kill, *b.* eat, *c.* dress, *d.* drink)
3. DAY : NIGHT :: DIURNAL : (*a.* nocturnal, *b.* eternal, *c.* vernal, *d.* external)
4. (*a.* Howard, *b.* Phineas, *c.* Ernest, *d.* Millard) : FILLMORE :: THOMAS : JEFFERSON
5. APRIL : 2 × 15 :: FEBRUARY : (*a.* 2 × 14, *b.* 2 × 15, *c.* 2 × 16, *d.* 2 × 17)
6. COMPARATIVE : (*a.* good, *b.* better, *c.* best, *d.* great) :: SUPERLATIVE : BEST
7. WINE : FRUIT :: BEER : (*a.* grape, *b.* hay, *c.* grain, *d.* lemon)
8. OTHELLO : JEALOUS :: HAMLET : (*a.* greedy, *b.* reflective, *c.* unintelligent, *d.* joyous)
9. (*a.* skirmish, *b.* war, *c.* disaster, *d.* truce) : BATTLE :: DRIZZLE : RAINFALL
10. SHETLAND : (*a.* monkey, *b.* lion, *c.* chicken, *d.* pony) :: HOLSTEIN : COW
11. (*a.* donkey, *b.* horse, *c.* bulldog, *d.* cougar) : DEMOCRAT :: ELEPHANT : REPUBLICAN

12. (*a.* green, *b.* red, *c.* blue, *d.* yellow) : CARDINAL :: ORANGE : ORIOLE

13. GERIATRICS : (*a.* old age, *b.* childhood, *c.* adolescence, *d.* adulthood) :: PEDIATRICS : CHILDHOOD

14. DOVE : PEACE :: (*a.* falcon, *b.* hawk, *c.* bluejay, *d.* vulture) : WAR

15. CHECK : (*a.* account, *b.* finesse, *c.* no trump, *d.* checkmate) :: TENTATIVE : FINAL

16. PHENOMENOLOGIST : HUSSERL :: EXISTENTIALIST : (*a.* Camus, *b.* Russell, *c.* Ryle, *d.* Quine)

17. GONDOLA : (*a.* canal, *b.* air, *c.* ocean, *d.* hangar) :: TRAIN : TRACK

18. (*a.* Babylonia, *b.* Phoenecia, *c.* Egypt, *d.* India) : PHARAOH :: ROMAN EMPIRE : EMPEROR

19. ACHILLES : TROJANS :: SAMSON : (*a.* Egyptians, *b.* Canaanites, *c.* Philistines, *d.* Moabites)

20. SPUMONI : TORTONI :: PARMESAN : (*a.* amontillado, *b.* mozzarella, *c.* manzanilla, *d.* maraschino)

21. HYPERBOLE : (*a.* geometric object, *b.* exaggeration, *c.* understatement, *d.* metaphysical object) :: HYPOCRITE : PRETENDER

22. MOOT COURT : HYPOTHETICAL CASES :: (*a.* kangaroo court, *b.* monkey court, *c.* cabbage court, *d.* dandelion court) : IRREGULAR PROCEDURES

23. ETHYL : METHYL :: GRAIN : (*a.* petrol, *b.* alcohol, *c.* sulfur, *d.* wood)

24. NEAPOLITAN : ITALY :: MUSCOVITE : (*a.* U.S.A., *b.* Hungary, *c.* Russia, *d.* Turkey)

25. APEX : SUMMIT :: ZENITH : (*a.* nadir, *b.* end, *c.* top, *d.* beginning)

26. (*a.* temporary, *b.* porous, *c.* impenetrable, *d.* permanent) : IMPERMEABLE :: COMMENCE : COMPLETE

27. PHILE : (*a.* love, *b.* hate, *c.* trust, *d.* distrust) :: PHOBE : FEAR

28. SOCRATES : (*a.* dagger, *b.* suffocation, *c.* noose, *d.* hemlock) :: GARFIELD : BULLET

29. OCHLOCRACY : MOB :: AUTOCRACY : (*a.* intellectual elite, *b.* rich, *c.* dictator, *d.* senate)

30. MOOR : PIN :: ROOM : (*a.* cue, *b.* nip, *c.* swim, *d.* thread)

31. FIREWATER : (*a.* acid, *b.* fire, *c.* liquor, *d.* lye) : : POTLATCH : FESTIVAL

32. (*a.* voluble, *b.* mum, *c.* lively, *d.* deaf) : MUTE : : SILENT : TACITURN

33. ATOM : MOLECULE :: CELL : (*a.* DNA, *b.* cytoplasm, *c.* tissue, *d.* ectoplasm)

34. AZURE : (*a.* blue, *b.* red, *c.* yellow, *d.* brown) :: MAGENTA : PURPLE

35. (*a.* quail, *b.* turkey, *c.* duck, *d.* pheasant) : DRAKE :: CHICKEN : ROOSTER

36. CIRRHOSIS : LIVER :: NEPHROSIS : (*a.* gall bladder, *b.* diaphragm, *c.* pancreas, *d.* kidneys)

37. IMPEACH : HOUSE :: (*a.* protect, *b.* convict, *c.* rebut, *d.* remand) : SENATE

38. (*a.* metabolism, *b.* anabolism, *c.* menabolism, *d.* atabolism) : CONSTRUCTION :: CATABOLISM : DESTRUCTION

39. GALAHAD : (*a.* size, *b.* cowardice, *c.* nobility, *d.* lechery) :: GRISELDA : PATIENCE

40. INDUCTION : DEDUCTION :: (*a.* synthetic, *b.* inferential, *c.* a priori, *d.* a fortiori) : ANALYTIC

41. FLOOZY : DISREPUTABLE :: FLIBBERTIGIBBET : (*a.* immoral, *b.* unintelligent, *c.* mentally unbalanced, *d.* flighty)

42. RED : LONGEST :: (*a.* blue, *b.* yellow, *c.* violet, *d.* green) : SHORTEST

43. STABLE : TABLE :: START : (*a.* motion, *b.* horse, *c.* stop, *d.* tart)

44. IN VIVO : (*a.* in vitro, *b.* in moribus, *c.* in extremis, *d.* in vacuo) :: LIVING ORGANISM : TEST TUBE

45. f'' : f' :: (*a.* speed, *b.* distance, *c.* time, *d.* acceleration) : VELOCITY

46. UNICYCLE : BICYCLE :: BICYCLE : (*a.* locomotive, *b.* dirigible, *c.* motorcycle, *d.* automobile)

47. SPELUNKER : (*a.* deserts, *b.* caves, *c.* glaciers, *d.* forests) :: ALPINIST : MOUNTAINS

48. APOTHECARY : (*a.* doctor, *b.* pharmacist, *c.* drug addict, *d.* patient) :: LAWYER : ATTORNEY

49. (*a.* Daniel Boone, *b.* The Headless Horseman, *c.* Paul Bunyan, *d.* Tonto) : BABE :: LONE RANGER : SILVER

50. SCULPTOR : STATUE :: (*a.* composer, *b.* politician, *c.* psychiatrist, *d.* blacksmith) : FUGUE

51. JOURNEYMAN : APPRENTICE :: ASSOCIATE PROFESSOR : (*a.* professor, *b.* research associate, *c.* assistant professor, *d.* teacher)

52. HOLMES : (*a.* Mason, *b.* Baker, *c.* Watson, *d.* Moriarty) :: CRUSOE : FRIDAY

53. FILLY : MARE :: GIRL : (*a.* adult, *b.* human, *c.* mother, *d.* woman)

54. IMPECUNIOUS : (*a.* generous, *b.* poor, *c.* wealthy, *d.* greedy) :: OBESE : CORPULENT

55. WAR BETWEEN THE STATES : CIVIL WAR :: GREAT WAR : (*a.* American Revolution, *b.* Hundred Years War, *c.* World War I, *d.* World War II)

56. HISTOLOGIST : TISSUE :: GRAPHOLOGIST : (*a.* maps, *b.* weather, *c.* handwriting, *d.* earthquakes)

57. (*a.* to play, *b.* will have played, *c.* playing, *d.* having played) : INFINITIVE :: WAITING : PARTICIPLE

58. PEDOMETER : (*a.* breaths, *b.* steps, *c.* heart beats, *d.* salivations) : : PROTRACTOR : DEGREES

59. ANGLE OF INCIDENCE : 45° :: ANGLE OF REFLECTION : (*a.* 0°, *b.* 22.5°, *c.* 45°, *d.* 90°)

60. (*a.* professional, *b.* hireling, *c.* journeyman, *d.* tyro) : NOVICE :: AMATEUR : BEGINNER

61. (*a.* novella, *b.* trial, *c.* soliloquy, *d.* epic) : POETRY :: NOVEL : PROSE

62. CONGLOMERATION : AGGLOMERATION :: CLUSTER : (*a.* heap, *b.* dispersion, *c.* hierarchy, *d.* aggrandizement)

63. (*a.* Jackson, *b.* Jefferson, *c.* Howe, *d.* Taylor) : DAVIS :: SHERMAN : LINCOLN

64. UMBRAGE : (*a.* offense, *b.* defense, *c.* innocence, *d.* responsibility) :: GUILT : CULPABILITY

65. PERFECT : PREFECT :: FLAWLESS : (*a.* caretaker, *b.* government official, *c.* refectory, *d.* preface)

66. DOZEN : 12 :: BAKER'S DOZEN : (*a.* 8, *b.* 11, *c.* 13, *d.* 16)

67. (*a.* tawdry, *b.* dehiscent, *c.* seraphic, *d.* edacious) : GAUDY :: NADIR : BOTTOM

68. PLUTO : (*a.* Hades, *b.* Thanatos, *c.* heaven, *d.* purgatory) :: SATAN : HELL

69. DEMONSTRATE : SHOW :: FORSWEAR : (*a.* promise, *b.* curse, *c.* renounce, *d.* conceal)

70. SHEEP : SHEEP :: (*a.* rhinocerii, *b.* rhinoceres, *c.* rhinoceroses, *d.* rhinocerae) : RHINOCEROS

71. PRETEND : PORTEND :: FEIGN : (*a.* fain, *b.* act realistically, *c.* presage, *d.* look back on)

72. UNIVERSAL DONOR : (*a.* A, *b.* B, *c.* O, *d.* Rh⁻) :: UNIVERSAL RECIPIENT : AB

73. (*a.* landscape, *b.* portrait, *c.* madonna, *d.* still life) : CLAUDE LORRAIN :: CARICATURE : HONORÉ DAUMIER

74. BRUNET : DARK BROWN :: HOARY : (*a.* red, *b.* white, *c.* black, *d.* blonde)

75. POINT : LINE :: LINE : (*a.* solid, *b.* plane, *c.* hypersphere, *d.* polygon)

76. LA BOHEME : PUCCINI :: LA TRAVIATA : (*a.* Berlioz, *b.* Menotti, *c.* Verdi, *d.* Rossini)

77. PESETA : SPANIARDS :: SHEKEL : (*a.* Chinese, *b.* Israelis, *c.* French, *d.* Indians)

78. (*a.* Declaration of Independence, *b.* Articles of Confederation, *c.* Declaration of Rights and Grievances, *d.* Townshend Acts) : U.S. CONSTITUTION :: LEAGUE OF NATIONS : UNITED NATIONS

79. MILLIMETER : CENTIMETER :: CENTIMETER : (*a.* decimeter, *b.* meter, *c.* decameter, *d.* kilometer)

80. ENSIGN : NAVY :: (*a.* private, *b.* sergeant, *c.* second lieutenant, *d.* colonel) : ARMY

81. COLT : REVOLVER :: NOBEL : (*a.* A-bomb, *b.* tear gas, *c.* rifle, *d.* dynamite)

82. HYDRATED : WATER :: ORGANIC : (*a.* hydrogen, *b.* nitrogen, *c.* oxygen, *d.* carbon)

83. (*a.* doctors, *b.* officers, *c.* clergymen, *d.* saboteurs) : FIFTH COLUMN :: SPIES : INTELLIGENCE

84. PING-PONG : BADMINTON :: TENNIS : (*a.* lacrosse, *b.* football, *c.* handball, *d.* soccer)

85. (*a.* Aegisthus, *b.* Priam, *c.* Agamemnon, *d.* Theseus) : PARIS :: DAEDALUS : ICARUS

86. BLACKSTONE : (*a.* medicine, *b.* politics, *c.* law, *d.* teaching) :: ROBERTS : PARLIAMENTARY PROCEDURE

87. WIFE OF BATH : (*a.* Chaucer, *b.* Milton, *c.* Wordsworth, *d.* Spenser) :: BELINDA : POPE

88. CATTON : CIVIL WAR :: (*a.* Plutarch, *b.* Thucydides, *c.* Herodotus, *d.* Pliny the Elder) : PELOPONNESIAN WAR

89. JEHOVAH'S WITNESSES : RUSSELL :: MORMONS : (*a.* Wesley, *b.* Smith, *c.* Thomas, *d.* Kirby)

90. 10 : OCTAL :: (*a.* 1, *b.* 1000, *c.* 111, *d.* 101) : BINARY

91. NEW JERSEY : THIRD :: (*a.* Virginia, *b.* New York, *c.* Delaware, *d.* New Hampshire) : FIRST

92. URIAH HEEP : HYPOCRITICALLY HUMBLE :: WILKINS MICAWBER : (*a.* poor but optimistic, *b.* poor and pessimistic, *c.* rich and optimistic, *d.* rich but pessimistic)

93. ABBOTT : FLATLAND :: DANTE : (*a.* China, *b.* Purgatory, *c.* Never-Never Land, *d.* Moonland)

94. (*a.* catharsis, *b.* tragedy, *c.* bathos, *d.* ethos) : UNIVERSAL :: PATHOS : PERSONAL

95. CANTOR : RABBI :: MUEZZIN : (*a.* minaret, *b.* guru, *c.* Brahman, *d.* imam)

96. ORPHEUS : RETURN OF EURYDICE TO HADES :: WIFE OF LOT : (*a.* transformation into a star, *b.* return to Sodom, *c.* transformation into a pillar of salt, *d.* return to Canaan)

97. CENTIGRADE : 100 :: KELVIN : (*a.* 132, *b.* 100, *c.* 0, *d.* 373)

98. LA GIACONDA : (*a.* Mona Lisa, *b.* Pieta, *c.* Madonna, *d.* Venus de Milo) :: ARRANGEMENT IN BLACK AND GRAY : WHISTLER'S MOTHER

99. EMPIRICIST : UTILITARIAN :: HUME : (*a.* Spinoza, *b.* Leibnitz, *c.* Kant, *d.* Mill)

100. BLOOMFIELD : SURFACE STRUCTURE :: (*a.* Whorf, *b.* Sapir, *c.* Skinner, *d.* Chomsky) : DEEP STRUCTURE

Answer Key for Practice Test 1

1. *d*	11. *a*	21. *b*	31. *c*	41. *d*	51. *c*	61. *d*	71. *c*	81. *d*	91. *c*
2. *d*	12. *b*	22. *a*	32. *b*	42. *c*	52. *c*	62. *a*	72. *c*	82. *d*	92. *a*
3. *a*	13. *a*	23. *d*	33. *c*	43. *d*	53. *d*	63. *a*	73. *a*	83. *d*	93. *b*
4. *d*	14. *b*	24. *c*	34. *a*	44. *a*	54. *b*	64. *a*	74. *b*	84. *a*	94. *d*
5. *a*	15. *d*	25. *c*	35. *c*	45. *d*	55. *c*	65. *b*	75. *b*	85. *b*	95. *d*
6. *b*	16. *a*	26. *b*	36. *d*	46. *d*	56. *c*	66. *c*	76. *c*	86. *c*	96. *c*
7. *c*	17. *a*	27. *a*	37. *b*	47. *b*	57. *a*	67. *a*	77. *b*	87. *a*	97. *d*
8. *b*	18. *c*	28. *d*	38. *b*	48. *b*	58. *b*	68. *a*	78. *b*	88. *b*	98. *a*
9. *a*	19. *c*	29. *c*	39. *c*	49. *c*	59. *c*	69. *c*	79. *a*	89. *b*	99. *d*
10. *d*	20. *b*	30. *b*	40. *a*	50. *a*	60. *d*	70. *c*	80. *c*	90. *b*	100. *d*

Explanation of Answers for Practice Test 1

1. CANARY : (*a.* red, *b.* blue, *c.* brown, ***d.* yellow**) :: POLAR BEAR : WHITE

   (d) A canary is usually yellow; a polar bear is generally white.
   General Information—Description

2. SHIRT : WEAR :: BLOODY MARY : (*a.* kill, *b.* eat, *c.* dress, ***d.* drink**)

   (d) One wears a shirt; one drinks a Bloody Mary.
   General Information—Description

3. DAY: NIGHT :: DIURNAL : (***a.* nocturnal**, *b.* eternal, *c.* vernal, *d.* external)

   (a) *Diurnal* refers to the daytime, while *nocturnal* refers to the nighttime.
   Vocabulary—Similarity/Contrast

4. (*a.* Howard, *b.* Phineas, *c.* Ernest, ***d.* Millard**) : FILLMORE :: THOMAS : JEFFERSON

   (d) Millard Fillmore and Thomas Jefferson were both presidents of the United States.
   Humanities—Completion

5. APRIL : 2 × 15 :: FEBRUARY : (***a.* 2 × 14**, *b.* 2 × 15, *c.* 2 × 16, *d.* 2 × 17)

   (a) April has 2 × 15, or 30 days; February usually has 2 × 14, or 28 days.
   General Information—Description

6. COMPARATIVE : (*a.* good, ***b.* better**, *c.* best, *d.* great) :: SUPERLATIVE : BEST

   (b) *Better* is the comparative form and *best* the superlative form of the adjective *good.*
   General Information—Description

7. WINE : FRUIT :: BEER : (*a.* grape, *b.* hay, ***c.* grain**, *d.* lemon)

   (c) Wine is fermented fruit; beer is fermented grain.
   General Information—Description

8. OTHELLO : JEALOUS :: HAMLET : (*a.* greedy, ***b.* reflective**, *c.* unintelligent, *d.* joyous)

   (b) In the respective Shakespearean plays in which they appear, Othello is a jealous character and Hamlet a reflective one.
   Humanities—Description

9. (***a.* skirmish**, *b.* war, *c.* disaster, *d.* truce) : BATTLE :: DRIZZLE : RAINFALL

   (a) A skirmish is a minor battle; a drizzle is a minor rainfall.
   Vocabulary—Class

10. SHETLAND : (*a.* monkey, *b.* lion, *c.* chicken, ***d.* pony**) :: HOLSTEIN : COW

(d) A Shetland is a type of pony; a Holstein is a type of cow.
General Information—Class

11. (***a.* donkey**, *b.* horse, *c.* bulldog, *d.* cougar) : DEMOCRAT :: ELEPHANT : REPUBLICAN

(a) A donkey is the symbol of the Democratic Party, while an elephant is the symbol of the Republican Party.
General Information—Description

12. (*a.* green, ***b.* red**, *c.* blue, *d.* yellow) : CARDINAL :: ORANGE : ORIOLE

(b) A cardinal is red; an oriole is orange.
General Information—Description

13. GERIATRICS : (***a.* old age**, *b.* childhood, *c.* adolescence, *d.* adulthood) :: PEDIATRICS : CHILDHOOD

(a) Geriatrics is the branch of medicine dealing with old age; pediatrics is the branch of medicine dealing with childhood.
Natural Science—Description

14. DOVE : PEACE :: (*a.* falcon, ***b.* hawk**, *c.* bluejay, *d.* vulture) : WAR

(b) A dove is a symbol of peace; a hawk is a symbol of war.
General Information—Description

15. CHECK : (*a.* account, *b.* finesse, *c.* no trump, ***d.* checkmate**) :: TENTATIVE : FINAL

(d) In the game of chess, a king is in tentative danger when in check, and in final danger when in checkmate.
General Information—Description

16. PHENOMENOLOGIST : HUSSERL :: EXISTENTIALIST : (***a.* Camus**, *b.* Russell, *c.* Ryle, *d.* Quine)

(a) In modern philosophy, Husserl is identified with the phenomenologist movement, Camus with the existentialist movement.
Humanities—Description

17. GONDOLA : (***a.* canal**, *b.* air, *c.* ocean, *d.* hangar) :: TRAIN : TRACK

(a) A gondola moves along a canal; a train moves along a track.
General Information—Description

18. (*a.* Babylonia, *b.* Phoenecia, ***c.* Egypt**, *d.* India) : PHARAOH :: ROMAN EMPIRE : EMPEROR

(c) In ancient times, Egypt was ruled by a pharaoh and the Roman Empire was ruled by an emperor.
Humanities—Description

19. ACHILLES : TROJANS :: SAMSON : (*a.* Egyptians, *b.* Canaanites, ***c.* Philistines**, *d.* Moabites)

(**c**) Achilles fought against the Trojans, Samson against the Philistines.
Humanities—Description

20. SPUMONI : TORTONI :: PARMESAN : (*a.* amontillado, ***b.* mozzarella**, *c.* manzanilla, *d.* maraschino)

(**b**) Spumoni and tortoni are both Italian ice-cream desserts; Parmesan and mozzarella are both Italian cheeses.
General Information—Class

21. HYPERBOLE : (*a.* geometric object, ***b.* exaggeration**, *c.* understatement, *d.* metaphysical object) :: HYPOCRITE : PRETENDER

(**b**) A hyperbole is an exaggeration; a hypocrite is a pretender.
Vocabulary—Similarity/Contrast

22. MOOT COURT : HYPOTHETICAL CASES :: (***a.* kangaroo court**, *b.* monkey court, *c.* cabbage court, *d.* dandelion court) : IRREGULAR PROCEDURES

(**a**) A moot court tries hypothetical cases; a kangaroo court exhibits irregular procedures.
Social Science—Description

23. ETHYL : METHYL :: GRAIN : (*a.* petrol, *b.* alcohol, *c.* sulfur, ***d.* wood**)

(**d**) Ethyl alcohol is grain alcohol; methyl alcohol is wood alcohol.
Natural Science—Description

24. NEAPOLITAN : ITALY :: MUSCOVITE : (*a.* U.S.A., *b.* Hungary, ***c.* Russia**, *d.* Turkey)

(**c**) A Neapolitan is a resident of Naples, and thus lives in Italy. A Muscovite is a resident of Moscow, and therefore lives in Russia.
General Information—Description

25. APEX : SUMMIT :: ZENITH : (*a.* nadir, *b.* end, ***c.* top**, *d.* beginning)

(**c**) *Apex*, *summit*, *zenith*, and *top* are all synonyms.
Vocabulary—Similarity/Contrast

26. (*a.* temporary, ***b.* porous**, *c.* impenetrable, *d.* permanent) : IMPERMEABLE :: COMMENCE : COMPLETE

(**b**) *Porous* and *impermeable* are antonyms, as are *commence* and *complete*.
Vocabulary—Similarity/Contrast

27. PHILE : (***a.* love**, *b.* hate, *c.* trust, *d.* distrust) :: PHOBE : FEAR

(**a**) *-Phile* is a suffix denoting love for something, while *-phobe* is a suffix denoting fear of something.
Vocabulary—Description

28. SOCRATES : (*a.* dagger, *b.* suffocation, *c.* noose, ***d.* hemlock**) :: GARFIELD : BULLET

(d) Socrates died from drinking hemlock, Garfield from being shot with a bullet.
Humanities—Description

29. OCHLOCRACY : MOB :: AUTOCRACY : (*a.* intellectual elite, *b.* rich, ***c.* dictator**, *d.* senate)

(c) Ochlocracy is rule by a mob; autocracy is rule by a single dictator.
Social Science—Description

30. MOOR : PIN :: ROOM : (*a.* cue, ***b.* nip**, *c.* swim, *d.* thread)

(b) *Room* is *moor* spelled backwards; *nip* is *pin* spelled backwards.
Nonsemantic

31. FIREWATER : (*a.* acid, *b.* fire, ***c.* liquor**, *d.* lye) :: POTLATCH : FESTIVAL

(c) *Potlatch* was an Indian name for a winter festival; *firewater* was an Indian name for liquor.
General Information—Similarity/Contrast

32. (*a.* voluble, ***b.* mum**, *c.* lively, *d.* deaf) : MUTE :: SILENT : TACITURN

(b) *Mum* and *mute* are synonyms, as are *silent* and *tactiturn.*
Vocabulary—Similarity/Contrast

33. ATOM : MOLECULE :: CELL : (*a.* DNA, *b.* cytoplasm, ***c.* tissue**, *d.* ectoplasm)

(c) Atoms combine to form molecules. Cells combine to form tissue.
Natural Science—Part/Whole

34. AZURE : (***a.* blue**, *b.* red, *c.* yellow, *d.* brown) :: MAGENTA : PURPLE

(a) Azure is a shade of blue; magenta is a shade of purple.
General Information—Description

35. (*a.* quail, *b.* turkey, ***c.* duck**, *d.* pheasant) : DRAKE :: CHICKEN : ROOSTER

(c) A drake is a male duck; a rooster is a male chicken.
General Information—Description

36. CIRRHOSIS : LIVER :: NEPHROSIS : (*a.* gall bladder, *b.* diaphragm, *c.* pancreas, ***d.* kidneys**)

(d) Cirrhosis is a disease that usually strikes the liver; nephrosis is a disease of the kidneys.
Natural Science—Description

37. IMPEACH : HOUSE :: (*a.* protect, ***b.* convict**, *c.* rebut, *d.* remand) : SENATE

(b) The House has the power to impeach the President, while the Senate has the power to convict him or her.
Social Science—Description

38. (*a.* metabolism, ***b.* anabolism**, *c.* menabolism, *d.* atabolism) : CONSTRUCTION :: CATABOLISM : DESTRUCTION

    (b) Anabolism is constructive metabolism, while catabolism is destructive metabolism.
    Natural Science—Description

39. GALAHAD : (*a.* size, *b.* cowardice, ***c.* nobility**, *d.* lechery) :: GRISELDA : PATIENCE

    (c) Galahad was distinguished for his nobility, Griselda for her patience.
    Humanities—Description

40. INDUCTION : DEDUCTION :: (***a.* synthetic**, *b.* inferential, *c.* a priori, *d.* a fortiori) : ANALYTIC

    (a) Induction is a synthetic form of thinking, while deduction is an analytic form of thinking.
    Humanities—Class

41. FLOOZY : DISREPUTABLE :: FLIBBERTIGIBBET : (*a.* immoral, *b.* unintelligent, *c.* mentally unbalanced, ***d.* flighty**)

    (d) A floozy is disreputable, while a flibbertigibbet is flighty.
    Vocabulary—Description

42. RED : LONGEST :: (*a.* blue, *b.* yellow, ***c.* violet**, *d.* green) : SHORTEST

    (c) Red light waves are the longest in the spectrum; violet waves, the shortest.
    Natural Science—Description

43. STABLE : TABLE :: START : (*a.* motion, *b.* horse, *c.* stop, ***d.* tart**)

    (d) The word *table* is the same as the word *stable*, but without the initial *s*. Similarly, the word *tart* is the same as the word *start*, again without the initial *s*.
    Nonsemantic

44. IN VIVO : (***a.* in vitro**, *b.* in moribus, *c.* in extremes, *d.* in vacuo) :: LIVING ORGANISM : TEST TUBE

    (a) Something grown *in vivo* is grown inside a living organism. Something grown *in vitro* is grown inside a test tube.
    Natural Science—Description

45. f″ : f′ :: (*a.* speed, *b.* distance, *c.* time, ***d.* acceleration**) : VELOCITY

    (d) The second derivative of a function, f'', can be used to determine acceleration. The first derivative, f', can be used to determine velocity.
    Natural Science—Description

46. UNICYCLE : BICYCLE :: BICYCLE : (*a.* locomotive, *b.* dirigible, *c.* motorcycle, ***d.* automobile**)

(d) A bicycle has twice as many wheels as a unicycle. An automobile has twice as many wheels as a bicycle.
General Information—Equality/Negation

47. SPELUNKER : (*a.* deserts, ***b.* caves**, *c.* glaciers, *d.* forests) :: ALPINIST : MOUNTAINS

(b) A spelunker explores caves; an alpinist climbs mountains.
General Information—Description

48. APOTHECARY : (*a.* doctor, ***b.* pharmacist**, *c.* drug addict, *d.* patient) :: LAWYER : ATTORNEY

(b) An apothecary is a pharmacist; a lawyer is an attorney.
General Information—Similarity/Contrast

49. (*a.* Daniel Boone, *b.* The Headless Horseman, ***c.* Paul Bunyan**, *d.* Tonto) : BABE :: LONE RANGER : SILVER

(c) Babe was an animal (ox) belonging to Paul Bunyan. Silver was an animal (horse) belonging to the Lone Ranger.
Humanities—Description

50. SCULPTOR : STATUE :: (***a.* composer**, *b.* politician, *c.* psychiatrist, *d.* blacksmith) : FUGUE

(a) A statue is a work of art created by a sculptor; a fugue is a work of art created by a composer.
Humanities—Description

51. JOURNEYMAN : APPRENTICE :: ASSOCIATE PROFESSOR : (*a.* professor, *b.* research associate, ***c.* assistant professor**, *d.* teacher)

(c) In craft guilds, a journeyman is one step above an apprentice. In colleges and universities, an associate professor is one step above an assistant professor.
General Information—Description

52. HOLMES : (*a.* Mason, *b.* Baker, ***c.* Watson**, *d.* Moriarty) :: CRUSOE : FRIDAY

(c) In their respective exploits, Holmes was assisted by Watson, Crusoe by Friday.
Humanities—Description

53. FILLY : MARE :: GIRL : (*a.* adult, *b.* human, *c.* mother, ***d.* woman**)

(d) A filly grows into a mare; a girl grows into a woman.
General Information—Description

54. IMPECUNIOUS : (*a.* generous, ***b.* poor**, *c.* wealthy, *d.* greedy) :: OBESE : CORPULENT

(b) *Impecunious* and *poor* are synonyms, as are *obese* and *corpulent*.
Vocabulary—Similarity/Contrast

55. WAR BETWEEN THE STATES : CIVIL WAR :: GREAT WAR : (*a)* American Revolution, *b.* Hundred Years War, **c. World War I**, *d.* World War II)

    (c) The Civil War is often called the War Between the States. World War I is often called the Great War.
    Humanities—Similarity/Contrast

56. HISTOLOGIST : TISSUE :: GRAPHOLOGIST : (*a.* maps, *b.* weather, **c. handwriting**, *d.* earthquakes)

    (c) A histologist studies tissue; a graphologist studies handwriting.
    General Information—Description

57. (**a. to play**, *b.* will have played, *c.* playing, *d.* having played) : INFINITIVE :: WAITING : PARTICIPLE

    (a) *To play* is an infinitive; *waiting* is a participle.
    General Information—Description

58. PEDOMETER : (*a.* breaths, **b. steps**, *c.* heart beats, *d.* salivations) :: PROTRACTOR : DEGREES

    (b) A pedometer measures numbers of steps; a protractor measures numbers of degrees.
    General Information—Description

59. ANGLE OF INCIDENCE : 45° :: ANGLE OF REFLECTION : (*a.* 0°, *b.* 22.5°, **c. 45°**, *d.* 90°)

    (c) If the angle of incidence of a light ray is 45°, its angle of reflection is also 45°.
    Natural Science—Equality/Negation

60. (*a.* professional, *b.* hireling, *c.* journeyman, **d. tyro**) : NOVICE :: AMATEUR : BEGINNER

    (d) *Tyro*, *novice*, *amateur*, and *beginner* are all synonymous.
    Vocabulary—Similarity/Contrast

61. (*a.* novella, *b.* trial, *c.* soliloquy, **d. epic**) : POETRY :: NOVEL : PROSE

    (d) An epic is a form of poetry; a novel is a form of prose.
    Humanities—Description

62. CONGLOMERATION : AGGLOMERATION :: CLUSTER : (**a. heap**, *b.* dispersion, *c.* hierarchy, *d.* aggrandizement)

    (a) A conglomeration is a cluster; an agglomeration, a heap.
    Vocabulary—Similarity/Contrast

63. (**a. Jackson**, *b.* Jefferson, *c.* Howe, *d.* Taylor) : DAVIS :: SHERMAN : LINCOLN

(**a**) Stonewall Jackson was a Confederate general under Jefferson Davis, while William Sherman was a Union general under Abraham Lincoln.
Humanities—Description

64. UMBRAGE : (***a.* offense**, *b.* defense, *c.* innocence, *d.* responsibility) :: GUILT : CULPABILITY

(**a**) *Umbrage* and *offense* are synonymous, as are *guilt* and *culpability.*
Vocabulary—Similarity/Contrast

65. PERFECT : PREFECT :: FLAWLESS : (*a.* caretaker, ***b.* government official**, *c.* refectory, *d.* preface)

(**b**) Something that is perfect is flawless. A prefect is a government official.
General Information—Similarity/Contrast

66. DOZEN : 12 :: BAKER'S DOZEN : (*a.* 8, *b.* 11, ***c.* 13**, *d.* 16)

(**c**) There are 12 objects in a dozen, and 13 objects in a baker's dozen.
General Information—Equality/Negation

67. (***a.* tawdry**, *b.* dehiscent, *c.* seraphic, *d.* edacious) : GAUDY :: NADIR : BOTTOM

(**a**) *Tawdry* and *gaudy* are synonyms, as are *nadir* and *bottom.*
Vocabulary—Similarity/Contrast

68. PLUTO : (***a.* Hades**, *b.* Thanatos, *c.* heaven, *d.* purgatory) :: SATAN : HELL

(**a**) According to Roman mythology, Pluto resided in Hades. According to certain Christian doctrine, Satan resides in hell.
Humanities—Description

69. DEMONSTRATE : SHOW :: FORSWEAR : (*a.* promise, *b.* curse, ***c.* renounce**, *d.* conceal)

(**c**) *Demonstrate* and *show* are synonyms, as are *forswear* and *renounce.*
Vocabulary—Similarity/Contrast

70. SHEEP : SHEEP :: (*a.* rhinocerii, *b.* rhinoceres, ***c.* rhinoceroses**, *d.* rhinocerae) : RHINOCEROS

(**c**) *Sheep* is the plural form of *sheep*; *rhinoceroses* is the preferred plural form of *rhinoceros.*
Nonsemantic

71. PRETEND : PORTEND :: FEIGN : (*a.* fain, *b.* act realistically, ***c.* presage**, *d.* look back on)

(**c**) *Pretend* and *feign* are synonyms, as are *portend* and *presage.*
Vocabulary—Similarity/Contrast

72. UNIVERSAL DONOR : (*a.* A, *b.* B, ***c.* O**, *d.* Rh^-) :: UNIVERSAL RECIPIENT : AB

(c) Persons with blood type O are called universal donors, while those with blood type AB are called universal recipients.
Natural Science—Description

73. (***a.* landscape**, *b.* portrait, *c.* madonna, *d.* still life) : CLAUDE LORRAIN :: CARICATURE : HONORÉ DAUMIER

(a) Claude Lorrain is best known for his landscapes, Honoré Daumier for his caricatures.
Humanities—Description

74. BRUNET : DARK BROWN :: HOARY : (*a.* red, ***b.* white**, *c.* black, *d.* blonde)

(b) Brunet coloring is dark brown, while hoary coloring is white.
General Information—Similarity/Contrast

75. POINT : LINE :: LINE : (*a.* solid, ***b.* plane**, *c.* hypersphere, *d.* polygon)

(b) An infinite collection of consecutive points forms a line. An infinite collection of consecutive lines forms a plane.
Mathematics—Part/Whole

76. LA BOHEME : PUCCINI :: LA TRAVIATA : (*a.* Berlioz, *b.* Menotti, ***c.* Verdi**, *d.* Rossini)

(c) *La Boheme* is an opera composed by Puccini; *La Traviata* is an opera composed by Verdi.
Humanities—Description

77. PESETA: SPANIARDS :: SHEKEL : (*a.* Chinese, ***b.* Israelis**, *c.* French, *d.* Indians)

(b) A peseta is a coin used by Spaniards; a shekel is a coin used by Israelis.
Humanities—Description

78. (*a.* Declaration of Independence, ***b.* Articles of Confederation**, *c.* Declaration of Rights and Grievances, *d.* Townshend Acts) : U.S. CONSTITUTION:: LEAGUE OF NATIONS : UNITED NATIONS

(b) The U.S. Constitution replaced the Articles of Confederation. The United Nations replaced the League of Nations.
Humanities—Description

79. MILLIMETER : CENTIMETER :: CENTIMETER : (***a.* decimeter**, *b.* meter, *c.* decameter, *d.* kilometer)

(a) There are 10 millimeters in a centimeter, and 10 centimeters in a decimeter.
Mathematics—Part/Whole

80. ENSIGN : NAVY :: (*a.* private, *b.* sergeant, ***c.* second lieutenant**, *d.* colonel) : ARMY

(c) An ensign is the lowest ranking commissioned officer in the Navy; a second lieutenant is the lowest ranking commissioned officer in the Army.
General Information—Description

81. COLT : REVOLVER :: NOBEL : (*a.* A-bomb, *b.* tear gas, *c.* rifle, ***d.* dynamite**)

    (d) Colt invented a type of revolver; Nobel invented dynamite.
    General Information—Description

82. HYDRATED : WATER :: ORGANIC : (*a.* hydrogen, *b.* nitrogen, *c.* oxygen, ***d.* carbon**)

    (d) A hydrated substance contains water; an organic substance contains carbon.
    Natural Science—Description

83. (*a.* doctors, *b.* officers, *c.* clergymen, ***d.* saboteurs**) : FIFTH COLUMN :: SPIES : INTELLIGENCE

    (d) During a war, saboteurs comprise a network that is often called a fifth column. Spies work in an intelligence network.
    General Information—Description

84. PING-PONG : BADMINTON :: TENNIS : (***a.* lacrosse**, *b.* football, *c.* handball, *d.* soccer)

    (a) The games of Ping-Pong, badminton, tennis, and lacrosse are all played with rackets.
    General Information—Class

85. (*a.* Aegisthus, ***b.* Priam**, *c.* Agamemnon, *d.* Theseus) : PARIS :: DAEDALUS : ICARUS

    (b) Priam was the father of Paris; Daedalus was the father of Icarus.
    Humanities—Description

86. BLACKSTONE : (*a.* medicine, *b.* politics, ***c.* law**, *d.* teaching) :: ROBERTS : PARLIAMENTARY PROCEDURE

    (c) Blackstone is known for his work on law, Roberts for his work on parliamentary procedure.
    Social Science—Description

87. WIFE OF BATH : (***a.* Chaucer**, *b.* Milton, *c.* Wordsworth, *d.* Spenser) :: BELINDA : POPE

    (a) The Wife of Bath is a literary character created by Chaucer, while Belinda was created by Pope.
    Humanities—Description

88. CATTON : CIVIL WAR :: (*a.* Plutarch, ***b.* Thucydides**, *c.* Herodotus, *d.* Pliny the Elder) : PELOPONNESIAN WAR

    (b) Catton is known for his historical writing on the Civil War, Thucydides for his historical work on the Peloponnesian War.
    Humanities—Description

89. JEHOVAH'S WITNESSES : RUSSELL :: MORMONS : (*a.* Wesley, ***b.* Smith**, *c.* Thomas, *d.* Kirby)

(b) The Jehovah's Witnesses sect was founded by Charles Russell; the Mormons were founded by Joseph Smith.
Humanities—Description

90. 10 : OCTAL :: (*a.* 1, ***b.* 1000**, *c.* 111, *d.* 101) : BINARY

(b) 10 in octal is equal to 1000 in binary; both are equal to 8 in conventional decimal notation.
Mathematics—Equality/Negation

91. NEW JERSEY : THIRD :: (*a.* Virginia, *b.* New York, ***c.* Delaware**, *d.* New Hampshire) : FIRST

(c) New Jersey was the third state to join the Union; Delaware was the first.
Humanities—Description

92. URIAH HEEP : HYPOCRITICALLY HUMBLE :: WILKINS MICAWBER : (***a.* poor but optimistic**, *b.* poor and pessimistic, *c.* rich and optimistic, *d.* rich but pessimistic)

(a) In Charles Dickens' *David Copperfield,* Uriah Heep is a character who is hypocritically humble, while Wilkins Micawber is poor but optimistic.
Humanities—Description

93. ABBOTT : FLATLAND :: DANTE : (*a.* China, ***b.* Purgatory**, *c.* Never-Never Land, *d.* Moonland)

(b) Abbott wrote a narrative describing his travels in Flatland; Dante wrote *The Divine Comedy,* describing in the second part of the trilogy his travels in Purgatory.
Humanities—Description

94. (*a.* catharsis, *b.* tragedy, *c.* bathos, ***d.* ethos**) : UNIVERSAL :: PATHOS : PERSONAL

(d) Ethos describes universal elements in a work of art, while pathos describes personal ones.
Humanities—Description

95. CANTOR : RABBI :: MUEZZIN : (*a.* minaret, *b.* guru, *c.* Brahman, ***d.* imam**)

(d) A cantor and a rabbi are both religious functionaries in the Jewish religion, while a muezzin and an imam are both functionaries in Islam.
Humanities—Class

96. ORPHEUS : RETURN OF EURYDICE TO HADES :: WIFE OF LOT : (*a.* transformation into a star, *b.* return to Sodom, ***c.* transformation into a pillar of salt**, *d.* return to Canaan)

(c) As a result of Orpheus' looking back, Eurydice was forced to return to Hades. As a result of Lot's wife's looking back, she was transformed into a pillar of salt.
Humanities—Description

97. CENTIGRADE : 100 :: KELVIN : (*a.* 132, *b.* 100, *c.* 0, ***d.* 373**)

(**d**) The boiling point of water is 100° Centigrade, and (to the nearest unit) 373 Kelvins.
Natural Science—Description

98. LA GIACONDA : (***a.* Mona Lisa**, *b.* La Pieta, *c.* Madonna, *d.* Venus de Milo) :: ARRANGEMENT IN BLACK AND GRAY : WHISTLER'S MOTHER

(**a**) *La Gioconda* and *Mona Lisa* refer to the same painting by Leonardo da Vinci. *Arrangement in Black and Gray* and *Whistler's Mother* refer to the same painting by Whistler.
Humanities—Similarity/Contrast

99. EMPIRICIST : UTILITARIAN :: HUME : (*a.* Spinoza, *b.* Leibnitz, *c.* Kant, ***d.* Mill**)

(**d**) Hume was an empiricist philosopher; Mill, a utilitarian philosopher.
Humanities—Description

100. BLOOMFIELD : SURFACE STRUCTURE :: (*a.* Whorf, *b.* Sapir, *c.* Skinner, ***d.* Chomsky**) : DEEP STRUCTURE

(**d**) In their respective linguistic analyses, Bloomfield theorized on the basis of surface structure, while Chomsky has theorized primarily on the basis of deep structure.
Social Science—Description

Item Classification Chart

Practice Test 1

CONTENT	RELATIONSHIP: Similarity/ Contrast	Description	Class	Completion	Part/ Whole	Equality/ Negation	Nonsemantic
Vocabulary	3, 21, 25, 26, 54, 67, 69, 60, 62, 64, 71	27, 41	9				
General Information	31, 32, 48, 65, 74	1, 2, 5, 6, 7, 11, 12, 14, 15, 17, 24, 34, 35, 38, 47, 51, 53, 56, 57, 58, 80, 81, 83	10, 20, 84			46, 66	
Humanities	55, 98	8, 16, 18, 19, 28, 39, 49, 50, 52, 61, 63, 68, 73, 76, 77, 78, 85, 87, 88, 89, 91, 92, 93, 94, 96, 99	40, 95	4			
Social Science		22, 29, 37, 86, 100					
Natural Science		13, 23, 36, 42, 44, 45, 72, 82, 97			33	59	
Mathematics					75, 79	90	
Nonsemantic							30, 43, 70

Miller Analogies Test PRACTICE TEST 2

DIRECTIONS: In each of the following questions, you will find three initial terms and, in parentheses, four answer options designated *a*, *b*, *c*, and *d*. You are to select from the four answer options the one that best completes the analogy with the three initial terms. To record your answers, use the answer sheet at the back of the book.

TIME: *50 minutes*

1. CANDLE : TALLOW :: TIRE : (*a.* automobile, *b.* round, *c.* rubber, *d.* hollow)
2. TERRESTRIAL : (*a.* palatial, *b.* partial, *c.* martial, *d.* celestial) :: EARTH : HEAVEN
3. (*a.* father, *b.* uncle, *c.* brother, *d.* son) : SIBLING :: HUSBAND : SPOUSE
4. 3.6% : (*a.* 0.0036, *b.* 0.036, *c.* 0.36, *d.* 3.6) :: 480% : 4.8
5. PERIODIC : INTERMITTENT :: CONSTANT : (*a.* incessant, *b.* occasional, *c.* infrequent, *d.* never)
6. DARWIN : (*a.* gravity, *b.* planetary orbits, *c.* evolution, *d.* magnetism) :: EINSTEIN : RELATIVITY
7. COMPOSER : SONATA :: (*a.* physicist, *b.* artist, *c.* sculptor, *d.* author) : LITHOGRAPH
8. HUNGRY : LION :: BUSY : (*a.* squirrel, *b.* beaver, *c.* hare, *d.* chipmunk)
9. MATRICIDE : MOTHER :: FRATRICIDE : (*a.* uncle, *b.* father, *c.* brother, *d.* son)
10. (*a.* United, *b.* League, *c.* National, *d.* NFL) : DODGERS :: AMERICAN : YANKEES
11. KNOCK : PIGEON :: KNEED : (*a.* toed, *b.* waisted, *c.* armed, *d.* headed)
12. (*a.* Memorial Day, *b.* Thanksgiving, *c.* Christmas, *d.* Labor Day) : DECORATION DAY :: VETERANS' DAY : ARMISTICE DAY
13. HANG : NOOSE :: BEHEAD : (*a.* guillotine, *b.* Savonarola, *c.* Robespierre, *d.* ablation)
14. APPROPRIATE : INAPPROPRIATE :: APROPOS : (*a.* inapropos, *b.* misapropos, *c.* anapropos, *d.* malapropos)

15. (*a.* gases, *b.* good eating, *c.* intestinal tract, *d.* gasoline) : GASTRONOMY :: HEAVENLY BODIES : ASTRONOMY

16. CONGRESS : UNITED STATES :: (*a.* UNICEF, *b.* Secretary-General, *c.* Security Council, *d.* General Assembly) : UNITED NATIONS

17. EXECUTOR : (*a.* executriss, *b.* executress, *c.* executrex, *d.* executrix) :: ACTOR : ACTRESS

18. CANCEROUS : NONCANCEROUS :: MALIGNANT : (*a.* benign, *b.* benevolent, *c.* beneficent, *d.* latent)

19. (*a.* syllogism, *b.* intellect, *c.* troop movements, *d.* weapons) : LOGISTICS :: LANGUAGE : LINGUISTICS

20. SUBWAY : NEW YORK :: (*a.* Metro, *b.* monorail, *c.* cable car, *d.* airplane) : PARIS

21. (*a.* velocity, *b.* humidity, *c.* pressure, *d.* THI) : BAROMETER :: MILEAGE : ODOMETER

22. KANSAS : WHEAT :: (*a.* Nebraska, *b.* Arkansas, *c.* Wisconsin, *d.* Idaho) : POTATO

23. HYPO : DERMIC :: UNDER : (*a.* skin, *b.* medicine, *c.* blood, *d.* syringe)

24. PECCADILLO : (*a.* stutter, *b.* pretense, *c.* amnesia, *d.* sin) :: MISDEMEANOR : CRIME

25. MISANTHROPE : (*a.* life, *b.* religion, *c.* women, *d.* people) :: MISOGAMIST : MARRIAGE

26. OSTENTATIOUS : (*a.* showy, *b.* proud, *c.* modest, *d.* fickle) :: ONEROUS : BURDENSOME

27. NATURE : NURTURE :: HEREDITY : (*a.* gene, *b.* progenitor, *c.* evolution, *d.* environment)

28. HURRY : SCURRY :: HURLY : (*a.* burly, *b.* curly, *c.* gurly, *d.* wurly)

29. STEM : METS :: (*a.* tab, *b.* ball, *c.* team, *d.* root) : BAT

30. SATAN : BEELZEBUB :: DEVIL : (*a.* Charon, *b.* Pandemonium, *c.* Lucifer, *d.* Hades)

31. FORT SUMTER : CIVIL WAR :: (*a.* Valley Forge, *b.* Princeton, *c.* Lexington, *d.* Trenton) : AMERICAN REVOLUTION

32. (*a.* chameleon, *b.* salamander, *c.* tadpole, *d.* chamois) : FICKLE :: MULE : STUBBORN

33. NEW AMSTERDAM : NEW YORK :: CONSTANTINOPLE : (*a.* Budapest, *b.* Istanbul, *c.* Cairo, *d.* Baghdad)

34. ANESTHESIA : FEEL :: (*a.* eyeball, *b.* eyes, *c.* glasses, *d.* blindness) : SEE

35. CORPORAL : BEAT :: CAPITAL : (*a.* stun, *b.* maim, *c.* kill, *d.* shock)

36. (*a.* neutron, *b.* electron, *c.* nucleon, *d.* positron) : PROTON :: NEGATIVE : POSITIVE

37. CARPE : DIEM :: CAVEAT : (*a.* corpus, *b.* emptor, *c.* deum, *d.* mandamus)

38. RAIN : (*a.* tempest, *b.* frost, *c.* hail, *d.* dry ice) :: WATER : ICE

39. FEINT : (*a.* fall, *b.* remove, *c.* pretend, *d.* authenticate) :: SEVER : SEPARATE

40. 10 : COMMANDMENTS :: (*a.* 5, *b.* 7, *c.* 10, *d.* 12) : DEADLY SINS

41. DOUBLE ENTENDRE : (*a.* ambiguity, *b.* treachery, *c.* meaninglessness, *d.* misperception) :: DOUBLE TAKE : DELAYED REACTION

42. (*a.* nominalism, *b.* phenomenalism, *c.* determinism, *d.* rationalism) : FATALISM :: EXISTENTIALISM : FREE WILL

43. (*a.* carmine, *b.* yellow, *c.* brown, *d.* orange) : RED :: AZURE : BLUE

44. FRAME : PICTURE :: (*a.* cell wall, *b.* endoplasmic reticulum, *c.* cytoplasm, *d.* nuclear envelope) : CELL

45. (*a.* keno, *b.* kalaha, *c.* wari, *d.* soma) : CRAPS :: ROULETTE : TWENTY-ONE

46. HECTOR : (*a.* Rome, *b.* Carthage, *c.* Sicily, *d.* Troy) :: ACHILLES : GREECE

47. PICA : (*a.* piezo, *b.* elite, *c.* 10-point, *d.* tiny) :: LARGE : SMALL

48. SWARM : BEES :: (*a.* colony, *b.* covey, *c.* pack, *d.* pride) : QUAIL

49. BITUMINOUS : ANTHRACITE :: (*a.* wood, *b.* lead, *c.* lignite, *d.* oil) : STEEL

50. CARRY NATION : (*a.* women's suffrage, *b.* low-income housing, *c.* temperance, *d.* abolition of child labor) :: MARTIN LUTHER KING, JR. : CIVIL RIGHTS

51. STENCIL : LETTERS :: COMPASS : (*a.* time, *b.* direction, *c.* northwest, *d.* circle)

52. (*a.* proposal, *b.* talk, *c.* dissertation, *d.* dialogue) : ORATION :: QUIZ : EXAMINATION

53. ANTERIOR : POSTERIOR :: (*a*. ventral, *b*. lateral, *c*. external, *d*. internal) : DORSAL

54. IMMIGRATION : EMIGRATION :: ENTRY : (*a*. expulsion, *b*. migration, *c*. egress, *d*. estuary)

55. SATRAP : (*a*. ruler, *b*. bush, *c*. miser, *d*. loner) :: TRAP : AMBUSH

56. ELEGY : LAMENTING :: EPIGRAM : (*a*. inane, *b*. abstruse, *c*. witty, *d*. obtuse)

57. REFORMATION : PROTESTANTS :: COUNTER-REFORMATION : (*a*. Catholics, *b*. Protestants, *c*. Anglicans, *d*. Jews)

58. (*a*. beriberi, *b*. rickets, *c*. anemia, *d*. pellagra) : D :: SCURVY : C

59. GO DUTCH : PAY YOUR OWN EXPENSES :: IN DUTCH : (*a*. in luck, *b*. in trouble, *c*. rich, *d*. poor)

60. FOOL'S GOLD : (*a*. ore, *b*. pyrite, *c*. bauxite, *d*. manganese) :: PENCIL LEAD : GRAPHITE

61. MILL : (*a*. franc, *b*. centime, *c*. shilling, *d*. cent) :: PENNY : DIME

62. (*a*. Spain, *b*. Italy, *c*. Israel, *d*. Lebanon) : RUSSIA :: EL AL : AEROFLOT

63. GAUGUIN : (*a*. England, *b*. U.S.A., *c*. Tahiti, *d*. Madagascar) :: GOYA : SPAIN

64. (*a*. entrecote, *b*. legume, *c*. glace, *d*. poulet) : STEAK :: ESCARGOTS : SNAILS

65. TEMERITY : AUDACITY :: (*a*. softness, *b*. boldness, *c*. shyness, *d*. depravity) : BRAVERY

66. CALORIE : (*a*. weight, *b*. basal metabolism, *c*. fat, *d*. energy) :: DECADE : TIME

67. PETROLOGY : (*a*. sandstone, *b*. Brontosaurus, *c*. moth, *d*. nylon) :: BOTANY : ROSE

68. HANSEL : GRETEL :: ORESTES : (*a*. Jocasta, *b*. Electra, *c*. Ophelia, *d*. Alicia)

69. (*a*. rude, *b*. talkative, *c*. immodest, *d*. brash) : GARRULOUS :: PETULANT : PEEVISH

70. PONCE DE LEON : (*a*. Atlantic Ocean, *b*. Mexico, *c*. Georgia, *d*. Florida) :: BALBOA : PACIFIC OCEAN

71. ATTENUATE : (*a*. disprove, *b*. weaken, *c*. prove, *d*. strengthen) :: ATTRACT : REPEL

72. CEREBRUM : THINKING :: CEREBELLUM : (*a.* olfaction, *b.* muscular coordination, *c.* glandular secretion, *d.* audition)

73. BEHAVIORISM : U.S.A. :: GESTALT : (*a.* France, *b.* England, *c.* Switzerland, *d.* Germany)

74. MONROE : (*a.* Treatise, *b.* Edict, *c.* Decree, *d.* Code) :: DOCTRINE : NAPOLEON

75. LXII : CLXXXVI :: D : (*a.* M, *b.* MC, *c.* MD, *d.* MM)

76. (*a.* loudness, *b.* compression, *c.* brightness, *d.* hardness) : MOHS :: TEMPERATURE : KELVIN

77. FOX : OWL :: (*a.* Saul, *b.* David, *c.* Iago, *d.* Lear) : SOLOMON

78. 1 : LINE :: 2 : (*a.* length, *b.* ellipse, *c.* point, *d.* sphere)

79. EXOSKELETON : LOBSTER :: ENDOSKELETON : (*a.* oyster, *b.* tiger, *c.* barnacle, *d.* worm)

80. FEZ : SOMBRERO :: BERET : (*a.* phylactery, *b.* millinery, *c.* muffler, *d.* fedora)

81. (a. angry, *b.* sanguine, *c.* dejected, *d.* pale) : PESSIMISTIC :: HOPEFUL : DISPIRITED

82. $4^{1/2} : 9^{1/2} : 36^{1/2}$ :: (*a.* 6, *b.* 9, *c.* 12, *d.* 81)

83. INCUBUS : (*a.* faccubus, *b.* excubus, *c.* succubus, *d.* maccubus) :: WOMEN : MEN

84. HEAD MONEY : (*a.* warn, *b.* punish, *c.* capture, *d.* bribe) :: HUSH MONEY : SILENCE

85. SUSTAIN : OVERRULE :: IN CAMERA : (*a.* in trouble, *b.* in public, *c.* in court, *d.* out of court)

86. CRONUS : SATURN :: (*a.* Poseidon, *b.* Ares, *c.* Zeus, *d.* Hermes) : MARS

87. D MINOR : F MAJOR :: (*a.* E minor, *b.* F minor, *c.* F# minor, *d.* G# minor) : A MAJOR

88. TAME : MATE :: LAME : (*a.* female, *b.* injured, *c.* male, *d.* excuse)

89. (*a.* spinal, *b.* neutral, *c.* temporal, *d.* spatial) : PARIETAL :: OCCIPITAL : FRONTAL

90. PARADISE : LOST :: JERUSALEM : (*a.* Sanctified, *b.* Discovered, *c.* Delivered, *d.* Vanquished)

91. PENN : PENNSYLVANIA :: CALVERT : (*a*. South Carolina, *b*. Vermont, *c*. Maryland, *d*. Rhode Island)

92. ETEOCLES : (*a*. Theseus, *b*. Laius, *c*. Oedipus, *d*. Polynices) :: ANTIGONE : ISMENE

93. DECIMAL : 10 :: DUODECIMAL : (*a*. 2, *b*. 8, *c*. 12, *d*. 16)

94. RATIONALIST : EMPIRICIST :: (*a*. Berkeley, *b*. Hume, *c*. Mill, *d*. Leibniz) : LOCKE

95. (*a*. Ivan Karamazov, *b*. Anna Karenina, *c*. Nicolai Gogol, *d*. Grigory Smirnov) : DOSTOYEVSKY :: THÉRÈSE : MAURIAC

96. PALESTRINA : 16th :: (*a*. Beethoven, *b*. Bach, *c*. Tchaikovsky, *d*. Stravinsky) : 20th

97. NICHOLAS II : RUSSIAN REVOLUTION :: (*a*. Louis XIV, *b*. Louis XV, *c*. Louis XVI, *d*. Louis XVII) : FRENCH REVOLUTION

98. VAN CLIBURN : PIANO :: PABLO CASALS : (*a*. piano, *b*. violin, *c*. cello, *d*. clarinet)

99. (*a*. Versailles, *b*. Xanadu, *c*. St. Malo, *d*. Rouen) : LOUIS XIV :: AMBOISE : FRANCIS II

100. ISHMAEL : (*a*. Hagar, *b*. Rebeccah, *c*. Esther, *d*. Sophia) :: ISAAC : SARAH

Answer Key for Practice Test 2

1. *c*	11. *a*	21. *c*	31. *c*	41. *a*	51. *d*	61. *d*	71. *d*	81. *b*	91. *c*
2. *d*	12. *a*	22. *d*	32. *a*	42. *c*	52. *b*	62. *c*	72. *b*	82. *b*	92. *d*
3. *c*	13. *a*	23. *a*	33. *b*	43. *a*	53. *a*	63. *c*	73. *d*	83. *c*	93. *c*
4. *b*	14. *d*	24. *d*	34. *d*	44. *a*	54. *c*	64. *a*	74. *d*	84. *c*	94. *d*
5. *a*	15. *b*	25. *d*	35. *c*	45. *a*	55. *a*	65. *b*	75. *c*	85. *b*	95. *a*
6. *c*	16. *d*	26. *a*	36. *b*	46. *d*	56. *c*	66. *d*	76. *d*	86. *b*	96. *d*
7. *b*	17. *d*	27. *d*	37. *b*	47. *b*	57. *a*	67. *a*	77. *c*	87. *c*	97. *c*
8. *b*	18. *a*	28. *a*	38. *c*	48. *b*	58. *b*	68. *b*	78. *b*	88. *c*	98. *c*
9. *c*	19. *c*	29. *a*	39. *c*	49. *b*	59. *b*	69. *b*	79. *b*	89. *c*	99. *a*
10. *c*	20. *a*	30. *c*	40. *b*	50. *c*	60. *b*	70. *d*	80. *d*	90. *c*	100. *a*

Explanation of Answers for Practice Test 2

1. CANDLE : TALLOW :: TIRE : (*a.* automobile, *b.* round, ***c.* rubber**, *d.* hollow)

   (c) A candle is frequently made of tallow. A tire is frequently made of rubber.
   General Information—Description

2. TERRESTRIAL : (*a.* palatial, *b.* partial, *c.* martial, ***d.* celestial**) :: EARTH : HEAVEN

   (d) Something that is terrestrial is of the earth. Something that is celestial is of heaven.
   Vocabulary—Description

3. (*a.* father, *b.* uncle, ***c.* brother**, *d.* son) : SIBLING :: HUSBAND : SPOUSE

   (c) A brother is a sibling. A husband is a spouse.
   Vocabulary—Description

4. 3.6% : (*a.* 0.0036, ***b.* 0.036**, *c.* 0.36, *d.* 3.6) :: 480% : 4.8

   (b) 3.6% is equal to 0.036. 480% is equal to 4.8.
   Mathematics—Equality/Negation

5. PERIODIC : INTERMITTENT :: CONSTANT : (***a.* incessant**, *b.* occasional, *c.* infrequent, *d.* never)

   (a) *Periodic* and *intermittent* are synonyms, as are *constant* and *incessant*.
   Vocabulary—Similarity/Contrast

6. DARWIN : (*a.* gravity, *b.* planetary orbits, ***c.* evolution**, *d.* magnetism) :: EINSTEIN : RELATIVITY

   (c) Charles Darwin is primarily responsible for the theory of evolution, while Albert Einstein is primarily responsible for relativity theory.
   Natural Science—Description

7. COMPOSER : SONATA :: (*a.* physicist, ***b.* artist**, *c.* sculptor, *d.* author) : LITHOGRAPH

   (b) A sonata is the creation of a composer. A lithograph is the creation of an artist.
   Humanities—Description

8. HUNGRY : LION :: BUSY : (*a.* squirrel, ***b.* beaver**, *c.* hare, *d.* chipmunk)

   (b) "Hungry as a lion" and "busy as a beaver" are both common similes used in everyday speech.
   General Information—Description

9. MATRICIDE : MOTHER :: FRATRICIDE : (*a.* uncle, *b.* father, ***c.* brother**, *d.* son)

(c) The act of killing one's mother is called matricide. The act of killing one's brother is called fratricide.
Vocabulary—Description

10. (*a.* United, *b.* League, ***c.* National** *d.* NFL) : DODGERS :: AMERICAN : YANKEES

(c) The Dodgers are a National League baseball team, while the Yankees are an American League team.
General Information—Description

11. KNOCK : PIGEON :: KNEED : (***a.* toed**, *b.* waisted, *c.* armed, *d.* headed)

(a) A person may be referred to as knock-kneed or pigeon-toed.
General Information—Completion

12. (***a.* Memorial Day**, *b.* Thanksgiving, *c.* Christmas, *d.* Labor Day) : DECORATION DAY :: VETERANS' DAY : ARMISTICE DAY

(a) Memorial Day and Decoration Day are two names for the same holiday. Veterans' Day and Armistice Day are also two names for the same holiday.
General Information—Similarity/Contrast

13. HANG : NOOSE :: BEHEAD : (***a.* guillotine**, *b.* Savonarola, *c.* Robespierre, *d.* ablation)

(a) A person is hanged with a noose, but beheaded with a guillotine.
General Information—Description

14. APPROPRIATE : INAPPROPRIATE :: APROPOS : (*a.* inapropos, *b.* misapropos, *c.* anapropos, ***d.* malapropos**)

(d) Something that is not appropriate is inappropriate. Something that is not apropos is malapropos.
Vocabulary—Similarity/Contrast

15. (*a.* gases, ***b.* good eating**, *c.* intestinal tract, *d.* gasoline) : GASTRONOMY :: HEAVENLY BODIES : ASTRONOMY

(b) Gastronomy is the study of good eating. Astronomy is the study of heavenly bodies.
General Information—Description

16. CONGRESS : UNITED STATES :: (*a.* UNICEF, *b.* Secretary-General, *c.* Security Council, ***d.* General Assembly**) : UNITED NATIONS

(d) The Congress is the main legislative body of the United States. The General Assembly is the main legislative body of the United Nations.
General Information—Description

17. EXECUTOR : (*a.* executriss, *b.* executress, *c.* executrex, ***d.* executrix**) :: ACTOR : ACTRESS

(d) The feminine form of *executor* is *executrix*. The feminine form of *actor* is *actress*.
General Information—Class

18. CANCEROUS : NONCANCEROUS :: MALIGNANT : (***a.* benign**, *b.* benevolent, *c.* beneficent, *d.* latent)

    (**a**) A cancerous tumor is called malignant. A noncancerous tumor is called benign.
    General Information—Similarity/Contrast

19. (*a.* syllogism, *b.* intellect, ***c.* troop movements**, *d.* weapons) : LOGISTICS :: LANGUAGE : LINGUISTICS

    (**c**) Logistics is the study of troop movements. Linguistics is the study of language.
    General Information—Description

20. SUBWAY : NEW YORK :: (***a.* Metro**, *b.* monorail, *c.* cable car, *d.* airplane) : PARIS

    (**a**) What is called a subway in New York is called the Metro in Paris.
    General Information—Description

21. (*a.* velocity, *b.* humidity, ***c.* pressure**, *d.* THI) : BAROMETER :: MILEAGE : ODOMETER

    (**c**) A barometer measures pressure. An odometer measures mileage.
    General Information—Description

22. KANSAS : WHEAT :: (*a.* Nebraska, *b.* Arkansas, *c.* Wisconsin, ***d.* Idaho**) : POTATO

    (**d**) Kansas is known for its wheat fields, Idaho for its potato fields.
    General Information—Description

23. HYPO : DERMIC :: UNDER : (***a.* skin**, *b.* medicine, *c.* blood, *d.* syringe)

    (**a**) A hypodermic needle goes under (hypo) the skin (dermis).
    Vocabulary—Similarity/Contrast

24. PECCADILLO : (*a.* stutter, *b.* pretense, *c.* amnesia, ***d.* sin**) :: MISDEMEANOR : CRIME

    (**d**) A peccadillo is a minor sin. A misdemeanor is a minor crime.
    Vocabulary—Description

25. MISANTHROPE : (*a.* life, *b.* religion, *c.* women, ***d.* people**) :: MISOGAMIST : MARRIAGE

    (**d**) A misanthrope detests people. A misogamist detests marriage.
    Vocabulary—Description

26. OSTENTATIOUS : (***a.* showy**, *b.* proud, *c.* modest, *d.* fickle) :: ONEROUS : BURDENSOME

    (**a**) *Ostentatious* means showy. *Onerous* means burdensome.
    Vocabulary—Similarity/Contrast

27. NATURE : NURTURE :: HEREDITY : (*a.* gene, *b.* progenitor, *c.* evolution, ***d.* environment**)

(**d**) A "nature-nurture" controversy is one between the effects of heredity and environment.
General Information—Description

28. HURRY : SCURRY :: HURLY : (***a.* burly**, *b.* curly, *c.* gurly, *d.* wurly)

(**a**) *Hurry-scurry* and *hurly-burly* both refer to disorder and confusion.
Vocabulary—Completion

29. STEM : METS :: (***a.* tab**, *b.* ball, *c.* team, *d.* root) : BAT

(**a**) *Stem* spelled backwards is *mets*. *Tab* spelled backwards is *bat*.
Nonsemantic

30. SATAN : BEELZEBUB :: DEVIL : (*a.* Charon, *b.* Pandemonium, ***c.* Lucifer**, *d.* Hades)

(**c**) Satan, Beelzebub, the Devil, and Lucifer are all different names for the same entity.
Humanities—Similarity/Contrast

31. FORT SUMTER : CIVIL WAR :: (*a.* Valley Forge, *b.* Princeton, ***c.* Lexington**, *d.* Trenton) : AMERICAN REVOLUTION

(**c**) Fort Sumter was the scene of the first battle of the Civil War. Lexington was the scene of the first battle of the American Revolution.
Humanities—Description

32. (***a.* chameleon**, *b.* salamander, *c.* tadpole, *d.* chamois) : FICKLE :: MULE : STUBBORN

(**a**) A chameleon is fickle; a mule, stubborn.
General Information—Description

33. NEW AMSTERDAM : NEW YORK :: CONSTANTINOPLE : (*a.* Budapest, ***b.* Istanbul**, *c.* Cairo, *d.* Baghdad)

(**b**) New Amsterdam is a former name of New York City. Constantinople is a former name of Istanbul.
General Information—Similarity/Contrast

34. ANESTHESIA : FEEL :: (*a.* eyeball, *b.* eyes, *c.* glasses, ***d.* blindness**) : SEE

(**d**) Anesthesia is a state in which one does not feel. Blindness is a state in which one does not see.
General Information—Description

35. CORPORAL : BEAT :: CAPITAL : (*a.* stun, *b.* maim, ***c.* kill**, *d.* shock)

(**c**) In corporal punishment, a person is beaten. In capital punishment, a person is killed.
General Information—Description

36. (*a.* neutron, ***b.* electron**, *c.* nucleon, *d.* positron) : PROTON :: NEGATIVE : POSITIVE

    (b) An electron has a negative electrical charge. A proton has a positive electrical charge.
    Natural Science—Description

37. CARPE : DIEM :: CAVEAT : (*a.* corpus, ***b.* emptor**, *c.* deum, *d.* mandamus)

    (b) *Carpe diem* (seize the opportunity—literally, the day) and *caveat emptor* (let the buyer beware) are both Latinisms used in English.
    Vocabulary—Completion

38. RAIN : (*a.* tempest, *b.* frost, ***c.* hail**, *d.* dry ice) :: WATER : ICE

    (c) Hail is frozen rain; ice is frozen water.
    General Information—Class

39. FEINT : (*a.* fall, *b.* remove, ***c.* pretend**, *d.* authenticate) :: SEVER : SEPARATE

    (c) To feint is to pretend. To sever is to separate.
    Vocabulary—Similarity/Contrast

40. 10 : COMMANDMENTS :: (*a.* 5, ***b.* 7**, *c.* 10, *d.* 12) : DEADLY SINS

    (b) There are 10 Commandments and 7 deadly sins.
    General Information—Class

41. DOUBLE ENTENDRE : (***a.* ambiguity**, *b.* treachery, *c.* meaninglessness, *d.* misperception) :: DOUBLE TAKE : DELAYED REACTION

    (a) A double entendre is characterized by ambiguity. A double take is characterized by a delayed reaction.
    Vocabulary—Similarity/Contrast

42. (*a.* nominalism, *b.* phenomenalism, ***c.* determinism**, *d.* rationalism) : FATALISM :: EXISTENTIALISM : FREE WILL

    (c) The philosophical doctrine of determinism argues for fatalism. The doctrine of existentialism argues for free will.
    Humanities—Description

43. (***a.* carmine**, *b.* yellow, *c.* brown, *d.* orange) : RED :: AZURE : BLUE

    (a) Carmine is a shade of red. Azure is a shade of blue.
    General Information—Class

44. FRAME : PICTURE :: (***a.* cell wall**, *b.* endoplasmic reticulum, *c.* cytoplasm, *d.* nuclear envelope) : CELL

    (a) A frame surrounds a picture. A cell wall surrounds a cell.
    Natural Science—Description

45. (***a.* keno**, *b.* kalaha, *c.* wari, *d.* soma) : CRAPS :: ROULETTE : TWENTY-ONE

(a) Keno, craps, roulette, and twenty-one are all gambling games.
General Information—Class

46. HECTOR : (*a.* Rome, *b.* Carthage, *c.* Sicily, ***d.* Troy**) :: ACHILLES : GREECE

(d) In the Trojan War, Hector fought for Troy and Achilles fought for Greece.
Humanities—Description

47. PICA : (*a.* piezo, ***b.* elite**, *c.* 10-point, *d.* tiny) :: LARGE : SMALL

(b) On a typewriter, pica is large type and elite is small type.
General Information—Description

48. SWARM : BEES :: (*a.* colony, ***b.* covey**, *c.* pack, *d.* pride) : QUAIL

(b) A group of bees is referred to as a swarm. A group of quail is referred to as a covey.
General Information—Description

49. BITUMINOUS : ANTHRACITE :: (*a.* wood, ***b.* lead**, *c.* lignite, *d.* oil) : STEEL

(b) Bituminous coal is soft, and anthracite coal is hard. Lead is a soft metal, and steel a hard metal.
General Information—Class

50. CARRY NATION : (*a.* women's suffrage, *b.* low-income housing, ***c.* temperance**, *d.* abolition of child labor) :: MARTIN LUTHER KING, JR. : CIVIL RIGHTS

(c) Carry Nation fought for temperance, while Martin Luther King, Jr. fought for civil rights.
Humanities—Description

51. STENCIL : LETTERS :: COMPASS : (*a.* time, *b.* direction, *c.* northwest, ***d.* circle**)

(d) A stencil is used to draw letters. A compass is used to draw a circle.
Mathematics—Description

52. (*a.* proposal, ***b.* talk**, *c.* dissertation, *d.* dialogue) : ORATION :: QUIZ : EXAMINATION

(b) An oration is a large-scale talk. An examination is a large-scale quiz.
Vocabulary—Description

53. ANTERIOR : POSTERIOR :: (***a.* ventral**, *b.* lateral, *c.* external, *d.* internal) : DORSAL

(a) In humans, the anterior and ventral sides are the front. The posterior and dorsal sides are the rear.
Natural Science—Similarity/Contrast

54. IMMIGRATION : EMIGRATION :: ENTRY : (*a.* expulsion, *b.* migration, ***c.* egress**, *d.* estuary)

    (c) Immigration is entry into a country, while emigration is egress from a country.
    Vocabulary—Similarity/Contrast

55. SATRAP : (***a.* ruler**, *b.* bush, *c.* miser, *d.* loner) :: TRAP : AMBUSH

    (a) A satrap is one kind of ruler. A trap is one kind of ambush.
    Vocabulary—Similarity/Contrast

56. ELEGY : LAMENTING :: EPIGRAM : (*a.* inane, *b.* abstruse, ***c.* witty**, *d.* obtuse)

    (c) An elegy is lamenting. An epigram is witty.
    Vocabulary—Description

57. REFORMATION : PROTESTANTS :: COUNTER-REFORMATION : (***a.* Catholics**, *b.* Protestants, *c.* Anglicans, *d.* Jews)

    (a) The Reformation was staged by Protestants, while the Counter-Reformation was staged by Catholics.
    Humanities—Description

58. (*a.* beriberi, ***b.* rickets**, *c.* anemia, *d.* pellagra) : D :: SCURVY : C

    (b) Rickets is caused by a deficiency of vitamin D. Scurvy is caused by a deficiency of vitamin C.
    Natural Sciences—Description

59. GO DUTCH : PAY YOUR OWN EXPENSES :: IN DUTCH : (*a.* in luck, ***b.* in trouble**, *c.* rich, *d.* poor)

    (b) To go Dutch is to pay your own expenses. To be in Dutch is to be in trouble.
    Vocabulary—Similarity/Contrast

60. FOOL'S GOLD : (*a.* ore, ***b.* pyrite**, *c.* bauxite, *d.* manganese) :: PENCIL LEAD : GRAPHITE

    (b) Fool's gold is pyrite. Pencil lead is graphite.
    General Information—Similarity/Contrast

61. MILL : (*a.* franc, *b.* centime, *c.* shilling, ***d.* cent**) :: PENNY : DIME

    (d) A mill is a tenth of a cent. A penny is a tenth of a dime.
    General Information—Part/Whole

62. (*a.* Spain, *b.* Italy, ***c.* Israel**, *d.* Lebanon) : RUSSIA :: EL AL : AEROFLOT

    (c) El Al is an Israeli airline, while Aeroflot is an airline of Russia.
    General Information—Description

63. GAUGUIN : (*a.* England, *b.* U.S.A., ***c.* Tahiti**, *d.* Madagascar) :: GOYA : SPAIN

(c) Gauguin is famous for his paintings relating to Tahiti. Goya is famous for his paintings relating to Spain.
Humanities—Description

64. (***a.* entrecote**, *b.* legume, *c.* glace, *d.* poulet) : STEAK :: ESCARGOTS : SNAILS

(a) In France, steak is called entrecote, while snails are called escargots.
General Information—Similarity/Contrast

65. TEMERITY : AUDACITY :: (*a.* softness, ***b.* boldness**, *c.* shyness, *d.* depravity) : BRAVERY

(b) *Temerity, audacity, boldness*, and *bravery* are synonyms.
Vocabulary—Similarity/Contrast

66. CALORIE : (*a.* weight, *b.* basal metabolism, *c.* fat, ***d.* energy**) :: DECADE : TIME

(d) A calorie is a measure of energy. A decade is a measure of time.
Natural Science—Description

67. PETROLOGY : (***a.* sandstone**, *b.* Brontosaurus, *c.* moth, *d.* nylon) :: BOTANY : ROSE

(a) Petrology is the study of rocks, among which is sandstone. Botany is the study of plants, among which is a rose.
Natural Science—Description

68. HANSEL : GRETEL :: ORESTES : (*a.* Jocasta, ***b.* Electra**, *c.* Ophelia, *d.* Alicia)

(b) Hansel and Gretel were brother and sister, as were Orestes and Electra.
Humanities—Class

69. (*a.* rude, ***b.* talkative**, *c.* immodest, *d.* brash) : GARRULOUS :: PETULANT : PEEVISH

(b) A garrulous person is talkative; a petulant person is peevish.
Vocabulary—Similarity/Contrast

70. PONCE DE LEON : (*a.* Atlantic Ocean, *b.* Mexico, *c.* Georgia, ***d.* Florida**) : BALBOA : PACIFIC OCEAN

(d) Ponce de Leon discovered Florida; Balboa discovered the Pacific Ocean.
Humanities—Description

71. ATTENUATE : (*a.* disprove, *b.* weaken, *c.* prove, ***d.* strengthen**) :: ATTRACT : REPEL

(d) *Attenuate* and *strengthen* are antonyms, as are *attract* and *repel.*
Vocabulary—Similarity/Contrast

72. CEREBRUM : THINKING :: CEREBELLUM : (*a.* olfaction, ***b.* muscular coordination**, *c.* glandular secretion, *d.* audition)

(b) In the brain, the cerebrum controls thinking, while the cerebellum controls muscular coordination.
Natural Sciences—Description

73. BEHAVIORISM : U.S.A. :: GESTALT : (*a.* France, *b.* England, *c.* Switzerland, ***d.* Germany**)

(d) In psychology, behaviorism originated in the United States, while the Gestalt movement originated in Germany.
Social Science—Description

74. MONROE : (*a.* Treatise, *b.* Edict, *c.* Decree, ***d.* Code**) :: DOCTRINE : NAPOLEON

(d) The Monroe Doctrine and the Code Napoleon were both policy statements.
Humanities—Completion

75. LXII : CLXXXVI :: D : (*a.* M, *b.* MC, ***c.* MD**, *d.* MM)

(c) 62 is to 186 as 500 is to 1500.
Mathematics—Equality/Negation

76. (*a.* loudness, *b.* compression, *c.* brightness, ***d.* hardness**) : MOHS :: TEMPERATURE : KELVIN

(d) The Mohs scale measures hardness, while the Kelvin scale measures temperature.
Natural Science—Description

77. FOX : OWL :: (*a.* Saul, *b.* David, ***c.* Iago**, *d.* Lear) : SOLOMON

(c) Iago was cunning, as a fox is supposed to be. Solomon was wise, as an owl is supposed to be.
Humanities—Description

78. 1 : LINE :: 2 : (*a.* length, ***b.* ellipse**, *c.* point, *d.* sphere)

(b) A line is one-dimensional, while an ellipse is two-dimensional.
Mathematics—Description

79. EXOSKELETON : LOBSTER :: ENDOSKELETON : (*a.* oyster, ***b.* tiger**, *c.* barnacle, *d.* worm)

(b) A lobster has an exoskeleton; a tiger has an endoskeleton.
Natural Science—Description

80. FEZ : SOMBRERO :: BERET : (*a.* phylactery, *b.* millinery, *c.* muffler, ***d.* fedora**)

(d) A fez, a sombrero, a beret, and a fedora are all forms of headgear.
General Information—Class

81. (*a.* angry, ***b.* sanguine**, *c.* dejected, *d.* pale) : PESSIMISTIC :: HOPEFUL : DISPIRITED

(**b**) *Sanguine* means *hopeful*; *pessimistic* means *dispirited*.
Vocabulary—Similarity/Contrast

82. $4^{1/2} : 9^{1/2} :: 36^{1/2}$: (*a*. 6, ***b*. 9**, *c*. 12, *d*. 81)

(**b**) 2 is to 3 as 6 is to 9.
Mathematics—Equality/Negation

83. INCUBUS : (*a*. faccubus, *b*. excubus, ***c*. succubus**, *d*. maccubus) :: WOMEN : MEN

(**c**) An incubus was once thought to be a demon that sought to have intercourse with sleeping women. A succubus sought to have intercourse with sleeping men.
General Information—Description

84. HEAD MONEY : (*a*. warn, *b*. punish, ***c*. capture**, *d*. bribe) :: HUSH MONEY : SILENCE

(**c**) Head money is used as payment for capture. Hush money is used as payment for silence.
General Information—Description

85. SUSTAIN : OVERRULE :: IN CAMERA : (*a*. in trouble, ***b*. in public**, *c*. in court, *d*. out of court)

(**b**) *Sustain* and *overrule* are opposites, as are *in camera* and *in public*.
Social Science—Similarity/Contrast

86. CRONUS : SATURN :: (*a*. Poseidon, ***b*. Ares**, *c*. Zeus, *d*. Hermes) : MARS

(**b**) Cronus is the Greek name, and Saturn the Roman name, for the god of agriculture. Ares is the Greek name, and Mars the Roman name, for the god of war.
Humanities—Similarity/Contrast

87. D MINOR : F MAJOR :: (*a*. E minor, *b*. F minor, ***c*. F# minor**, *d*. G# minor) : A MAJOR

(**c**) The musical keys of D minor and F major both have one flat, while the keys of F# minor and A major both have three sharps.
Humanities—Description

88. TAME : MATE :: LAME : (*a*. female, *b*. injured, ***c*. male**, *d*. excuse)

(**c**) *Mate* can be obtained from *tame* by reversing the initial three letters. *Male* can be obtained from *lame*, also by reversing the initial three letters.
Nonsemantic

89. (*a*. spinal, *b*. neutral, ***c*. temporal**, *d*. spatial) : PARIETAL :: OCCIPITAL : FRONTAL

(**c**) Four lobes of the brain are the temporal, parietal, occipital, and frontal.
Natural Science—Class

90. PARADISE : LOST :: JERUSALEM : (*a.* Sanctified, *b.* Discovered, ***c.* Delivered**, *d.* Vanquished)

(**c**) *Paradise Lost* and *Jerusalem Delivered* are both epics, the former by Milton and the latter by Tasso.
Humanities—Completion

91. PENN : PENNSYLVANIA :: CALVERT : (*a.* South Carolina, *b.* Vermont, ***c.* Maryland**, *d.* Rhode Island)

(**c**) Penn founded Pennsylvania, while Calvert founded Maryland.
Humanities—Description

92. ETEOCLES : (*a.* Theseus, *b.* Laius, *c.* Oedipus, ***d.* Polynices**) :: ANTIGONE : ISMENE

(**d**) Eteocles and Polynices were siblings, as were Antigone and Ismene.
Humanities—Class

93. DECIMAL : 10 :: DUODECIMAL : (*a.* 2, *b.* 8, ***c.* 12**, *d.* 16)

(**c**) The decimal system has 10 as its base. The duodecimal system has 12 as its base.
Mathematics—Description

94. RATIONALIST : EMPIRICIST :: (*a.* Berkeley, *b.* Hume, *c.* Mill, ***d.* Leibniz**) : LOCKE

(**d**) Leibniz was a famous rationalist philosopher. Locke was a famous empiricist.
Humanities—Description

95. (***a.* Ivan Karamazov**, *b.* Anna Karenina, *c.* Nicolai Gogol, *d.* Grigory Smirnov) : DOSTOYEVSKY :: THÉRÈSE : MAURIAC

(**a**) Ivan Karamazov is a literary character created by Dostoyevsky. Thérèse is a literary character created by Mauriac.
Humanities—Description

96. PALESTRINA : 16th :: (*a.* Beethoven, *b.* Bach, *c.* Tchaikovsky, ***d.* Stravinsky**) : 20th

(**d**) Palestrina was a 16th century composer; Stravinsky was a 20th century composer.
Humanities—Description

97. NICHOLAS II : RUSSIAN REVOLUTION :: (*a.* Louis XIV, *b.* Louis XV, ***c.* Louis XVI**, *d.* Louis XVII) : FRENCH REVOLUTION

(**c**) The Russian Revolution overthrew Nicholas II. The French Revolution overthrew Louis XVI.
Humanities—Description

98. VAN CLIBURN : PIANO :: PABLO CASALS : (*a.* piano, *b.* violin, ***c.* cello**, *d.* clarinet)

(c) Van Cliburn is a famous pianist; Casals was a famous cellist.
Humanities—Description

99. (***a.* Versailles**, *b.* Xanadu, *c.* St. Malo, *d.* Rouen) : LOUIS XIV :: AMBOISE : FRANCIS II

(a) Amboise is the location of the palace of Francis II. Versailles is the location of the palace of Louis XIV.
Humanities—Description

100. ISHMAEL : (***a.* Hagar**, *b.* Rebeccah, *c.* Esther, *d.* Sophia) :: ISAAC : SARAH

(a) According to the Bible, Ishmael was the son of Hagar and Abraham, while Isaac was the son of Sarah and Abraham.
Humanities—Description

Item Classification Chart

Practice Test 2	RELATIONSHIP						
CONTENT	Similarity/ Contrast	Description	Class	Completion	Part/ Whole	Equality/ Negation	Nonsemantic
Vocabulary	5, 14, 23, 26, 39, 41, 54, 55, 59, 65, 69, 71, 81	2, 3, 9, 24, 25, 52, 56		28, 37			
General Information	12, 18, 33, 60, 64	1, 8, 10, 13, 15, 16, 19, 20, 21, 22, 27, 32, 34 35, 47, 48, 62, 83, 84	17, 38, 40, 43, 45, 49	11	61		
Humanities	30, 86	7, 31, 42, 46, 50, 57, 63, 70, 77, 87, 91, 94, 95, 96, 97, 98, 99, 100	68, 80, 92	74, 90			
Social Science	85	73					
Natural Science	53	6, 36, 44, 58, 66, 67, 72, 76, 79	89				
Mathematics		51, 78, 93				4, 75, 82	
Nonsemantic							29, 88

Miller Analogies Test 3
PRACTICE TEST

DIRECTIONS: In each of the following questions, you will find three initial terms and, in parentheses, four answer options designated *a*, *b*, *c*, and *d*. You are to select from the four answer options the one that best completes the analogy with the three initial terms. To record your answers, use the answer sheet at the back of the book.

TIME: *50 minutes*

1. LAMB : (*a.* goat, *b.* sheep, *c.* mule, *d.* cow) :: COLT : HORSE
2. DOCTOR : ACCOUNTANT :: PATIENT : (*a.* judge, *b.* client, *c.* jury, *d.* district attorney)
3. IRELAND : EIRE :: (*a.* Holland, *b.* Switzerland, *c.* Denmark, *d.* Germany) : DEUTSCHLAND
4. DEFICIT : RED :: SURPLUS : (*a.* black, *b.* green, *c.* brown, *d.* white)
5. LEMON : SOUR :: TOBACCO : (*a.* tasty, *b.* sour, *c.* bitter, *d.* salty)
6. YELLOW : (*a.* blue, *b.* white, *c.* green, *d.* red) :: COWARDLY : GLOOMY
7. HOUDINI : (*a.* magician, *b.* surgeon, *c.* lawyer, *d.* detective) :: FRANKLIN : STATESMAN
8. CURRIER : (*a.* Loewe, *b.* Ives, *c.* Cowe, *d.* Best) :: GILBERT : SULLIVAN
9. DE FACTO : IN FACT :: (*a.* de jure, *b.* de legibus, *c.* ex facto, *d.* ex legato) : IN LAW
10. SQUARE : CUBE :: CIRCLE : (*a.* rectangle, *b.* solid, *c.* ellipse, *d.* sphere)
11. FIDDLER : PRAYING :: (*a.* bow, *b.* bear, *c.* violinist, *d.* crab) : MANTIS
12. WINCHESTER : SHOOT :: CAT-O'-NINE-TAILS : (*a.* stab, *b.* whip, *c.* poison, *d.* drown)
13. FULTON : (*a.* locomotive, *b.* steamboat, *c.* incandescent lamp, *d.* crystal radio) :: WHITNEY: COTTON GIN
14. (*a.* jugular, *b.* carotid, *c.* thorax, *d.* sclerotic) : VEIN :: AORTA : ARTERY
15. HISTRIONICS : (*a.* geriatrics, *b.* hysterics, *c.* theatrics, *d.* pediatrics) :: PATRONYMICS : SURNAMES

16. NUN : HABIT :: (*a.* postal carrier, *b.* surgeon, *c.* knight, *d.* solicitor) : COAT OF MAIL

17. (*a.* people, *b.* automobiles, *c.* horses, *d.* bicycles) : INDIANAPOLIS 500 :: HORSES : KENTUCKY DERBY

18. LOBBYIST : LEGISLATOR :: (*a.* lawyer, *b.* judge, *c.* court stenographer, *d.* foreman) : JURY

19. CONGRESSIONAL MEDAL OF HONOR : SOLDIER :: PULITZER PRIZE : (*a.* lawyer, *b.* journalist, *c.* chemist, *d.* doctor)

20. PART : TRAP :: (*a.* good-bye, *b.* whole, *c.* bait, *d.* tar) : RAT

21. BARTON : (*a.* Candy, *b.* Helen, *c.* Clara, *d.* Elsa) :: NIGHTINGALE : FLORENCE

22. EMERALD : MINE :: PEARL : (*a.* oyster, *b.* clam, *c.* mine, *d.* river)

23. BIOGRAPHY : AUTOBIOGRAPHY :: (*a.* first, *b.* third, *c.* fourth, *d.* fifth) : FIRST

24. DUET : PAIR :: DIALOGUE : (*a.* monologue, *b.* quandary, *c.* bipolar, *d.* quartet)

25. (*a.* foot, *b.* ball, *c.* skate, *d.* stick) : HOCKEY :: BAT : BASEBALL

26. (*a.* chroma, *b.* violet, *c.* rainbow, *d.* black) : COLOR :: VACUUM : AIR

27. FLORIDA : PENINSULA :: CUBA : (*a.* state, *b.* gulf, *c.* nation, *d.* island)

28. URBAN : RURAL :: URBANE : (*a.* lazy, *b.* suburban, *c.* boorish, *d.* effete)

29. (*a.* air, *b.* earth, *c.* fire, *d.* plastic) : PYRO :: WATER : HYDRO

30. (*a.* sailor, *b.* mountebank, *c.* salesman, *d.* villain) : CHARLATAN :: FRAUD : QUACK

31. RULER : LINE SEGMENT :: PROTRACTOR : (*a.* distance, *b.* angle, *c.* perimeter, *d.* velocity)

32. WILLIAMS : (*a.* Massachusetts, *b.* Vermont, *c.* New Hampshire, *d.* Rhode Island) :: PENN : PENNSYLVANIA

33. OLD : (*a.* Two, *b.* Twenty, *c.* Forty, *d.* Sixty) :: MAID : ONE

34. (*a.* princess, *b.* worker, *c.* drone, *d.* servant) : QUEEN :: GANDER : GOOSE

35. XL : LX :: CC : (*a.* CCC, *b.* CD, *c.* DC, *d.* CM)

36. CASTOR : (*a.* Pisces, *b.* Orion, *c.* Pollux, *d.* Andromeda) :: JACOB : ESAU

37. KEYNES : (*a.* psychology, *b.* economics, *c.* anthropology, *d.* ecology) :: EINSTEIN : PHYSICS

38. (*a.* New Jersey, *b.* Missouri, *c.* Indian, *d.* Byrd) : ANTARCTIC :: HUDSON : MISSISSIPPI

39. SPRINGS : PALM :: (*a.* Old, *b.* Mineral, *c.* York, *d.* Tree) : NEW

40. MEGAPHONE : CONE :: (*a.* funnel, *b.* cloud, *c.* hurricane, *d.* dictaphone) : TORNADO

41. HARVARD : CAMBRIDGE :: CAMBRIDGE : (*a.* Oxford, *b.* Yale, *c.* Cambridge, *d.* Gloucester)

42. ACTUAL : VIRTUAL :: IN FACT : (*a.* in cause, *b.* in time, *c.* in truth, *d.* in effect)

43. BRAVE NEW WORLD : (*a.* Winston, *b.* Huxley, *c.* O'Brian, *d.* Wells) :: 1984 : ORWELL

44. CANINE : DOG :: EQUINE : (*a.* cow, *b.* goat, *c.* horse, *d.* pig)

45. CENSURE : (*a.* expurgate, *b.* condemn, *c.* praise, *d.* oppose) :: OBTUSE : DULL

46. USHER : POE :: (*a.* ill Repute, *b.* Seven Gables, *c.* Tara, *d.* No Return) : HAWTHORNE

47. NUMISMATIST : PHILATELIST :: (*a.* coins, *b.* numbers, *c.* rocks, *d.* trinkets) : STAMPS

48. CASTLE : BISHOP :: HORIZONTAL : (*a.* vertical, *b.* diagonal, *c.* cathedral, *d.* abbey)

49. (*a.* endemic, *b.* mercurial, *c.* unabating, *d.* retrogressive) : CONSTANT :: CHANGEABLE : IMMUTABLE

50. TRAGEDY : MELODRAMA :: PATHOS : (*a.* bathos, *b.* ethos, *c.* comedy, *d.* catharsis)

51. PERVADE : PERMEATE :: (*a.* trusting, *b.* mistrustful, *c.* favorable, *d.* unfavorable) : AUSPICIOUS

52. GOOSE : GEESE :: MOOSE : (*a.* moosen, *b.* meese, *c.* mooses, *d.* moose)

53. (*a.* passenger pigeon, *b.* sphinx, *c.* phoenix, *d.* humming bird) : DODO :: RAVEN : SPARROW

54. EASTERN STANDARD : 8 A.M. :: PACIFIC STANDARD : (*a.* 5 A.M., *b.* 6 A.M., *c.* 10 A.M., *d.* 11 A.M.)

55. CENTIGRADE : 100 :: CELSIUS : (*a.* –173, *b.* 0, *c.* 100, *d.* 212)

56. SURFEIT : EXCESS :: EVANESCENT : (*a.* silent, *b.* eternal, *c.* ephemeral, *d.* celestial)

57. PLUTARCH : (*a.* drama, *b.* biography, *c.* epic, *d.* oration) :: AESOP : FABLE

58. HYDRO : AQUA :: (*a.* air, *b.* gas, *c.* liquid, *d.* water) : WATER

59. REMISS : (*a.* negligent, *b.* careful, *c.* auspicious, *d.* remote) :: DARK : LIGHT

60. FUSTIAN : GALATEA :: MUSLIN : (*a.* grandam, *b.* lydgate, *c.* gabardine, *d.* rhodium)

61. BLUE : STRAW :: RASP : (*a.* yellow, *b.* hay, *c.* black, *d.* shriek)

62. BUFFALO BILL : (*a.* Cody, *b.* James, *c.* Bowman, *d.* Broderick) :: WILD BILL : HICKOK

63. MOURNER : TEARS :: (*a.* hypochondriac, *b.* lover, *c.* troglodyte, *d.* hypocrite) : CROCODILE TEARS

64. CEDE : SEED :: (*a.* run, *b.* win, *c.* yield, *d.* go) : PLANT

65. INGENUOUS : (*a.* clever, *b.* innocent, *c.* pastoral, *d.* hopeful) :: INFRACTION : VIOLATION

66. SECULAR : (*a.* sacred, *b.* ecclesiastical, *c.* lay, *d.* regular) :: BISHOP : MONK

67. EXTIRPATE : (*a.* evade, *b.* examine, *c.* exude, *d.* eradicate) :: BUOY : ENCOURAGE

68. THREE : (*a.* Two, *b.* Five, *c.* Seven, *d.* Ten) :: MUSKETEERS : LITTLE PEPPERS

69. WEND : END :: (*a.* food, *b.* wait, *c.* tend, *d.* beginning) : ATE

70. VOLT : POTENTIAL DIFFERENCE :: WATT : (*a.* resistance, *b.* brightness, *c.* power, *d.* actual difference)

71. POINT : 0 :: HEXAGON : (*a.* 1, *b.* 2, *c.* 3, *d.* 4)

72. (*a.* Troy, *b.* Athens, *c.* Carthage, *d.* Milan) : PUNIC :: SPARTA : PELOPONNESIAN

73. WINDY CITY : CHICAGO :: GOTHAM : (*a.* San Francisco, *b.* Paris, *c.* New York City, *d.* London)

74. INCANDESCENT : FILAMENT :: FLUORESCENT : (*a.* air, *b.* vacuum, *c.* energy, *d.* phosphor)

75. CABAL : (*a.* trivia, *b.* plot, *c.* wire, *d.* quibble) :: CAPABLE : COMPETENT

76. ORDER : (*a.* Human, *b.* Primates, *c.* erectus, *d.* Mammalia) :: SPECIES : SAPIENS

77. GRENDEL : BEOWULF :: HYDRA : (*a.* Achilles, *b.* Vulcan, *c.* Atlas, *d.* Hercules)

78. 2^{-2} : 2^{-1} :: 2^{2} : (*a.* 2^{0}, *b.* 2^{1}, *c.* 2^{2}, *d.* 2^{3})

79. DEARTH : SHORTAGE :: PLETHORA : (*a.* abundance, *b.* scarcity, *c.* excess, *d.* necessity)

80. WANDERING JEW : EARTH :: FLYING DUTCHMAN : (*a.* seas, *b.* stars, *c.* heaven, *d.* hell)

81. ASTROLABE : SEXTANT :: SUNDIAL : (*a.* time, *b.* electric clock, *c.* ruler, *d.* light rays)

82. VENAL : (*a.* rigid, *b.* cold, *c.* humorless, *d.* mercenary) :: VENIAL : EXCUSABLE

83. E# : Fb :: B : (*a.* Cb, *b.* Bb, *c.* C, *d.* B)

84. MELIORATE : AMELIORATE :: HASTEN : (*a.* speed up, *b.* slow down, *c.* better, *d.* worsen)

85. MACHIAVELLI : PRINCE :: CASTIGLIONE : (*a.* Knight, *b.* Courtier, *c.* King, *d.* Yeoman)

86. NOSTRUM : (*a.* pedestal, *b.* disease, *c.* panacea, *d.* pabulum) :: VERACIOUS : HONEST

87. DWARF : PITUITARY :: CRETIN : (*a.* endocrine, *b.* thyroid, *c.* thalamus, *d.* hypothalamus)

88. (*a.* barometer, *b.* tachometer, *c.* hydrometer, *d.* voltmeter) : THERMOMETER :: SPEED : TEMPERATURE

89. FROWARD : BACKWARD :: (*a.* dilatory, *b.* upside down, *c.* refractory, *d.* right side up) : REVERSED

90. LEWIN : (*a.* attribution theory, *b.* dissonance theory, *c.* field theory, *d.* psychoanalytic theory) :: JUNG : ANALYTIC THEORY

91. BUNSEN BURNER : GAS :: AUTOCLAVE : (*a.* oil, *b.* electricity, *c.* steam, *d.* solar energy)

92. BACH : (*a.* invention, *b.* symphony, *c.* waltz, *d.* polyphony) :: CHOPIN : MAZURKA

93. BANISHMENT : COUNTRY :: DEFENESTRATION : (*a.* ceiling, *b.* floor, *c.* city, *d.* window)

94. CADMEAN : (*a.* Caesarian, *b.* Augustan, *c.* Napoleonic, *d.* Pyrrhic) :: EXPENSIVE : COSTLY

95. MOSES : (*a.* Abraham, *b.* Joseph, *c.* Joshua, *d.* Gideon) :: ROOSEVELT : TRUMAN

96. PARASYMPATHETIC : (*a.* sympathetic, *b.* protosympathetic, *c.* asympathetic, *d.* prosympathetic) :: SLOW DOWN : SPEED UP

97. (*a.* Galileo, *b.* Newton, *c.* Galen, *d.* Ptolemy) : COPERNICUS :: GEOCENTRIC : HELIOCENTRIC

98. TOSCANINI : (*a.* Fournier, *b.* Ormandy, *c.* Goodman, *d.* Heifetz) :: VAN CLIBURN : RUBENSTEIN

99. RICHELIEU : CARDINAL :: (*a.* Henry IV, *b.* Louis XIII, *c.* Francis I, *d.* Napoleon III) : KING

100. JAMES : FUNCTIONALISM :: (*a.* Dewey, *b.* Levi-Strauss, *c.* Watson, *d.* Klineberg) : STRUCTURALISM

Answer Key for Practice Test 3

1. *b*	11. *d*	21. *c*	31. *b*	41. *c*	51. *c*	61. *c*	71. *b*	81. *b*	91. *c*
2. *b*	12. *b*	22. *a*	32. *d*	42. *d*	52. *d*	62. *a*	72. *c*	82. *d*	92. *a*
3. *d*	13. *b*	23. *b*	33. *b*	43. *b*	53. *a*	63. *d*	73. *c*	83. *b*	93. *d*
4. *a*	14. *a*	24. *c*	34. *c*	44. *c*	54. *a*	64. *c*	74. *d*	84. *a*	94. *d*
5. *c*	15. *c*	25. *d*	35. *a*	45. *b*	55. *c*	65. *b*	75. *b*	85. *b*	95. *c*
6. *a*	16. *c*	26. *d*	36. *c*	46. *b*	56. *c*	66. *d*	76. *b*	86. *c*	96. *a*
7. *a*	17. *b*	27. *d*	37. *b*	47. *a*	57. *b*	67. *d*	77. *d*	87. *b*	97. *d*
8. *b*	18. *a*	28. *c*	38. *c*	48. *b*	58. *d*	68. *b*	78. *d*	88. *b*	98. *b*
9. *a*	19. *b*	29. *c*	39. *c*	49. *b*	59. *b*	69. *b*	79. *c*	89. *c*	99. *b*
10. *d*	20. *d*	30. *b*	40. *a*	50. *a*	60. *c*	70. *c*	80. *a*	90. *c*	100. *b*

Explanation of Answers for Practice Test 3

1. LAMB : (*a.* goat, ***b.* sheep**, *c.* mule, *d.* cow) :: COLT : HORSE

   (b) A lamb is a young sheep; a colt is a young horse.
   General Information—Description

2. DOCTOR : ACCOUNTANT :: PATIENT : (*a.* judge, ***b.* client**, *c.* jury, *d.* district attorney)

   (b) A doctor serves patients; an accountant serves clients.
   General Information—Description

3. IRELAND : EIRE :: (*a.* Holland, *b.* Switzerland, *c.* Denmark, ***d.* Germany**) : DEUTSCHLAND

   (d) Ireland and Eire are the same country, as are Germany and Deutschland.
   General Information—Similarity/Contrast

4. DEFICIT : RED :: SURPLUS : (***a.* black**, *b.* green, *c.* brown, *d.* white)

   (a) To be in the red is to show a deficit, while to be in the black is to show a surplus.
   General Information—Similarity/Contrast

5. LEMON : SOUR :: TOBACCO : (*a.* tasty, *b.* sour, ***c.* bitter**, *d.* salty)

   (c) A lemon is sour; tobacco is bitter.
   General Information—Description

6. YELLOW : (***a.* blue**, *b.* white, *c.* green, *d.* red) :: COWARDLY : GLOOMY

   (a) A cowardly person is sometimes referred to as "yellow." A gloomy person is sometimes referred to as feeling "blue."
   General Information—Similarity/Contrast

7. HOUDINI : (***a.* magician**, *b.* surgeon, *c.* lawyer, *d.* detective) :: FRANKLIN : STATESMAN

   (a) Harry Houdini was a magician; Benjamin Franklin, a statesman.
   General Information—Description

8. CURRIER : (*a.* Loewe, ***b.* Ives**, *c.* Cowe, *d.* Best) :: GILBERT : SULLIVAN

   (b) Currier and Ives were a team of artists, while Gilbert and Sullivan were a team who wrote operettas.
   Humanities—Class

9. DE FACTO : IN FACT :: (***a.* de jure**, *b.* de legibus, *c.* ex facto, *d.* ex legato) : IN LAW

   (a) *De facto* means *in fact*. *De jure* means *in law*.
   Vocabulary—Similarity/Contrast

10. SQUARE : CUBE :: CIRCLE : (*a.* rectangle, *b.* solid, *c.* ellipse, ***d.* sphere**)

    (d) A two-dimensional "slice" through a cube yields a square. A two-dimensional "slice" through a sphere yields a circle.
    Mathematics—Description

11. FIDDLER : PRAYING :: (*a.* bow, *b.* bear, *c.* violinist, ***d.* crab**) : MANTIS

    (d) The fiddler crab and praying mantis are both types of animal.
    Natural Science—Completion

12. WINCHESTER : SHOOT :: CAT-O'-NINE-TAILS : (*a.* stab, ***b.* whip**, *c.* poison, *d.* drown)

    (b) A Winchester can be used to shoot someone. A cat-o'-nine-tails can be used to whip someone.
    General Information—Description

13. FULTON : (*a.* locomotive, ***b.* steamboat**, *c.* incandescent lamp, *d.* crystal radio) :: WHITNEY : COTTON GIN

    (b) Robert Fulton invented the steamboat. Eli Whitney invented the cotton gin.
    Social Science—Description

14. (***a.* jugular**, *b.* carotid, *c.* thorax, *d.* sclerotic) : VEIN :: AORTA : ARTERY

    (a) The jugular is a vein; the aorta is an artery.
    Natural Science—Class

15. HISTRIONICS : (*a.* geriatrics, *b.* hysterics, ***c.* theatrics**, *d.* pediatrics) :: PATRONYMICS : SURNAMES

    (c) Histrionics are theatrics; patronymics are surnames.
    Vocabulary—Similarity/Contrast

16. NUN : HABIT :: (*a.* postal carrier, *b.* surgeon, ***c.* knight**, *d.* solicitor) : COAT OF MAIL

    (c) A nun sometimes wears a habit. A knight wore a coat of mail.
    General Information—Similarity/Contrast

17. (*a.* people, ***b.* automobiles**, *c.* horses, *d.* bicycles) : INDIANAPOLIS 500 :: HORSES : KENTUCKY DERBY

    (b) The Indianapolis 500 is an automobile race. The Kentucky Derby is a horse race.
    General Information—Description

18. LOBBYIST : LEGISLATOR :: (***a.* lawyer**, *b.* judge, *c.* court stenographer, *d.* foreman) : JURY

    (a) The job of a lobbyist is to persuade a legislator. The job of a lawyer is to persuade a jury.
    General Information—Description

19. CONGRESSIONAL MEDAL OF HONOR : SOLDIER :: PULITZER PRIZE : (*a.* lawyer, ***b.* journalist**, *c.* chemist, *d.* doctor)

    (b) The Congressional Medal of Honor is given to outstanding soldiers. The Pulitzer Prize is given to outstanding journalists.
    General Information—Description

20. PART : TRAP :: (*a.* good-bye, *b.* whole, *c.* bait, ***d.* tar**) : RAT

    (d) *Part* is *trap* spelled backwards. *Tar* is *rat* spelled backwards.
    Nonsemantic

21. BARTON : (*a.* Candy, *b.* Helen, ***c.* Clara**, *d.* Elsa) :: NIGHTINGALE : FLORENCE

    (c) Clara Barton and Florence Nightingale are both famous for their work in nursing.
    General Information—Completion

22. EMERALD : MINE :: PEARL : (***a.* oyster**, *b.* clam, *c.* mine, *d.* river)

    (a) Emeralds are found in mines. Pearls are found in oysters.
    Natural Science—Description

23. BIOGRAPHY : AUTOBIOGRAPHY :: (*a.* first, ***b.* third**, *c.* fourth, *d.* fifth) : FIRST

    (b) A biography is written in third person. An autobiography is written in first person.
    Humanities—Description

24. DUET : PAIR :: DIALOGUE : (*a.* monologue, *b.* quandary, ***c.* bipolar**, *d.* quartet)

    (c) *Duet, pair, dialogue,* and *bipolar* all refer to two of something.
    General Information—Similarity/Contrast

25. (*a.* foot, *b.* ball, *c.* skate, ***d.* stick**) : HOCKEY :: BAT : BASEBALL

    (d) In hockey, players hit a puck with a stick. In baseball, players hit a ball with a bat.
    General Information—Description

26. (*a.* chroma, *b.* violet, *c.* rainbow, ***d.* black**) : COLOR :: VACUUM : AIR

    (d) Black is an absence of color. A vacuum is an absence of air.
    Natural Science—Description

27. FLORIDA : PENINSULA :: CUBA : (*a.* state, *b.* gulf, *c.* nation, ***d.* island**)

    (d) Florida is a peninsula. Cuba is an island.
    General Information—Description

28. URBAN : RURAL :: URBANE : (*a.* lazy, *b.* suburban, ***c.* boorish**, *d.* effete)

    (c) *Urban* and *rural* are antonyms, as are *urbane* and *boorish*.
    Vocabulary—Similarity/Contrast

29. (*a.* air, *b.* earth, **c. fire**, *d.* plastic) : PYRO :: WATER : HYDRO

    (c) *Pyro-* is a prefix meaning *fire*, while *hydro-* is a prefix meaning *water.*
    Vocabulary—Similarity/Contrast

30. (*a.* sailor, ***b.* mountebank**, *c.* salesman, *d.* villain) : CHARLATAN :: FRAUD : QUACK

    (b) A mountebank is a charlatan, and a fraud is a quack.
    Vocabulary—Similarity/Contrast

31. RULER : LINE SEGMENT :: PROTRACTOR : (*a.* distance, ***b.* angle**, *c.* perimeter, *d.* velocity)

    (b) A ruler is used to measure a line segment, while a protractor is used to measure an angle.
    Mathematics—Description

32. WILLIAMS : (*a.* Massachusetts, *b.* Vermont, *c.* New Hampshire, ***d.* Rhode Island**) :: PENN : PENNSYLVANIA

    (d) Roger Williams founded the state of Rhode Island; William Penn founded the state of Pennsylvania.
    Humanities—Description

33. OLD : (*a.* Two, ***b.* Twenty**, *c.* Forty, *d.* Sixty) :: MAID : ONE

    (b) Old Maid and Twenty-One are both card games.
    General Information—Completion

34. (*a.* princess, *b.* worker, **c. drone**, *d.* servant) : QUEEN :: GANDER : GOOSE

    (c) A drone is a male bee, and a queen is a female bee. A gander is a male, and a goose is a female.
    Natural Science—Class

35. XL : LX :: CC : (***a.* CCC**, *b.* CD, *c.* DC, *d.* CM)

    (a) 40 is to 60 as 200 is to 300.
    Mathematics—Equality/Negation

36. CASTOR : (*a.* Pisces, *b.* Orion, **c. Pollux**, *d.* Andromeda) :: JACOB : ESAU

    (c) Castor and Pollux were twins, as were Jacob and Esau.
    Humanities—Class

37. KEYNES : (*a.* psychology, ***b.* economics**, *c.* anthropology, *d.* ecology) :: EINSTEIN : PHYSICS

    (b) John Maynard Keynes revolutionized economic theory, while Albert Einstein revolutionized theory in physics.
    Social Science—Description

38. (*a.* New Jersey, *b.* Missouri, **c. Indian**, *d.* Byrd) : ANTARCTIC :: HUDSON : MISSISSIPPI

(**c**) The Indian and the Antarctic are both oceans. The Hudson and the Mississippi are both rivers.
General Information—Class

39. SPRINGS : PALM :: (*a.* Old, *b.* Mineral, ***c.* York**, *d.* Tree) : NEW

(**c**) Palm Springs and New York are both major cities.
General Information—Completion

40. MEGAPHONE : CONE :: (***a.* funnel**, *b.* cloud, *c.* hurricane, *d.* dictaphone) : TORNADO

(**a**) A megaphone, a funnel, a cone, and a tornado all have approximately the same shape.
General Information—Class

41. HARVARD : CAMBRIDGE :: CAMBRIDGE : (*a.* Oxford, *b.* Yale, ***c.* Cambridge**, *d.* Gloucester)

(**c**) Harvard University is in Cambridge, Massachusetts, and Cambridge University is in Cambridge, England.
General Information—Description

42. ACTUAL : VIRTUAL :: IN FACT : (*a.* in cause, *b.* in time, *c.* in truth, ***d.* in effect**)

(**d**) *Actual* means *in fact*. *Virtual* means *in effect*.
Vocabulary—Similarity/Contrast

43. BRAVE NEW WORLD : (*a.* Winston, ***b.* Huxley**, *c.* O'Brian, *d.* Wells) :: 1984 : ORWELL

(**b**) *Brave New World* is a novel by Huxley; *1984* is a novel by Orwell. (Both describe nightmarish societies of the future.)
Humanities—Description

44. CANINE : DOG :: EQUINE : (*a.* cow, *b.* goat, ***c.* horse**, *d.* pig)

(**c**) *Canine* means *doglike*. *Equine* means *horselike*.
General Information—Description

45. CENSURE : (*a.* expurgate, ***b.* condemn**, *c.* praise, *d.* oppose) :: OBTUSE : DULL

(**b**) To censure is to condemn. To be obtuse is to be dull.
Vocabulary—Similarity/Contrast

46. USHER : POE :: (*a.* ill Repute, ***b.* Seven Gables**, *c.* Tara, *d.* No Return) : HAWTHORNE

(**b**) Poe wrote about the House of Usher; Hawthorne wrote about the House of the Seven Gables.
Humanities—Description

47. NUMISMATIST : PHILATELIST :: (***a.* coins**, *b.* numbers, *c.* rocks, *d.* trinkets) : STAMPS

(a) A numismatist collects coins; a philatelist collects stamps.
General Information—Description

48. CASTLE : BISHOP :: HORIZONTAL : (*a.* vertical, ***b.* diagonal**, *c.* cathedral, *d.* abbey)

(b) In the game of chess, a castle is capable of horizontal movement, while a bishop is capable of diagonal movement.
General Information—Description

49. (*a.* endemic, ***b.* mercurial**, *c.* unabating, *d.* retrogressive) : CONSTANT :: CHANGEABLE : IMMUTABLE

(b) *Mercurial* and *constant* are antonyms, as are *changeable* and *immutable.*
Vocabulary—Similarity/Contrast

50. TRAGEDY : MELODRAMA :: PATHOS : (***a.* bathos**, *b.* ethos, *c.* comedy, *d.* catharsis)

(a) Tragedy expresses pathos, while melodrama expresses bathos.
Humanities—Description

51. PERVADE : PERMEATE :: (*a.* trusting, *b.* mistrustful, ***c.* favorable**, *d.* unfavorable) : AUSPICIOUS

(c) *Pervade* and *permeate* are synonyms, as are *favorable* and *auspicious.*
Vocabulary—Similarity/Contrast

52. GOOSE : GEESE :: MOOSE : (*a.* moosen, *b.* meese, *c.* mooses, ***d.* moose**)

(d) The plural of *goose* is *geese*. The plural of *moose* is *moose.*
Nonsemantic

53. (***a.* passenger pigeon**, *b.* sphinx, *c.* phoenix, *d.* humming bird) : DODO :: RAVEN : SPARROW

(a) The passenger pigeon and the dodo are both extinct species of birds. The raven and the sparrow are not extinct.
Natural Science—Class

54. EASTERN STANDARD : 8 A.M. :: PACIFIC STANDARD : (***a.* 5 A.M.**, *b.* 6 A.M., *c.* 10 A.M., *d.* 11 A.M.)

(a) When it is 8 A.M. Eastern Standard Time, it is 5 A.M. Pacific Standard Time.
General Information—Similarity/Contrast

55. CENTIGRADE : 100 :: CELSIUS : (*a.* –173, *b.* 0, ***c.* 100**, *d.* 212)

(c) The centigrade and Celsius temperature scales are identical, so 100 degrees centigrade equals 100 degrees Celsius.
Natural Science—Equality/Negation

56. SURFEIT : EXCESS :: EVANESCENT : (*a.* silent, *b.* eternal, ***c.* ephemeral**, *d.* celestial)

(c) *Surfeit* and *excess* are synonyms, as are *evanescent* and *ephemeral.*
Vocabulary—Similarity/Contrast

57. PLUTARCH : (*a.* drama, ***b.* biography**, *c.* epic, *d.* oration) :: AESOP : FABLE

(b) Plutarch is famous as a writer of biography. Aesop is famous as a writer of fables.
Humanities—Description

58. HYDRO : AQUA :: (*a.* air, *b.* gas, *c.* liquid, ***d.* water**) : WATER

(d) *Hydro-* and *aqua-* are both prefixes meaning *water.*
Vocabulary—Similarity/Contrast

59. REMISS : (*a.* negligent, ***b.* careful**, *c.* auspicious, *d.* remote) :: DARK : LIGHT

(b) *Remiss* is the opposite of *careful*; *dark* is the opposite of *light.*
Vocabulary—Similarity/Contrast

60. FUSTIAN : GALATEA :: MUSLIN : (*a.* grandam, *b.* lydgate, ***c.* gabardine**, *d.* rhodium)

(c) Fustian, galatea, muslin, and gabardine are all types of cloth.
General Information—Class

61. BLUE : STRAW :: RASP : (*a.* yellow, *b.* hay, ***c.* black**, *d.* shriek)

(c) A blueberry, a strawberry, a raspberry, and a blackberry are all types of berries.
General Information—Class

62. BUFFALO BILL : (***a.* Cody**, *b.* James, *c.* Bowman, *d.* Broderick) :: WILD BILL : HICKOK

(a) Buffalo Bill Cody and Wild Bill Hickok were both famous cowboys.
General Information—Completion

63. MOURNER : TEARS :: (*a.* hypochondriac, *b.* lover, *c.* troglodyte, ***d.* hypocrite**) : CROCODILE TEARS

(d) A mourner sheds tears. A hypocrite sheds crocodile tears.
Vocabulary—Description

64. CEDE : SEED :: (*a.* run, *b.* win, ***c.* yield**, *d.* go) : PLANT

(c) To cede is to yield. To seed is to plant.
Vocabulary—Similarity/Contrast

65. INGENUOUS : (*a.* clever, ***b.* innocent**, *c.* pastoral, *d.* hopeful) :: INFRACTION : VIOLATION

(b) *Ingenuous* and *innocent* are synonyms, as are *infraction* and *violation.*
Vocabulary—Similarity/Contrast

66. SECULAR : (*a.* sacred, *b.* ecclesiastical, *c.* lay, ***d.* regular**) :: BISHOP : MONK

(d) A bishop is a member of the secular clergy. A monk is a member of the regular clergy.
Humanities—Class

67. EXTIRPATE : (*a.* evade, *b.* examine, *c.* exude, ***d.* eradicate**) :: BUOY : ENCOURAGE

(d) To extirpate is to eradicate. To buoy is to encourage.
Vocabulary—Similarity/Contrast

68. THREE : (*a.* Two, ***b.* Five**, *c.* Seven, *d.* Ten) :: MUSKETEERS : LITTLE PEPPERS

(b) There were, so the stories go, three musketeers, but five little Peppers.
Humanities—Completion

69. WEND : END :: (*a.* food, ***b.* wait**, *c.* tend, *d.* beginning) : ATE

(b) *Wend* is pronounced like end, except for the added initial *w* consonant sound. *Wait* is pronounced like *ate*, also except for the initial *w* consonant sound.
Nonsemantic

70. VOLT : POTENTIAL DIFFERENCE :: WATT : (*a.* resistance, *b.* brightness, ***c.* power**, *d.* actual difference)

(c) The volt is a measure of potential difference. The watt is a measure of power.
Natural Science—Description

71. POINT : 0 :: HEXAGON : (*a.* 1, ***b.* 2**, *c.* 3, *d.* 4)

(b) A point occupies 0 dimension, while a hexagon occupies 2 dimensions.
Mathematics—Description

72. (*a.* Troy, *b.* Athens, ***c.* Carthage**, *d.* Milan) : PUNIC :: SPARTA : PELOPONNESIAN

(c) Carthage was one of the opposing sides in the Punic Wars, while Sparta was one of the opposing sides in the Peloponnesian War.
Humanities—Description

73. WINDY CITY : CHICAGO :: GOTHAM : (*a.* San Francisco, *b.* Paris, ***c.* New York City**, *d.* London)

(c) Windy City is another name for Chicago. Gotham is another name for New York City.
General Information—Similarity/Contrast

74. INCANDESCENT : FILAMENT :: FLUORESCENT : (*a.* air, *b.* vacuum, *c.* energy, ***d.* phosphor**)

(d) The filament glows in an incandescent lamp. The phosphor glows in a fluorescent lamp.
Natural Science—Description

75. CABAL : (*a.* trivia, ***b.* plot**, *c.* wire, *d.* quibble) :: CAPABLE : COMPETENT

(b) *Cabal* and *plot* are synonyms, as are *capable* and *competent.*
Vocabulary—Similarity/Contrast

76. ORDER : (*a.* Human, ***b.* Primates**, *c.* erectus, *d.* Mammalia) :: SPECIES : SAPIENS

(b) Human beings are of order Primates and species *sapiens.*
Natural Science—Class

77. GRENDEL : BEOWULF :: HYDRA : (*a.* Achilles, *b.* Vulcan, *c.* Atlas, ***d.* Hercules**)

(d) Beowulf slew Grendel; Hercules slew Hydra.
Humanities—Description

78. $2^{-2} : 2^{-1} :: 2^{2}$: (*a.* 2^0, *b.* 2^1, *c.* 2^2, ***d.* 2^3**)

(d) ¼ is to ½ as 4 is to 8.
Mathematics—Class

79. DEARTH : SHORTAGE :: PLETHORA : (*a.* abundance, *b.* scarcity, ***c.* excess**, *d.* necessity)

(c) A dearth is a shortage. A plethora is an excess.
Vocabulary—Similarity/Contrast

80. WANDERING JEW : EARTH :: FLYING DUTCHMAN : (***a.* seas**, *b.* stars, *c.* heaven, *d.* hell)

(a) The Wandering Jew was doomed to wander the earth. The Flying Dutchman was doomed to wander the seas.
Humanities—Description

81. ASTROLABE : SEXTANT :: SUNDIAL : (*a.* time, ***b.* electric clock**, *c.* ruler, *d.* light rays)

(b) The sextant replaced the astrolabe; the electric clock replaced the sundial.
Natural Science—Description

82. VENAL : (*a.* rigid, *b.* cold, *c.* humorless, ***d.* mercenary**) :: VENIAL : EXCUSABLE

(d) *Venal* and *mercenary* are synonyms, as are *venial* and *excusable.*
Vocabulary—Similarity/Contrast

83. E# : Fb :: B : (*a.* Cb, ***b.* B_b**, *c.* C, *d.* B)

(b) E# is a half-tone higher than F_b. B is a half-tone higher than B_b.
Humanities—Description

84. MELIORATE : AMELIORATE :: HASTEN : (***a.* speed up**, *b.* slow down, *c.* better, *d.* worsen)

(**a**) *Meliorate* and *ameliorate* mean the same thing, as do *hasten* and *speed up*.
Vocabulary—Similarity/Contrast

85. MACHIAVELLI : PRINCE :: CASTIGLIONE : (*a.* Knight, ***b.* Courtier**, *c.* King, *d.* Yeoman)

(**b**) Machiavelli is the author of *The Prince*. Castiglione is the author of *The Courtier.*
Humanities—Description

86. NOSTRUM : (*a.* pedestal, *b.* disease, ***c.* panacea**, *d.* pabulum) :: VERACIOUS : HONEST

(**c**) A nostrum is a panacea. A veracious person is an honest person.
Vocabulary—Similarity/Contrast

87. DWARF : PITUITARY :: CRETIN : (*a.* endocrine, ***b.* thyroid**, *c.* thalamus, *d.* hypothalamus)

(**b**) A dwarf has a malfunctioning pituitary gland. A cretin has a malfunctioning thyroid gland.
Natural Science—Description

88. (*a.* barometer, ***b.* tachometer**, *c.* hydrometer, *d.* voltmeter) : THERMOMETER :: SPEED : TEMPERATURE

(**b**) A tachometer measures speed. A thermometer measures temperature.
Natural Science—Description

89. FROWARD : BACKWARD :: (*a.* dilatory, *b.* upside down, ***c.* refractory**, *d.* right side up) : REVERSED

(**c**) *Froward* means *refractory*. *Backward* means *reversed*.
Vocabulary—Similarity/Contrast

90. LEWIN : (*a.* attribution theory, *b.* dissonance theory, ***c.* field theory**, *d.* psychoanalytic theory) :: JUNG : ANALYTIC THEORY

(**c**) Lewin's theory of personality is classified as a field theory. Jung's theory of personality is called analytic theory.
Social Science—Description

91. BUNSEN BURNER : GAS :: AUTOCLAVE : (*a.* oil, *b.* electricity, ***c.* steam**, *d.* solar energy)

(**c**) A Bunsen burner produces heat through gas. An autoclave produces heat through steam.
Natural Science—Description

92. BACH : (***a.* invention**, *b.* symphony, *c.* waltz, *d.* polyphony) :: CHOPIN : MAZURKA

(**a**) Bach was a composer of inventions. Chopin was a composer of mazurkas.
Humanities—Description

93. BANISHMENT : COUNTRY :: DEFENESTRATION : (*a.* ceiling, *b.* floor, *c.* city, ***d.* window**)

(**d**) Banishment occurs when someone is thrown out of a country. Defenestration occurs when someone is thrown out of a window.
Vocabulary—Description

94. CADMEAN : (*a.* Caesarian, *b.* Augustan, *c.* Napoleonic, ***d.* Pyrrhic**) :: EXPENSIVE : COSTLY

(**d**) Both a Cadmean and a Pyrrhic victory are excessively (costly) types of victory.
Humanities—Similarity/Contrast

95. MOSES : (*a.* Abraham, *b.* Joseph, ***c.* Joshua**, *d.* Gideon) :: ROOSEVELT : TRUMAN

(**c**) Joshua succeeded Moses as leader of the Israelites. Truman succeeded Roosevelt as president of the United States.
Humanities—Description

96. PARASYMPATHETIC : (***a.* sympathetic**, *b.* protosympathetic, *c.* asympathetic, *d.* prosympathetic) :: SLOW DOWN : SPEED UP

(**a**) The parasympathetic nervous system slows down the heartbeat, while the sympathetic nervous system speeds it up.
Natural Science—Description

97. (*a.* Galileo, *b.* Newton, *c.* Galen, ***d.* Ptolemy**) : COPERNICUS :: GEOCENTRIC : HELIOCENTRIC

(**d**) Ptolemy is known for his geocentric theory of the solar system, while Copernicus is known for his heliocentric theory.
Natural Science—Description

98. TOSCANINI : (*a.* Fournier, ***b.* Ormandy**, *c.* Goodman, *d.* Heifetz) :: VAN CLIBURN : RUBENSTEIN

(**b**) Toscanini and Ormandy attained fame as conductors; Van Cliburn and Rubenstein became famous as pianists.
Humanities—Class

99. RICHELIEU : CARDINAL :: (*a.* Henry IV, ***b.* Louis XIII**, *c.* Francis I, *d.* Napoleon III) : KING

(**b**) Richelieu was cardinal when Louis XIII was king.
Humanities—Description

100. JAMES : FUNCTIONALISM :: (*a.* Dewey, ***b.* Levi-Strauss**, *c.* Watson, *d.* Klineberg) : STRUCTURALISM

(**b**) James was a functionalist; Levi-Strauss, a structuralist.
Social Science—Description

Item Classification Chart

Practice Test 3	RELATIONSHIP						
CONTENT	**Similarity/ Contrast**	**Description**	**Class**	**Completion**	**Part/ Whole**	**Equality/ Negation**	**Nonsemantic**
Vocabulary	9, 15, 28, 29 30, 42, 45 49, 51, 56 58, 59, 64 65, 67, 75 79, 82, 84 86, 89	63, 93					
General Information	3, 4, 6, 16, 24, 54, 73	1, 2, 5, 7, 12, 17, 18, 19, 25, 27, 41, 44, 47, 48	38, 40, 60, 61	21, 33, 39, 62			
Humanities	94	23, 32, 43, 46, 50, 57, 72, 77, 80, 83, 85, 92, 95, 99	8, 36, 66, 98	68			
Social Science		13, 37, 90, 100					
Natural Science		22, 26, 70, 74, 81, 87, 88, 91, 96, 97	14, 34, 53, 76	11		55	
Mathematics		10, 31, 71	78			35	
Nonsemantic							20, 52, 69

Miller Analogies Test
PRACTICE TEST 4

DIRECTIONS: In each of the following questions, you will find three initial terms and, in parentheses, four answer options designated *a*, *b*, *c*, and *d*. You are to select from the four answer options the one that best completes the analogy with the three initial terms. To record your answers, use the answer sheet at the back of the book.

TIME: *50 minutes*

1. POLAND : POLISH :: (*a.* Holland, *b.* Dublin, *c.* Denmark, *d.* Dansk) : DANISH
2. UNION : (*a.* green, *b.* brown, *c.* blue, *d.* white) :: CONFEDERACY : GRAY
3. ARTICLE : (*a.* preposition, *b.* conjunction, *c.* adjective, *d.* verb) :: THE : AND
4. SAFETY : 2 :: TOUCHDOWN : (*a.* 2, *b.* 4, *c.* 6, *d.* 8)
5. CIRCLE : ELLIPSE :: SQUARE : (*a.* triangle, *b.* rectangle, *c.* pentagon, *d.* hexagon)
6. BIRD : (*a.* nest, *b.* worm, *c.* wings, *d.* fly) :: GENIE : MAGIC CARPET
7. FOXHOLE : (*a.* foxes, *b.* gunfire, *c.* discovery, *d.* earthquakes) :: RAINCOAT : RAIN
8. FOOLISH : OWL :: (*a.* timid, *b.* large, *c.* wise, *d.* temperamental) : LION
9. SINBAD : (*a.* sailor, *b.* squire, *c.* sinner, *d.* poet) :: ARTHUR : KING
10. SOLOMON : WISE :: NERO : (*a.* stupid, *b.* bold, *c.* just, *d.* cruel)
11. GRAPE : VINE :: RUBBER : (*a.* tree, *b.* conifer, *c.* root, *d.* leaf)
12. (*a.* Georgia, *b.* Massachusetts, *c.* New Jersey, *d.* Ohio) : MIDDLE ATLANTIC :: VERMONT : NEW ENGLAND
13. BALD : HAIR :: ALBINO : (*a.* height, *b.* pain, *c.* sight, *d.* pigment)
14. BOW : (*a.* arrow, *b.* curtsey, *c.* stern, *d.* fore) :: FRONT : REAR
15. MONOGYNY : POLYGYNY :: ONE : (*a.* none, *b.* two, *c.* eight, *d.* many)

16. (*a.* chlorine, *b.* ferrous, *c.* aluminum, *d.* sodium) : IRON :: NITROUS : NITROGEN

17. (*a.* secret codes, *b.* inscriptions on church vaults, *c.* science fiction, *d.* religious rituals) : CRYPTOGRAPHY :: DICTIONARIES : LEXICOGRAPHY

18. $E = MC^2$: EINSTEIN :: $C^2 = A^2 + B^2$: (*a.* Bernoulli, *b.* Cauchy, *c.* Descartes, *d.* Pythagoras)

19. GREEK : GREEK :: ROMAN : (*a.* Indo-European, *b.* Latin, *c.* Mediterranean, *d.* Romanish)

20. (*a.* Jesus, *b.* hell, *c.* heaven, *d.* Satan) : CHRISTIANITY :: NIRVANA : BUDDHISM

21. U.S. CALENDAR : U.S. FISCAL CALENDAR :: JANUARY : (*a.* December, *b.* March, *c.* July, *d.* September)

22. PHOTOMETER : (*a.* light, *b.* distance, *c.* magnetism, *d.* velocity) :: AUDIOMETER : SOUND

23. (*a.* believable, *b.* wrong, *c.* fanciful, *d.* humorous) : INCREDIBLE :: AUGMENT : DIMINISH

24. INFINITIVE : (*a.* having eaten, *b.* to sleep, *c.* has tried, *d.* to the store) :: PARTICIPLE : WALKING

25. MARX : COMMUNISM :: (*a.* Hamilton, *b.* Lenin, *c.* Smith, *d.* Davis) : CAPITALISM

26. (*a.* Iambic, *b.* Doric, *c.* Spartan, *d.* Grecian) : CORINTHIAN :: SONATA : CONCERTO

27. SOCCER : BALL :: (*a.* cricket, *b.* rugby, *c.* hockey, *d.* lacrosse) : PUCK

28. (*a.* sheep, *b.* plasma, *c.* vulture, *d.* harass) : BLOOD :: DOG : HOUND

29. (*a.* hawk, *b.* owl, *c.* bluejay, *d.* ostrich) : NOCTURNAL :: ROBIN : DIURNAL

30. PHLEGM : PHLEGMATIC :: BILE : (*a.* bilious, *b.* billiard, *c.* binding, *d.* bilabial)

31. HEAVY-HANDED : (*a.* uncoordinated, *b.* tactless, *c.* strong, *d.* coordinated) :: HEAVY-FOOTED : PLODDING

32. PALEFACE : WHITE :: BLUENOSE : (*a.* frigid, *b.* tough, *c.* unkind, *d.* puritanical)

33. PROTON : NEUTRON :: POSITIVE : (*a.* negative, *b.* uncharged, *c.* positive, *d.* nucleonic)

34. SPHINX : (*a.* pterodactyl, *b.* dodo, *c.* vulture, *d.* phoenix) :: LION : EAGLE

35. OCARINA : SWEET POTATO :: INDIAN CORN : (*a.* rye, *b.* barley, *c.* maize, *d.* peppercorn)

36. RADIUS : 4 :: DIAMETER : (*a.* 16, *b.* 8, *c.* 87π, *d.* 167π)

37. PIKE : (*a.* sturgeon, *b.* lion, *c.* whale, *d.* buffalo) :: COW : PIG

38. WASSERMANN : (*a.* heart disease, *b.* diabetes, *c.* syphilis, *d.* lung cancer) :: PAP : CERVICAL CANCER

39. COMPLEMENTARY : SUPPLEMENTARY :: (*a.* 0, *b.* 45, *c.* 90, *d.* 360) : 180

40. E.G. : FOR EXAMPLE :: VIZ. : (*a.* namely, *b.* except for, *c.* according to, *d.* generally)

41. GRAPE : WINE :: (*a.* apple, *b.* potato, *c.* pomegranate, *d.* malt) : VODKA

42. RISING : FALLING :: (*a.* bull, *b.* bird, *c.* sparrow, *d.* antelope) : BEAR

43. XX : FEMALE :: (*a.* XY, *b.* YY, *c.* XZ, *d.* ZZ) : MALE

44. RESPECT : (*a.* love, *b.* protect, *c.* revere, *d.* obey) :: DISLIKE : HATE

45. PARLIAMENT : LORDS :: (*a.* House of Representatives, *b.* Congress, *c.* White House, *d.* Supreme Court) : SENATE

46. (*a.* parsing, *b.* gender, *c.* case, *d.* declension) : NOUN :: CONJUGATION : VERB

47. MC : MD :: MMCC : (*a.* MCM, *b.* MGM, *c.* MDM, *d.* MMM)

48. (*a.* dour, *b.* caustic, *c.* sweet, *d.* mild) : ACRID :: BITTER : ACRIMONIOUS

49. PORCINE : (*a.* porcupine, *b.* goat, *c.* dog, *d.* pig) :: FELINE : CAT

50. TIPPECANOE : AND TYLER TOO :: FIFTY-FOUR FORTY : (*a.* forever, *b.* or fight, *c.* and forward, *d.* to fortune)

51. IMPEACH : (*a.* prove the guilt of, *b.* overturn, *c.* acquit, *d.* accuse) :: CONVICT : FIND GUILTY

52. CITY OF SEVEN HILLS : ROME :: CITY OF GOD : (*a.* heaven, *b.* Jerusalem, *c.* Bethlehem, *d.* Jericho)

53. WOOD : PAPER :: LATEX : (*a.* cotton, *b.* plastic, *c.* rayon, *d.* rubber)

54. TEXTILE : RAYON :: GEM : (*a.* sapphire, *b.* diamond, *c.* spinel, *d.* quartz)

55. SIAM : (*a.* Mongolia, *b.* China, *c.* Thailand, *d.* Nepal) :: PERSIA : IRAN

56. HABEAS CORPUS : LAW :: EXEUNT OMNES : (*a.* medicine, *b.* drama, *c.* law, *d.* political theory)

57. PENTHOUSE APARTMENT : TOP FLOOR :: DUPLEX APARTMENT : (*a.* two rooms, *b.* two floors, *c.* two bedrooms, *d.* two persons)

58. XENOPHOBIA : (*a.* foreigners, *b.* death, *c.* insanity, *d.* live burial) :: CLAUSTROPHOBIA : CONFINED PLACES

59. LOCKJAW : TETANUS :: HYDROPHOBIA : (*a.* encephalitis, *b.* malaria, *c.* syphilis, *d.* rabies)

60. ENGLISH : CANADA :: (*a.* Italian, *b.* Portuguese, *c.* Brazilian, *d.* French) : BRAZIL

61. MITIGATE : ASSUAGE :: MODERATE : (*a.* lessen, *b.* make worse, *c.* disprove, *d.* approve)

62. 1^0 : 1^{10} :: 10^0 : (*a.* 10^0, *b.* 10^1, *c.* 10^2, *d.* 10^{10})

63. PUSILLANIMOUS : AUDACIOUS :: (*a.* brave, *b.* purposive, *c.* cowardly, *d.* evanescent) : BOLD

64. HANNIBAL : (*a.* Theseus, *b.* Scipio, *c.* Cicero, *d.* Marcion) :: NAPOLEON : WELLINGTON

65. EPITOME : (*a.* monologue, *b.* prevarication, *c.* summary, *d.* diatribe) :: PREFACE : PROLOGUE

66. (*a.* wave, *b.* radian, *c.* alpha, *d.* roentgen) : RADIATION :: MINUTE : TIME

67. VERACIOUS : (*a.* repeated, *b.* horizontal, *c.* diagonal, *d.* truthful) :: CONTINUAL : INCESSANT

68. SOLAR : SUN :: (*a.* lunar, *b.* diurnal, *c.* stellar, *d.* nocturnal) : MOON

69. LINCOLN STEFFENS : POLITICAL MACHINES :: UPTON SINCLAIR : (*a.* meat-packing industry, *b.* financial speculators, *c.* railroad magnates, *d.* patent medicine quacks)

70. FAMILY : HOMINIDAE :: (*a.* sapiens, *b.* species, *c.* genus, *d.* class) : HOMO

71. OVERWEENING : (*a.* conceited, *b.* modest, *c.* spoiled, *d.* underprotected) :: BLUNT : SHARP

72. HEARSAY : GOSSIP :: GAINSAY : (*a.* oppose, *b.* protect, *c.* lose, *d.* take)

73. (*a.* thin, *b.* analogy, *c.* happy, *d.* fat) : FIAT :: SMILE : SIMILE

74. ROUNDHEAD : SHORT HAIR :: (*a.* Tory, *b.* Whig, *c.* Royalist, *d.* Cavalier) : LONG HAIR

75. EUGENICS : HEREDITY :: (*a.* euthanasia, *b.* euthenics, *c.* mnemonics, *d.* dialectics) : ENVIRONMENT

76. THERMO : (*a.* cryo, *b.* iso, *c.* crypto, *d.* paleo) :: HOT : COLD

77. (*a.* North Carolina, *b.* South Carolina, *c.* Georgia, *d.* Florida) : OGLETHORPE :: PENNSYLVANIA : PENN

78. BANEFUL : (*a.* baleful, *b.* salutary, *c.* promiscuous, *d.* remorseful) :: PERSONABLE : HANDSOME

79. WERTHEIMER : GESTALT :: (*a.* Watson, *b.* Kohler, *c.* Koffka, *d.* Piaget) : BEHAVIORIST

80. (*a.* depilate, *b.* dampen, *c.* derogate, *d.* desiccate) : DRY :: MOISTEN : WET

81. GLUCOSE : (*a.* comatose, *b.* malactose, *c.* lactose, *d.* adipose) :: SUCROSE : FRUCTOSE

82. ABLE : MELBA :: (*a.* colt, *b.* peach, *c.* era, *d.* willing) : MARE

83. (*a.* Mars, *b.* Jupiter, *c.* Venus, *d.* Pluto) : PROSERPINA :: ZEUS : HERA

84. FLEET STREET : (*a.* press, *b.* police, *c.* amusement, *d.* high fashion) :: DOWNING STREET : GOVERNMENT

85. ARTUR RUBENSTEIN : PIANO :: ISAAC STERN : (*a.* piano, *b.* violin, *c.* trumpet, *d.* oboe)

86. DURKHEIM : (*a.* Homocide, *b.* Matricide, *c.* Suicide, *d.* Genocide) :: BECKER : OUTSIDERS

87. JOHN WESLEY : METHODIST :: MARY BAKER EDDY : (*a.* Presbyterian, *b.* Baha'i, *c.* Jehovah's Witness, *d.* Christian Science)

88. BACH : BAROQUE :: GRIEG : (*a.* classical, *b.* modern, *c.* romantic, *d.* medieval)

89. (*a.* Husserl, *b.* Heidegger, *c.* Comte, *d.* Camus) : POSITIVISM :: SARTRE : EXISTENTIALISM

90. F# : Gb :: B : (*a.* C_b, *b.* A_b, *c.* G#, *d.* G_b)

91. SECOND : THIRD :: (*a.* clergy, *b.* king, *c.* commoners, *d.* nobility) : BOURGEOISIE

92. ALEXANDER : GREAT :: JULIAN : (*a.* Ingenious, *b.* Meek, *c.* Bold, *d.* Apostate)

93. (*a.* Helen, *b.* Jezebel, *c.* Una, *d.* Archimago) : DUESSA :: GOOD : EVIL

94. D : R × T :: (*a.* A, *b.* C, *c.* F, *d.* H) : M × A

95. PURLOINED : (*a.* Melville, *b.* Doyle, *c.* Poe, *d.* Conrad) :: SCARLET : HAWTHORNE

96. PROPHASE : METAPHASE :: ANAPHASE : (*a.* meiophase, *b.* telophase, *c.* mitophase, *d.* protophase)

97. NEWBERY : (*a.* Wohlenberg, *b.* Caldecott, *c.* Pulitzer, *d.* Thompsen) :: STORY : ARTWORK

98. COUNTESS AURELIA : THE MADWOMAN OF CHAILLOT :: (*a.* Lear, *b.* Othello, *c.* Antonio, *d.* Iago) : THE MERCHANT OF VENICE

99. PICASSO : GUERNICA :: (*a.* Manet, *b.* Raphael, *c.* David, *d.* Leger) : LUNCHEON ON THE GRASS

100. RACINE : MOLIÈRE :: SOPHOCLES : (*a.* Zeno, *b.* Aristophanes, *c.* Plato, *d.* Aristotle)

Answer Key for Practice Test 4

1. *c*	11. *a*	21. *c*	31. *b*	41. *b*	51. *d*	61. *a*	71. *b*	81. *c*	91. *d*
2. *c*	12. *c*	22. *a*	32. *d*	42. *a*	52. *a*	62. *a*	72. *a*	82. *c*	92. *d*
3. *b*	13. *d*	23. *a*	33. *b*	43. *a*	53. *d*	63. *c*	73. *d*	83. *d*	93. *c*
4. *c*	14. *c*	24. *b*	34. *d*	44. *c*	54. *c*	64. *b*	74. *d*	84. *a*	94. *c*
5. *b*	15. *d*	25. *c*	35. *c*	45. *b*	55. *c*	65. *c*	75. *b*	85. *b*	95. *c*
6. *c*	16. *b*	26. *b*	36. *b*	46. *d*	56. *b*	66. *d*	76. *a*	86. *c*	96. *b*
7. *b*	17. *a*	27. *c*	37. *a*	47. *d*	57. *b*	67. *d*	77. *c*	87. *d*	97. *b*
8. *a*	18. *d*	28. *a*	38. *c*	48. *b*	58. *a*	68. *a*	78. *a*	88. *c*	98. *c*
9. *a*	19. *b*	29. *b*	39. *c*	49. *d*	59. *d*	69. *a*	79. *a*	89. *c*	99. *a*
10. *d*	20. *c*	30. *a*	40. *a*	50. *b*	60. *b*	70. *c*	80. *d*	90. *a*	100. *b*

Explanation of Answers for Practice Test 4

1. POLAND : POLISH :: (*a.* Holland, *b.* Dublin, ***c.* Denmark**, *d.* Dansk) : DANISH

   (c) A Polish person is from Poland; a Danish person is from Denmark.
   General Information—Description

2. UNION : (*a.* green, *b.* brown, ***c.* blue**, *d.* white) :: CONFEDERACY : GRAY

   (c) During the Civil War, Union soldiers wore blue uniforms and soldiers of the Confederacy wore gray uniforms.
   Humanities—Description

3. ARTICLE : (*a.* preposition, ***b.* conjunction**, *c.* adjective, *d.* verb) :: THE : AND

   (b) *The* is an article; *and* is a conjunction.
   Humanities—Description

4. SAFETY : 2 :: TOUCHDOWN : (*a.* 2, *b.* 4, ***c.* 6**, *d.* 8)

   (c) In football, a safety is worth 2 points and a touchdown is worth 6 points.
   General Information—Description

5. CIRCLE : ELLIPSE :: SQUARE : (*a.* triangle, ***b.* rectangle**, *c.* pentagon, *d.* hexagon)

   (b) Both a circle and an ellipse are closed curves. Both a square and a rectangle are polygons with four sides.
   Mathematics—Class

6. BIRD : (*a.* nest, *b.* worm, ***c.* wings**, *d.* fly) :: GENIE : MAGIC CARPET

   (c) A bird flies by means of its wings. A genie flies by means of a magic carpet.
   General Information—Description

7. FOXHOLE : (*a.* foxes, ***b.* gunfire**, *c.* discovery, *d.* earthquakes) :: RAINCOAT : RAIN

   (b) A foxhole provides protection from gunfire. A raincoat provides protection from rain.
   General Information—Description

8. FOOLISH : OWL :: (***a.* timid**, *b.* large, *c.* wise, *d.* temperamental) : LION

   (a) An owl is reputed to be wise, which is the opposite of foolish. A lion is reputed to be bold, which is the opposite of timid.
   General Information—Description

9. SINBAD : (***a.* sailor**, *b.* squire, *c.* sinner, *d.* poet) :: ARTHUR : KING

(**a**) Sinbad was a sailor, Arthur a king.
Humanities—Description

10. SOLOMON : WISE :: NERO : (*a*. stupid, *b*. bold, *c*. just, ***d*. cruel**)

(**d**) Solomon was wise; Nero was cruel.
Humanities—Description

11. GRAPE : VINE :: RUBBER : (***a*. tree**, *b*. conifer, *c*. root, *d*. leaf)

(**a**) Grapes come from a vine; rubber comes from a tree.
General Information—Description

12. (*a*. Georgia, *b*. Massachusetts, ***c*. New Jersey**, *d*. Ohio) : MIDDLE ATLANTIC :: VERMONT : NEW ENGLAND

(**c**) New Jersey is a Middle Atlantic state. Vermont is a New England state.
General Information—Description

13. BALD : HAIR :: ALBINO : (*a*. height, *b*. pain, *c*. sight, ***d*. pigment**)

(**d**) A bald person lacks hair. An albino lacks pigment.
General Information—Description

14. BOW : (*a*. arrow, *b*. curtsey, ***c*. stern**, *d*. fore) :: FRONT : REAR

(**c**) The bow is the front of a ship; the stern is the rear.
General Information—Similarity/Contrast

15. MONOGYNY : POLYGYNY :: ONE : (*a*. none, *b*. two, *c*. eight, ***d*. many**)

(**d**) Monogyny is marriage to one spouse. Polygyny is marriage to many spouses.
Social Science—Description

16. (*a*. chlorine, ***b*. ferrous**, *c*. aluminum, *d*. sodium) : IRON :: NITROUS : NITROGEN

(**b**) A ferrous compound contains iron. A nitrous compound contains nitrogen.
Natural Science—Description

17. (***a*. secret codes**, *b*. inscriptions on church vaults, *c*. science fiction, *d*. religious rituals) : CRYPTOGRAPHY :: DICTIONARIES : LEXICOGRAPHY

(**a**) Cryptography is the art of writing secret codes. Lexicography is the art of writing dictionaries.
General Information—Description

18. $E = mc^2$: EINSTEIN :: $C^2 = A^2 + B^2$: (*a*. Bernoulli, *b*. Cauchy, *c*. Descartes, ***d*. Pythagoras**)

(**d**) The equation $E = mc^2$ is attributable to Einstein. The equation $C^2 = A^2 + B^2$ is attributable to Pythagoras.
Mathematics—Description

19. GREEK : GREEK :: ROMAN : (*a.* Indo-European, ***b.* Latin**, *c.* Mediterranean, *d.* Romansh)

(**b**) The ancient Greeks spoke Greek. The ancient Romans spoke Latin.
Humanities—Description

20. (*a.* Jesus, *b.* Hell, ***c.* Heaven**, *d.* Satan) : CHRISTIANITY :: NIRVANA : BUDDHISM

(**c**) The concept of heaven in Christianity serves a function similar to that of nirvana in Buddhism.
Humanities—Description

21. U.S. CALENDAR : U.S. FISCAL CALENDAR :: JANUARY : (*a.* December, *b.* March, ***c.* July**, *d.* September)

(**c**) The first month of the U.S. calendar is January. The first month of the U.S. fiscal calendar is July.
General Information—Description

22. PHOTOMETER : (***a.* light**, *b.* distance, *c.* magnetism, *d.* velocity) :: AUDIOMETER : SOUND

(**a**) A photometer is used to measure light; an audiometer is used to measure sound.
Natural Science—Description

23. (***a.* believable**, *b.* wrong, *c.* fanciful, *d.* humorous) : INCREDIBLE :: AUGMENT : DIMINISH

(**a**) *Incredible* and *believable* are antonyms, as are *augment* and *diminish.*
Vocabulary—Similarity/Contrast

24. INFINITIVE : (*a.* having eaten, ***b.* to sleep**, *c.* has tried, *d.* to the store) :: PARTICIPLE : WALKING

(**b**) *To sleep* is an infinitive. *Walking* is a participle.
Humanities—Class

25. MARX : COMMUNISM :: (*a.* Hamilton, *b.* Lenin, ***c.* Smith**, *d.* Davis) : CAPITALISM

(**c**) Karl Marx is famous for his writing on communism. Adam Smith is famous for his writing on capitalism.
Social Science—Description

26. (*a.* Iambic, ***b.* Doric**, *c.* Spartan, *d.* Grecian) : CORINTHIAN :: SONATA : CONCERTO

(**b**) Doric and Corinthian are both types of columns. A sonata and a concerto are both types of musical compositions.
Humanities—Class

27. SOCCER : BALL :: (*a.* cricket, *b.* rugby, ***c.* hockey**, *d.* lacrosse) : PUCK

(c) Soccer is played with a ball, hockey with a puck.
General Information—Description

28. (***a.* sheep**, *b.* plasma, *c.* vulture, *d.* harass) : BLOOD :: DOG : HOUND

(a) A sheep dog and a bloodhound are both types of dogs.
General Information—Completion

29. (*a.* hawk, ***b.* owl**, *c.* bluejay, *d.* ostrich) : NOCTURNAL :: ROBIN : DIURNAL

(b) An owl is a nocturnal bird; a robin is a diurnal bird.
Natural Science—Description

30. PHLEGM : PHLEGMATIC :: BILE : (***a.* bilious**, *b.* billiard, *c.* binding, *d.* bilabial)

(a) The word *phlegmatic* derives from *phlegm*. The word *bilious* derives from *bile*.
Vocabulary—Description

31. HEAVY-HANDED : (*a.* uncoordinated, ***b.* tactless**, *c.* strong, *d.* coordinated) :: HEAVY-FOOTED : PLODDING

(b) Someone who is heavy-handed is tactless. Someone who is heavy-footed is plodding.
Vocabulary—Similarity/Contrast

32. PALEFACE : WHITE :: BLUENOSE : (*a.* frigid, *b.* tough, *c.* unkind, ***d.* puritanical**)

(d) A paleface is a white person. A bluenose is puritanical.
General Information—Description

33. PROTON : NEUTRON :: POSITIVE : (*a.* negative, ***b.* uncharged**, *c.* positive, *d.* nucleonic)

(b) A proton has a positive electrical charge. A neutron is uncharged.
Natural Science—Description

34. SPHINX : (*a.* pterodactyl, *b.* dodo, *c.* vulture, ***d.* phoenix**) :: LION : EAGLE

(d) A sphinx and a phoenix are both mythological animals. A lion and an eagle are both real animals.
Humanities—Class

35. OCARINA : SWEET POTATO :: INDIAN CORN : (*a.* rye, *b.* barley, ***c.* maize**, *d.* peppercorn)

(c) Another name for an ocarina is "sweet potato." Another name for Indian corn is maize.
General Information—Similarity/Contrast

36. RADIUS : 4 :: DIAMETER : (*a.* 16, ***b.* 8**, *c.* 87π, *d.* 167π)

(b) If the radius of a circle is 4, the circle's diameter is 8.
Mathematics—Description

37. PIKE : (***a.* sturgeon**, *b.* lion, *c.* whale, *d.* buffalo) :: COW : PIG

(a) A pike and a sturgeon are both fishes. A cow and a pig are both mammals.
Natural Science—Class

38. WASSERMANN : (*a.* heart disease, *b.* diabetes, ***c.* syphilis**, *d.* lung cancer) :: PAP : CERVICAL CANCER

(c) The Wassermann test is for syphilis. The Pap test is for cervical cancer.
Natural Science—Description

39. COMPLEMENTARY : SUPPLEMENTARY :: (*a.* 0, *b.* 45, ***c.* 90**, *d.* 360) : 180

(c) Complementary angles sum to 90 degrees. Supplementary angles sum to 180 degrees.
Mathematics—Description

40. E.G. : FOR EXAMPLE :: VIZ. : (***a.* namely**, *b.* except for, *c.* according to, *d.* generally)

(a) The abbreviation *e.g.* means *for example*; *viz.* means *namely.*
General Information—Similarity/Contrast

41. GRAPE : WINE :: (*a.* apple, ***b.* potato**, *c.* pomegranate, *d.* malt) : VODKA

(b) Grapes are used to make wine, potatoes to make vodka.
General Information—Description

42. RISING : FALLING :: (***a.* bull**, *b.* bird, *c.* sparrow, *d.* antelope) : BEAR

(a) A rising market is a bull market. A falling market is a bear market.
Social Science—Similarity/Contrast

43. XX : FEMALE :: (***a.* XY**, *b.* YY, *c.* XZ, *d.* ZZ) : MALE

(a) A female is distinguished by an XX chromosome. A male is distinguished by an XY chromosome.
Natural Science—Description

44. RESPECT : (*a.* love, *b.* protect, ***c.* revere**, *d.* obey) :: DISLIKE : HATE

(c) To revere is to respect a great deal. To hate is to dislike a great deal.
Vocabulary—Description

45. PARLIAMENT : LORDS :: (*a.* House of Representatives, ***b.* Congress**, *c.* White House, *d.* Supreme Court) : SENATE

(b) The House of Lords is the upper chamber of the British Parliament. The Senate is the upper chamber of the U.S. Congress.
Social Science—Description

46. (*a.* parsing, *b.* gender, *c.* case, ***d.* declension**) : NOUN :: CONJUGATION : VERB

    (d) Nouns may belong to a declension, verbs to a conjugation.
    Humanities—Description

47. MC : MD :: MMCC : (*a.* MCM, *b.* MGM, *c.* MDM, ***d.* MMM**)

    (d) 1100 is to 1500 as 2200 is to 3000.
    Mathematics—Equality/Negation

48. (*a.* dour, ***b.* caustic**, *c.* sweet, *d.* mild) : ACRID :: BITTER : ACRIMONIOUS

    (b) *Caustic*, *acrid*, *bitter,* and *acrimonious* all mean the same thing.
    Vocabulary—Similarity/Contrast

49. PORCINE : (*a.* porcupine, *b.* goat, *c.* dog, ***d.* pig**) :: FELINE : CAT

    (d) *Porcine* means *piglike*. *Feline* means *catlike*.
    Vocabulary—Description

50. TIPPECANOE : AND TYLER TOO :: FIFTY-FOUR FORTY : (*a.* forever, ***b.* or fight**, *c.* and forward, *d.* to fortune)

    (b) "Tippecanoe and Tyler too" and "Fifty-four forty or fight" were both slogans in the American past.
    Humanities—Completion

51. IMPEACH : (*a.* prove the guilt of, *b.* overturn, *c.* acquit, ***d.* accuse**) :: CONVICT : FIND GUILTY

    (d) To impeach is to accuse. To convict is to find guilty.
    Vocabulary—Similarity/Contrast

52. CITY OF SEVEN HILLS : ROME :: CITY OF GOD : (***a.* heaven**, *b.* Jerusalem, *c.* Bethlehem, *d.* Jericho)

    (a) Rome is the City of Seven Hills. Heaven is the City of God.
    Humanities—Similarity/Contrast

53. WOOD : PAPER :: LATEX : (*a.* cotton, *b.* plastic, *c.* rayon, ***d.* rubber**)

    (d) Wood is used to make paper. Latex is used to make rubber.
    Natural Science—Description

54. TEXTILE : RAYON :: GEM : (*a.* sapphire, *b.* diamond, ***c.* spinel**, *d.* quartz)

    (c) Rayon is a synthetic textile. Spinel is a synthetic gem.
    Natural Science—Class

55. SIAM : (*a.* Mongolia, *b.* China, ***c.* Thailand**, *d.* Nepal) :: PERSIA : IRAN

    (c) Siam is the former name of Thailand. Persia is the former name of Iran.
    General Information—Similarity/Contrast

56. HABEAS CORPUS : LAW :: EXEUNT OMNES : (*a.* medicine, ***b.* drama**, *c.* law, *d.* political theory)

(**b**) *Habeas corpus* is an expression used in law. *Exeunt omnes* is an expression used in drama.
Humanities—Description

57. PENTHOUSE APARTMENT : TOP FLOOR :: DUPLEX APARTMENT : (*a.* two rooms, ***b.* two floors**, *c.* two bedrooms, *d.* two persons)

(**b**) A penthouse apartment is on the top floor. A duplex apartment has two floors.
General Information—Description

58. XENOPHOBIA : (***a.* foreigners**, *b.* death, *c.* insanity, *d.* live burial) :: CLAUSTROPHOBIA : CONFINED PLACES

(**a**) Xenophobia is a fear of foreigners. Claustrophobia is a fear of confined places.
Vocabulary—Description

59. LOCKJAW : TETANUS :: HYDROPHOBIA : (*a.* encephalitis, *b.* malaria, *c.* syphilis, ***d.* rabies**)

(**d**) Tetanus is sometimes called lockjaw. Rabies is sometimes called hydrophobia.
Natural Science—Similarity/Contrast

60. ENGLISH : CANADA :: (*a.* Italian, ***b.* Portuguese**, *c.* Brazilian, *d.* French) : BRAZIL

(**b**) English is the most widely spoken language in Canada. Portuguese is the most widely spoken language in Brazil.
General Information—Description

61. MITIGATE : ASSUAGE :: MODERATE : (***a.* lessen**, *b.* make worse, *c.* disprove, *d.* approve)

(**a**) *Mitigate*, *assuage*, *moderate*, and *lessen* can all be used interchangeably.
Vocabulary—Similarity/Contrast

62. $1^0 : 1^{10} :: 10^0$: (***a.*** $\mathbf{10^0}$, *b.* 10^1, *c.* 10^2, *d.* 10^{10})

(**a**) 1 is to 1 as 1 is to 1.
Mathematics—Equality/Negation

63. PUSILLANIMOUS : AUDACIOUS :: (*a.* brave, *b.* purposive, ***c.* cowardly**, *d.* evanescent) : BOLD

(**c**) *Pusillanimous* and *cowardly* are synonyms, as are *audacious* and *bold.*
Vocabulary—Similarity/Contrast

64. HANNIBAL : (*a.* Theseus, ***b.* Scipio**, *c.* Cicero, *d.* Marcion) :: NAPOLEON : WELLINGTON

(**b**) Hannibal was defeated by Scipio. Napoleon was defeated by Wellington.
Humanities—Description

65. EPITOME : (*a.* monologue, *b.* prevarication, ***c.* summary**, *d.* diatribe) :: PREFACE : PROLOGUE

    (c) An epitome is a summary. A preface is a prologue.
    Vocabulary—Similarity/Contrast

66. (*a.* wave, *b.* radian, *c.* alpha, ***d.* roentgen**) : RADIATION :: MINUTE : TIME

    (d) A roentgen is a unit of radiation. A minute is a unit of time.
    Natural Science—Description

67. VERACIOUS : (*a.* repeated, *b.* horizontal, *c.* diagonal, ***d.* truthful**) :: CONTINUAL : INCESSANT

    (d) *Veracious* means *truthful. Continual* means *incessant.*
    Vocabulary—Similarity/Contrast

68. SOLAR : SUN :: (***a.* lunar**, *b.* diurnal, *c.* stellar, *d.* nocturnal) : MOON

    (a) The word *solar* derives from Sol, the Roman god of the sun. The word *lunar* derives from Luna, the Roman goddess of the moon.
    Humanities—Description

69. LINCOLN STEFFENS : POLITICAL MACHINES :: UPTON SINCLAIR : (***a.* meat-packing industry**, *b.* financial speculators, *c.* railroad magnates, *d.* patent medicine quacks)

    (a) Lincoln Steffens was a muckraker who exposed political machines. Upton Sinclair was a muckraker who exposed the sordid conditions in the meat-packing industry.
    Humanities—Description

70. FAMILY : HOMINIDAE :: (*a.* sapiens, *b.* species, ***c.* genus**, *d.* class) : HOMO

    (c) Human beings are of family Hominidae and genus *Homo.*
    Natural Science—Class

71. OVERWEENING : (*a.* conceited, ***b.* modest**, *c.* spoiled, *d.* underprotected) :: BLUNT : SHARP

    (b) *Overweening* is the opposite of *modest. Blunt* is the opposite of *sharp.*
    Vocabulary—Similarity/Contrast

72. HEARSAY : GOSSIP :: GAINSAY : (***a.* oppose**, *b.* protect, *c.* lose, *d.* take)

    (a) Hearsay is gossip. To gainsay is to oppose.
    Vocabulary—Similarity/Contrast

73. (*a.* thin, *b.* analogy, *c.* happy, ***d.* fat**) : FIAT :: SMILE : SIMILE

    (d) *Simile* is *smile* with an *i* added to the interior of the word. *Fiat* is *fat* with an *i* added to the interior of the word.
    Nonsemantic

74. ROUNDHEAD : SHORT HAIR :: (*a.* Tory, *b.* Whig, *c.* Royalist, ***d.* Cavalier**) : LONG HAIR

(d) The Roundheads were known for their short hair. The Cavaliers were known for their long hair.
Humanities—Description

75. EUGENICS : HEREDITY :: (*a.* euthanasia, ***b.* euthenics**, *c.* mnemonics, *d.* dialectics) : ENVIRONMENT

(b) Eugenics studies how to "improve" the human "race" through the manipulation of heredity. Euthenics studies how to do the same through the manipulation of the environment.
Vocabulary—Description

76. THERMO : (***a.* cryo**, *b.* iso, *c.* crypto, *d.* paleo) :: HOT : COLD

(a) *Thermo-* is a prefix meaning *heat*. *Cryo-* is a prefix meaning *cold.*
Vocabulary—Similarity/Contrast

77. (*a.* North Carolina, *b.* South Carolina, ***c.* Georgia**, *d.* Florida) : OGLETHORPE :: PENNSYLVANIA : PENN

(c) Oglethorpe founded Georgia. Penn founded Pennsylvania.
Humanities—Description

78. BANEFUL : (***a.* baleful**, *b.* salutary, *c.* promiscuous, *d.* remorseful) :: PERSONABLE : HANDSOME

(a) *Baneful* means *baleful*. *Personable* means *handsome*.
Vocabulary—Similarity/Contrast

79. WERTHEIMER : GESTALT :: (***a.* Watson**, *b.* Kohler, *c.* Koffka, *d.* Piaget) : BEHAVIORIST

(a) Wertheimer was a leading psychologist in the Gestalt movement. Watson was a leading psychologist in the behaviorist movement.
Social Science—Description

80. (*a.* depilate, *b.* dampen, *c.* derogate, ***d.* desiccate**) : DRY :: MOISTEN : WET

(d) To desiccate is to dry. To moisten is to wet.
Vocabulary—Similarity/Contrast

81. GLUCOSE : (*a.* comatose, *b.* malactose, ***c.* lactose**, *d.* adipose) :: SUCROSE : FRUCTOSE

(c) Glucose, lactose, sucrose, and fructose are all sugars.
Natural Science—Class

82. ABLE : MELBA :: (*a.* colt, *b.* peach, ***c.* era**, *d.* willing) : MARE

(c) *Melba* is *able* spelled backwards, with an added initial *m*. *Mare* is *era* spelled backwards, with an added initial *m*.
Nonsemantic

83. (*a.* Mars, *b.* Jupiter, *c.* Venus, ***d.* Pluto**) : PROSERPINA :: ZEUS : HERA

(d) In Greek mythology, Proserpina was the wife of Pluto, Hera the wife of Zeus.
Humanities—Class

84. FLEET STREET : (***a.* press**, *b.* police, *c.* amusement, *d.* high fashion) :: DOWNING STREET : GOVERNMENT

(a) In London, Fleet Street has many of the offices of the press, while Downing Street has many of the offices of the government.
General Information—Description

85. ARTUR RUBENSTEIN : PIANO :: ISAAC STERN : (*a.* piano, ***b.* violin**, *c.* trumpet, *d.* oboe)

(b) Artur Rubenstein is a pianist. Isaac Stern is a violinist.
Humanities—Description

86. DURKHEIM : (*a.* Homocide, *b.* Matricide, ***c.* Suicide**, *d.* Genocide) :: BECKER : OUTSIDERS

(c) Durkheim is the author of the sociological work *Suicide.* Becker is the author of the sociological study *Outsiders.*
Social Science—Description

87. JOHN WESLEY : METHODIST :: MARY BAKER EDDY : (*a.* Presbyterian, *b.* Baha'i, *c.* Jehovah's Witness, ***d.* Christian Science**)

(d) John Wesley was the founder of the Methodist church. Mary Baker Eddy was the founder of the Christian Science church.
Humanities—Description

88. BACH : BAROQUE :: GRIEG : (*a.* classical, *b.* modern, ***c.* romantic**, *d.* medieval)

(c) Bach was a composer in the baroque period of music. Grieg was a romantic composer.
Humanities—Description

89. (*a.* Husserl, *b.* Heidegger, ***c.* Comte**, *d.* Camus) : POSITIVISM :: SARTRE : EXISTENTIALISM

(c) Comte helped shape the movement in philosophy now known as positivism. Sartre was a major shaper of existentialism.
Humanities—Description

90. F# : Gb :: B : (***a.* C_b**, *b.* A_b, *c.* G#, *d.* G_b)

(a) F# is the same as G_b. B is the same as C_b.
Humanities—Similarity/Contrast

91. SECOND : THIRD :: (*a.* clergy, *b.* king, *c.* commoners, ***d.* nobility**) : BOURGEOISIE

(d) The nobility comprised the Second Estate of the French Estates-General. The bourgeoisie comprised the Third Estate.
Humanities—Description

92. ALEXANDER : GREAT :: JULIAN : (*a.* Ingenious, *b.* Meek, *c.* Bold, ***d.* Apostate**)

(**d**) Alexander was called the Great. Julian was called the Apostate.
Humanities—Description

93. (*a.* Helen, *b.* Jezebel, ***c.* Una**, *d.* Archimago) : DUESSA :: GOOD : EVIL

(**c**) In Spenser's poem, *The Faerie Queene*, Una represents the forces of good and Duessa the forces of evil.
Humanities—Description

94. D : R × T :: (*a.* A, *b.* C, ***c.* F**, *d.* H) : M × A

(**c**) In physics, Distance = Rate × Time and Force = Mass × Acceleration.
Natural Science—Equality/Negation

95. PURLOINED : (*a.* Melville, *b.* Doyle, ***c.* Poe**, *d.* Conrad) :: SCARLET : HAWTHORNE

(**c**) *The Purloined Letter* is a story by Poe. *The Scarlet Letter* is a story by Hawthorne.
Humanities—Description

96. PROPHASE : METAPHASE :: ANAPHASE : (*a.* meiophase, ***b.* telophase**, *c.* mitophase, *d.* protophase)

(**b**) Prophase, metaphase, anaphase, and telophase are all stages in mitosis (a form of cell division).
Natural Science—Class

97. NEWBERY : (*a.* Wohlenberg, ***b.* Caldecott**, *c.* Pulitzer, *d.* Thompsen) :: STORY : ARTWORK

(**b**) The Newbery Medal is awarded annually to a distinguished children's story book. The Caldecott Medal is also awarded annually for distinguished artwork in a children's book.
General Information—Description

98. COUNTESS AURELIA : THE MADWOMAN OF CHAILLOT :: (*a.* Lear, *b.* Othello, ***c.* Antonio**, *d.* Iago) : THE MERCHANT OF VENICE

(**c**) Countess Aurelia is the Madwoman of Chaillot in the play by the same name. Antonio is the Merchant of Venice in the play by the same name.
Humanities—Similarity/Contrast

99. PICASSO : GUERNICA :: (***a.* Manet**, *b.* Raphael, *c.* David, *d.* Leger) : LUNCHEON ON THE GRASS

(**a**) Picasso is the artist who painted *Guernica*. Manet is the artist who painted *Luncheon on the Grass.*
Humanities—Description

100. RACINE : MOLIÈRE :: SOPHOCLES : (*a.* Zeno, ***b.* Aristophanes**, *c.* Plato, *d.* Aristotle)

(b) Racine was a French playwright who wrote tragedies, while Molière was a French playwright who wrote comedies. Sophocles was a Greek playwright who wrote tragedies, while Aristophanes was a Greek playwright who wrote comedies.
Humanities—Class

Item Classification Chart

Practice Test 4	RELATIONSHIP						
CONTENT	Similarity/ Contrast	Description	Class	Completion	Part/ Whole	Equality/ Negation	Nonsemanti
Vocabulary	23, 31, 48 51, 61, 63, 65, 67, 71, 72, 76, 78, 80	30, 44, 49 58, 75					
General Information	14, 35, 40, 55	1, 4, 6, 7, 8, 11, 12, 13, 17, 21, 27, 32, 41, 57, 60, 84, 97		28			
Humanities	52, 90, 98	2, 3, 9, 10, 19, 20, 46, 56, 64, 68, 69, 74, 77, 85, 87, 88, 89, 91, 92, 93, 95, 99	24, 26, 34, 83, 100	50			
Social Science	42	15, 25, 45, 79, 86					
Natural Science	59	16, 22, 29, 33, 38, 43, 53, 66	37, 54, 70, 81, 96			94	
Mathematics		18, 36, 39	5			47, 62	
Nonsemantic							73, 82

Miller Analogies Test PRACTICE TEST 5

DIRECTIONS: In each of the following questions, you will find three initial terms and, in parentheses, four answer options designated *a*, *b*, *c*, and *d*. You are to select from the four answer options the one that best completes the analogy with the three initial terms. To record your answers, use the answer sheet at the back of the book.

TIME: *50 minutes*

1. BOW : (*a.* arrow, *b.* grenade, *c.* quiver, *d.* target) :: RIFLE : BULLET
2. MARK TWAIN : HANNIBAL :: (*a.* Ernest Hemingway, *b.* Stephen Crane, *c.* William Shakespeare, *d.* Victor Hugo) : STRATFORD-UPON-AVON
3. UNITED : STAND :: DIVIDED : (*a.* fall, *b.* sit, *c.* lie, *d.* rise)
4. (*a.* Asia, *b.* South America, *c.* Africa, *d.* North America) : SAHARA :: NORTH AMERICA : PAINTED
5. TARANTULA : (*a.* spider, *b.* rabbit, *c.* cat, *d.* cockroach) :: COBRA : SNAKE
6. (*a.* 6, *b.* 9, *c.* 12, *d.* 15) : BASEBALL :: 5 : BASKETBALL
7. SEINE : (*a.* Canada, *b.* Holland, *c.* Germany, *d.* France) :: THAMES : ENGLAND
8. PLIABLE : BEND :: (*a.* brittle, *b.* transparent, *c.* opaque, *d.* flexible) : BREAK
9. ADVERB : HAPPILY :: PREPOSITION : (*a.* the, *b.* or, *c.* on, *d.* none)
10. RIGHT ANGLE : (*a.* 0, *b.* 45, *c.* 90, *d.* 360) :: STRAIGHT ANGLE : 180
11. AUTHOR : PEN :: PAINTER : (*a.* brush, *b.* paint, *c.* canvas, *d.* picture)
12. ASTRONAUT : ROCKET SHIP :: WITCH : (*a.* cauldron, *b.* vulture, *c.* black cat, *d.* broomstick)
13. (*a.* achievement, *b.* permission, *c.* month, *d.* desire) : ABILITY :: MAY : CAN
14. GPO : GENERAL POST OFFICE :: GOP : (*a.* Government Printing Office, *b.* Government Oceanographic Party, *c.* Republican Party, *d.* Democratic Party)
15. (*a.* earthling, *b.* earthian, *c.* earthing, *d.* earthan) : EARTH :: MARTIAN : MARS

16. ASBESTOS : FIRE :: (*a.* vinyl, *b.* air, *c.* cotton, *d.* faucet) : WATER

17. DAVY JONES : (*a.* Great Britain, *b.* Planet Earth, *c.* the sun, *d.* the sea) :: LAND OF THE RISING SUN : JAPAN

18. PAIR : PARE :: COUPLE : (*a.* several, *b.* one, *c.* pear, *d.* prune)

19. ASCETIC : (*a.* businessman, *b.* monk, *c.* carpenter, *d.* policeman) :: CRAFTY : CONFIDENCE MAN

20. GUILLOTINE : ROBESPIERRE :: (*a.* noose, *b.* poison, *c.* knife, *d.* illness) : SOCRATES

21. GIN : BLACK :: (*a.* apple, *b.* whiskey, *c.* cotton, *d.* rummy) : JACK

22. PESO : MEXICO :: (*a.* ounce, *b.* pound, *c.* ruble, *d.* mark) : ENGLAND

23. SILVER : GOLD :: (*a.* Si, *b.* Sl, *c.* Ag, *d.* Hg) : Au

24. VALEDICTORIAN : SALUTATORIAN :: PRIME : (*a.* excellent, *b.* good, *c.* choice, *d.* alternative)

25. CHEROKEE : (*a.* Indian, *b.* aborigine, *c.* Seminole, *d.* pariah) :: APACHE : NAVAHO

26. (*a.* musical instruments, *b.* books, *c.* weather systems, *d.* diseases) : DEWEY :: LIVING THINGS : LINNAEUS

27. IVAN : TERRIBLE :: PETER : (*a.* Hairy, *b.* Reformer, *c.* Great, *d.* Awful)

28. SQUARE : 360 :: RECTANGLE : (*a.* 90, *b.* 180, *c.* 270, *d.* 360)

29. WHALE : (*a.* mammal, *b.* reptile, *c.* amphibian, *d.* fish) :: LIZARD : REPTILE

30. LINCOLN : (*a.* 1, *b.* 5, *c.* 10, *d.* 16) :: JACKSON : 20

31. CONJUNCTION : DISJUNCTION :: AND : (*a.* but, *b.* if . . . then, *c.* or, *d.* because)

32. AENEAS : (*a.* Virgil, *b.* Plutarch, *c.* Caesar, *d.* Demosthenes) :: ODYSSEUS : HOMER

33. CLAUSTROPHOBIA : AGORAPHOBIA :: CONFINED PLACES : (*a.* heights, *b.* water, *c.* open spaces, *d.* darkness)

34. GRIMM : (*a.* Donne, *b.* Petrarch, *c.* Nash, *d.* Andersen) :: CHAUCER : BOCCACCIO

35. CYCLONE : TORNADO :: HURRICANE : (*a.* storm, *b.* typhoon, *c.* rain, *d.* miasma)

36. GREENHOUSE : PLANTS :: AVIARY : (*a.* birds, *b.* bees, *c.* rodents, *d.* fish)

37. (*a.* $A \cap B$, *b.* $B \cap A$, *c.* $A \cup B$, *d.* $B \cup A$) : $B \cup A$ :: $X \wedge Y : Y \vee X$

38. OFFER : JOB :: TENDER : (*a.* resignation, *b.* retirement, *c.* delicate, *d.* rough)

39. HICCUP : HICCOUGH :: EYE : (*a.* light, *b.* ice, *c.* I, *d.* iris)

40. (*a.* black, *b.* white, *c.* orange, *d.* brown) : BLUE :: RED : GREEN

41. ASPIRIN : (*a.* anaphoric, *b.* mycin, *c.* antibiotic, *d.* analgesic) :: PENICILLIN : ANTIBIOTIC

42. (*a.* Istanbul, *b.* Dar es Salaam, *c.* Jerusalem, *d.* Mecca) : MOHAMMED :: BETHLEHEM : JESUS

43. CETANE : DIESEL FUEL OIL :: (*a.* octane, *b.* heptane, *c.* methane, *d.* propane) : GASOLINE

44. DEAD DUCK : GONER :: LAME DUCK : (*a.* one who finishes a term after failing re-election, *b.* one who gives up easily, *c.* one who invests cautiously, *d.* one who complains incessantly)

45. ARGONAUTS : (*a.* Francis Marion, *b.* Jason, *c.* Achilles, *d.* George Washington) :: GREEN MOUNTAIN BOYS : ETHAN ALLEN

46. LYNX : CAT :: BOAR : (*a.* hog, *b.* dog, *c.* goat, *d.* ram)

47. LENIN : BOLSHEVIK :: (*a.* Stalin, *b.* Kerensky, *c.* Trotsky, *d.* Marx) : MENSHEVIK

48. (*a.* oak, *b.* walnut, *c.* balsa, *d.* corundum) : HICKORY :: TIN : STEEL

49. ROCK : ROCKET :: (*a.* coat, *b.* cloth, *c.* jack, *d.* wasp) : JACKET

50. MALARIA : CHILLS :: GOITER : (*a.* pockmarks, *b.* swelling, *c.* fever, *d.* hypertension)

51. PIZARRO : INCA :: (*a.* Ponce de Leon, *b.* Hudson, *c.* Velásquez, *d.* Cortez) : AZTEC

52. ASTROLOGY : (*a.* astronomy, *b.* physics, *c.* pharmacology, *d.* phrenology) :: ASTRONOMY : ANATOMY

53. DUET : SEXTET :: SOLO : (*a.* quartet, *b.* quintet, *c.* chorus, *d.* trio)

54. ANDES : (*a.* Asia, *b.* Africa, *c.* South America, *d.* Europe) :: ALPS : EUROPE

55. MYOPIA : (*a.* hyperopia, *b.* scotopia, *c.* photopia, *d.* metropia) :: NEARSIGHTED : FARSIGHTED

56. PASTORAL : (*a.* religious, *b.* rustic, *c.* metropolitan, *d.* worldly) :: URBAN : CITIFIED

57. SEA : TIGER :: LION : (*a.* land, *b.* fauna, *c.* lily, *d.* heart)

58. ASTRONAUT : SPACESUIT :: (*a.* judge, *b.* baker, *c.* ballerina, *d.* monk) : HABIT

59. MONOGAMY : BIGAMY :: BIPED : (*a.* unipod, *b.* pedate, *c.* millepede, *d.* quadruped)

60. POPE : ROMAN :: (*a.* Metropolitan, *b.* Patriarch, *c.* Cardinal, *d.* Bishop) : GREEK ORTHODOX

61. SEXTANT : (*a.* navigator, *b.* architect, *c.* archeologist, *d.* priest) :: SCALPEL : SURGEON

62. PRIDE : PREJUDICE :: SENSE : (*a.* Folly, *b.* Pretense, *c.* Sensibility, *d.* Sanity)

63. PACIFIST : PEACE :: (*a.* revolutionary, *b.* diplomat, *c.* charlatan, *d.* traitor) : WAR

64. (*a.* brown, *b.* gray, *c.* purple, *d.* blue) : UMBER :: GREEN : CHARTREUSE

65. INCREASE : LESSEN :: (*a.* fair, *b.* final, *c.* incipient, *d.* unfair) : INCHOATE

66. EXCALIBUR : (*a.* sword, *b.* pony, *c.* lioness, *d.* cannon) :: LASSIE : DOG

67. (*a.* Berne, *b.* Geneva, *c.* Zurich, *d.* Lucerne) : SWITZERLAND :: NEW DELHI : INDIA

68. SILVER-TONGUED : ELOQUENT :: JANUS-FACED : (*a.* duplicitous, *b.* versatile, *c.* incredibly ugly, *d.* honest)

69. PRESENT : FUTURE PERFECT :: GO : (*a.* would go, *b.* will go, *c.* will have gone, *d.* would have gone)

70. AMPLITUDE : FREQUENCY :: RATE : (*a.* distance, *b.* velocity, *c.* acceleration, *d.* time)

71. GREENHORN : NOVICE :: NEOPHYTE : (*a.* expert, *b.* priest, *c.* beginner, *d.* novelist)

72. PANEGYRIC : (*a.* prayer, *b.* joke, *c.* threat, *d.* eulogy) :: TEMPEST : STORM

73. CARMEN : (*a.* Verdi, *b.* Bizet, *c.* Gounod, *d.* Wagner) :: BARBER OF SEVILLE : ROSSINI

74. PALPITATE : QUIVER :: MASTICATE : (*a.* abuse, *b.* remove, *c.* stomp, *d.* chew)

75. BOLÍVAR : (*a.* Venezuela, *b.* Spain, *c.* United States, *d.* Mexico) :: WASHINGTON : ENGLAND

76. CORNUCOPIA : (*a.* horn of plenty, *b.* horn of Roland, *c.* hornpipe, *d.* hornstone) :: TENET : PRECEPT

77. SHRIMP : CRUSTACEAN :: (*a.* snail, *b.* lobster, *c.* goldfish, *d.* brine) : MOLLUSK

78. NEW AMSTERDAM : NEW YORK :: SIAM : (*a.* Thailand, *b.* Cambodia, *c.* Laos, *d.* China)

79. HIRSUTE : (*a.* pleasantly plump, *b.* well-dressed, *c.* handsome, *d.* hairy) :: EXTROVERTED : OUTGOING

80. EYE : LIP :: ELBOW : (*a.* forehead, *b.* nose, *c.* foot, *d.* chest)

81. (*a.* feldspar, *b.* talc, *c.* quartz, *d.* topaz) : 1 :: DIAMOND : 10

82. TORTUOUS : (*a.* painless, *b.* painful, *c.* straight, *d.* winding) :: SOBER : INEBRIATED

83. NONPLUS : (*a.* perplexity, *b.* disappointment, *c.* deletion, *d.* elation) :: NONPAREIL : UNEQUALED

84. CROCKETT : ALAMO :: BONAPARTE : (*a.* Madrid, *b.* St. Helena, *c.* Rome, *d.* London)

85. EL GRECO : (*a.* impressionist, *b.* mannerist, *c.* expressionist, *d.* realist) :: DAVID : NEOCLASSICIST

86. GRAY : COUNTRY CHURCHYARD :: (*a.* Keats, *b.* Poe, *c.* Byron, *d.* Longfellow) : GRECIAN URN

87. MITER : (*a.* dancer, *b.* cartoonist, *c.* queen, *d.* bishop) :: CROWN : KING

88. $2^0 : 2^{-2} :: 2^2$: (*a.* $2^{1/4}$, *b.* 2^0, *c.* 2^1, *d.* 2^{-1})

89. FLOWER : GARDEN :: (*a.* pinnacle, *b.* stalamite, *c.* cavern, *d.* explorer) : CAVE

90. LEVITICUS : OLD :: (*a.* Deuteronomy, *b.* Isaiah, *c.* Numbers, *d.* Ephesians) : NEW

91. LOUVRE : PARIS :: PRADO : (*a.* Madrid, *b.* Seville, *c.* Florence, *d.* Chartres)

92. CUL-DE-SAC : BLIND ALLEY :: SANGFROID : (*a.* carelessness, *b.* timidity, *c.* courage, *d.* imperturbability)

93. ENCOMIUM : TRIBUTE :: (*a.* admonition, *b.* excoriation, *c.* benison, *d.* exegesis) : CRITICAL ANALYSIS

94. CARPETBAGGER : NORTH :: (*a.* Granger, *b.* Scalawag, *c.* Bull Moose, *d.* Tweedy Pie) : SOUTH

95. MERCURIAL : (*a.* pretty, *b.* plutonic, *c.* hateful, *d.* hermetic) :: MARTIAL : AREOLOGY

96. LEGATO : BOW :: PIZZICATO : (*a.* fingers, *b.* bow, *c.* reed, *d.* feet)

97. NICK ADAMS : (*a.* Fitzgerald, *b.* Faulkner, *c.* Hemingway, *d.* Joyce) :: ARROWSMITH : LEWIS

98. (*a.* Burgundian, *b.* Prussian, *c.* Turkish, *d.* Bulgarian) : OTTOMAN :: FRENCH : BOURBON

99. ORPHEUS : EURYDICE :: DAPHNIS : (*a.* Pyramus, *b.* Thisbe, *c.* Chloe, *d.* Helen)

100. (*a.* darling, *b.* wench, *c.* harridan, *d.* myrmidon) : SHREW :: MOLLYCODDLE : SISSY

Answer Key for Practice Test 5

1. *a*	11. *a*	21. *d*	31. *c*	41. *d*	51. *d*	61. *a*	71. *c*	81. *b*	91. *a*
2. *c*	12. *d*	22. *b*	32. *a*	42. *d*	52. *d*	62. *c*	72. *d*	82. *c*	92. *d*
3. *a*	13. *b*	23. *c*	33. *c*	43. *a*	53. *d*	63. *a*	73. *b*	83. *a*	93. *d*
4. *c*	14. *c*	24. *c*	34. *d*	44. *a*	54. *c*	64. *a*	74. *d*	84. *b*	94. *b*
5. *a*	15. *a*	25. *c*	35. *b*	45. *b*	55. *a*	65. *b*	75. *b*	85. *b*	95. *d*
6. *b*	16. *a*	26. *b*	36. *a*	46. *a*	56. *b*	66. *a*	76. *a*	86. *a*	96. *a*
7. *d*	17. *d*	27. *c*	37. *a*	47. *b*	57. *c*	67. *a*	77. *a*	87. *d*	97. *c*
8. *a*	18. *d*	28. *d*	38. *a*	48. *c*	58. *d*	68. *a*	78. *a*	88. *b*	98. *c*
9. *c*	19. *b*	29. *a*	39. *c*	49. *c*	59. *d*	69. *c*	79. *d*	89. *b*	99. *c*
10. *c*	20. *b*	30. *b*	40. *c*	50. *b*	60. *b*	70. *d*	80. *c*	90. *d*	100. *c*

Explanation of Answers for Practice Test 5

1. BOW : (***a*. arrow**, *b*. grenade, *c*. quiver, *d*. target) :: RIFLE : BULLET

   (a) An arrow is shot from a bow; a bullet is shot from a rifle.
   General Information—Description

2. MARK TWAIN : HANNIBAL :: (*a*. Ernest Hemingway, *b*. Stephen Crane, ***c*. William Shakespeare**, *d*. Victor Hugo) : STRATFORD-UPON-AVON

   (c) Mark Twain was born in Hannibal, Missouri. William Shakespeare was born in Stratford-upon-Avon, England.
   Humanities—Description

3. UNITED : STAND :: DIVIDED : (***a*. fall**, *b*. sit, *c*. lie, *d*. rise)

   (a) "United we stand, divided we fall" is a familiar saying.
   General Information—Completion

4. (*a*. Asia, *b*. South America, ***c*. Africa**, *d*. North America) : SAHARA :: NORTH AMERICA : PAINTED

   (c) The Sahara Desert is in Africa. The Painted Desert is in North America.
   General Information—Description

5. TARANTULA : (***a*. spider**, *b*. rabbit, *c*. cat, *d*. cockroach) :: COBRA : SNAKE

   (a) A tarantula is a type of spider; a cobra is a type of snake.
   Natural Science—Class

6. (*a*. 6, ***b*. 9**, *c*. 12, *d*. 15) : BASEBALL :: 5 : BASKETBALL

   (b) There are 9 players on a baseball team, and 5 on a basketball team.
   General Information—Description

7. SEINE : (*a*. Canada, *b*. Holland, *c*. Germany, ***d*. France**) :: THAMES : ENGLAND

   (d) The Seine River is in France, while the Thames River is in England.
   General Information—Description

8. PLIABLE : BEND :: (***a*. brittle**, *b*. transparent, *c*. opaque, *d*. flexible) : BREAK

   (a) A pliable object will easily bend, while a brittle substance will easily break.
   General Information—Description

9. ADVERB : HAPPILY :: PREPOSITION : (*a*. the, *b*. or, ***c*. on**, *d*. none)

   (c) *Happily* is an adverb. *On* is a preposition.
   Humanities—Description

10. RIGHT ANGLE : (*a.* 0, *b.* 45, ***c.* 90**, *d.* 360) :: STRAIGHT ANGLE : 180

    (c) A right angle is 90 degrees; a straight angle is 180 degrees.
    Mathematics—Description

11. AUTHOR : PEN :: PAINTER : (***a.* brush**, *b.* paint, *c.* canvas, *d.* picture)

    (a) An author does his or her writing with a pen; a painter does his or her painting with a brush.
    General Information—Description

12. ASTRONAUT : ROCKET SHIP :: WITCH : (*a.* cauldron, *b.* vulture, *c.* black cat, ***d.* broomstick**)

    (d) An astronaut flies by rocket ship. A witch "flies" by broomstick.
    General Information—Description

13. (*a.* achievement, ***b.* permission**, *c.* month, *d.* desire) : ABILITY :: MAY : CAN

    (b) Someone who can do something is able to do it. Someone who may do something has permission to do it.
    General Information—Description

14. GPO : GENERAL POST OFFICE :: GOP : (*a.* Government Printing Office, *b.* Government Oceanographic Party, ***c.* Republican Party**, *d.* Democratic Party)

    (c) GPO is a common abbreviation for General Post Office. GOP is an abbreviation for the Grand Old Party, which is the Republican Party.
    General Information—Similarity/Contrast

15. (***a.* earthling**, *b.* earthian, *c.* earthing, *d.* earthan) : EARTH :: MARTIAN : MARS

    (a) An earthling is an inhabitant of the Earth. A Martian is an inhabitant of Mars.
    General Information—Description

16. ASBESTOS : FIRE :: (***a.* vinyl**, *b.* air, *c.* cotton, *d.* faucet) : WATER

    (a) Asbestos is fireproof. Vinyl is waterproof.
    General Information—Description

17. DAVY JONES : (*a.* Great Britain, *b.* Planet Earth, *c.* the sun, ***d.* the sea**) :: LAND OF THE RISING SUN : JAPAN

    (d) Davy Jones is the sea. The Land of the Rising Sun is Japan.
    General Information—Similarity/Contrast

18. PAIR : PARE :: COUPLE : (*a.* several, *b.* one, *c.* pear, ***d.* prune**)

    (d) A pair is a couple. To pare is to prune.
    Vocabulary—Similarity/Contrast

19. ASCETIC : (*a.* businessman, ***b.* monk**, *c.* carpenter, *d.* policeman) :: CRAFTY : CONFIDENCE MAN

(**b**) A monk is ascetic. A confidence man is crafty.
General Information—Description

20. GUILLOTINE : ROBESPIERRE :: (*a.* noose, ***b.* poison**, *c.* knife, *d.* illness) : SOCRATES

(**b**) Robespierre was killed by the guillotine. Socrates was killed by poison.
Humanities—Description

21. GIN : BLACK :: (*a.* apple, *b.* whiskey, *c.* cotton, ***d.* rummy**) : JACK

(**d**) Gin rummy and blackjack are both card games.
General Information—Completion

22. PESO : MEXICO :: (*a.* ounce, ***b.* pound**, *c.* ruble, *d.* mark) : ENGLAND

(**b**) The peso is the unit of currency in Mexico. The pound is the unit of currency in England.
General Information—Description

23. SILVER : GOLD :: (*a.* Si, *b.* Sl, ***c.* Ag**, *d.* Hg) : Au

(**c**) The chemical symbol for silver is Ag; that for gold is Au.
Natural Science—Similarity/Contrast

24. VALEDICTORIAN : SALUTATORIAN :: PRIME : (*a.* excellent, *b.* good, ***c.* choice**, *d.* alternative)

(**c**) A valedictorian is the highest-ranking student in a class, while a salutatorian is the second highest. Prime meat is the highest-ranked type of meat, while choice meat is the second highest-ranked.
General Information—Class

25. CHEROKEE : (*a.* Indian, *b.* aborigine, ***c.* Seminole**, *d.* pariah) :: APACHE : NAVAHO

(**c**) The Cherokee, Seminole, Apache, and Navaho are all tribes of American Indians.
Social Science—Class

26. (*a.* musical instruments, ***b.* books**, *c.* weather systems, *d.* diseases) : DEWEY :: LIVING THINGS : LINNAEUS

(**b**) Dewey devised a system for classifying books. Linnaeus devised a system for classifying living things.
Humanities—Description

27. IVAN : TERRIBLE :: PETER : (*a.* Hairy, *b.* Reformer, ***c.* Great**, *d.* Awful)

(**c**) Ivan the Terrible and Peter the Great were both rulers of Russia.
Humanities—Completion

28. SQUARE : 360 :: RECTANGLE : (*a.* 90, *b.* 180, *c.* 270, ***d.* 360**)

(**d**) Both a square and a rectangle have interior angles summing to 360 degrees.
Mathematics—Description

29. WHALE : (***a.* mammal**, *b.* reptile, *c.* amphibian, *d.* fish) :: LIZARD : REPTILE

(**a**) A whale is a mammal; a lizard is a reptile.
Natural Science—Class

30. LINCOLN : (*a.* 1, ***b.* 5**, *c.* 10, *d.* 16) :: JACKSON : 20

(**b**) President Lincoln's portrait appears on a $5 bill; President Jackson's portrait appears on a $20 bill.
General Information—Description

31. CONJUNCTION : DISJUNCTION :: AND : (*a.* but, *b.* if . . . then, ***c.* or**, *d.* because)

(**c**) In logic, *and* expresses conjunction and *or* expresses disjunction.
Mathematics—Class

32. AENEAS : (***a.* Virgil**, *b.* Plutarch, *c.* Caesar, *d.* Demosthenes) :: ODYSSEUS : HOMER

(**a**) Virgil wrote about the travels of Aeneas; Homer wrote about the travels of Odysseus.
Humanities—Description

33. CLAUSTROPHOBIA : AGORAPHOBIA :: CONFINED PLACES : (*a.* heights, *b.* water, ***c.* open spaces**, *d.* darkness)

(**c**) Claustrophobia is a fear of confined places. Agoraphobia is a fear of open spaces.
Vocabulary—Description

34. GRIMM : (*a.* Donne, *b.* Petrarch, *c.* Nash, ***d.* Andersen**) :: CHAUCER : BOCCACCIO

(**d**) Grimm and Andersen both wrote fairy tales. Chaucer and Boccaccio both wrote collections of tales told by groups of people.
Humanities—Class

35. CYCLONE : TORNADO :: HURRICANE : (*a.* storm, ***b.* typhoon**, *c.* rain, *d.* miasma)

(**b**) Cyclone, tornado, hurricane, and typhoon are all types of major storms.
Natural Science—Class

36. GREENHOUSE : PLANTS :: AVIARY : (***a.* birds**, *b.* bees, *c.* rodents, *d.* fish)

(**a**) A greenhouse houses plants. An aviary houses birds.
Natural Science—Description

37. (***a.*** $\mathbf{A \cap B}$, *b.* $B \cap A$, *c.* $A \cup B$, *d.* $B \cup A$) : $B \cup A$ :: $X \wedge Y$: $Y \vee X$

(a) $A \cap B$ and $X \wedge Y$ are equivalent, as are $B \cup A$ and $Y \vee X$.
Mathematics—Equality/Negation

38. OFFER : JOB :: TENDER : (***a.* resignation**, *b.* retirement, *c.* delicate, *d.* rough)

    (a) One offers a job, but tenders a resignation.
    General Information—Description

39. HICCUP : HICCOUGH :: EYE : (*a.* light, *b.* ice, ***c.* I**, *d.* iris)

    (c) *Hiccup* and *hiccough* are pronounced identically, as are *eye* and *I.*
    Nonsemantic

40. (*a.* black, *b.* white, ***c.* orange**, *d.* brown) : BLUE :: RED : GREEN

    (c) Orange and blue are complementary colors, as are red and green.
    Natural Science—Similarity/Contrast

41. ASPIRIN : (*a.* anaphoric, *b.* mycin, *c.* antibiotic, ***d.* analgesic**) :: PENICILLIN : ANTIBIOTIC

    (d) Aspirin is an analgesic, while penicillin is an antibiotic.
    Natural Science—Class

42. (*a.* Istanbul, *b.* Dar es Salaam, *c.* Jerusalem, ***d.* Mecca**) : MOHAMMED :: BETHLEHEM : JESUS

    (d) Mecca was the birthplace of Mohammed, while Bethlehem was the birthplace of Jesus.
    Humanities—Description

43. CETANE : DIESEL FUEL OIL :: (***a.* octane**, *b.* heptane, *c.* methane, *d.* propane) : GASOLINE

    (a) Diesel fuel oil is given a cetane rating as an index of quality, while gasoline is given an octane rating for the same purpose.
    Natural Science—Description

44. DEAD DUCK : GONER :: LAME DUCK : (***a.* one who finishes a term after failing re-election**, *b.* one who gives up easily, *c.* one who invests cautiously, *d.* one who complains incessantly)

    (a) A dead duck is a goner; a lame duck is an elected official who finishes his or her term after failing re-election.
    General Information—Similarity/Contrast

45. ARGONAUTS : (*a.* Francis Marion, ***b.* Jason**, *c.* Achilles, *d.* George Washington) :: GREEN MOUNTAIN BOYS : ETHAN ALLEN

    (b) The Argonauts accompanied Jason in his exploits; the Green Mountain Boys accompanied Ethan Allen in his exploits.
    Humanities—Description

46. LYNX : CAT :: BOAR : (***a.* hog**, *b.* dog, *c.* goat, *d.* ram)

(a) A lynx is a type of wild cat. A boar is a type of wild hog.
Natural Science—Class

47. LENIN : BOLSHEVIK :: (*a.* Stalin, ***b.* Kerensky**, *c.* Trotsky, *d.* Marx) : MENSHEVIK

(b) After the Russian Revolution, Lenin led the Bolsheviks and Kerensky led the Mensheviks.
Humanities—Description

48. (*a.* oak, *b.* walnut, ***c.* balsa**, *d.* corundum) : HICKORY :: TIN : STEEL

(c) Balsa is a soft wood, hickory a hard wood. Tin is a soft metal, steel a hard metal.
Natural Science—Class

49. ROCK : ROCKET :: (*a.* coat, *b.* cloth, ***c.* jack**, *d.* wasp) : JACKET

(c) Rocket is rock with *-et* at the end. *Jacket* is *jack* with *-et* at the end.
Nonsemantic

50. MALARIA : CHILLS :: GOITER : (*a.* pockmarks, ***b.* swelling**, *c.* fever, *d.* hypertension)

(b) Malaria results in chills. Goiter results in swelling.
Natural Science—Description

51. PIZARRO : INCA :: (*a.* Ponce de Leon, *b.* Hudson, *c.* Velásquez, ***d.* Cortez**) : AZTEC

(d) Pizarro conquered the Inca Indians. Cortez conquered the Aztecs.
Humanities—Description

52. ASTROLOGY : (*a.* astronomy, *b.* physics, *c.* pharmacology, ***d.* phrenology**) :: ASTRONOMY : ANATOMY

(d) Astrology and phrenology are commonly considered pseudosciences, while astronomy and anatomy are accepted as natural sciences.
Natural Science—Class

53. DUET : SEXTET :: SOLO : (*a.* quartet, *b.* quintet, *c.* chorus, ***d.* trio**)

(d) Two is to six as one is to three.
Mathematics—Equality/Negation

54. ANDES : (*a.* Asia, *b.* Africa, ***c.* South America**, *d.* Europe) :: ALPS : EUROPE

(c) The Andes mountain range is in South America; the Alps are in Europe.
General Information—Description

55. MYOPIA : (***a.* hyperopia**, *b.* scotopia, *c.* photopia, *d.* metropia) :: NEARSIGHTED : FARSIGHTED

(**a**) A nearsighted person has myopia, while a farsighted person has hyperopia.
Natural Science—Description

56. PASTORAL : (*a.* religious, ***b.* rustic**, *c.* metropolitan, *d.* worldly) :: URBAN : CITIFIED

(**b**) *Pastoral* and *rustic* are synonyms, as are *urban* and *citified.*
Vocabulary—Similarity/Contrast

57. SEA : TIGER :: LION : (*a.* land, *b.* fauna, ***c.* lily**, *d.* heart)

(**c**) A sea lion and a tiger lily are both living things.
General Information—Class

58. ASTRONAUT : SPACESUIT :: (*a.* judge, *b.* baker, *c.* ballerina, ***d.* monk**) : HABIT

(**d**) An astronaut wears a spacesuit; a monk wears a habit.
General Information—Description

59. MONOGAMY : BIGAMY :: BIPED : (*a.* unipod, *b.* pedate, *c.* millepede, ***d.* quadruped**)

(**d**) One is to two as two is to four.
Mathematics—Class

60. POPE : ROMAN :: (*a.* Metropolitan, ***b.* Patriarch**, *c.* Cardinal, *d.* Bishop) : GREEK ORTHODOX

(**b**) The Pope is the spiritual leader of the Roman Catholic Church, while the Patriarch is the spiritual leader of the Greek Orthodox Catholic Church.
Humanities—Description

61. SEXTANT : (***a.* navigator**, *b.* architect, *c.* archeologist, *d.* priest) :: SCALPEL : SURGEON

(**a**) A sextant is used by a navigator, while a scalpel is used by a surgeon.
Natural Science—Description

62. PRIDE : PREJUDICE :: SENSE : (*a.* Folly, *b.* Pretense, ***c.* Sensibility**, *d.* Sanity)

(**c**) *Pride and Prejudice* and *Sense and Sensibility* are both novels by Jane Austen.
Humanities—Completion

63. PACIFIST : PEACE :: (***a.* revolutionary**, *b.* diplomat, *c.* charlatan, *d.* traitor) : WAR

(**a**) A pacifist seeks peace; a revolutionary seeks war.
Vocabulary—Description

64. (***a.* brown**, *b.* gray, *c.* purple, *d.* blue) : UMBER :: GREEN : CHARTREUSE

(**a**) Umber is a shade of brown; chartreuse is a shade of green.
Vocabulary—Class

65. INCREASE : LESSEN :: (*a.* fair, ***b.* final**, *c.* incipient, *d.* unfair) : INCHOATE

(**b**) *Increase* and *lessen* are antonyms, as are *final* and *inchoate.*
Vocabulary—Similarity/Contrast

66. EXCALIBUR : (***a.* sword**, *b.* pony, *c.* lioness, *d.* cannon) :: LASSIE : DOG

(**a**) Excalibur was the name of a sword (King Arthur's). Lassie was the name of a dog (Jeff Miller's).
Humanities—Description

67. (***a.* Berne**, *b.* Geneva, *c.* Zurich, *d.* Lucerne) : SWITZERLAND :: NEW DELHI : INDIA

(**a**) Berne is the capital of Switzerland; New Delhi is the capital of India.
General Information—Description

68. SILVER-TONGUED : ELOQUENT :: JANUS-FACED : (***a.* duplicitous**, *b.* versatile, *c.* incredibly ugly, *d.* honest)

(**a**) A silver-tongued person is eloquent. A Janus-faced person is duplicitous—literally, two-faced.
Vocabulary—Similarity/Contrast

69. PRESENT : FUTURE PERFECT :: GO : (*a.* would go, *b.* will go, ***c.* will have gone**, *d.* would have gone)

(**c**) *Go* is the present tense, and *will have gone* the future perfect tense, of the same verb.
Humanities—Description

70. AMPLITUDE : FREQUENCY :: RATE : (*a.* distance, *b.* velocity, *c.* acceleration, ***d.* time**)

(**d**) Amplitude and frequency of a wave are inversely related, as are rate and time traveled by an object.
Natural Science—Equality/Negation

71. GREENHORN : NOVICE :: NEOPHYTE : (*a.* expert, *b.* priest, ***c.* beginner**, *d.* novelist)

(**c**) *Greenhorn*, *novice, neophyte*, and *beginner* are all synonymous.
Vocabulary—Similarity/Contrast

72. PANEGYRIC : (*a.* prayer, *b.* joke, *c.* threat, ***d.* eulogy**) :: TEMPEST : STORM

(**d**) A panegyric is a eulogy. A tempest is a storm.
Vocabulary—Similarity/Contrast

73. CARMEN : (*a.* Verdi, ***b.* Bizet**, *c.* Gounod, *d.* Wagner) :: BARBER OF SEVILLE : ROSSINI

(**b**) *Carmen* is an opera by Bizet. *The Barber of Seville* is an opera by Rossini.
Humanities—Description

74. PALPITATE : QUIVER :: MASTICATE : (*a.* abuse, *b.* remove, *c.* stomp, ***d.* chew**)

(**d**) To palpitate is to quiver. To masticate is to chew.
Vocabulary—Similarity/Contrast

75. BOLÍVAR : (*a.* Venezuela, ***b.* Spain**, *c.* United States, *d.* Mexico) :: WASHINGTON : ENGLAND

(**b**) Simon Bolivar fought against Spain for the liberation of South American countries. George Washington fought against England for the liberation of the newly formed United States.
Humanities—Description

76. CORNUCOPIA : (***a.* horn of plenty**, *b.* horn of Roland, *c.* hornpipe, *d.* hornstone) :: TENET : PRECEPT

(**a**) A cornucopia is a horn of plenty. A tenet is a precept.
Vocabulary—Similarity/Contrast

77. SHRIMP : CRUSTACEAN :: (***a.* snail**, *b.* lobster, *c.* goldfish, *d.* brine) : MOLLUSK

(**a**) A shrimp is a form of crustacean. A snail is a form of mollusk.
Natural Science—Class

78. NEW AMSTERDAM : NEW YORK :: SIAM : (***a.* Thailand**, *b.* Cambodia, *c.* Laos, *d.* China)

(**a**) New York was formerly called New Amsterdam. Thailand was formerly called Siam.
General Information—Similarity/Contrast

79. HIRSUTE : (*a.* pleasantly plump, *b.* well-dressed, *c.* handsome, ***d.* hairy**) :: EXTROVERTED : OUTGOING

(**d**) A hirsute person is hairy. An extroverted person is outgoing.
Vocabulary—Similarity/Contrast

80. EYE : LIP :: ELBOW : (*a.* forehead, *b.* nose, ***c.* foot**, *d.* chest)

(**c**) A normal human being has two eyes, lips, elbows, and feet.
General Information—Class

81. (*a.* feldspar, ***b.* talc**, *c.* quartz, *d.* topaz) : 1 :: DIAMOND : 10

(**b**) On the Mohs scale of hardness, talc is rated 1 (softest) and diamond is rated 10 (hardest).
Natural Science—Description

82. TORTUOUS : (*a.* painless, *b.* painful, ***c.* straight**, *d.* winding) :: SOBER : INEBRIATED

(c) *Tortuous* and *straight* are opposites, as are *sober* and *inebriated.*
Vocabulary—Similarity/Contrast

83. NONPLUS : (***a.* perplexity**, *b.* disappointment, *c.* deletion, *d.* elation) :: NONPAREIL : UNEQUALED

(a) Nonplus is perplexity. Something that is nonpareil is unequaled.
Vocabulary—Similarity/Contrast

84. CROCKETT : ALAMO :: BONAPARTE : (*a.* Madrid, ***b.* St. Helena**, *c.* Rome, *d.* London)

(b) Davy Crockett died at the Alamo. Napoleon Bonaparte died on St. Helena.
Humanities—Description

85. EL GRECO : (*a.* impressionist, ***b.* mannerist**, *c.* expressionist, *d.* realist) :: DAVID : NEOCLASSICIST

(b) El Greco was a mannerist painter. David was a neoclassicist painter.
Humanities—Description

86. GRAY : COUNTRY CHURCHYARD :: (***a.* Keats**, *b.* Poe, *c.* Byron, *d.* Longfellow) : GRECIAN URN

(a) Thomas Gray is famous for his "Elegy in a Country Churchyard," while John Keats is famous for his "Ode on a Grecian Urn."
Humanities—Description

87. MITER : (*a.* dancer, *b.* cartoonist, *c.* queen, ***d.* bishop**) :: CROWN : KING

(d) A miter is a headpiece worn by a bishop. A crown is a headpiece worn by a king.
General Information—Description

88. $2^0 : 2^{-2} :: 2^2 :$ (*a.* $2^{1/4}$, ***b.*** $\mathbf{2^0}$, *c.* 2^1, *d.* 2^{-1})

(b) 1 is to ¼ as 4 is to 1.
Mathematics—Equality/Negation

89. FLOWER : GARDEN :: (*a.* pinnacle, ***b.* stalagmite**, *c.* cavern, *d.* explorer) : CAVE

(b) Flowers grow up from a garden; stalagmites "grow" up from the floor of a cave.
Natural Science—Description

90. LEVITICUS : OLD :: (*a.* Deuteronomy, *b.* Isaiah, *c.* Numbers, ***d.* Ephesians**) : NEW

(d) Leviticus is a book in the Old Testament, while Ephesians is a book in the New Testament.
Humanities—Description

91. LOUVRE : PARIS :: PRADO : (***a.* Madrid**, *b.* Seville, *c.* Florence, *d.* Chartres)

(a) The Louvre is an art museum in Paris; the Prado is an art museum in Madrid.
Humanities—Description

92. CUL-DE-SAC : BLIND ALLEY :: SANGFROID : (*a.* carelessness, *b.* timidity, *c.* courage, ***d.* imperturbability**)

(d) A cul-de-sac is a blind alley. Sangfroid is imperturbability.
Vocabulary—Similarity/Contrast

93. ENCOMIUM : TRIBUTE :: (*a.* admonition, *b.* excoriation, *c.* benison, ***d.* exegesis**) : CRITICAL ANALYSIS

(d) An encomium is a tribute. An exegesis is a critical analysis.
Vocabulary—Similarity/Contrast

94. CARPETBAGGER : NORTH :: (*a.* Granger, ***b.* Scalawag**, *c.* Bull Moose, *d.* Tweedy Pie) : SOUTH

(b) After the Civil War, intruders from the North were called carpetbaggers, and Northern sympathizers (usually Republicans) from the South were called scalawags.
Humanities—Description

95. MERCURIAL : (*a.* pretty, *b.* plutonic, *c.* hateful, ***d.* hermetic**) :: MARTIAL : AREOLOGY

(d) The word *mercurial* is derived from the Roman name and the word *hermetic* from the Greek name, for the messenger of the gods (Mercury or Hermes, respectively). The word *martial* is derived from the Roman name, and the word *areology* from the Greek name, for the god of war (Mars or Ares, respectively).
Humanities—Description

96. LEGATO : BOW :: PIZZICATO : (***a.* fingers**, *b.* bow, *c.* reed, *d.* feet)

(a) On a string instrument, legato notes are played with a bow, while pizzicato notes are played with the fingers.
Humanities—Description

97. NICK ADAMS : (*a.* Fitzgerald, *b.* Faulkner, ***c.* Hemingway**, *d.* Joyce) :: ARROWSMITH : LEWIS

(c) Nick Adams was a character in stories by Ernest Hemingway. Arrowsmith was a character in a novel by Sinclair Lewis.
Humanities—Description

98. (*a.* Burgundian, *b.* Prussian, ***c.* Turkish**, *d.* Bulgarian) : OTTOMAN :: FRENCH : BOURBON

(c) The Ottomans were Turkish; the Bourbons were French.
Humanities—Description

99. ORPHEUS : EURYDICE :: DAPHNIS : (*a.* Pyramus, *b.* Thisbe, ***c.* Chloe**, *d.* Helen)

(c) Orpheus and Eurydice were lovers, as were Daphnis and Chloe.
Humanities—Class

100. (*a.* darling, *b.* wench, ***c.* harridan**, *d.* myrmidon) : SHREW :: MOLLYCODDLE : SISSY

(c) A harridan is a shrew. A mollycoddle is a sissy.
Vocabulary—Similarity/Contrast

Item Classification Chart

Practice Test 5	RELATIONSHIP						
CONTENT	Similarity/ Contrast	Description	Class	Completion	Part/ Whole	Equality/ Negation	Nonsemantic
Vocabulary	18, 56, 65 68, 71, 72, 74, 76, 79 82, 83, 92, 93, 100	33, 63	64				
General Information	14, 17, 44, 78	1, 4, 6, 7, 8, 11, 12, 13, 15, 16, 19, 22, 30, 38, 54, 58, 67, 87	24, 57, 80	3, 21			
Humanities		2, 9, 20, 26, 32, 42, 45, 47, 51, 60, 66, 69, 73, 75, 84, 85 86, 90, 91, 94, 95, 96, 97, 98	34, 99	27, 62			
Social Science			25				
Natural Science	23, 40	36, 43, 50, 55, 61, 81, 89	5, 29, 35, 41, 46, 48, 52, 77			70	
Mathematics		10, 28	31, 59			37, 53, 88	
Nonsemantic							39, 49

Miller Analogies Test PRACTICE TEST 6

Directions: In each of the following questions, you will find three initial terms and, in parentheses, four answer options designated *a*, *b*, *c*, and *d*. You are to select from the four answer options the one that best completes the analogy with the three initial terms. To record your answers, use the answer sheet at the back of the book.

Time: *50 minutes*

1. LETTER : WORD :: (*a.* paragraph, *b.* word, *c.* period, *d.* meaning) : SENTENCE

2. GIVEN NAME : FIRST :: (*a.* Christian name, *b.* real name, *c.* nickname, *d.* surname) : LAST

3. JUDICIARY : (*a.* Circuit Court, *b.* Supreme Court, *c.* District Court, *d.* Court of Appeals) :: LEGISLATIVE : CONGRESS

4. (*a.* magna cum laude, *b.* optima cum laude, *c.* puella cum laude, *d.* summa cum laude) : HIGHEST HONOR :: CUM LAUDE : HONOR

5. WILLIAM JAMES : PHILOSOPHER :: HENRY JAMES : (*a.* chemist, *b.* novelist, *c.* lawyer, *d.* politician)

6. OUNCE : PREVENTION :: POUND : (*a.* remedy, *b.* prophylaxis, *c.* medicine, *d.* cure)

7. (*a.* decline, *b.* recline, *c.* acclaim, *d.* reclaim) : ASCEND :: INCLINE : DESCEND

8. CARNIVORE : ANIMALS :: (*a.* omnivore, *b.* herbivore, *c.* carnivore, *d.* vegetivore) : VEGETABLES

9. COLD : (*a.* caress, *b.* shiver, *c.* legs, *d.* shoulder) :: OPEN : ARMS

10. DROUGHT : (*a.* desert, *b.* thirst, *c.* rain, *d.* crops) :: FAMINE : FOOD

11. WESTMINSTER ABBEY : ENGLAND :: TAJ MAHAL : (*a.* Iran, *b.* India, *c.* Pakistan, *d.* China)

12. LEGISLATOR : MAKES :: POLICE OFFICER : (*a.* interprets, *b.* enforces, *c.* breaks, *d.* enacts)

13. DIRECT : INDIRECT :: HIM : (*a.* him, *b.* his, *c.* he, *d.* he'd)

14. ZIP : LETTER :: AREA : (*a.* volume, *b.* πr^2, *c.* post box, *d.* telephone call)

15. COURSE : COARSE :: (*a.* ruffle, *b.* direction, *c.* jagged, *d.* golf) : ROUGH

16. DIRIGIBLE : (*a.* air, *b.* sea, *c.* land, *d.* underground) :: AUTOMOBILE : LAND

17. MENDEL : (*a.* inequality, *b.* dominance, *c.* depression, *d.* orbits) :: MENDELEEV : PERIODICITY

18. LIVID : ASHEN :: JAUNDICED : (*a.* white, *b.* black, *c.* red, *d.* yellow)

19. AMIABLE : UNFRIENDLY :: AFFABLE : (*a.* unpleasant, *b.* ugly, *c.* beautiful, *d.* kindly)

20. JUNEAU : ALASKA :: (*a.* Waikiki, *b.* Honolulu, *c.* Oahu, *d.* Hawaii) : HAWAII

21. EAT : DRINK :: EDIBLE : (*a.* palpable, *b.* potable, *c.* lacteal, *d.* labile)

22. WHITE LIE : LIE :: (*a.* hurricane, *b.* drizzle, *c.* storm, *d.* humidity) : RAINFALL

23. (*a.* net, *b.* ten, *c.* met, *d.* end) : TEND :: MEN : MEND

24. FLAPJACK : (*a.* pumpkin pie, *b.* pancake, *c.* sponge cake, *d.* paddycake) :: GRIDDLECAKE : HOTCAKE

25. BINOMIAL : POLYNOMIAL :: TWO : (*a.* four, *b.* eight, *c.* all, *d.* many)

26. SAUDI ARABIA : OIL :: (*a.* Iran, *b.* Brazil, *c.* Hungary, *d.* Guatemala) : COFFEE

27. MONARCHY : ONE :: OLIGARCHY : (*a.* two, *b.* three, *c.* several, *d.* multitudes)

28. PASADENA : FOOTBALL :: WIMBLEDON : (*a.* tennis, *b.* boxing, *c.* golf, *d.* basketball)

29. MOLEHILL : EARTH :: DUNE : (*a.* rock, *b.* desert, *c.* mud, *d.* sand)

30. (*a.* plankton, *b.* gizzard, *c.* oyster, *d.* dinosaur) : REPTILE :: FROG : AMPHIBIAN

31. (*a.* Andersen, *b.* Grimm, *c.* Milne, *d.* Alcott) : WINNIE :: DISNEY : MICKEY

32. PATRICIAN : PLEBEIAN :: NOBILITY : (*a.* clergy, *b.* lordship, *c.* proletariat, *d.* bourgeoisie)

33. (*a.* fungi, *b.* water, *c.* gases, *d.* algae) : HYDROLOGY :: LIFE : BIOLOGY

34. GOTHIC : POINTED :: ROMANESQUE : (*a.* rounded, *b.* scalloped, *c.* squared, *d.* buttressed)

35. (*a.* 7, *b.* 9, *c.* 10, *d.* 12) : PLAGUES :: 7 : DEADLY SINS

36. STEP : PETS :: REEL : (*a.* fishes, *b.* rod, *c.* leer, *d.* real)

37. HAWK : PREY :: SWINDLER : (*a.* dupe, *b.* dodge, *c.* doll, *d.* dolt)

38. SOPORIFIC : (*a.* pain, *b.* sleepiness, *c.* hunger, *d.* thirst) :: APHRODISIAC : SEXUAL DESIRE

39. PASTEURIZE : (*a.* chemically treat, *b.* strain, *c.* chill, *d.* partially sterilize) :: HOMOGENIZE : MAKE UNIFORM

40. DECLARATIVE : . :: INTERROGATIVE : (*a.* !, *b.* :, *c.* –, *d.* ?)

41. ALLEGRO : (*a.* largo, *b.* presto, *c.* crescendo, *d.* cantabile) :: FAST : SLOW

42. PENCE : POUND :: CENTS : (*a.* nickel, *b.* dime, *c.* quarter, *d.* dollar)

43. CLANDESTINE : (*a.* surreptitious, *b.* tacit, *c.* sanguine, *d.* outgoing) :: SHY : DIFFIDENT

44. INCOGNITO : (*a.* ignorant, *b.* uninterested, *c.* unofficial, *d.* disguised) :: SATISFACTORY : ADEQUATE

45. ANTIDOTE : POISON :: (*a.* mycin, *b.* antibiotic, *c.* analgesic, *d.* antigen) : BACTERIA

46. DIRTY : LINEN :: FILTHY : (*a.* flax, *b.* burlap, *c.* lummox, *d.* lucre)

47. POLAR : (*a.* equatorial, *b.* mammoth, *c.* coordinate, *d.* grizzly) :: FORD : CHEVROLET

48. ONTOLOGY : BEING :: EPISTEMOLOGY : (*a.* spirit, *b.* knowledge, *c.* metaphysics, *d.* causality)

49. RECORDER : (*a.* flute, *b.* magnetic tape, *c.* player piano, *d.* trombone) :: LUTE : GUITAR

50. MILLIMETER : METER :: METER : (*a.* centimeter, *b.* decimeter, *c.* decameter, *d.* kilometer)

51. GENDARMES : FRANCE :: CARABINIERI : (*a.* Spain, *b.* Italy, *c.* Switzerland, *d.* Turkey)

52. RENOIR : IMPRESSIONIST :: (*a.* Braque, *b.* Matisse, *c.* Monet, *d.* Stella) : CUBIST

53. SCOTLAND YARD : CRIME :: EXCHEQUER : (*a.* agriculture, *b.* industry, *c.* defense, *d.* money)

54. (*a.* magician, *b.* tycoon, *c.* adventurer, *d.* usurer) : GENTLEMAN OF FORTUNE :: ATTENDANT : GENTLEMAN IN WAITING

55. HALCYON : (*a.* tranquil, *b.* agitated, *c.* bounteous, *d.* impoverished) :: FORTUITOUS : PLANNED

56. UTOPIA : (*a.* More, *b.* Plato, *c.* Becket, *d.* Aquinas) :: LILLIPUT : SWIFT

57. MERIDIAN : LONGITUDE :: (*a.* meridian, *b.* prime, *c.* parallel, *d.* perpendicular) : LATITUDE

58. CENTURY : HUNDRED :: MILLENIUM : (*a.* A.D. 1, *b.* eternity, *c.* thousand, *d.* million)

59. COLD-BLOODED : HARD-HEARTED :: HOT-BLOODED : (*a.* cruel, *b.* listless, *c.* cold-hearted, *d.* excitable)

60. ASSIDUOUS : (*a.* ambitious, *b.* favorable, *c.* diligent, *d.* evergreen) :: ASSIMILATE : ABSORB

61. SUTHERLAND : SOPRANO :: CARUSO : (*a.* soprano, *b.* contralto, *c.* tenor, *d.* bass)

62. CARDINAL : ORDINAL :: 8 : (*a.* –2, *b.* 60%, *c.* 5th, *d.* 9)

63. VALJEAN : (*a.* Mauriac, *b.* Balzac, *c.* Hugo, *d.* Molière) :: GORIOT : BALZAC

64. MAUVE : (*a.* brown, *b.* red, *c.* purple, *d.* green) :: TAN : BROWN

65. RANGERS : (*a.* basketball, *b.* polo, *c.* football, *d.* hockey) :: CARDINALS : BASEBALL

66. CARTIER : (*a.* Hudson, *b.* Missouri, *c.* St. Lawrence, *d.* Cartesian) :: MARQUETTE : MISSISSIPPI

67. BUCOLIC : (*a.* rural, *b.* urban, *c.* spicy, *d.* mild) :: TIMID : SHY

68. MERSEAULT : (*a.* Betty, *b.* Suzanne, *c.* Jacqueline, *d.* Marie) :: TOM : BECKY

69. (*a.* scrupulous, *b.* shrewd, *c.* ingenuous, *d.* indigenous) : WILY :: NAIVE : SOPHISTICATED

70. MAXIM : (*a.* chisel, *b.* saw, *c.* palindrome, *d.* deed) :: ADAGE : PROVERB

71. BUCKINGHAM PALACE : MONARCH OF ENGLAND :: PANDEMONIUM : (*a.* Neptune, *b.* Genghis Khan, *c.* Satan, *d.* Citizen Kane)

72. TAXONOMY : LIFE FORMS :: NOSOLOGY : (*a.* noses, *b.* laws, *c.* coins, *d.* diseases)

73. PENOLOGY : OENOLOGY :: PEAL : (*a.* wine, *b.* oil, *c.* poll, *d.* eel)

74. FATHERS : SONS :: SONS (*a.* Daughters, *b.* Lovers, *c.* Strangers, *d.* Mothers)

75. CATATONIC : HEBEPHRENIC :: ANAL : (*a.* genital, *b.* phallic, *c.* oral, *d.* Oedipal)

76. (*a.* Joyce, *b.* Wilde, *c.* James, *d.* O'Henry) : DORIAN GRAY :: JOYCE : ARTIST AS A YOUNG MAN

77. EISENHOWER : REPUBLICAN :: (*a.* T. Roosevelt, *b.* Harrison, *c.* Fillmore, *d.* Wilson) : BULL MOOSE

78. TANGENT X : COTANGENT X :: X : (*a.* X^2, *b.* 1/X, *c.* X – 1, *d.* tan X – sin X)

79. (*a.* mammals, *b.* life, *c.* fish, *d.* humans) : PALEOZOIC :: DINOSAURS : MESOZOIC

80. CITY OF SEVEN HILLS : ROME :: CITY OF LIGHT : (*a.* New York, *b.* Paris, *c.* London, *d.* Venice)

81. SLEEP : SOMNAMBULIST :: (*a.* pimp, *b.* crime, *c.* street, *d.* bed) : PROSTITUTE

82. CELSIUS : 0 :: KELVINS : (*a.* 32, *b.* 0, *c.* –100, *d.* 273)

83. DIONYSUS : DAMOCLES :: (*a.* Zeus, *b.* Pandora, *c.* Ares, *d.* Cronus) : PROMETHEUS

84. PENCIL LEAD : GRAPHITE :: CHALK : (*a.* limestone, *b.* sandstone, *c.* talc, *d.* gypsum)

85. MAUDLIN : (*a.* immature, *b.* humorous, *c.* munificent, *d.* mawkish) :: MODERATE : TEMPERATE

86. RHEOSTAT : ELECTRICITY :: (*a.* automobile, *b.* traffic light, *c.* car-counter, *d.* bottleneck) : TRAFFIC

87. CHAUCER : SWEET SHOWERS :: ELIOT : (*a.* stinging rain, *b.* sweet breath, *c.* swich licour, *d.* cruellest month)

88. 8^{-1} : 8^{1} :: –1 : (*a.* –64, *b.* –8, *c.* 8, *d.* 64)

89. BIGOT : ZEALOT :: TROGLODYTE : (*a.* cave dweller, *b.* hero, *c.* traitor, *d.* reformer)

90. TEMPER : (*a.* piano, *b.* moisture, *c.* docility, *d.* tape recorder) :: FOCUS : CAMERA

91. ZEUS : HERA :: (*a.* Ulysses, *b.* Orestes, *c.* Agamemnon, *d.* Paris) : CLYTEMNESTRA

92. TRITIUM : HYDROGEN :: OZONE : (*a.* oxygen, *b.* nitrogen, *c.* carbon dioxide, *d.* cesium)

93. METROPOLITAN MUSEUM : NEW YORK :: RIJKSMUSEUM : (*a.* Utrecht, *b.* Munich, *c.* Paris, *d.* Amsterdam)

94. POSEIDON : (*a.* Uranus, *b.* Mars, *c.* Saturn, *d.* Neptune) :: ZEUS : JUPITER

95. (*a.* zz, *b.* Zuider, *c.* zero, *d.* zee) : ZED :: BAR : PUB

96. (*a.* hot, *b.* bacterium, *c.* virus, *d.* lungs) : TUBERCULOSIS :: VIRUS : COLD

97. MOLLY : (*a.* Madison, *b.* Monroe, *c.* Maguire, *d.* Malone) :: KNOW : NOTHING

98. ANEMOMETER : WIND SPEED :: MANOMETER : (*a.* blood pressure, *b.* heart rate, *c.* visual acuity, *d.* auditory acuity)

99. HERODOTUS : (*a.* history, *b.* medicine, *c.* his city, *d.* Greece) :: WASHINGTON : HIS COUNTRY

100. (*a.* Washington, *b.* Jackson, *c.* Eisenhower, *d.* Polk) : HOWE :: GRANT : LEE

Answer Key for Practice Test 6

1. *b*	11. *b*	21. *b*	31. *c*	41. *a*	51. *b*	61. *c*	71. *c*	81. *c*	91. *c*
2. *d*	12. *b*	22. *b*	32. *c*	42. *d*	52. *a*	62. *c*	72. *d*	82. *d*	92. *a*
3. *b*	13. *a*	23. *b*	33. *b*	43. *a*	53. *d*	63. *c*	73. *d*	83. *a*	93. *d*
4. *d*	14. *d*	24. *b*	34. *a*	44. *d*	54. *c*	64. *c*	74. *b*	84. *a*	94. *d*
5. *b*	15. *b*	25. *d*	35. *c*	45. *b*	55. *b*	65. *d*	75. *c*	85. *d*	95. *d*
6. *d*	16. *a*	26. *b*	36. *c*	46. *d*	56. *a*	66. *c*	76. *b*	86. *b*	96. *b*
7. *a*	17. *b*	27. *c*	37. *a*	47. *d*	57. *c*	67. *a*	77. *a*	87. *d*	97. *c*
8. *b*	18. *d*	28. *a*	38. *b*	48. *b*	58. *c*	68. *d*	78. *b*	88. *a*	98. *a*
9. *d*	19. *a*	29. *d*	39. *d*	49. *a*	59. *d*	69. *c*	79. *c*	89. *a*	99. *a*
10. *c*	20. *b*	30. *d*	40. *d*	50. *d*	60. *c*	70. *b*	80. *b*	90. *a*	100. *a*

Explanation of Answers for Practice Test 6

1. LETTER : WORD :: (*a.* paragraph, ***b.* word**, *c.* period, *d.* meaning) : SENTENCE

   (b) A word is composed of letters. A sentence is composed of words.
   General Information—Part/Whole

2. GIVEN NAME : FIRST :: (*a.* Christian name, *b.* real name, *c.* nickname, ***d.* surname**) : LAST

   (d) A given name is a first name. A surname is a last name.
   Vocabulary—Similarity/Contrast

3. JUDICIARY : (*a.* Circuit Court, ***b.* Supreme Court**, *c.* District Court, *d.* Court of Appeals) :: LEGISLATIVE : CONGRESS

   (b) The Supreme Court is the highest judiciary body in the United States. The Congress is the highest legislative body in the United States.
   Social Science—Description

4. (*a.* magna cum laude, *b.* optima cum laude, *c.* puella cum laude, ***d.* summa cum laude**) : HIGHEST HONOR :: CUM LAUDE : HONOR

   (d) *Summa cum laude* denotes highest honor; *cum laude*, honor.
   General Information—Similarity/Contrast

5. WILLIAM JAMES : PHILOSOPHER :: HENRY JAMES : (*a.* chemist, ***b.* novelist**, *c.* lawyer, *d.* politician)

   (b) William James was a philosopher; his brother Henry was a novelist.
   Humanities—Description

6. OUNCE : PREVENTION :: POUND : (*a.* remedy, *b.* prophylaxis, *c.* medicine, ***d.* cure**)

   (d) "An ounce of prevention is worth a pound of cure," or so the saying goes.
   General Information—Completion

7. (***a.* decline**, *b.* recline, *c.* acclaim, *d.* reclaim) : ASCEND :: INCLINE : DESCEND

   (a) *Decline* and *incline* are antonyms, as are *ascend* and *descend.*
   Vocabulary—Similarity/Contrast

8. CARNIVORE : ANIMALS :: (*a.* omnivore, ***b.* herbivore**, *c.* carnivore, *d.* vegetivore) : VEGETABLES

   (b) A carnivore eats (the flesh of) animals; an herbivore eats vegetables.
   Vocabulary—Description

9. COLD : (*a.* caress, *b.* shiver, *c.* legs, ***d.* shoulder**) :: OPEN : ARMS

(d) A person may be greeted either with a cold shoulder or with open arms.
General Information—Completion

10. DROUGHT : (*a.* desert, *b.* thirst, ***c.* rain**, *d.* crops) :: FAMINE : FOOD

    (c) A drought is caused by lack of rain; a famine is caused by lack of food.
    Vocabulary—Description

11. WESTMINSTER ABBEY : ENGLAND :: TAJ MAHAL : (*a.* Iran, ***b.* India**, *c.* Pakistan, *d.* China)

    (b) Westminster Abbey is in England. The Taj Mahal is in India.
    General Information—Description

12. LEGISLATOR : MAKES :: POLICE OFFICER : (*a.* interprets, ***b.* enforces**, *c.* breaks, *d.* enacts)

    (b) A legislator makes laws; a police officer enforces them.
    General Information—Description

13. DIRECT : INDIRECT :: HIM : (***a.* him**, *b.* his, *c.* he, *d.* he'd)

    (a) *Him* is the correct form of the personal pronoun for use as either a direct or an indirect object.
    Humanities—Description

14. ZIP : LETTER :: AREA : (*a.* volume, *b.* πr^2, *c.* post box, ***d.* telephone call**)

    (d) A zip code is used for a letter, while an area code is used for a telephone call.
    General Information—Description

15. COURSE : COARSE :: (*a.* ruffle, ***b.* direction**, *c.* jagged, *d.* golf) : ROUGH

    (b) *Course* and *direction* are synonyms, as are *coarse* and *rough.*
    Vocabulary—Similarity/Contrast

16. DIRIGIBLE : (***a.* air**, *b.* sea, *c.* land, *d.* underground) :: AUTOMOBILE : LAND

    (a) A dirigible travels by air, while an automobile travels by land.
    General Information—Description

17. MENDEL : (*a.* inequality, ***b.* dominance**, *c.* depression, *d.* orbits) :: MENDELEEV : PERIODICITY

    (b) Mendel formulated the law of dominance; Mendeleev formulated the law of periodicity.
    Natural Science—Description

18. LIVID : ASHEN :: JAUNDICED : (*a.* white, *b.* black, *c.* red, ***d.* yellow**)

    (d) Something that is livid is ashen. Something that is jaundiced is yellow.
    Vocabulary—Similarity/Contrast

19. AMIABLE : UNFRIENDLY :: AFFABLE : (***a.* unpleasant**, *b.* ugly, *c.* beautiful, *d.* kindly)

    (a) *Amiable* and *unfriendly* are opposites, as are *affable* and *unpleasant.*
    Vocabulary—Similarity/Contrast

20. JUNEAU : ALASKA :: (*a.* Waikiki, ***b.* Honolulu**, *c.* Oahu, *d.* Hawaii) : HAWAII

    (b) Juneau is the capital of Alaska; Honolulu is the capital of Hawaii.
    General Information—Description

21. EAT : DRINK :: EDIBLE : (*a.* palpable, ***b.* potable**, *c.* lacteal, *d.* labile)

    (b) One can eat what is edible and drink what is potable.
    Vocabulary—Description

22. WHITE LIE : LIE :: (*a.* hurricane, ***b.* drizzle**, *c.* storm, *d.* humidity) : RAINFALL

    (b) A white lie is a minor lie; a drizzle is a minor rainfall.
    Vocabulary—Description

23. (*a.* net, ***b.* ten**, *c.* met, *d.* end) : TEND :: MEN : MEND

    (b) *Tend* is pronounced as *ten,* but with an added *d* consonant sound at the end. *Mend* is pronounced as *men*, but again with an added *d* consonant sound at the end.
    Nonsemantic

24. FLAPJACK : (*a.* pumpkin pie, ***b.* pancake**, *c.* sponge cake, *d.* paddycake) :: GRIDDLECAKE : HOTCAKE

    (b) Flapjack, pancake, griddlecake, and hotcake are all names for the same food.
    General Information—Similarity/Contrast

25. BINOMIAL : POLYNOMIAL :: TWO : (*a.* four, *b.* eight, *c.* all, ***d.* many**)

    (d) A binomial is an equation with two terms. A polynomial is an equation with many terms.
    Mathematics—Description

26. SAUDI ARABIA : OIL :: (*a.* Iran, ***b.* Brazil**, *c.* Hungary, *d.* Guatemala) : COFFEE

    (b) Saudi Arabia is a major source of oil. Brazil is a major source of coffee.
    General Information—Description

27. MONARCHY : ONE :: OLIGARCHY : (*a.* two, *b.* three, ***c.* several**, *d.* multitudes)

    (c) A monarchy is a government of one ruler; an oligarchy is a government several individuals rule jointly.
    Social Science—Description

28. PASADENA : FOOTBALL :: WIMBLEDON : (***a.* tennis**, *b.* boxing, *c.* golf, *d.* basketball)

    (a) Pasadena is the location of a major football game (the Rose Bowl). Wimbledon is the location of a major tennis match.
    General Information—Description

29. MOLEHILL : EARTH :: DUNE : (*a.* rock, *b.* desert, *c.* mud, ***d.* sand)**

    (d) A molehill is composed of earth. A dune is composed of sand.
    General Information—Description

30. (*a.* plankton, *b.* gizzard, *c.* oyster, ***d.* dinosaur**) : REPTILE :: FROG : AMPHIBIAN

    (d) A dinosaur is a form of reptile. A frog is a form of amphibian.
    Natural Science—Class

31. (*a.* Andersen, *b.* Grimm, ***c.* Milne**, *d.* Alcott) : WINNIE :: DISNEY : MICKEY

    (c) A. A. Milne created the character Winnie (the Pooh). Walt Disney created the character Mickey (Mouse).
    Humanities—Description

32. PATRICIAN : PLEBEIAN :: NOBILITY : (*a.* clergy, *b.* lordship, ***c.* proletariat**, *d.* bourgeoisie)

    (c) In ancient Rome, the patricians were members of the nobility and the plebeians were members of the proletariat.
    Humanities—Similarity/Contrast

33. (*a.* fungi, ***b.* water**, *c.* gases, *d.* algae) : HYDROLOGY :: LIFE : BIOLOGY

    (b) Hydrology is the study of water; biology is the study of life.
    Natural Science—Description

34. GOTHIC : POINTED :: ROMANESQUE : (***a.* rounded**, *b.* scalloped, *c.* squared, *d.* buttressed)

    (a) Gothic arches are pointed, while Romanesque arches are rounded.
    Humanities—Description

35. (*a.* 7, *b.* 9, ***c.* 10**, *d.* 12) : PLAGUES :: 7 : DEADLY SINS

    (c) There were 10 plagues in Egypt, and there are 7 deadly sins.
    Humanities—Description

36. STEP : PETS :: REEL : (*a.* fishes, *b.* rod, ***c.* leer**, *d.* real)

    (c) *Pets* is *step* spelled backwards. *Leer* is *reel* spelled backwards.
    Nonsemantic

37. HAWK : PREY :: SWINDLER : (***a.* dupe**, *b.* dodge, *c.* doll, *d.* dolt)

    (a) A hawk victimizes prey. A swindler victimizes dupes.
    General Information—Description

38. SOPORIFIC : (*a.* pain, ***b.* sleepiness**, *c.* hunger, *d.* thirst) :: APHRODISIAC : SEXUAL DESIRE

(b) A soporific induces sleepiness. An aphrodisiac induces sexual desire.
Vocabulary—Description

39. PASTEURIZE : (*a.* chemically treat, *b.* strain, *c.* chill, ***d.* partially sterilize**) :: HOMOGENIZE : MAKE UNIFORM

(d) To pasteurize milk is to partially sterilize it. To homogenize milk is to make it uniform.
General Information—Similarity/Contrast

40. DECLARATIVE : . :: INTERROGATIVE : (*a.* !, *b.* :, *c.* –, ***d.* ?**)

(d) A declarative sentence ends with a period (.). An interrogative sentence ends with a question mark (?).
Humanities—Description

41. ALLEGRO : (***a.* largo**, *b.* presto, *c.* crescendo, *d.* cantabile) :: FAST : SLOW

(a) In music, an allegro tempo is a fast one, while a largo tempo is a slow one.
Humanities—Similarity/Contrast

42. PENCE : POUND :: CENTS : (*a.* nickel, *b.* dime, *c.* quarter, ***d.* dollar**)

(d) There are 100 pence in a pound (in English currency) and 100 cents in a dollar (in American currency).
General Information—Part/Whole

43. CLANDESTINE : (***a.* surreptitious**, *b.* tacit, *c.* sanguine, *d.* outgoing) :: SHY : DIFFIDENT

(a) *Clandestine* means *surreptitious*. *Shy* means *diffident*.
Vocabulary—Similarity/Contrast

44. INCOGNITO : (*a.* ignorant, *b.* uninterested, *c.* unofficial, ***d.* disguised**) :: SATISFACTORY : ADEQUATE

(d) *Incognito* means *disguised*. *Satisfactory* means *adequate*.
Vocabulary—Similarity/Contrast

45. ANTIDOTE : POISON :: (*a.* mycin, ***b.* antibiotic**, *c.* analgesic, *d.* antigen) : BACTERIA

(b) An antidote is a cure for the effects of poison; an antibiotic is a remedy for the effects of bacteria.
Natural Science—Description

46. DIRTY : LINEN :: FILTHY : (*a.* flax, *b.* burlap, *c.* lummox, ***d.* lucre**)

(d) *Dirty linen* and *filthy lucre* are two common English expressions.
General Information—Completion

47. POLAR : (*a.* equatorial, *b.* mammoth, *c.* coordinate, ***d.* grizzly**) :: FORD : CHEVROLET

(**d**) A polar bear and a grizzly bear are two types of bears. A Ford and a Chevrolet are two types of cars.
General Information—Class

48. ONTOLOGY : BEING :: EPISTEMOLOGY : (*a.* spirit, ***b.* knowledge**, *c.* metaphysics, *d.* causality)

(**b**) Ontology is the study of being; epistemology, the study of knowledge.
Humanities—Description

49. RECORDER : (***a.* flute**, *b.* magnetic tape, *c.* player piano, *d.* trombone) :: LUTE : GUITAR

(**a**) A recorder is an early form of flute; a lute is an early form of guitar.
Humanities—Class

50. MILLIMETER : METER :: METER : (*a.* centimeter, *b.* decimeter, *c.* decameter, ***d.* kilometer**)

(**d**) There are 1000 millimeters in a meter, and 1000 meters in a kilometer.
Mathematics—Part/Whole

51. GENDARMES : FRANCE :: CARABINIERI : (*a.* Spain, ***b.* Italy**, *c.* Switzerland, *d.* Turkey)

(**b**) Police officers in France are called gendarmes; in Italy, they are called carabinieri.
General Information—Description

52. RENOIR : IMPRESSIONIST :: (***a.* Braque**, *b.* Matisse, *c.* Monet, *d.* Stella) : CUBIST

(**a**) Renoir was an impressionist painter; Braque, a cubist.
Humanities—Description

53. SCOTLAND YARD : CRIME :: EXCHEQUER : (*a.* agriculture, *b.* industry, *c.* defense, ***d.* money**)

(**d**) In England, Scotland Yard is charged with the control of crime, the Exchequer with the control of money.
General Information—Description

54. (*a.* magician, *b.* tycoon, ***c.* adventurer**, *d.* usurer) : GENTLEMAN OF FORTUNE :: ATTENDANT : GENTLEMAN IN WAITING

(**c**) A gentleman of fortune is an adventurer. A gentleman in waiting is an attendant.
General Information—Similarity/Contrast

55. HALCYON : (*a.* tranquil, ***b.* agitated**, *c.* bounteous, *d.* impoverished) :: FORTUITOUS : PLANNED

(**b**) *Halcyon* is an antonym of *agitated. Fortuitous* is an antonym of *planned.*
Vocabulary—Similarity/Contrast

56. UTOPIA : (***a*. More**, *b*. Plato, *c*. Becket, *d*. Aquinas) :: LILLIPUT : SWIFT

(**a**) Utopia is a land invented by More; Lilliput is a land invented by Swift.
Humanities—Description

57. MERIDIAN : LONGITUDE :: (*a*. meridian, *b*. prime, ***c*. parallel**, *d*. perpendicular) : LATITUDE

(**c**) A meridian is a line of longitude; a parallel is a line of latitude.
General Information—Description

58. CENTURY : HUNDRED :: MILLENIUM : (*a*. A.D. 1, *b*. eternity, ***c*. thousand**, *d*. million)

(**c**) A century is one hundred years; a millenium is one thousand years.
General Information—Description

59. COLD-BLOODED : HARD-HEARTED :: HOT-BLOODED : (*a*. cruel, *b*. listless, *c*. cold-hearted, ***d*. excitable**)

(**d**) *Cold-blooded* means *hard-hearted. Hot-blooded* means *excitable.*
Vocabulary—Similarity/Contrast

60. ASSIDUOUS : (*a*. ambitious, *b*. favorable, ***c*. diligent**, *d*. evergreen) :: ASSIMILATE : ABSORB

(**c**) *Assiduous* is a synonym of *diligent. Assimilate* is a synonym of *absorb.*
Vocabulary—Similarity/Contrast

61. SUTHERLAND : SOPRANO :: CARUSO : (*a*. soprano, *b*. contralto, ***c*. tenor**, *d*. bass)

(**c**) Joan Sutherland is a renowned soprano; Caruso was a renowned tenor.
Humanities—Description

62. CARDINAL : ORDINAL :: 8 : (*a*. –2, *b*. 60%, ***c*. 5th**, *d*. 9)

(**c**) 8 is a cardinal number, and 5th is an ordinal number.
Mathematics—Class

63. VALJEAN : (*a*. Mauriac, *b*. Balzac, ***c*. Hugo**, *d*. Molière) :: GORIOT : BALZAC

(**c**) Jean Valjean is a character created by the French novelist Victor Hugo. Père Goriot is a character created by the French novelist Honoré de Balzac.
Humanities—Description

64. MAUVE : (*a*. brown, *b*. red, ***c*. purple**, *d*. green) :: TAN : BROWN

(**c**) Mauve is a shade of purple; tan is a shade of brown.
General Information—Class

65. RANGERS : (*a.* basketball, *b.* polo, *c.* football, ***d.* hockey**) :: CARDINALS : BASEBALL

    (d) The Rangers are a hockey team. The Cardinals are a baseball team.
    General Information—Description

66. CARTIER : (*a.* Hudson, *b.* Missouri, ***c.* St. Lawrence**, *d.* Cartesian) :: MARQUETTE : MISSISSIPPI

    (c) Cartier explored the St. Lawrence River; Marquette explored the Mississippi River.
    Humanities—Description

67. BUCOLIC : (***a.* rural**, *b.* urban, *c.* spicy, *d.* mild) :: TIMID : SHY

    (a) *Bucolic* means *rural*; *timid* means *shy*.
    Vocabulary—Similarity/Contrast

68. MERSEAULT : (*a.* Betty, *b.* Suzanne, *c.* Jacqueline, ***d.* Marie**) :: TOM : BECKY

    (d) In *The Stranger,* Marie is the girlfriend of Merseault. In *Tom Sawyer*, Becky is the girlfriend of Tom.
    Humanities—Class

69. (*a.* scrupulous, *b.* shrewd, ***c.* ingenuous**, *d.* indigenous) : WILY :: NAIVE : SOPHISTICATED

    (c) *Ingenuous* and *wily* are opposites, as are *naive* and *sophisticated.*
    Vocabulary—Similarity/Contrast

70. MAXIM : (*a.* chisel, ***b.* saw**, *c.* palindrome, *d.* deed) :: ADAGE : PROVERB

    (b) *Maxim*, *saw*, *adage*, and *proverb* are all synonymous.
    Vocabulary—Similarity/Contrast

71. BUCKINGHAM PALACE : MONARCH OF ENGLAND :: PANDEMONIUM : (*a.* Neptune, *b.* Genghis Khan, ***c.* Satan**, *d.* Citizen Kane)

    (c) Buckingham Palace is the palace of the monarch of England. Pandemonium, in *Paradise Lost*, is the palace of Satan.
    Humanities—Description

72. TAXONOMY : LIFE FORMS :: NOSOLOGY : (*a.* noses, *b.* laws, *c.* coins, ***d.* diseases**)

    (d) Taxonomy is classification of life forms. Nosology is classification of diseases.
    Natural Science—Description

73. PENOLOGY : OENOLOGY :: PEAL : (*a.* wine, *b.* oil, *c.* poll, ***d.* eel**)

    (d) *Penology* and *oenology* have the same initial vowel sound, as do *peal* and *eel.*
    Nonsemantic

74. FATHERS : SONS :: SONS (*a.* Daughters, ***b.* Lovers**, *c.* Strangers, *d.* Mothers)

(**b**) *Fathers and Sons* is a novel by Ivan Turgenev. *Sons and Lovers* is a novel by D. H. Lawrence.
Humanities—Completion

75. CATATONIC : HEBEPHRENIC :: ANAL : (*a.* genital, *b.* phallic, ***c.* oral**, *d.* Oedipal)

(**c**) A catatonic shows anal symptomatology. A hebephrenic shows oral symptomatology.
Social Science—Description

76. (*a.* Joyce, ***b.* Wilde**, *c.* James, *d.* O'Henry) : DORIAN GRAY :: JOYCE : ARTIST AS A YOUNG MAN

(**b**) Oscar Wilde wrote *The Picture of Dorian Gray*. James Joyce wrote *A Portrait of the Artist as a Young Man.*
Humanities—Description

77. EISENHOWER : REPUBLICAN :: (***a.* T. Roosevelt**, *b.* Harrison, *c.* Fillmore, *d.* Wilson) : BULL MOOSE

(**a**) President Eisenhower was a member of the Republican Party. President T. (Theodore) Roosevelt was a member of the Bull Moose Party.
Social Science—Description

78. TANGENT X : COTANGENT X :: X : (*a.* X^2, ***b.* 1/X**, *c.* X – 1, *d.* tan X – sin X)

(**b**) The cotangent of *X* is equal to 1 divided by the tangent of *X*.
Mathematics—Description

79. (*a.* mammals, *b.* life, ***c.* fish**, *d.* humans) : PALEOZOIC :: DINOSAURS : MESOZOIC

(**c**) Fish first appeared in the Paleozoic Era. Dinosaurs first appeared in the Mesozoic Era.
Natural Science—Description

80. CITY OF SEVEN HILLS : ROME :: CITY OF LIGHT : (*a.* New York, ***b.* Paris**, *c.* London, *d.* Venice

(**b**) Rome is the City of Seven Hills; Paris is the City of Light.
Humanities—Similarity/Contrast

81. SLEEP : SOMNAMBULIST :: (*a.* pimp, *b.* crime, ***c.* street**, *d.* bed) : PROSTITUTE

(**c**) A somnambulist walks in his or her sleep. A prostitute walks in the streets.
General Information—Description

82. CELSIUS : 0 :: KELVINS : (*a.* 32, *b.* 0, *c.* –100, ***d.* 273**)

(**d**) Zero degrees Celsius is equal to 273 kelvins (to the nearest unit).
Natural Science—Equality/Negation

83. DIONYSUS : DAMOCLES :: (***a.* Zeus**, *b.* Pandora, *c.* Ares, *d.* Cronus) : PROMETHEUS

(**a**) Dionysus punished Damocles (by hanging a sword over his head). Zeus punished Prometheus (by chaining him to a rock).
Humanities—Description

84. PENCIL LEAD : GRAPHITE :: CHALK : (***a.* limestone**, *b.* sandstone, *c.* talc, *d.* gypsum)

(**a**) Pencil lead is made of graphite. Chalk is made of limestone.
General Information—Description

85. MAUDLIN : (*a.* immature, *b.* humorous, *c.* munificent, ***d.* mawkish**) :: MODERATE : TEMPERATE

(**d**) *Maudlin* means *mawkish*. *Moderate* means *temperate*.
Vocabulary—Similarity/Contrast

86. RHEOSTAT : ELECTRICITY :: (*a.* automobile, ***b.* traffic light**, *c.* car-counter, *d.* bottleneck) : TRAFFIC

(**b**) A rheostat regulates the flow of electricity. A traffic light regulates the flow of traffic.
Natural Science—Description

87. CHAUCER : SWEET SHOWERS :: ELIOT : (*a.* stinging rain, *b.* sweet breath, *c.* swich licour, ***d.* cruellest month**)

(**d**) In the opening line of *The Canterbury Tales*, Chaucer mentions April in the context of its sweet showers. In the opening line of *The Wasteland*, Eliot alludes to Chaucer, but changes things by mentioning April as the cruellest month.
Humanities—Description

88. $8^{-1} : 8^{1}$ :: –1 : (***a.* –64**, *b.* –8, *c.* 8, *d.* 64)

(**a**) ⅛ is to 8 as –1 is to –64.
Mathematics—Equality/Negation

89. BIGOT : ZEALOT :: TROGLODYTE : (***a.* cave dweller**, *b.* hero, *c.* traitor, *d.* reformer)

(**a**) A bigot is a zealot; a troglodyte was a cave dweller.
Vocabulary—Similarity/Contrast

90. TEMPER : (***a.* piano**, *b.* moisture, *c.* docility, *d.* tape recorder) :: FOCUS : CAMERA

(**a**) One tempers a piano; one focuses a camera.
General Information—Description

91. ZEUS : HERA :: (*a.* Ulysses, *b.* Orestes, ***c.* Agamemnon**, *d.* Paris) : CLYTEMNESTRA

(c) In Greek mythology, Zeus was the husband of Hera. In Greek literature, Agamemnon was the husband of Clytemnestra.
Humanities—Class

92. TRITIUM : HYDROGEN :: OZONE : (***a.* oxygen**, *b.* nitrogen, *c.* carbon dioxide, *d.* cesium)

(a) Tritium is a form of hydrogen, H_3. Ozone is a form of oxygen, O_3.
Natural Science—Class

93. METROPOLITAN MUSEUM : NEW YORK :: RIJKSMUSEUM : (*a.* Utrecht, *b.* Munich, *c.* Paris, ***d.* Amsterdam**)

(d) The Metropolitan Museum is in New York. The Rijksmuseum is in Amsterdam.
General Information—Description

94. POSEIDON : (*a.* Uranus, *b.* Mars, *c.* Saturn, ***d.* Neptune**) :: ZEUS : JUPITER

(d) Poseidon was the Greek name, and Neptune the Roman name, for the god of the sea. Zeus was the Greek name, and Jupiter the Roman name, for the king of the gods.
Humanities—Similarity/Contrast

95. (*a.* zz, *b.* Zuider, *c.* zero, ***d.* zee**) : ZED :: BAR : PUB

(d) The British call zed what Americans call zee (the letter *Z*). The British call a pub what Americans call a bar.
General Information—Similarity/Contrast

96. (*a.* hot, ***b.* bacterium**, *c.* virus, *d.* lungs) : TUBERCULOSIS :: VIRUS : COLD

(b) Tuberculosis is caused by a bacterium; a cold is caused by a virus.
Natural Science—Description

97. MOLLY : (*a.* Madison, *b.* Monroe, ***c.* Maguire**, *d.* Malone) :: KNOW : NOTHING

(c) The Molly Maguires and the Know-Nothings were both secret political action groups.
Social Science—Completion

98. ANEMOMETER : WIND SPEED :: MANOMETER : (***a.* blood pressure**, *b.* heart rate, *c.* visual acuity, *d.* auditory acuity)

(a) An anemometer measures wind speed; a manometer measures blood pressure.
Natural Science—Description

99. HERODOTUS : (***a.* history**, *b.* medicine, *c.* his city, *d.* Greece) :: WASHINGTON : HIS COUNTRY

(**a**) Herodotus is sometimes called the Father of History. George Washington is sometimes called the Father of His Country.
Social Science—Description

100. (***a.* Washington**, *b.* Jackson, *c.* Eisenhower, *d.* Polk) : HOWE :: GRANT : LEE

(**a**) General Howe surrendered to George Washington. General Lee surrendered to Ulysses S. Grant.
Humanities—Description

Item Classification Chart

Practice Test 6	RELATIONSHIP						
CONTENT	Similarity/ Contrast	Description	Class	Completion	Part/ Whole	Equality/ Negation	Nonsemantic
Vocabulary	2, 7, 15, 18, 19, 43, 44, 55, 59, 60, 67, 69, 70, 85, 89	8, 10, 21, 22, 38					
General Information	4, 24, 39, 54, 95	11, 12, 14, 16, 20, 26, 28, 29, 37, 51, 53, 57, 58, 65, 81, 84, 90, 93	47, 64	6, 9, 46	1, 42		
Humanities	32, 41, 80, 94	5, 13, 31, 34, 35, 40, 48, 52, 56, 61, 63, 66, 71, 76, 83, 87, 100	49, 68, 91	74			
Social Science		3, 27, 75, 77, 97, 99					
Natural Science		17, 33, 45, 72, 79, 86, 96, 98	30, 92			82	
Mathematics		25, 78	62		50	88	
Nonsemantic							23, 36, 73

Miller Analogies Test PRACTICE TEST 7

DIRECTIONS: In each of the following questions, you will find three initial terms and, in parentheses, four answer options designated *a*, *b*, *c*, and *d*. You are to select from the four answer options the one that best completes the analogy with the three initial terms. To record your answers, use the answer sheet at the back of the book.

TIME: *50 minutes*

1. SUFFOCATION : AIR :: DEHYDRATION : (*a.* food, *b.* shelter, *c.* water, *d.* sunlight)

2. RISE : (*a.* set, *b.* raise, *c.* sit, *d.* decrease) :: EAST : WEST

3. (*a.* greedy, *b.* pleasure-seeking, *c.* lazy, *d.* warlike) : SPARTA :: CULTURED : ATHENS

4. CUBE : SQUARE :: (*a.* ellipsis, *b.* ellipsoid, *c.* oblong, *d.* tetrahedron) : ELLIPSE

5. INFRARED : BELOW :: (*a.* maroon, *b.* aquamarine, *c.* chartreuse, *d.* ultraviolet) : ABOVE

6. (*a.* NW, *b.* SW, *c.* NE, *d.* SE) : SE :: S : N

7. DIASTOLIC : DILATATION :: (*a.* anatolic, *b.* controlic, *c.* catatolic, *d.* systolic) : CONTRACTION

8. CAVALRY : HORSE :: INFANTRY : (*a.* platoon, *b.* stallion, *c.* tank, *d.* foot)

9. MADISON : (*a.* American Revolution, *b.* French-Indian War, *c.* War of 1812, *d.* Spanish-American War) :: LINCOLN : CIVIL WAR

10. SHEEP : (*a.* sheeps, *b.* sheep, *c.* sheepes, *d.* sheepses) :: LIFE : LIVES

11. MICKEY : MOUSE :: POLYPHEMOUS : (*a.* Scylla, *b.* Cyclops, *c.* daemon, *d.* satyr)

12. LABOUR : (*a.* Conservative, *b.* Federalist, *c.* Socialist, *d.* Progressive) :: DEMOCRAT : REPUBLICAN

13. A.M. : (*a.* ab, *b.* ante, *c.* amon, *d.* annuo) :: P.M. : post

14. JUDAISM : TORAH :: (*a.* Hinduism, *b.* Buddhism, *c.* Islam, *d.* Confucianism) : KORAN

15. (*a.* gin, *b.* rummy, *c.* check, *d.* mate) : GIN RUMMY :: CHECKMATE : CHESS

16. SAWYER : THATCHER :: TOM : (*a.* Susie, *b.* Becky, *c.* Janey, *d.* Judy)

17. PRAIRIE SCHOONER : (*a.* covered wagon, *b.* horse, *c.* mule, *d.* railroad train) :: PRAIRIE WOLF : COYOTE

18. YEN : JAPAN :: MARK : (*a.* Germany, *b.* Sweden, *c.* Holland, *d.* France)

19. GENOTYPE : PHENOTYPE :: (*a.* expected, *b.* ontogeny, *c.* philogeny, *d.* environmental) : OBSERVED

20. HOLLAND : NETHERLANDS :: FORMOSA : (*a.* Kemoy, *b.* Matsu, *c.* Taiwan, *d.* Oahu)

21. TABLE : ABLE :: TRACK : (*a.* field, *b.* willing, *c.* rack, *d.* truck)

22. MIDWIFE : (*a.* marriage, *b.* birth, *c.* disease, *d.* death) :: SHERIFF : LAW ENFORCEMENT

23. PRISONER : RELEASE :: SOLDIER : (*a.* draft, *b.* fight, *c.* enlist, *d.* discharge)

24. YELLOW : (*a.* coat, *b.* chicken, *c.* hornet, *d.* jacket) :: BUMBLE : BEE

25. AMERICAN : (*a.* British, *b.* Swiss, *c.* Colombian, *d.* Belgian) :: PARMESAN : CAMEMBERT

26. (*a.* hawk, *b.* dove, *c.* eagle, *d.* robin) : U.S.A. :: MAPLE LEAF : CANADA

27. CIRCE : SWINE :: MEDUSA : (*a.* jackal, *b.* stone, *c.* gold, *d.* snake)

28. (*a.* bones, *b.* skin, *c.* muscles, *d.* blood) : DERMATOLOGY :: IMMUNITY : IMMUNOLOGY

29. TWIDDLE : TWADDLE :: (*a.* jambo, *b.* jimbo, *c.* mumbo, *d.* rumbo) : JUMBO

30. OLFACTORY : (*a.* mouth, *b.* ears, *c.* nose, *d.* fingers) :: VISUAL : EYES

31. ECUADOR : SOUTH AMERICA :: EGYPT : (*a.* Africa, *b.* Asia, *c.* Europe, *d.* India)

32. RED CROSS : RELIEF FROM DISASTERS :: BLUE CROSS : (*a.* health insurance, *b.* relief from tyranny, *c.* relief from mental illness, *d.* medical supplies)

33. EEG : BRAIN :: EKG : (*a.* heart, *b.* brain, *c.* gall bladder, *d.* vagus nerve)

34. ABRAHAM : SARAH :: PUNCH : (*a.* Judy, *b.* Paula, *c.* Pat, *d.* Joanie)

35. MPH : RPM :: MILES : (*a.* rotations, *b.* revolutions, *c.* minutes, *d.* hours)

36. ORDAIN : MINISTER :: (*a.* approve, *b.* obey, *c.* admit, *d.* certify) : TEACHER

37. WATER : HYDROGEN :: TABLE SALT : (*a.* chlorine, *b.* potassium, *c.* nitrogen, *d.* oxygen)

38. ELBOW : ARM :: (*a.* shin, *b.* thigh, *c.* calf, *d.* knee) : LEG

39. NUMBER : GENDER :: SINGULAR : (*a.* plural, *b.* feminine, *c.* nominative, *d.* present)

40. PATRICIDE : FATHER :: GENOCIDE : (*a.* enemy, *b.* group, *c.* mother, *d.* brother)

41. INCA : (*a.* Mexico, *b.* Panama, *c.* Honduras, *d.* Peru) :: AZTEC : MEXICO

42. ODIOUS : (*a.* burdensome, *b.* easy, *c.* pleasing, *d.* disgusting) :: HONORABLE : DISGRACEFUL

43. SITTING BULL : CUSTER :: (*a.* Eddington, *b.* Howe, *c.* Sheridan, *d.* Wellington) : NAPOLEON BONAPARTE

44. LOG 10 : 1 :: LOG 100 : (*a.* 2, *b.* 5, *c.* 10, *d.* 90)

45. HOMING PIGEON : CARRIER PIGEON :: STOOL PIGEON : (*a.* fool, *b.* informer, *c.* loser, *d.* passenger pigeon)

46. STOP : POTS :: NOON : (*a.* morning, *b.* noon, *c.* night, *d.* never)

47. EBENEEZER SCROOGE : MISERLY :: SIMON LEGREE : (*a.* humane, *b.* generous, *c.* stingy, *d.* cruel)

48. PALEONTOLOGIST : (*a.* vertebrates, *b.* rocks, *c.* earthquakes, *d.* fossils) :: ZOOLOGIST : ANIMALS

49. (*a.* emperor, *b.* pharaoh, *c.* shah, *d.* diet) : CONGRESS :: PRIME MINISTER : PRESIDENT

50. B_1 : THIAMINE :: (*a.* B_2, *b.* B_6, *c.* C, *d.* D) : RIBOFLAVIN

51. GUERNSEY : (*a.* York, *b.* Jersey, *c.* British, *d.* French) :: CHESHIRE : SIAMESE

52. TOURNEY : TOURNAMENT :: TEMPORARY : (*a.* permanent, *b.* sudden, *c.* transitory, *d.* temptation)

53. STOMACH : DIGESTION :: ANATOMY : (*a.* cartography, *b.* biology, *c.* physiology, *d.* proctology)

54. PRE : PRIOR :: PRETER : (*a*. beyond, *b*. as if, *c*. therefore, *d*. only)

55. LINCOLN : KENNEDY :: (*a*. Tyler, *b*. Johnson, *c*. Eisenhower, *d*. Garfield) : McKINLEY

56. FORTE : LOUD :: (*a*. largo, *b*. rubato, *c*. violin, *d*. piano) : SOFT

57. LATIN ALPHABET : FRENCH :: CYRILLIC ALPHABET : (*a*. Russian, *b*. Sanskrit, *c*. Greek, *d*. Chinese)

58. CENTRIFUGAL : (*a*. centripetal, *b*. centrigonal, *c*. centrobaric, *d*. centrosomal) :: AWAY FROM : TOWARD

59. ICHTHYOLOGY : (*a*. insects, *b*. reptiles, *c*. arthropods, *d*. fish) :: ORNITHOLOGY : BIRDS

60. (*a*. wool, *b*. synthetic, *c*. dinosaur, *d*. gasoline) : PETROL :: U.S.A. : BRITAIN

61. (*a*. overindulge, *b*. persevere, *c*. quit, *d*. deprive) : SURFEIT :: CLOY : SATIATE

62. (*a*. Hesse, *b*. Joyce, *c*. Mann, *d*. Proust) : DEATH IN VENICE :: SHAKESPEARE : MERCHANT OF VENICE

63. ROOK : CASTLE :: HORSE : (*a*. knight, *b*. track, *c*. chess, *d*. winner)

64. (*a*. Greuze, *b*. Utrillo, *c*. Seurat, *d*. Manet) : POINTILLISM :: DAVID : NEOCLASSICISM

65. BILL : BEAK :: (*a*. finger, *b*. leg, *c*. hand, *d*. kneecap) : DIGIT

66. GEWGAW : (*a*. trinket, *b*. bottle, *c*. rhinestone, *d*. candy) :: TACITURN : QUIET

67. (*a*. fortunate, *b*. entreat, *c*. unfortunate, *d*. order) : IMPORTUNE :: IMPREGNABLE : UNSHAKABLE

68. CULPABLE : GUILTY :: (*a*. preculpable, *b*. exculpable, *c*. multiculpable, *d*. malculpable) : ACQUITTED

69. FOX : (*a*. bovine, *b*. vulpine, *c*. porcine, *d*. equine) :: CAT : FELINE

70. AGONY : ECSTASY :: SOUND : (*a*. Light, *b*. Trumpet, *c*. Signpost, *d*. Fury)

71. LANG SYNE : (*a*. bygone days, *b*. future days, *c*. here and now, *d*. nonexistent times) :: IMMEDIATELY : AT ONCE

72. (*a*. India, *b*. Brazil, *c*. Mexico, *d*. Spain) : GUANAJUATO :: CANADA : MANITOBA

73. VERDI : AIDA :: (*a*. Bach, *b*. Mozart, *c*. Beethoven, *d*. Brahms) : FIDELIO

74. TORTUOUS : (*a.* winding, *b.* barbaric, *c.* long, *d.* incomprehensible) :: HAPPY : FELICITOUS

75. (*a.* present, *b.* past, *c.* recent, *d.* never) : CURRENT :: ERSTWHILE : FORMER

76. DAVID : GOLIATH :: HOLMES : (*a.* Moriarty, *b.* Watson, *c.* Doyle, *d.* Devlin)

77. LUGUBRIOUS : (*a.* shallow, *b.* cheerful, *c.* expensive, *d.* fatuous) :: PONDEROUS : LIGHT

78. EXPLETIVE : (*a.* interrogative, *b.* factotum, *c.* oath, *d.* lie) :: EXPOSÉ : DISCLOSURE

79. 11 : BINARY :: (*a.* 2, *b.* 3, *c.* 4, *d.* 10) : DECIMAL

80. CHALICE : GOBLET :: LEAF : (*a.* plant, *b.* tree, *c.* sheet, *d.* gold)

81. (*a.* nut, *b.* fruit, *c.* root, *d.* berry) : TURNIP :: STEM : CELERY

82. ABRAM : ABRAHAM :: (*a.* Sarabelle, *b.* Sarai, *c.* Salome, *d.* Sharon) : SARAH

83. VELÁSQUEZ : MAIDS OF HONOR :: (*a.* Botticelli, *b.* Bellini, *c.* Bosch, *d.* Uccello) : THE BIRTH OF VENUS

84. CIVIL : (*a.* misdemeanor, *b.* larceny, *c.* tort, *d.* perjury) :: CRIMINAL : FELONY

85. GREGORIAN : NOVEMBER :: FRENCH REVOLUTIONARY : (*a.* Novembre, *b.* February, *c.* Julian, *d.* Thermidor)

86. GOLDEN RULE : LUKE :: CATEGORICAL IMPERATIVE : (*a.* Hegel, *b.* Kant, *c.* Ardrey, *d.* Lorenz)

87. EQUIVOCATION : (*a.* perversity, *b.* exultation, *c.* veracity, *d.* perjury) :: UNCERTAINTY : CERTAINTY

88. TIMBREL : (*a.* cymbals, *b.* zither, *c.* flute, *d.* tambourine) :: LUTE : GUITAR

89. (*a.* Apollo, *b.* Phaeton, *c.* Furies, *d.* Sirens) : EUMENIDES :: PLUTO : HADES

90. JOSEPH K. : TRIAL :: GREGOR SAMSA : (*a.* Hunger Artist, *b.* Death in Venice, *c.* The Flies, *d.* Metamorphosis)

91. $\sqrt{2}$: $\sqrt{18}$: : 1 : (*a.* 2, *b.* 3, *c.* 6, *d.* 9)

92. TRANSUBSTANTIATION : ACTUAL :: (*a.* insubstantiation, *b.* absubstantiation, *c.* consubstantiation, *d.* desubstantiation) : SYMBOLIC

93. ABACUS : COMPUTER :: DAGUERROTYPE : (*a.* stereo, *b.* photograph, *c.* tape recorder, *d.* telephone)

94. DECLARATION OF INDEPENDENCE : PHILADELPHIA :: MAGNA CARTA : (*a.* Gloucester, *b.* Runnymede, *c.* Canterbury, *d.* Norwalk)

95. MINTON : ROYAL DOULTON :: MIKASA : (*a.* Sony, *b.* Rosenthal, *c.* Lenox, *d.* Noritake)

96. SHYLOCK : SCROOGE :: DON JUAN : (*a.* Antonio, *b.* Don Giovanni, *c.* Lothario, *d.* Don Quixote)

97. SKINNER : EMPIRICIST :: (*a.* Watson, *b.* Aristotle, *c.* Chomsky, *d.* Locke) : RATIONALIST

98. MOHAWK : IROQUOIS :: (*a.* Apache, *b.* Zuni, *c.* Seminole, *d.* Creek) : PUEBLO

99. (*a.* half-life, *b.* radioactivity, *c.* atomic mass, *d.* atomic number) : ISOTOPE :: ATOMIC WEIGHT : ISOBAR

100. SARACEN : (*a.* Hindu, *b.* Muslim, *c.* Shintoist, *d.* Taoist) :: EPISCOPALIAN : ANGLICAN

Answer Key for Practice Test 7

1. *c*	11. *b*	21. *c*	31. *a*	41. *d*	51. *b*	61. *a*	71. *a*	81. *c*	91. *b*
2. *a*	12. *a*	22. *b*	32. *a*	42. *c*	52. *c*	62. *c*	72. *c*	82. *b*	92. *c*
3. *d*	13. *b*	23. *d*	33. *a*	43. *d*	53. *c*	63. *a*	73. *c*	83. *a*	93. *b*
4. *b*	14. *c*	24. *d*	34. *a*	44. *a*	54. *a*	64. *c*	74. *a*	84. *c*	94. *b*
5. *d*	15. *a*	25. *b*	35. *b*	45. *b*	55. *d*	65. *a*	75. *a*	85. *d*	95. *d*
6. *a*	16. *b*	26. *c*	36. *d*	46. *b*	56. *d*	66. *a*	76. *a*	86. *b*	96. *c*
7. *d*	17. *a*	27. *b*	37. *a*	47. *d*	57. *a*	67. *b*	77. *b*	87. *c*	97. *c*
8. *d*	18. *a*	28. *b*	38. *d*	48. *d*	58. *a*	68. *b*	78. *c*	88. *d*	98. *b*
9. *c*	19. *a*	29. *c*	39. *b*	49. *d*	59. *d*	69. *b*	79. *b*	89. *c*	99. *d*
10. *b*	20. *c*	30. *c*	40. *b*	50. *a*	60. *d*	70. *d*	80. *c*	90. *d*	100. *b*

Explanation of Answers for Practice Test 7

1. SUFFOCATION : AIR :: DEHYDRATION : (*a.* food, *b.* shelter, ***c.* water**, *d.* sunlight)

   (c) Suffocation is caused by lack of air. Dehydration is caused by lack of water.
   Natural Science—Description

2. RISE : (***a.* set**, *b.* raise, *c.* sit, *d.* decrease) :: EAST : WEST

   (a) The sun rises in the east and sets in the west.
   General Information—Description

3. (*a.* greedy, *b.* pleasure-seeking, *c.* lazy, ***d.* warlike**) : SPARTA :: CULTURED : ATHENS

   (d) In ancient Greece, the people of Sparta were known to be warlike, while the people of Athens were known to be cultured.
   Humanities—Description

4. CUBE : SQUARE :: (*a.* ellipsis, ***b.* ellipsoid**, *c.* oblong, *d.* tetrahedron) : ELLIPSE

   (b) When a plane is passed through a cube at a right angle, the intersection is a square. When a plane is passed through an ellipsoid at a right angle, the intersection is an ellipse.
   Mathematics—Part/Whole

5. INFRARED : BELOW :: (*a.* maroon, *b.* aquamarine, *c.* chartreuse, ***d.* ultraviolet**) : ABOVE

   (d) Infrared light is below the visible spectrum for human beings; ultraviolet light is above the visible spectrum.
   Natural Science—Description

6. (***a.* NW**, *b.* SW, *c.* NE, *d.* SE) : SE :: S : N

   (a) NW (northwest) and SE (southeast) are opposing directions, as are S (south) and N (north).
   General Information—Similarity/Contrast

7. DIASTOLIC : DILATATION :: (*a.* anatolic, *b.* controlic, *c.* catatolic, ***d.* systolic**) : CONTRACTION

   (d) Diastolic blood pressure refers to the dilatation of the heart, while systolic blood pressure refers to the contraction of the heart.
   Natural Science—Description

8. CAVALRY : HORSE :: INFANTRY : (*a.* platoon, *b.* stallion, *c.* tank, ***d.* foot**)

   (d) In an army, the cavalry travels by horse, the infantry by foot.
   General Information—Description

9. MADISON : (*a.* American Revolution, *b.* French-Indian War, ***c.* War of 1812**, *d.* Spanish-American War) :: LINCOLN : CIVIL WAR

   (c) Madison was president during the War of 1812; Lincoln was president during the Civil War.
   Social Science—Description

10. SHEEP : (*a.* sheeps, ***b.* sheep**, *c.* sheepes, *d.* sheepses) :: LIFE : LIVES

    (b) The plural of *sheep* is *sheep*. The plural of *life* is *lives.*
    Nonsemantic

11. MICKEY : MOUSE :: POLYPHEMOUS : (*a.* Scylla, ***b.* Cyclops**, *c.* daemon, *d.* satyr)

    (b) Mickey is the name of a fictional mouse; Polyphemous is the name of a fictional Cyclops (in Homer's *Odyssey*).
    Humanities—Description

12. LABOUR : (***a.* Conservative**, *b.* Federalist, *c.* Socialist, *d.* Progressive) :: DEMOCRAT : REPUBLICAN

    (a) In British politics, the Labour party has generally been a left of center political party opposing the right of center Conservative party. In U.S. politics, the more left-leaning Democrats have traditionally opposed the more right-leaning Republicans.
    Social Science—Class

13. A.M. : (*a.* ab, ***b.* ante**, *c.* amon, *d.* annuo) :: P.M. : post

    (b) The A in *A.M.* is an abbreviation for *ante*; the P in *P.M.* is an abbreviation for *post.*
    General Information—Description

14. JUDAISM : TORAH :: (*a.* Hinduism, *b.* Buddhism, ***c.* Islam**, *d.* Confucianism) : KORAN

    (c) The Torah is a holy book of Judaism, while the Koran is a holy book of Islam.
    Humanities—Description

15. (***a.* gin**, *b.* rummy, *c.* check, *d.* mate) : GIN RUMMY :: CHECKMATE : CHESS

    (a) The state of gin ends a gin rummy game, just as the state of checkmate ends a chess game.
    General Information—Description

16. SAWYER : THATCHER :: TOM : (*a.* Susie, ***b.* Becky**, *c.* Janey, *d.* Judy)

    (b) Tom Sawyer and Becky Thatcher are both characters in Mark Twain's novel *Tom Sawyer*.
    Humanities—Completion

17. PRAIRIE SCHOONER : (***a.* covered wagon**, *b.* horse, *c.* mule, *d.* railroad train) :: PRAIRIE WOLF : COYOTE

(a) A prairie schooner is a covered wagon; a prairie wolf is a coyote.
General Information—Similarity/Contrast

18. YEN : JAPAN :: MARK : (***a.* Germany**, *b.* Sweden, *c.* Holland, *d.* France)

(a) The yen is the unit of currency in Japan, while the mark is the unit of currency in Germany.
General Information—Description

19. GENOTYPE : PHENOTYPE :: (***a.* expected**, *b.* ontogeny, *c.* philogeny, *d.* environmental) : OBSERVED

(a) A genotype is what is expected on the basis of heredity, while a phenotype is what is observed on the basis of heredity, environment, and the interaction between them.
Natural Science—Description

20. HOLLAND : NETHERLANDS :: FORMOSA : (*a.* Kemoy, *b.* Matsu, ***c.* Taiwan**, *d.* Oahu)

(c) Holland and Netherlands refer to the same country, as do Formosa and Taiwan.
General Information—Similarity/Contrast

21. TABLE : ABLE :: TRACK : (*a.* field, *b.* willing, ***c.* rack**, *d.* truck)

(c) *Able* is *table* without the initial *t*; *rack* is *track* without the initial *t*.
Nonsemantic

22. MIDWIFE : (*a.* marriage, ***b.* birth**, *c.* disease, *d.* death) :: SHERIFF : LAW ENFORCEMENT

(b) The job of a midwife is to help in birth; the job of a sheriff is to help in law enforcement.
General Information—Description

23. PRISONER : RELEASE :: SOLDIER : (*a.* draft, *b.* fight, *c.* enlist, ***d.* discharge**)

(d) A prisoner receives a release from prison; a soldier receives a discharge from the army.
General Information—Description

24. YELLOW : (*a.* coat, *b.* chicken, *c.* hornet, ***d.* jacket**) :: BUMBLE : BEE

(d) A yellow jacket and a bumblebee are both types of insect.
General Information—Description

25. AMERICAN : (*a.* British, ***b.* Swiss**, *c.* Colombian, *d.* Belgian) :: PARMESAN : CAMEMBERT

(b) American, Swiss, Parmesan, and Camembert are all types of cheese.
General Information—Class

26. (*a.* hawk, *b.* dove, ***c.* eagle**, *d.* robin) : U.S.A. :: MAPLE LEAF : CANADA

(**c**) The eagle is an emblem of the United States, while the maple leaf is an emblem of Canada.
Social Science—Description

27. CIRCE : SWINE :: MEDUSA : (*a.* jackal, ***b.*** **stone**, *c.* gold, *d.* snake)

    (**b**) Circe transformed men into swine; Medusa transformed them into stone.
    Humanities—Description

28. (*a.* bones, ***b.*** **skin**, *c.* muscles, *d.* blood) : DERMATOLOGY :: IMMUNITY : IMMUNOLOGY

    (**b**) Dermatology is the branch of medicine dealing with the skin; immunology is the branch of medicine dealing with immunity.
    Natural Science—Description

29. TWIDDLE : TWADDLE :: (*a.* jambo, *b.* jimbo, ***c.*** **mumbo**, *d.* rumbo) : JUMBO

    (**c**) Twiddle twaddle and mumbo jumbo both refer to gibberish.
    Vocabulary—Completion

30. OLFACTORY : (*a.* mouth, *b.* ears, ***c.*** **nose**, *d.* fingers) :: VISUAL : EYES

    (**c**) The olfactory sense (smell) receives sensation through the nose; the visual sense (seeing) receives sensation through the eyes.
    Natural Science—Description

31. ECUADOR : SOUTH AMERICA :: EGYPT : (***a.*** **Africa**, *b.* Asia, *c.* Europe, *d.* India)

    (**a**) Ecuador is a country in South America. Egypt is a country in Africa.
    General Information—Description

32. RED CROSS : RELIEF FROM DISASTERS :: BLUE CROSS : (***a.*** **health insurance**, *b.* relief from tyranny, *c.* relief from mental illness, *d.* medical supplies)

    (**a**) The Red Cross organization provides relief from disasters; the Blue Cross organization provides health insurance.
    General Information—Description

33. EEG : BRAIN :: EKG : (***a.*** **heart**, *b.* brain, *c.* gall bladder, *d.* vagus nerve)

    (**a**) An EEG is a tracing of the changes in electric potential produced by the brain, while an EKG is a tracing of the changes in electric potential produced by the heart.
    Natural Science—Description

34. ABRAHAM : SARAH :: PUNCH : (***a.*** **Judy**, *b.* Paula, *c.* Pat, *d.* Joanie)

    (**a**) In the Bible, Abraham was the husband of Sarah. In a Punch-and-Judy puppet show, Punch is the husband of Judy.
    Humanities—Class

35. MPH : RPM :: MILES : (*a.* rotations, ***b.* revolutions**, *c.* minutes, *d.* hours)

(**b**) The *m* in *mph* is an abbreviation for *miles*. The *r* in *rpm* is an abbreviation for *revolutions*.
Natural Science—Description

36. ORDAIN : MINISTER :: (*a.* approve, *b.* obey, *c.* admit, ***d.* certify**) : TEACHER

(**d**) A minister is ordained before beginning to preach. A teacher is certified before beginning to teach.
General Information—Description

37. WATER : HYDROGEN :: TABLE SALT : (***a.* chlorine**, *b.* potassium, *c.* nitrogen, *d.* oxygen)

(**a**) Water is a chemical compound containing hydrogen, while table salt is a chemical compound containing chlorine.
Natural Science—Part/Whole

38. ELBOW : ARM :: (*a.* shin, *b.* thigh, *c.* calf, ***d.* knee**) : LEG

(**d**) The elbow is the joint separating the upper and lower arms. The knee is the joint separating the upper and lower legs.
Natural Science—Part/Whole

39. NUMBER : GENDER :: SINGULAR : (*a.* plural, ***b.* feminine**, *c.* nominative, *d.* present)

(**b**) In grammar, singular is an example of number, and feminine is an example of gender.
Humanities—Class

40. PATRICIDE : FATHER :: GENOCIDE : (*a.* enemy, ***b.* group**, *c.* mother, *d.* brother)

(**b**) Patricide is the murder of a father; genocide is the murder of a group.
Vocabulary—Description

41. INCA : (*a.* Mexico, *b.* Panama, *c.* Honduras, ***d.* Peru**) :: AZTEC : MEXICO

(**d**) The Inca Indians resided in Peru; the Aztecs resided in Mexico.
Social Science—Description

42. ODIOUS : (*a.* burdensome, *b.* easy, ***c.* pleasing**, *d.* disgusting) :: HONORABLE : DISGRACEFUL

(**c**) *Odious* and *pleasing* are antonyms, as are *honorable* and *disgraceful*.
Vocabulary—Similarity/Contrast

43. SITTING BULL : CUSTER :: (*a.* Eddington, *b.* Howe, *c.* Sheridan, ***d.* Wellington**) : NAPOLEON BONAPARTE

(**d**) Sitting Bull defeated General Custer. Wellington defeated Napoleon Bonaparte.
Humanities—Description

44. LOG 10 : 1 :: LOG 100 : (***a.* 2**, *b.* 5, *c.* 10, *d.* 90)

    (a) Log 10 is equal to 1. Log 100 is equal to 2.
    Mathematics—Equality/Negation

45. HOMING PIGEON : CARRIER PIGEON :: STOOL PIGEON : (*a.* fool, ***b.* informer**, *c.* loser, *d.* passenger pigeon)

    (b) A homing pigeon is a carrier pigeon. A stool pigeon is an informer.
    Vocabulary—Similarity/Contrast

46. STOP : POTS :: NOON : (*a.* morning, ***b.* noon**, *c.* night, *d.* never)

    (b) *Stop* spelled backwards is *pots. Noon* spelled backwards is *noon.*
    Nonsemantic

47. EBENEEZER SCROOGE : MISERLY :: SIMON LEGREE : (*a.* humane, *b.* generous, *c.* stingy, ***d.* cruel**)

    (d) The literary character Ebeneezer Scrooge was miserly, while the character Simon Legree was cruel.
    Humanities—Description

48. PALEONTOLOGIST : (*a.* vertebrates, *b.* rocks, *c.* earthquakes, ***d.* fossils**) :: ZOOLOGIST : ANIMALS

    (d) A paleontologist studies fossils; a zoologist studies animals.
    Natural Science—Description

49. (*a.* emperor, *b.* pharaoh, *c.* shah, ***d.* diet**) : CONGRESS :: PRIME MINISTER : PRESIDENT

    (d) A diet and a congress are both legislative bodies of government. A prime minister and a president are both executive officers of government.
    Social Science—Class

50. B_1 : THIAMINE :: (***a.* B_2**, *b.* B_6, *c.* C, *d.* D) : RIBOFLAVIN

    (a) Thiamine is vitamin B_1. Riboflavin is vitamin B_2.
    Natural Science—Similarity/Contrast

51. GUERNSEY : (*a.* York, ***b.* Jersey**, *c.* British, *d.* French) :: CHESHIRE : SIAMESE

    (b) Guernsey and Jersey are both types of cow. Cheshire and Siamese are both types of cat.
    General Information—Class

52. TOURNEY : TOURNAMENT :: TEMPORARY : (*a.* permanent, *b.* sudden, ***c.* transitory**, *d.* temptation)

    (c) *Tourney* and *tournament* are synonyms, as are *temporary* and *transitory.*
    Vocabulary—Similarity/Contrast

53. STOMACH : DIGESTION :: ANATOMY : (*a.* cartography, *b.* biology, ***c.* physiology**, *d.* proctology)

(c) Anatomy is the study of body structures, such as the stomach. Physiology is the study of body functions, such as digestion.
Natural Science—Description

54. PRE : PRIOR :: PRETER : (***a.* beyond**, *b.* as if, *c.* therefore, *d.* only)

(a) *Pre-* is a prefix meaning *prior*. *Preter-* is a prefix meaning *beyond.*
Vocabulary—Similarity/Contrast

55. LINCOLN : KENNEDY :: (*a.* Tyler, *b.* Johnson, *c.* Eisenhower, ***d.* Garfield**) : McKINLEY

(d) Presidents Lincoln, Garfield, McKinley, and Kennedy were all assassinated while in office.
Humanities—Class

56. FORTE : LOUD :: (*a.* largo, *b.* rubato, *c.* violin, ***d.* piano**) : SOFT

(d) In musical contexts, *forte* means loud and *piano* means soft.
Humanities—Similarity/Contrast

57. LATIN ALPHABET : FRENCH :: CYRILLIC ALPHABET : (***a.* Russian**, *b.* Sanskrit, *c.* Greek, *d.* Chinese)

(a) The Latin alphabet is used for writing French, while the Cyrillic alphabet is used for writing Russian.
Humanities—Description

58. CENTRIFUGAL : (***a.* centripetal**, *b.* centrigonal, *c.* centrobaric, *d.* centrosomal) :: AWAY FROM : TOWARD

(a) *Centrifugal* means *away from center*, while *centripetal* means *toward center.*
Natural Science—Description

59. ICHTHYOLOGY : (*a.* insects, *b.* reptiles, *c.* arthropods, ***d.* fish**) :: ORNITHOLOGY : BIRDS

(d) Ichthyology is the study of fish; ornithology is the study of birds.
Natural Science—Description

60. (*a.* wool, *b.* synthetic, *c.* dinosaur, ***d.* gasoline**) : PETROL :: U.S.A. : BRITAIN

(d) The fuel called gasoline in the United States is called petrol in Britain.
General Information—Similarity/Contrast

61. (***a.* overindulge**, *b.* persevere, *c.* quit, *d.* deprive) : SURFEIT :: CLOY : SATIATE

(a) *Overindulge, surfeit, cloy,* and *satiate* are synonyms.
Vocabulary—Similarity/Contrast

62. (*a.* Hesse, *b.* Joyce, ***c.* Mann**, *d.* Proust) : DEATH IN VENICE :: SHAKESPEARE : MERCHANT OF VENICE

(c) Mann is the author of *Death in Venice*; Shakespeare is the author of *The Merchant of Venice.*
Humanities—Description

63. ROOK : CASTLE :: HORSE : (*a.* **knight**, *b.* track, *c.* chess, *d.* winner)

(a) In the game of chess, *rook* and *castle* refer to the same piece, as do *knight* and *horse.*
General Information—Similarity/Contrast

64. (*a.* Greuze, *b.* Utrillo, ***c.* Seurat**, *d.* Manet) : POINTILLISM :: DAVID : NEOCLASSICISM

(c) Seurat was a leading member in the French school of pointillism. David was a leading member in the French school of neoclassicism.
Humanities—Description

65. BILL : BEAK :: (***a.* finger**, *b.* leg, *c.* hand, *d.* kneecap) : DIGIT

(a) A bill is a beak. A finger is a digit.
Vocabulary—Similarity/Contrast

66. GEWGAW : (***a.* trinket**, *b.* bottle, *c.* rhinestone, *d.* candy) :: TACITURN : QUIET

(a) A gewgaw is a trinket. A taciturn person is quiet.
Vocabulary—Similarity/Contrast

67. (*a.* fortunate, ***b.* entreat**, *c.* unfortunate, *d.* order) : IMPORTUNE :: IMPREGNABLE : UNSHAKABLE

(b) *Entreat* and *importune* are synonyms, as are *impregnable* and *unshakable.*
Vocabulary—Similarity/Contrast

68. CULPABLE : GUILTY :: (*a.* preculpable, ***b.* exculpable**, *c.* multiculpable, *d.* malculpable) : ACQUITTED

(b) Someone who is culpable is guilty; someone who is exculpable is acquitted.
Vocabulary—Similarity/Contrast

69. FOX : (*a.* bovine, ***b.* vulpine**, *c.* porcine, *d.* equine) :: CAT : FELINE

(b) *Vulpine* means foxlike, while *feline* means catlike.
Vocabulary—Description

70. AGONY : ECSTASY :: SOUND : (*a.* Light, *b.* Trumpet, *c.* Signpost, ***d.* Fury**)

(d) *The Agony and the Ecstasy* and *The Sound and the Fury* are both book titles.
Humanities—Completion

71. LANG SYNE : (***a.* bygone days**, *b.* future days, *c.* here and now, *d.* nonexistent times) :: IMMEDIATELY : AT ONCE

(a) *Lang syne* means *bygone days*; *immediately* means *at once*.
Vocabulary—Similarity/Contrast

72. (*a*. India, *b*. Brazil, ***c*. Mexico**, *d*. Spain) : GUANAJUATO :: CANADA : MANITOBA

(c) Guanajuato is a political subdivision of Mexico. Manitoba is a political subdivision of Canada.
Social Science—Part/Whole

73. VERDI : AIDA :: (*a*. Bach, *b*. Mozart, ***c*. Beethoven**, *d*. Brahms) : FIDELIO

(c) Verdi composed the opera *Aida*. Beethoven composed the opera *Fidelio*.
Humanities—Description

74. TORTUOUS : (***a*. winding**, *b*. barbaric, *c*. long, *d*. incomprehensible) :: HAPPY : FELICITOUS

(a) *Tortuous* and *winding* are synonyms, as are *happy* and *felicitous*.
Vocabulary—Similarity/Contrast

75. (***a*. present**, *b*. past, *c*. recent, *d*. never) : CURRENT :: ERSTWHILE : FORMER

(a) A present event is current; a former event is erstwhile.
Vocabulary—Similarity/Contrast

76. DAVID : GOLIATH :: HOLMES : (***a*. Moriarty**, *b*. Watson, *c*. Doyle, *d*. Devlin)

(a) Goliath was the mortal enemy of David; Moriarty was the mortal enemy of Holmes.
Humanities—Description

77. LUGUBRIOUS : (*a*. shallow, ***b*. cheerful**, *c*. expensive, *d*. fatuous) :: PONDEROUS : LIGHT

(b) *Lugubrious* and *cheerful* are antonyms, as are *ponderous* and *light*.
Vocabulary—Similarity/Contrast

78. EXPLETIVE : (*a*. interrogative, *b*. factotum, ***c*. oath**, *d*. lie) :: EXPOSÉ : DISCLOSURE

(c) An expletive is an oath. An exposé is a disclosure.
Vocabulary—Similarity/Contrast

79. 11 : BINARY :: (*a*. 2, ***b*. 3**, *c*. 4, *d*. 10) : DECIMAL

(b) The number 11 in binary notation is equal to the number 3 in decimal notation.
Mathematics—Equality/Negation

80. CHALICE : GOBLET :: LEAF : (*a*. plant, *b*. tree, ***c*. sheet**, *d*. gold)

(c) A chalice is a goblet. A leaf is a sheet (of paper).
Vocabulary—Similarity/Contrast

81. (*a.* nut, *b.* fruit, ***c.* root**, *d.* berry) : TURNIP :: STEM : CELERY

    (c) The stem of celery is edible, as is the root of turnip.
    General Information—Class

82. ABRAM : ABRAHAM :: (*a.* Sarabelle, ***b.* Sarai**, *c.* Salome, *d.* Sharon) : SARAH

    (b) After the Covenant with God, Abram's name was changed to Abraham, and Sarai's name was changed to Sarah.
    Humanities—Description

83. VELÁSQUEZ : MAIDS OF HONOR :: (***a.* Botticelli**, *b.* Bellini, *c.* Bosch, *d.* Uccello) : THE BIRTH OF VENUS

    (a) *Maids of Honor* is a famous painting by Velasque; *The Birth of Venus* is a famous painting by Botticelli.
    Humanities—Description

84. CIVIL : (*a.* misdemeanor, *b.* larceny, ***c.* tort**, *d.* perjury) :: CRIMINAL : FELONY

    (c) A tort is a civil offense, while a felony is a criminal offense.
    Social Science—Class

85. GREGORIAN : NOVEMBER :: FRENCH REVOLUTIONARY : (*a.* Novembre, *b.* February, *c.* Julian, ***d.* Thermidor**)

    (d) Thermidor in the French Revolutionary calendar corresponded to November in the conventional Gregorian calendar.
    Humanities—Similarity/Contrast

86. GOLDEN RULE : LUKE :: CATEGORICAL IMPERATIVE : (*a.* Hegel, ***b.* Kant**, *c.* Ardrey, *d.* Lorenz)

    (b) The golden rule—"Do unto others as you would have them do unto you"—is found in the Gospel of Luke. The categorical imperative—"One's behavior should be governed by the same principles that one would have govern other people's behavior"—is found in the philosophy of Kant.
    Humanities—Description

87. EQUIVOCATION : (*a.* perversity, *b.* exultation, ***c.* veracity**, *d.* perjury) :: UNCERTAINTY : CERTAINTY

    (c) *Equivocation* is the opposite of *veracity. Uncertainty* is the opposite of *certainty.*
    Vocabulary—Similarity/Contrast

88. TIMBREL : (*a.* cymbals, *b.* zither, *c.* flute, ***d.* tambourine**) :: LUTE : GUITAR

    (d) A timbrel is an early form of tambourine; a lute is an early form of guitar.
    Humanities—Class

89. (*a.* Apollo, *b.* Phaeton, ***c.* Furies**, *d.* Sirens) : EUMENIDES :: PLUTO : HADES

(c) The Furies and the Eumenides were one and the same; similarly, Pluto and Hades were one and the same.
Humanities—Similarity/Contrast

90. JOSEPH K. : TRIAL :: GREGOR SAMSA : (*a.* Hunger Artist, *b.* Death in Venice, *c.* The Flies, ***d.* Metamorphosis**)

(d) Joseph K. is the main character in Kafka's *The Trial*. Gregor Samsa is the main character in Kafka's *The Metamorphosis.*
Humanities—Description

91. $\sqrt{2}$: $\sqrt{18}$: : 1 : (*a.* 2, *b.* 3, *c.* 6, *d.* 9)

(b) The ratio of $\sqrt{2}$ to $\sqrt{18}$ is equal to the ratio of 1 to 3.
Mathematics—Equality/Negation

92. TRANSUBSTANTIATION : ACTUAL :: (*a.* insubstantiation, *b.* absubstantiation, ***c.* consubstantiation**, *d.* desubstantiation) : SYMBOLIC

(c) According to the doctrine of transubstantiation, the actual substances of the bread and of the wine in the Eucharist are changed into the body and blood of Christ; according to the doctrine of consubstantiation, the bread and wine are merely symbolic.
Humanities—Description

93. ABACUS : COMPUTER :: DAGUERROTYPE : (*a.* stereo, ***b.* photograph**, *c.* tape recorder, *d.* telephone)

(b) The abacus is a primitive computer; the daguerrotype is a primitive photograph.
Humanities—Description

94. DECLARATION OF INDEPENDENCE : PHILADELPHIA :: MAGNA CARTA : (*a.* Gloucester, ***b.* Runnymede**, *c.* Canterbury, *d.* Norwalk)

(b) The Declaration of Independence was signed in Philadelphia; the Magna Carta was signed at Runnymede.
Humanities—Description

95. MINTON : ROYAL DOULTON :: MIKASA : (*a.* Sony, *b.* Rosenthal, *c.* Lenox, ***d.* Noritake**)

(d) Minton and Royal Doulton are both English makers of fine china, while Mikasa and Noritake are both Japanese makers of fine china.
General Information—Class

96. SHYLOCK : SCROOGE :: DON JUAN : (*a.* Antonio, *b.* Don Giovanni, ***c.* Lothario**, *d.* Don Quixote)

(c) In literature, Shylock and Scrooge are both miserly characters, while Don Juan and Lothario are both "great lovers."
Humanities—Class

97. SKINNER : EMPIRICIST :: (*a.* Watson, *b.* Aristotle, ***c.* Chomsky**, *d.* Locke) : RATIONALIST

(c) Skinner is a philosophical empiricist, while Chomsky is a philosophical rationalist.
Social Science—Description

98. MOHAWK : IROQUOIS :: (*a.* Apache, ***b.* Zuni**, *c.* Seminole, *d.* Creek) : PUEBLO

(b) The Mohawks were one of the Iroquois Indian tribes; the Zuni were one of the Pueblo Indian tribes.
Social Science—Class

99. (*a.* half-life, *b.* radioactivity, *c.* atomic mass, ***d.* atomic number**) : ISOTOPE :: ATOMIC WEIGHT : ISOBAR

(d) Chemical isotopes have the same atomic number; chemical isobars have the same atomic weight.
Natural Science—Description

100. SARACEN : (*a.* Hindu, ***b.* Muslim**, *c.* Shintoist, *d.* Taoist) :: EPISCOPALIAN : ANGLICAN

(b) A Saracen is a Muslim. An Episcopalian is an Anglican.
Humanities—Similarity/Contrast

Item Classification Chart

Practice Test 7	RELATIONSHIP						
CONTENT	Similarity/ Contrast	Description	Class	Completion	Part/ Whole	Equality/ Negation	Nonsemantic
Vocabulary	42, 45, 52, 54, 61, 65, 66, 67, 68, 71, 74, 75, 77 78, 80, 87	40, 69		29			
General Information	6, 17, 20, 60, 63	2, 8, 13, 15, 18, 22, 23, 31, 32, 36	25, 51, 81, 95	24			
Humanities	56, 85, 89, 100	3, 11, 14, 27, 43, 47, 57, 62, 64, 73, 76, 82, 83, 86, 90, 92, 93, 94	34, 39, 55, 88, 96	16, 70			
Social Science		9, 26, 41, 97	12, 49, 84, 98		72		
Natural Science	50	1, 5, 7, 19, 28, 30, 33, 35, 48, 53, 58, 59, 99			37, 38		
Mathematics					4	44, 79, 91	
Nonsemantic							10, 21, 46

Miller Analogies Test PRACTICE TEST 8

Directions: In each of the following questions, you will find three initial terms and, in parentheses, four answer options designated *a*, *b*, *c*, and *d*. You are to select from the four answer options the one that best completes the analogy with the three initial terms. To record your answers, use the answer sheet at the back of the book.

Time: *50 minutes*

1. STOCKHOLM : (*a.* Switzerland, *b.* Austria, *c.* Finland, *d.* Sweden) :: PARIS : FRANCE
2. ESCARGOTS : FRENCH :: SUKIYAKI : (*a.* Japanese, *b.* German, *c.* Hungarian, *d.* Mexican)
3. COBBLER : SHOES :: TAILOR : (*a.* needles, *b.* clothes, *c.* threads, *d.* thimbles)
4. (*a.* black, *b.* yellow, *c.* red, *d.* blue) : SULFUR :: WHITE : GYPSUM
5. TRANSITIVE : HIT :: (*a.* expletive, *b.* intransitive, *c.* nominative, *d.* subjunctive) : IS
6. COMPOSITE : 8 :: PRIME : (*a.* 4, *b.* 6, *c.* 7, *d.* 9)
7. FRESCO : PLASTER :: TAPESTRY : (*a.* stone, *b.* metal, *c.* cloth, *d.* wood)
8. VEGETARIAN : MEAT :: TEETOTALER : (*a.* fruit, *b.* alcoholic beverages, *c.* cooked food, *d.* tobacco)
9. TRAFALGAR SQUARE : (*a.* London, *b.* Florence, *c.* Moscow, *d.* Paris) :: TIMES SQUARE : NEW YORK
10. (*a.* appliance, *b.* food, *c.* explosive, *d.* automobile) : TNT :: COUNTRY : U.S.A.
11. YELLOW : COWARDLY :: (*a.* blue, *b.* black, *c.* red, *d.* green) : INEXPERIENCED
12. 2 : QUART :: (*a.* 1, *b.* 4, *c.* 8, *d.* 16) : GALLON
13. RED FLAG : REVOLUTION :: WHITE FLAG : (*a.* victory, *b.* surrender, *c.* established order, *d.* purity)
14. ZEBRA : STRIPES :: LEOPARD : (*a.* spots, *b.* stripes, *c.* diagonals, *d.* zigzags)
15. (*a.* tyrant, *b.* wealthy merchant, *c.* explorer, *d.* pirate) : BUCCANEER :: SETTLER : PIONEER

16. CENTIGRADE : 100 :: FAHRENHEIT : (*a.* 0, *b.* 32, *c.* 100, *d.* 212)

17. (*a.* 1, *b.* 5, *c.* 20, *d.* 25) : SILVER :: 50 : GOLD

18. BEEF : STEER :: MUTTON : (*a.* ox, *b.* sheep, *c.* deer, *d.* goat)

19. ATOM : (*a.* molecule, *b.* electron, *c.* nucleus, *d.* gamma ray) :: TREE : FOREST

20. IGNORANCE : (*a.* intelligence, *b.* knowledge, *c.* foresight, *d.* attention) :: STUPIDITY : INTELLIGENCE

21. NONAGENARIAN : 90 :: OCTOGENARIAN : (*a.* 60, *b.* 70, *c.* 80, *d.* 100)

22. LISBON : (*a.* Spain, *b.* Portugal, *c.* Hungary, *d.* Denmark) :: THE HAGUE : NETHERLANDS

23. WAMPUM : (*a.* Dutchman, *b.* Portuguese, *c.* Pakistani, *d.* American Indian) :: DOUBLOON : SPANIARD

24. GREEK ALPHABET : GREEK :: LATIN ALPHABET : (*a.* Russian, *b.* Cyrillic, *c.* Sanskrit, *d.* English)

25. (*a.* 90, *b.* 180, *c.* 270, *d.* 360) : TRIANGLE :: 360 : SQUARE

26. COLUMBIA : (*a.* South America, *b.* North America, *c.* United States, *d.* Brazil) :: BRITANNIA : BRITAIN

27. FINALE : MUSICAL COMPOSITION :: (*a.* check, *b.* checkmate, *c.* rook, *d.* jeopardy) : CHESS

28. JEHOVAH : JUDAISM :: ALLAH : (*a* Islam, *b.* Judaism, *c.* Taoism, *d.* Confucianism)

29. (*a.* nominative, *b.* dative, *c.* accusative, *d.* ablative) : OBJECTIVE :: SHE : HIM

30. RECTANGLE : OCTAGON :: (*a.* triangle, *b.* square, *c.* pentagon, *d.* rhombus) : HEXAGON

31. (*a.* prize, *b.* damn, *c.* reflect, *d.* complete) : PRAISE :: COMPLEMENT : COMPLIMENT

32. SUB : BUS :: TAR : (*a.* car, *b.* road, *c.* vehicle, *d.* rat)

33. MANDATORY : (*a.* laudatory, *b.* damning, *c.* optional, *d.* compulsory) :: DEFINITE : UNCERTAIN

34. ONE : LAND :: TWO : (*a.* air, *b.* sea, *c.* ground, *d.* island)

35. (*a.* eat, *b.* drink, *c.* sever, *d.* mend) : CHALICE :: DIG : SHOVEL

36. CONSONANT : (*a.* syncopated, *b.* rhythmic, *c.* euphemistic, *d.* euphonious) :: DISSONANT : DISCORDANT

37. (*a.* Montague, *b.* Scali, *c.* Dunlop, *d.* Mineo) : ROMEO :: CAPULET : JULIET

38. EMANCIPATE : (*a.* emaciate, *b.* free, *c.* enslave, *d.* deliver) :: EMPTY : FULL

39. PALMISTRY : PALM :: PHRENOLOGY : (*a.* handwriting, *b.* EEG, *c.* eyes, *d.* skull)

40. (*a.* Columbia Gem, *b.* Union Jack, *c.* Royal Ensign, *d.* Fleur-de-Lis) : GREAT BRITAIN :: STARS AND STRIPES : U.S.A.

41. COMMON LOG : 10 :: NATURAL LOG : (*a.* π, *b.* e, *c.* i, *d.* 1)

42. MAE WEST : LIFE JACKET :: MICKEY FINN : (*a.* blackjack, *b.* Molotov cocktail, *c.* drugged liquor, *d.* time bomb)

43. EARTH : AIR :: (*a.* bile, *b.* carbon, *c.* phlogiston, *d.* fire) : WATER

44. CAMUS : STRANGER :: (*a.* Sartre, *b.* Camus, *c.* Mauriac, *d.* Ionesco) : PLAGUE

45. DOG : PIE :: HOT : (*a.* cold, *b.* cat, *c.* pizza, *d.* cake)

46. PIETÀ : MICHELANGELO :: THE KISS : (*a.* Rodin, *b.* Pisano, *c.* Ghiberti, *d.* da Vinci)

47. (*a.* Congress of Vienna, *b.* League of Nations, *c.* Warsaw Pact, *d.* NATO) : UNITED NATIONS :: GASLIGHT : ELECTRIC LIGHT

48. CARAT : (*a.* size, *b.* weight, *c.* brilliance, *d.* value) :: ACRE : AREA

49. $a + b : b + a :: a(b+a)b$: (*a.* $2a^2b^2$, *b.* $(a + b)^2$, *c.* $a^2b + ab^2$, *d.* $a^2b^2 + ab$)

50. FRANCIS CRICK : STRUCTURE OF DNA MOLECULE :: MARIE CURIE : (*a.* nobelium, *b.* uranium, *c.* radium, *d.* plutonium)

51. ANALOG : SLIDE RULE :: DIGITAL : (*a.* odometer, *b.* ruler, *c.* compass, *d.* protractor)

52. CHARLOTTE'S : PILGRIM'S :: WEB : (*a.* Follies, *b.* Progress, *c.* Pretense, *d.* Journey)

53. VOID : VACUUM :: FULL : (*a.* replete, *b.* deplete, *c.* compact, *d.* empty)

54. HIGH : DIE :: (*a.* gregarious, *b.* reticent, *c.* low, *d.* buy) : SHY

55. (*a.* retina, *b.* iris, *c.* lens, *d.* cone) : ROD :: CHROMATIC : ACHROMATIC

56. BOVINE : (*a*. jackal, *b*. monkey, *c*. ox, *d*. rabbit) :: URSINE : BEAR

57. (*a*. Plato, *b*. Aristotle, *c*. Leibniz, *d*. Locke) : REPUBLIC :: DESCARTES : MEDITATIONS

58. DEER : DEER :: CORPUS : (*a*. corpi, *b*. corpuses, *c*. corpora, *d*. corpes)

59. BUDAPEST : HANOI : : HUNGARY : (*a*. Cambodia, *b*. Laos, *c*. Thailand, *d*. Vietnam)

60. PROMISED LAND : CANAAN :: LAND OF NOD : (*a*. wakefulness, *b*. hell, *c*. sleep, *d*. heaven)

61. MISOGYNIST : WOMEN :: MISOGAMIST : (*a*. men, *b*. people, *c*. marriage, *d*. religion)

62. (*a*. Achilles, *b*. Hector, *c*. Paris, *d*. Troilus) : HELEN :: PLUTO : PROSERPINA

63. BENIGN : BENEVOLENT :: (*a*. beneficent, *b*. nefarious, *c*. tortuous, *d*. voracious) : MALEVOLENT

64. BLOCKHEAD : LUNKHEAD :: MUTTONHEAD : (*a*. fathead, *b*. sleepyhead, *c*. bighead, *d*. egghead)

65. UNCLE TOM : SERVILE :: DUTCH UNCLE : (*a*. hoary, *b*. kind, *c*. stern, *d*. stingy)

66. ALPHA : (*a*. gamma, *b*. zed, *c*. epsilon, *d*. omega) :: A : Z

67. THIAMINE : ASCORBIC ACID :: B_1 : (*a*. B_6, *b*. B_{12}, *c*. C, *d*. E)

68. BRAZIL : (*a*. Portuguese, *b*. Spanish, *c*. French, *d*. Brazilian) :: AUSTRIA : GERMAN

69. CENTURY : EON :: DOZEN : (*a*. one hundred, *b*. gross, *c*. zero, *d*. myriad)

70. SITTING BULL : SIOUX :: GERONIMO : (*a*. Apache, *b*. Pueblo, *c*. Mohawk, *d*. Seminole)

71. AUTOCRACY : AUTARCHY :: MONARCHY : (*a*. democracy, *b*. anarchy, *c*. oligarchy, *d*. kingdom)

72. GOGGLE-EYED : BULGING :: HOOK-NOSED : (*a*. opercular, *b*. oviparous, *c*. ovine, *d*. aquiline)

73. NEPTUNE : DIANA :: SEA : (*a*. hearth, *b*. sun, *c*. moon, *d*. home)

74. EXPEL : DRIVE AWAY :: EXPIATE : (*a*. atone for, *b*. talk at length, *c*. forgive, *d*. speak briefly)

75. LARGO : SLOW :: (*a.* moderato, *b.* allegro, *c.* piano, *d.* fortissimo) : FAST

76. (*a.* with faith, *b.* with truth, *c.* with passion, *d.* with authority) : EX CATHEDRA :: ON THE FACE : EX FACIE

77. FIFE : CLARINET :: TROMBONE : (*a.* lute, *b.* bagpipe, *c.* piano, *d.* violin)

78. PARASITE : LIVING :: (*a.* saprophyte, *b.* neophyte, *c.* pteridophyte, *d.* bryophyte) : DEAD

79. PRINCE : MACHIAVELLI :: PETIT PRINCE : (*a.* Saint-Exupéry, *b.* Mauriac, *c.* Camus, *d.* Lescaut)

80. ITALY : LIRA :: (*a.* Switzerland, *b.* Netherlands, *c.* Portugal, *d.* Sweden) : GUILDER

81. DEMOSTHENES : (*a.* Cicero, *b.* Socrates, *c.* Pericles, *d.* Ovid) :: HOMER : VIRGIL

82. (*a.* mg, *b.* gg, *c.* kg, *d.* cg) : g :: m : mm

83. CIPANGO : JAPAN :: CATHAY : (*a.* China, *b.* Tibet, *c.* Polynesia, *d.* Mongolia)

84. IMPROMPTU : EXTEMPORE :: PROBITY : (*a.* open-mindedness, *b.* dishonesty, *c.* narrow-mindedness, *d.* honesty)

85. FERMI : NUCLEAR PHYSICS :: JANE ADDAMS : (*a.* nursing, *b.* physics, *c.* social work, *d.* drama)

86. (*a.* Inferno, *b.* Decameron, *c.* The Wasteland, *d.* No Exit) : CANTERBURY TALES :: ANTHOLOGY : COLLECTION

87. RICHELIEU : (*a.* Cushing, *b.* Mazarin, *c.* Metternich, *d.* Marat) :: KENNEDY : JOHNSON

88. (*a.* uncertainty, *b.* luck, *c.* sample, *d.* variance) : POPULATION :: STATISTIC : PARAMETER

89. REGAN : GONERIL :: LEAH : (*a.* Jacob, *b.* Rebeccah, *c.* Isaac, *d.* Rachel)

90. TEMPUS : CARPE :: FUGIT : (*a.* cibus, *b.* mater, *c.* diem, *d.* tempum)

91. ERSATZ : (*a.* genuine, *b.* superior, *c.* inferior, *d.* fake) :: FRESH : RANCID

92. EVE : DEED :: MADAM : (*a.* cuckoo, *b.* swoon, *c.* noon, *d.* pool)

93. SLEEPY : SOMNOLENT :: GROGGY : (*a.* asleep, *b.* unsteady, *c.* awake, *d.* dead)

94. AXON : DEPART :: (*a.* neuron, *b.* ganglion, *c.* dendrites, *d.* plasma) : APPROACH

95. BUDGE : TENNIS :: LOUIS : (*a.* hockey, *b.* football, *c.* baseball, *d.* boxing)

96. BLOOD : MELANCHOLY :: CHOLER : (*a.* plasma, *b.* lymph, *c.* phlegm, *d.* saliva)

97. MEXICO : YORK :: CAROLINA : (*a.* Virginia, *b.* Oregon, *c.* Washington, *d.* Dakota)

98. ARGON : NEON :: XENON : (*a.* helium, *b.* oxygen, *c.* mercury, *d.* carbon)

99. HORN : ROLAND :: HARP : (*a.* Gideon, *b.* David, *c.* Moses, *d.* Samuel)

100. GLUTTON : FOOD :: SATYR : (*a.* punishment, *b.* glory, *c.* alcoholic beverages, *d.* sex)

Answer Key for Practice Test 8

1. *d*	11. *d*	21. *c*	31. *d*	41. *b*	51. *a*	61. *c*	71. *d*	81. *a*	91. *a*
2. *a*	12. *c*	22. *b*	32. *d*	42. *c*	52. *b*	62. *c*	72. *d*	82. *c*	92. *c*
3. *b*	13. *b*	23. *d*	33. *c*	43. *d*	53. *a*	63. *b*	73. *c*	83. *a*	93. *b*
4. *b*	14. *a*	24. *d*	34. *b*	44. *b*	54. *d*	64. *a*	74. *a*	84. *d*	94. *c*
5. *b*	15. *d*	25. *b*	35. *b*	45. *c*	55. *d*	65. *c*	75. *b*	85. *c*	95. *d*
6. *c*	16. *d*	26. *c*	36. *d*	46. *a*	56. *c*	66. *d*	76. *d*	86. *b*	96. *c*
7. *c*	17. *d*	27. *b*	37. *a*	47. *b*	57. *a*	67. *c*	77. *b*	87. *b*	97. *d*
8. *b*	18. *b*	28. *a*	38. *c*	48. *b*	58. *c*	68. *a*	78. *a*	88. *c*	98. *a*
9. *a*	19. *a*	29. *a*	39. *d*	49. *c*	59. *d*	69. *d*	79. *a*	89. *d*	99. *b*
10. *c*	20. *b*	30. *a*	40. *b*	50. *c*	60. *c*	70. *a*	80. *b*	90. *c*	100. *d*

Explanation of Answers for Practice Test 8

1. STOCKHOLM : (*a.* Switzerland, *b.* Austria, *c.* Finland, ***d.* Sweden**) :: PARIS : FRANCE

   (**d**) Stockholm is the capital of Sweden. Paris is the capital of France.
   General Information—Description

2. ESCARGOTS : FRENCH :: SUKIYAKI : (***a.* Japanese**, *b.* German, *c.* Hungarian, *d.* Mexican)

   (**a**) Escargots are a French food. Sukiyaki is a Japanese food dish.
   General Information—Description

3. COBBLER : SHOES :: TAILOR : (*a.* needles, ***b.* clothes**, *c.* threads, *d.* thimbles)

   (**b**) A cobbler mends shoes; a tailor mends clothes.
   General Information—Description

4. (*a.* black, ***b.* yellow**, *c.* red, *d.* blue) : SULFUR :: WHITE : GYPSUM

   (**b**) Sulfur is usually yellow; gypsum is usually white.
   Natural Science—Description

5. TRANSITIVE : HIT :: (*a.* expletive, ***b.* intransitive**, *c.* nominative, *d.* subjunctive) : IS

   (**b**) *Hit* is a transitive verb. *Is* is an intransitive verb.
   Humanities—Description

6. COMPOSITE : 8 :: PRIME : (*a.* 4, *b.* 6, ***c.* 7**, *d.* 9)

   (**c**) 8 is a composite number. 7 is a prime number.
   Mathematics—Description

7. FRESCO : PLASTER :: TAPESTRY : (*a.* stone, *b.* metal, ***c.* cloth**, *d.* wood)

   (**c**) A fresco is made of plaster. A tapestry is made of cloth.
   Humanities—Description

8. VEGETARIAN : MEAT :: TEETOTALER : (*a.* fruit, ***b.* alcoholic beverages**, *c.* cooked food, *d.* tobacco)

   (**b**) A vegetarian will not eat meat. A teetotaler will not drink alcoholic beverages.
   General Information—Description

9. TRAFALGAR SQUARE : (***a.* London**, *b.* Florence, *c.* Moscow, *d.* Paris) :: TIMES SQUARE : NEW YORK

   (**a**) Trafalgar Square is in London. Times Square is in New York.
   General Information—Description

10. (*a.* appliance, *b.* food, ***c.* explosive**, *d.* automobile) : TNT :: COUNTRY : U.S.A.

    (**c**) TNT is an explosive. The United States is a country.
    General Information—Class

11. YELLOW : COWARDLY :: (*a.* blue, *b.* black, *c.* red, ***d.* green**) : INEXPERIENCED

    (**d**) A cowardly person is sometimes referred to as yellow. An inexperienced person is sometimes referred to as green.
    General Information—Similarity/Contrast

12. 2 : QUART :: (*a.* 1, *b.* 4, ***c.* 8**, *d.* 16) : GALLON

    (**c**) There are 2 pints in a quart, and 8 pints in a gallon.
    Mathematics—Class

13. RED FLAG : REVOLUTION :: WHITE FLAG : (*a.* victory, ***b.* surrender**, *c.* established order, *d.* purity)

    (**b**) A red flag is often used to signify revolution, while a white flag is often used to signify surrender.
    General Information—Description

14. ZEBRA : STRIPES :: LEOPARD : (***a.* spots**, *b.* stripes, *c.* diagonals, *d.* zigzags)

    (**a**) A zebra has stripes; a leopard, spots.
    General Information—Description

15. (*a.* tyrant, *b.* wealthy merchant, *c.* explorer, ***d.* pirate**) : BUCCANEER :: SETTLER : PIONEER

    (**d**) A buccaneer is a pirate; a pioneer is a settler.
    General Information—Similarity/Contrast

16. CENTIGRADE : 100 :: FAHRENHEIT : (*a.* 0, *b.* 32, *c.* 100, ***d.* 212**)

    (**d**) One hundred degrees centigrade (the boiling point of water) is equal to 212 degrees Fahrenheit.
    Natural Science—Equality/Negation

17. (*a.* 1, *b.* 5, *c.* 20, ***d.* 25**) : SILVER :: 50 : GOLD

    (**d**) A 25th anniversary is often referred to as a silver anniversary, while a 50th anniversary is gold.
    General Information—Description

18. BEEF : STEER :: MUTTON : (*a.* ox, ***b.* sheep**, *c.* deer, *d.* goat)

    (**b**) Beef comes from a steer; mutton comes from a sheep.
    General Information—Description

19. ATOM : (***a.* molecule**, *b.* electron, *c.* nucleus, *d.* gamma ray) :: TREE : FOREST

(a) Atoms combine to form a molecule; trees combine to form a forest.
Natural Science—Part/Whole

20. IGNORANCE : (*a.* intelligence, ***b.* knowledge**, *c.* foresight, *d.* attention) :: STUPIDITY : INTELLIGENCE

(b) Ignorance is the absence of knowledge. Stupidity is the absence of intelligence.
Vocabulary—Similarity/Contast

21. NONAGENARIAN : 90 :: OCTOGENARIAN : (*a.* 60, *b.* 70, ***c.* 80**, *d.* 100)

(c) A nonagenarian has lived to the age of 90; an octogenarian has lived to the age of 80.
Vocabulary—Description

22. LISBON : (*a.* Spain, ***b.* Portugal**, *c.* Hungary, *d.* Denmark) :: THE HAGUE : NETHERLANDS

(b) Lisbon is the capital of Portugal; The Hague is the capital of the Netherlands.
General Information—Description

23. WAMPUM : (*a.* Dutchman, *b.* Portuguese, *c.* Pakistani, ***d.* American Indian**) :: DOUBLOON : SPANIARD

(d) Wampum was used as a coin by certain American Indian tribes; the doubloon was formerly a Spanish coin.
Humanities—Description

24. GREEK ALPHABET : GREEK :: LATIN ALPHABET : (*a.* Russian, *b.* Cyrillic, *c.* Sanskrit, ***d.* English**)

(d) The Greek language uses the Greek alphabet. The English language uses the Latin alphabet.
Humanities—Description

25. (*a.* 90, ***b.* 180**, *c.* 270, *d.* 360) : TRIANGLE :: 360 : SQUARE

(b) A triangle has 180 degrees; a square has 360 degrees.
Mathematics—Description

26. COLUMBIA : (*a.* South America, *b.* North America, ***c.* U.S.A.,** *d.* Brazil) :: BRITANNIA : BRITAIN

(c) Columbia is a poetic name for the United States; Britannia is a poetic name for Britain.
General Information—Similarity/Contrast

27. FINALE : MUSICAL COMPOSITION :: (*a.* check, ***b.* checkmate**, *c.* rook, *d.* jeopardy) : CHESS

(b) A finale ends a musical composition. Checkmate ends a game of chess.
General Information—Description

28. JEHOVAH : JUDAISM :: ALLAH : (***a.* Islam**, *b.* Judaism, *c.* Taoism, *d.* Confucianism)

    (a) The concept of Jehovah in Judaism is analogous to the concept of Allah in Islam.
    Humanities—Description

29. (***a.* nominative**, *b.* dative, *c.* accusative, *d.* ablative) : OBJECTIVE :: SHE : HIM

    (a) The word *she* is in the nominative case; the word *him* is in the objective case.
    General Information—Description

30. RECTANGLE : OCTAGON :: (***a.* triangle**, *b.* square, *c.* pentagon, *d.* rhombus) : HEXAGON

    (a) An octagon has twice as many sides as a rectangle; a hexagon has twice as many sides as a triangle.
    Mathematics—Equality/Negation

31. (*a.* prize, *b.* damn, *c.* reflect, ***d.* complete**) : PRAISE :: COMPLEMENT : COMPLIMENT

    (d) A complement completes something; a compliment praises something.
    Vocabulary—Similarity/Contrast

32. SUB : BUS :: TAR : (*a.* car, *b.* road, *c.* vehicle, ***d.* rat**)

    (d) *Bus* is *sub* spelled backwards; *rat* is *tar* spelled backwards.
    Nonsemantic

33. MANDATORY : (*a.* laudatory, *b.* damning, ***c.* optional**, *d.* compulsory) :: DEFINITE : UNCERTAIN

    (c) *Mandatory* and *optional* are antonyms; *definite* and *uncertain* are antonyms.
    Vocabulary—Similarity/Contrast

34. ONE : LAND :: TWO : (*a.* air, ***b.* sea**, *c.* ground, *d.* island)

    (b) Paul Revere was to be informed of the means by which British troops were coming through a system of shining lanterns. One lantern meant the British were coming by land; two meant they were coming by sea.
    Humanities—Description

35. (*a.* eat, ***b.* drink**, *c.* sever, *d.* mend) : CHALICE :: DIG : SHOVEL

    (b) One uses a chalice to drink from, and a shovel to dig with.
    Vocabulary—Description

36. CONSONANT : (*a.* syncopated, *b.* rhythmic, *c.* euphemistic, ***d.* euphonious**) :: DISSONANT : DISCORDANT

    (d) Consonant sounds are euphonious; dissonant sounds are discordant.
    Vocabulary—Similarity/Contrast

37. (***a.* Montague**, *b.* Scali, *c.* Dunlop, *d.* Mineo) : ROMEO :: CAPULET : JULIET

    (a) In Shakespeare's play, Montague is the surname of Romeo, Capulet the surname of Juliet.
    Humanities—Description

38. EMANCIPATE : (*a.* emaciate, *b.* free, ***c.* enslave**, *d.* deliver) :: EMPTY : FULL

    (c) *Emancipate* and *enslave* are antonyms, as are *empty* and *full.*
    Vocabulary—Similarity/Contrast

39. PALMISTRY : PALM :: PHRENOLOGY : (*a.* handwriting, *b.* EEG, *c.* eyes, ***d.* skull**)

    (d) Palmistry makes use of the palm in telling about a person; phrenology makes use of the skull.
    General Information—Description

40. (*a.* Columbia Gem, ***b.* Union Jack**, *c.* Royal Ensign, *d.* Fleur-de-Lis) : GREAT BRITAIN :: STARS AND STRIPES : U.S.A.

    (b) The Union Jack is the flag of Great Britain; the Stars and Stripes is the flag of the United States.
    Social Science—Description

41. COMMON LOG : 10 :: NATURAL LOG : (*a.* π, ***b.* e**, *c.* i, *d.* 1)

    (b) Common logs are to base 10. Natural logs are to base *e*.
    Mathematics—Description

42. MAE WEST : LIFE JACKET :: MICKEY FINN : (*a.* blackjack, *b.* Molotov cocktail, ***c.* drugged liquor**, *d.* time bomb)

    (c) A Mae West is a type of life jacket. A Mickey Finn is a form of drugged liquor.
    General Information—Similarity/Contrast

43. EARTH : AIR :: (*a.* bile, *b.* carbon, *c.* phlogiston, ***d.* fire**) : WATER

    (d) Earth, air, fire, and water were once believed to be the four basic elements from which every other substance is composed.
    Humanities—Class

44. CAMUS : STRANGER :: (*a.* Sartre, ***b.* Camus**, *c.* Mauriac, *d.* Ionesco) : PLAGUE

    (b) Camus is the author of both *The Stranger* and *The Plague.*
    Humanities—Description

45. DOG : PIE :: HOT : (*a.* cold, *b.* cat, ***c.* pizza**, *d.* cake)

    (c) A hotdog and a pizza pie are both forms of food.
    General Information—Completion

46. PIETÀ : MICHELANGELO :: THE KISS : (***a.* Rodin**, *b.* Pisano, *c.* Ghiberti, *d.* da Vinci)

    (a) *The Pietà* is a sculpture by Michelangelo. *The Kiss* is a sculpture by Rodin.
    Humanities—Description

47. (*a.* Congress of Vienna, ***b.* League of Nations**, *c.* Warsaw Pact, *d.* NATO) : UNITED NATIONS :: GASLIGHT : ELECTRIC LIGHT

    (b) The United Nations replaced the League of Nations. The electric light replaced the gaslight.
    General Information—Description

48. CARAT : (*a.* size, ***b.* weight**, *c.* brilliance, *d.* value) :: ACRE : AREA

    (b) A carat is a measure of weight. An acre is a measure of area.
    Natural Science—Description

49. a + b : b + a :: a(b + a)b : (*a.* $2a^2b^2$, *b.* $(a + b)^2$, ***c.*** $\mathbf{a^2b + ab^2}$, *d.* $a^2b^2 + ab$)

    (c) $a + b$ is equal to $b + a$. $a(b + a)b$ is equal to $a^2b + ab^2$.
    Mathematics—Equality/Negation

50. FRANCIS CRICK : STRUCTURE OF DNA MOLECULE :: MARIE CURIE : (*a.* nobelium, *b.* uranium, ***c.* radium**, *d.* plutonium)

    (c) Francis Crick was a codiscoverer of the structure of the DNA molecule. Marie Curie was a codiscoverer of the element radium.
    Natural Science—Description

51. ANALOG : SLIDE RULE :: DIGITAL : (***a.* odometer**, *b.* ruler, *c.* compass, *d.* protractor)

    (a) A slide rule is an analog device. An odometer is a digital device.
    Natural Science—Description

52. CHARLOTTE'S : PILGRIM'S :: WEB : (*a.* Follies, ***b.* Progress**, *c.* Pretense, *d.* Journey)

    (b) *Charlotte's Web* and *Pilgrim's Progress* are both titles of books.
    Humanities—Description

53. VOID : VACUUM :: FULL : (***a.* replete**, *b.* deplete, *c.* compact, *d.* empty)

    (a) *Void* and *vacuum* are synonyms, as are *full* and *replete.*
    Vocabulary—Similarity/Contrast

54. HIGH : DIE :: (*a.* gregarious, *b.* reticent, *c.* low, ***d.* buy**) : SHY

    (d) *High*, *die*, *buy*, and *shy* all rhyme.
    Nonsemantic

55. (*a.* retina, *b.* iris, *c.* lens, ***d.* cone**) : ROD :: CHROMATIC : ACHROMATIC

(**d**) In the visual system, the cones are responsible for chromatic vision, and the rods for achromatic vision.
Natural Science—Description

56. BOVINE : (*a.* jackal, *b.* monkey, ***c.* ox**, *d.* rabbit) :: URSINE : BEAR

(**c**) A bovine creature is oxlike. An ursine creature is bearlike.
General Information—Similarity/Contrast

57. (***a.* Plato**, *b.* Aristotle, *c.* Leibniz, *d.* Locke) : REPUBLIC :: DESCARTES : MEDITATIONS

(**a**) Plato is the author of the *Republic*. Descartes is the author of *Meditations.*
Humanities—Description

58. DEER : DEER :: CORPUS : (*a.* corpi, *b.* corpuses, ***c.* corpora**, *d.* corpes)

(**c**) *Deer* is the plural form of *deer*. *Corpora* is the plural form of *corpus.*
Nonsemantic

59. BUDAPEST : HANOI :: HUNGARY : (*a.* Cambodia, *b.* Laos, *c.* Thailand, ***d.* Vietnam**)

(**d**) Budapest is the capital of Hungary. Hanoi is the capital of Vietnam.
General Information—Description

60. PROMISED LAND : CANAAN :: LAND OF NOD : (*a.* wakefulness, *b.* hell, ***c.* sleep**, *d.* heaven)

(**c**) Canaan was the Promised Land for the Israelites. The Land of Nod is sleep.
Humanities—Similarity/Contrast

61. MISOGYNIST : WOMEN :: MISOGAMIST : (*a.* men, *b.* people, ***c.* marriage**, *d.* religion)

(**c**) A misogynist detests women. A misogamist detests marriage.
Vocabulary—Description

62. (*a.* Achilles, *b.* Hector, ***c.* Paris**, *d.* Troilus) : HELEN :: PLUTO : PROSERPINA

(**c**) Paris abducted Helen. Pluto abducted Proserpina.
Humanities—Description

63. BENIGN : BENEVOLENT :: (*a.* beneficent, ***b.* nefarious**, *c.* tortuous, *d.* voracious) : MALEVOLENT

(**b**) *Benign* and *benevolent* are synonyms, as are *nefarious* and *malevolent.*
Vocabulary—Similarity/Contrast

64. BLOCKHEAD : LUNKHEAD :: MUTTONHEAD : (***a.* fathead**, *b.* sleepyhead, *c.* bighead, *d.* egghead)

(a) A blockhead is a lunkhead is a muttonhead is a fathead.
Vocabulary—Similarity/Contrast

65. UNCLE TOM : SERVILE :: DUTCH UNCLE : (*a.* hoary, *b.* kind, ***c.* stern**, *d.* stingy)

(c) An Uncle Tom is servile. A Dutch uncle is stern.
Vocabulary—Description

66. ALPHA : (*a.* gamma, *b.* zed, *c.* epsilon, ***d.* omega**) :: A : Z

(d) *Alpha* is the first letter of the Greek alphabet, and *omega* is the last. *A* is the first letter of the English alphabet, and *Z* is the last.
Humanities—Similarity/Contrast

67. THIAMINE : ASCORBIC ACID :: B_1 : (*a.* B_6, *b.* B_{12}, ***c.* C**, *d.* E)

(c) Thiamine is vitamin B_1. Ascorbic acid is vitamin C.
Natural Science—Similarity/Contrast

68. BRAZIL : (***a.* Portuguese**, *b.* Spanish, *c.* French, *d.* Brazilian) :: AUSTRIA : GERMAN

(a) Portuguese is the principal language spoken in Brazil. German is the principal language spoken in Austria.
Social Science—Description

69. CENTURY : EON :: DOZEN : (*a.* one hundred, *b.* gross, *c.* zero, ***d.* myriad**)

(d) A century is a specified period of time, and an eon is a long, unspecified period of time. A dozen is a specified amount, and a myriad is a large, unspecified amount.
Vocabulary—Description

70. SITTING BULL : SIOUX :: GERONIMO : (***a.* Apache**, *b.* Pueblo, *c.* Mohawk, *d.* Seminole)

(a) Sitting Bull was a Sioux Indian chief; Geronimo was an Apache Indian chief.
Social Science—Description

71. AUTOCRACY : AUTARCHY :: MONARCHY : (*a.* democracy, *b.* anarchy, *c.* oligarchy, ***d.* kingdom**)

(d) An autocracy is an autarchy. A monarchy is a kingdom.
Social Science—Similarity/Contrast

72. GOGGLE-EYED : BULGING :: HOOK-NOSED : (*a.* opercular, *b.* oviparous, *c.* ovine, ***d.* aquiline**)

(d) Someone who is goggle-eyed has bulging eyes. Someone who is hook-nosed has an aquiline nose.
Vocabulary—Similarity/Contrast

73. NEPTUNE : DIANA :: SEA : (*a.* hearth, *b.* sun, ***c.* moon**, *d.* home)

(c) In Roman mythology, Neptune was the god of the sea and Diana the goddess of the moon.
Humanities—Description

74. EXPEL : DRIVE AWAY :: EXPIATE : (***a.* atone for**, *b.* talk at length, *c.* forgive, *d.* speak briefly)

(a) To expel is to drive away. To expiate is to atone for.
Vocabulary—Similarity/Contrast

75. LARGO : SLOW :: (*a.* moderato, ***b.* allegro**, *c.* piano, *d.* fortissimo) : FAST

(b) In music, largo signifies a slow tempo, allegro a fast tempo.
Humanities—Similarity/Contrast

76. (*a.* with faith, *b.* with truth, *c.* with passion, ***d.* with authority**) : EX CATHEDRA :: ON THE FACE : EX FACIE

(d) *Ex cathedra* means *with authority. Ex facie* means *on the face.*
Vocabulary—Similarity/Contrast

77. FIFE : CLARINET :: TROMBONE : (*a.* lute, ***b.* bagpipe**, *c.* piano, *d.* violin)

(b) A fife, a clarinet, a trombone, and a bagpipe are all wind instruments.
Humanities—Class

78. PARASITE : LIVING :: (***a.* saprophyte**, *b.* neophyte, *c.* pteridophyte, *d.* bryophyte) : DEAD

(a) A parasite lives off a living organism. A saprophyte lives off a dead organism.
Natural Science—Description

79. PRINCE : MACHIAVELLI :: PETIT PRINCE : (***a.* Saint-Exupéry**, *b.* Mauriac, *c.* Camus, *d.* Lescaut)

(a) *The Prince* was written by Machiavelli. *Le Petit Prince* was written by Saint-Exupéry.
Humanities—Description

80. ITALY : LIRA :: (*a.* Switzerland, ***b.* Netherlands**, *c.* Portugal, *d.* Sweden) : GUILDER

(b) The lira is the unit of currency in Italy. The guilder is the unit of currency in the Netherlands.
General Information—Description

81. DEMOSTHENES : (***a.* Cicero**, *b.* Socrates, *c.* Pericles, *d.* Ovid) :: HOMER : VIRGIL

(a) Demosthenes was a Greek orator, and Cicero a Roman orator. Homer was a Greek poet, and Virgil a Roman poet.
Humanities—Class

82. (*a.* mg, *b.* gg, ***c.* kg**, *d.* cg) : g :: m : mm

(c) There are 1000 grams (g) in a kilogram (kg). There are 1000 millimeters (mm) in a meter (m).
Mathematics—Part/Whole

83. CIPANGO : JAPAN :: CATHAY : (***a.* China**, *b.* Tibet, *c.* Polynesia, *d.* Mongolia)

(a) Cipango is a poetic name for Japan. Cathay is a poetic name for China.
Humanities—Similarity/Contrast

84. IMPROMPTU : EXTEMPORE :: PROBITY : (*a.* open-mindedness, *b.* dishonesty, *c.* narrow-mindedness, ***d.* honesty**)

(d) *Impromptu* and *extempore* are synonyms, as are *probity* and *honesty.*
Vocabulary—Similarity/Contrast

85. FERMI : NUCLEAR PHYSICS :: JANE ADDAMS : (*a.* nursing, *b.* physics, ***c.* social work**, *d.* drama)

(c) Fermi is famous for his work in nuclear physics. Jane Addams is famous for her social work.
Humanities—Description

86. (*a.* Inferno, ***b.* Decameron**, *c.* The Wasteland, *d.* No Exit) : CANTERBURY TALES :: ANTHOLOGY : COLLECTION

(b) *The Decameron* and *The Canterbury Tales* are both anthologies (collections) of stories.
Humanities—Class

87. RICHELIEU : (*a.* Cushing, ***b.* Mazarin**, *c.* Metternich, *d.* Marat) :: KENNEDY : JOHNSON

(b) Cardinal Mazarin succeeded Cardinal Richelieu in his French diplomatic role. Johnson succeeded Kennedy as president of the United States.
Social Science—Description

88. (*a.* uncertainty, *b.* luck, ***c.* sample**, *d.* variance) : POPULATION :: STATISTIC : PARAMETER

(c) A statistic is a sample value, while a parameter is a population value.
Mathematics—Description

89. REGAN : GONERIL :: LEAH : (*a.* Jacob, *b.* Rebeccah, *c.* Isaac, ***d.* Rachel**)

(d) Regan and Goneril were sisters (in *King Lear*), as were Leah and Rachel (in the Bible).
Humanities—Class

90. TEMPUS : CARPE :: FUGIT : (*a.* cibus, *b.* mater, ***c.* diem**, *d.* tempum)

(c) *Tempus fugit* and *carpe diem* are both Latinisms used in English. *Tempus fugit* means *time flies*, while *carpe diem* means *seize the opportunity*—literally, *the day.*
Vocabulary—Completion

91. ERSATZ : (***a.* genuine**, *b.* superior, *c.* inferior, *d.* fake) :: FRESH : RANCID

(**a**) *Ersatz* and *genuine* are antonyms, as are *fresh* and *rancid*.
Vocabulary—Similarity/Contrast

92. EVE : DEED :: MADAM : (*a.* cuckoo, *b.* swoon, ***c.* noon**, *d.* pool)

(**c**) *Eve*, *deed*, *madam*, and *noon* are all palindromes—they read the same whether spelled forward or backward.
Nonsemantic

93. SLEEPY : SOMNOLENT :: GROGGY : (*a.* asleep, ***b.* unsteady**, *c.* awake, *d.* dead)

(**b**) A sleepy person is somnolent; a groggy person is unsteady.
Vocabulary—Similarity/Contrast

94. AXON : DEPART :: (*a.* neuron, *b.* ganglion, ***c.* dendrites**, *d.* plasma) : APPROACH

(**c**) Nerve impulses depart from a cell body via the axon; they approach the cell body via the dendrites.
Natural Science—Description

95. BUDGE : TENNIS :: LOUIS : (*a.* hockey, *b.* football, *c.* baseball, ***d.* boxing**)

(**d**) Joe Louis was a famous boxer. Don Budge was a famous tennis player.
General Information—Description

96. BLOOD : MELANCHOLY :: CHOLER : (*a.* plasma, *b.* lymph, ***c.* phlegm**, *d.* saliva)

(**c**) Blood, phlegm, choler, and melancholy were once believed to be the four body humors (fluids).
Humanities—Class

97. MEXICO : YORK :: CAROLINA : (*a.* Virginia, *b.* Oregon, *c.* Washington, ***d.* Dakota**)

(**d**) Both (New) Mexico and (New) York are states. Both (North or South) Carolina and (North or South) Dakota are states.
General Information—Description

98. ARGON : NEON :: XENON : (***a.* helium**, *b.* oxygen, *c.* mercury, *d.* carbon)

(**a**) Argon, neon, xenon, and helium are all inert (noble) gases.
Natural Science—Class

99. HORN : ROLAND :: HARP : (*a.* Gideon, ***b.* David**, *c.* Moses, *d.* Samuel)

(**b**) Roland was famous for his horn, David for his harp.
Humanities—Description

100. GLUTTON : FOOD :: SATYR : (*a.* punishment, *b.* glory, *c.* alcoholic beverages, ***d.* sex**)

(**d**) A glutton overindulges in food, a satyr in sex.
General Information—Description

Item Classification Chart

Practice Test 8	RELATIONSHIP						
CONTENT	**Similarity/ Contrast**	**Description**	**Class**	**Completion**	**Part/ Whole**	**Equality/ Negation**	**Nonsemantic**
Vocabulary	20, 31, 33, 36, 38, 53, 63, 64, 72, 74, 76, 84, 91, 93	21, 35, 61, 65, 69		90			
General Information	11, 15, 26, 42, 56	1, 2, 3, 8, 9, 13, 14, 17, 18, 22, 27, 29, 39, 47, 59, 80, 95, 97, 100	10	45			
Humanities	60, 66, 75, 83	5, 7, 23, 24, 28, 34, 37, 44, 46, 52, 57, 62, 73, 79, 85, 99	43, 77, 81, 86, 89, 96				
Social Science	71	40, 68, 70, 87					
Natural Science	67	4, 48, 50, 51, 55, 78, 94	98		19	16	
Mathematics		6, 25, 41, 88	12		82	30, 49	
Nonsemantic							32, 54, 58, 92

Miller Analogies Test PRACTICE TEST 9

Directions: In each of the following questions, you will find three initial terms and, in parentheses, four answer options designated *a*, *b*, *c*, and *d*. You are to select from the four answer options the one that best completes the analogy with the three initial terms. To record your answers, use the answer sheet at the back of the book.

Time: *50 minutes*

1. POSTMAN : LETTER :: (*a*. surgeon, *b*. orthopedist, *c*. obstetrician, *d*. podiatrist) : BABY

2. CHLOROPHYLL : GREEN :: HEMOGLOBIN : (*a*. red, *b*. black, *c*. green, *d*. blue)

3. HAPPY : (*a*. sad, *b*. gay, *c*. indifferent, *d*. ecstatic) :: BRIGHT : BRILLIANT

4. PENCIL : PEN :: (*a*. wood, *b*. ballpoint, *c*. graphite, *d*. boron) : INK

5. ONE BIRD : HAND :: TWO BIRDS : (*a*. bush, *b*. foot, *c*. nest, *d*. head)

6. SILVER : TARNISH :: IRON : (*a*. oxidation, *b*. rust, *c*. magnet, *d*. tin)

7. BUTTERFLY : CATERPILLAR :: (*a*. amphibian, *b*. frog, *c*. salamander, *d*. larva) : TADPOLE

8. GREEN : (*a*. cowardice, *b*. viciousness, *c*. envy, *d*. delight) :: PURPLE : RAGE

9. JUDAS : JESUS :: (*a*. Augustus, *b*. Brutus, *c*. Lucius, *d*. Antony) : JULIUS CAESAR

10. JOLLY ROGER : (*a*. communists, *b*. fascists, *c*. pirates, *d*. anarchists) :: UNION JACK : UNITED KINGDOM

11. DIALECTIC : HEGEL :: DIALECTICAL MATERIALISM : (*a*. Marx, *b*. Fichte, *c*. Schelling, *d*. Kant)

12. (*a*. screen, *b*. camera, *c*. projector, *d*. frame) : MOVIE FILM :: LINK : CHAIN

13. PROLOGUE : (*a*. decalogue, *b*. epilogue, *c*. preface, *d*. forward) :: APPETIZER : DESSERT

14. HAMMERSTEIN : (*a*. Sondheim, *b*. Rodgers, *c*. Gilbert, *d*. Herman) :: LERNER : LOEWE

15. (*a.* dumb, *b.* stupid, *c.* loquacious, *d.* brilliant) : MUTE :: SMART : INTELLIGENT

16. ARCHIVES : (*a.* munitions, *b.* tombs, *c.* documents, *d.* animals) :: PANTRY : KITCHEN UTENSILS

17. DUNCAN : MACBETH :: MACBETH : (*a.* Lady Macbeth, *b.* Macduff, *c.* Polonius, *d.* Claudius)

18. V : X :: D : (*a.* I, *b.* M, *c.* D, *d.* C)

19. JACK SPRAT'S WIFE : LEAN :: VEGETARIAN : (*a.* meat, *b.* fat, *c.* vegetables, *d.* roots)

20. (*a.* politics, *b.* law, *c.* music, *d.* medicine) : HIPPOCRATES :: HISTORY : HERODOTUS

21. (*a.* Russia, *b.* China, *c.* Japan, *d.* Hungary) : BALALAIKA :: SCOTLAND : BAGPIPES

22. TAILPIPE : EXHAUST :: RADIUM : (*a.* beta rays, *b.* strontium, *c.* cosmic rays, *d.* lead)

23. ARGUS : 100 :: CYCLOPS : (*a.* 1000, *b.* 10, *c.* 5, *d.* 1)

24. CANNON : BIG BERTHA :: (*a.* battleship, *b.* bazooka, *c.* bell, *d.* church steeple) : BIG BEN

25. (*a.* pretty, *b.* pretentious, *c.* proud, *d.* portly) : PEACOCK :: SILLY : GOOSE

26. HYPOCRITICAL : INSINCERE :: HYPERCRITICAL : (*a.* overcritical, *b.* sincere, *c.* oversincere, *d.* critical)

27. (*a.* cross, *b.* aisle, *c.* refectory, *d.* nave) : TRANSEPT :: VERTICAL : HORIZONTAL

28. MNEMONIC : (*a.* nymph, *b.* elf, *c.* anger, *d.* knock) :: PNEUMATIC : GNOME

29. FAITH : JOB :: (*a.* wisdom, *b.* age, *c.* wickedness, *d.* courage) : METHUSELAH

30. MRS. GRUNDY : NARROW-MINDED :: POLLYANNA : (*a.* witty, *b.* dull, *c.* pessimistic, *d.* optimistic)

31. MIDNIGHT SUN : (*a.* Russia, *b.* Norway, *c.* China, *d.* South Pole) :: RISING SUN : JAPAN

32. RED-BLOODED : VIGOROUS :: BLUE-BLOODED : (*a.* cowardly, *b.* sickly, *c.* prudish, *d.* aristocratic)

33. (*a.* battle, *b.* artillery, *c.* ammunition, *d.* armory) : WEAPONS :: CLOSET : CLOTHING

34. CHARACTERISTIC : DEFINING :: USUALLY : (*a.* never, *b.* sometimes, *c.* rarely, *d.* always)

35. OBVIATE : (*a.* make unnecessary, *b.* make necessary, *c.* make obvious, *d.* make obscure) :: EXPUNGE : DELETE

36. BROBDINGNAGIAN : GIGANTIC :: (*a.* Lilliputian, *b.* Houyhnhnm, *c.* Vespasian, *d.* Yahoo) :: TINY

37. RUSSIA : (*a.* tsar, *b.* king, *c.* emperor, *d.* autarch) :: FRANCE : KING

38. MINOTAUR : BULL :: CENTAUR : (*a.* cow, *b.* horse, *c.* pig, *d.* goat)

39. INTEGRAL : (*a.* acceleration, *b.* length, *c.* area, *d.* velocity) :: DERIVATIVE : SLOPE

40. GUSTATORY : (*a.* taste, *b.* touch, *c.* sight, *d.* smell) :: AUDITORY : HEARING

41. OCTOPI : OCTOPUSES :: (*a.* cannona, *b.* cannon, *c.* cannones, *d.* cannonade) : CANNONS

42. CRIME : WAR :: PUNISHMENT : (*a.* Destruction, *b.* Treaty, *c.* Peace, *d.* Retribution)

43. SUPPLY : DEMAND :: RATE : (*a.* distance, *b.* time, *c.* velocity, *d.* price)

44. ICONOCLAST : (*a.* religious images, *b.* autocracy, *c.* democratic ideals, *d.* anarchy) :: NIHILIST : SOCIAL ORDER

45. QUIXOTIC : CERVANTES :: FAUSTIAN : (*a.* Hegel, *b.* Faust, *c.* Schiller, *d.* Goethe)

46. EXPEL : STUDENT :: (*a.* expire, *b.* expunge, *c.* expropriate, *d.* exorcise) : SPIRIT

47. (*a.* Julian, *b.* Augustan, *c.* Caesarian, *d.* Publican) : GREGORIAN :: NEWTONIAN : EINSTEINIAN

48. (*a.* Koch, *b.* Pasteur, *c.* Lister, *d.* Sabin) : RABIES :: SALK : POLIO

49. MINNEAPOLIS : ST. PAUL :: (*a.* Uncle, *b.* Rabbit, *c.* Abelard, *d.* Romulus) : REMUS

50. POSSE : SHERIFF :: SQUIRE : (*a.* queen, *b.* bourgeoisie, *c.* knight, *d.* vassal)

51. UNTOUCHABLE : (*a.* Hindu, *b.* Vishnu, *c.* Brahman, *d.* Krishna) :: FLOOR : CEILING

52. PENTAGON : DECAGON :: RECTANGLE : (*a*. square, *b*. pentagon, *c*. heptagon, *d*. octagon)

53. TOWARD : IN THE DIRECTION OF :: UNTOWARD : (*a*. at the location of, *b*. away from, *c*. unseemly, *d*. unsafe)

54. EXOGAMY : OUTBREEDING :: (*a*. endogamy, *b*. inogamy, *c*. anogamy, *d*. onogamy) : INBREEDING

55. GRAND : (*a*. pauvre, *b*. petit, *c*. standard, *d*. legal) :: INDICT : CONVICT

56. CHROMATIC : PASTEL :: ACHROMATIC : (*a*. oil, *b*. tempera, *c*. chiasma, *d*. chiaroscuro)

57. EQUATOR : LATITUDE :: (*a*. North Pole, *b*. apogee, *c*. Greenwich, *d*. meridian) : LONGITUDE

58. ROMEO : JULIET :: PYRAMUS : (*a*. Chloe, *b*. Thisbe, *c*. Helen, *d*. Daphne)

59. PETROLEUM : GASOLINE :: BAUXITE : (*a*. aluminum, *b*. tin, *c*. lead, *d*. fool's gold)

60. 0 : ADDITION :: (*a*. 0, *b*. 1, *c*. –1, *d*. ∞) : MULTIPLICATION

61. GALAHAD : (*a*. Beatrice, *b*. Round Table, *c*. Holy Grail, *d*. True Cross) :: JASON : GOLDEN FLEECE

62. RED HERRING : (*a*. lie, *b*. peccadillo, *c*. diversion, *d*. secret plot) :: BLUE RIBBON : FIRST PRIZE

63. WATERMARK : EARMARK :: (*a*. crops, *b*. tide, *c*. silver, *d*. paper) : ANIMAL

64. ETHER : STARS :: PHLOGISTON : (*a*. earth, *b*. metal, *c*. fire, *d*. water)

65. PARTY : (*a*. revel, *b*. fight, *c*. meeting, *d*. dance) :: SWINE : BOAR

66. RHODE ISLAND : ALASKA :: MERCURY : (*a*. Earth, *b*. Jupiter, *c*. Saturn, *d*. Uranus)

67. MERETRICIOUS : (*a*. egregious, *b*. excellent, *c*. gaudy, *d*. plain) :: APEX : SUMMIT

68. ANTONY : CLEOPATRA :: (*a*. Lancelot, *b*. Arthur, *c*. Merlin, *d*. Gawain) : GUINEVERE

69. MERITOCRACY : MERIT :: PLUTOCRACY : (*a*. wisdom, *b*. money, *c*. power, *d*. physical prowess)

70. INTREPID : (*a*. cowardly, *b*. bold, *c*. voluble, *d*. taciturn) :: AGILE : CLUMSY

71. (a. Mars, *b.* Saturn, *c.* Jupiter, *d.* Mercury) : HERMES :: VENUS : APHRODITE

72. COMPLEMENTARY ANGLES : 90° :: COMPLEMENTARY COLORS : (*a.* white, *b.* black, *c.* violet, *d.* red)

73. (*a.* Jefferson, b. Adams, *c.* Hamilton, *d.* Madison) : BURR :: LINCOLN : BOOTH

74. PUFFIN : (*a.* bird, *b.* reptile, *c.* mammal, *d.* amphibian) :: STURGEON : FISH

75. BRONZE : (*a.* aluminum, *b.* tin, *c.* gold, *d.* silver) :: BRASS : ZINC

76. G MAJOR : (*a.* B minor, *b.* C minor, *c.* D minor, *d.* E minor) :: C MAJOR : A MINOR

77. (*a.* cow, *b.* jackal, *c.* wolf, *d.* rabbit) : LUPINE :: DOG : CANINE

78. (*a.* one, *b.* few, *c.* ten, *d.* all) : ISOCRACY :: ONE : AUTOCRACY

79. LOG 10 : LOG 100 :: LOG 100 : (*a.* log 1,000, *b.* log 10,000, *c.* log 100,000, *d.* log 1,000,000)

80. HAPPINESS : SHANGRI-LA :: (*a.* wealth, *b.* happiness, *c.* gods, *d.* freedom) : EL DORADO

81. DRACONIAN : (*a.* cowardly, *b.* bold, *c.* cruel, *d.* kindly) :: STENTORIAN : LOUD

82. MANSION : HOUSE :: TOME : (*a.* boat, *b.* book, *c.* desk, *d.* church)

83. NEUTRAL : 7 :: (*a.* alkaline, *b.* acidic, *c* hydrated, *d.* oxidized) : 1

84. PERUSE : SKIM :: REPEL : (*a.* gloss, *b.* bowdlerize, *c.* drive back, *d.* attract)

85. NUCLEOLUS : NUCLEUS :: SET : (*a.* superset, *b.* set, *c.* subset, *d.* disjoint set)

86. HORSEBACK RIDING : EQUITATION :: (*a.* giving birth, *b.* skydiving, *c.* swimming, *d.* dancing) : NATATION

87. WHIGS : TORIES :: JACOBINS : (*a.* Fascists, *b.* Laborites, *c.* Roundheads, *d.* Girondists)

88. PRIME : (*a.* God, *b.* destiny, *c.* factum, *d.* mover) :: FIRST : CAUSE

89. FRANC : FRANCE :: (*a.* lira, *b.* mark, *c.* guilder, *d.* franc) : SWITZERLAND

90. (*a.* Jungfrau, *b.* Blanc, *c.* Matterhorn, *d.* Olympus) : ALPS :: EVEREST : HIMALAYAS

91. MELANCHOLY : (*a.* blue bile, *b.* green bile, *c.* red bile, *d.* black bile) :: CHOLER : YELLOW BILE

92. ORAL : ANAL :: DEPENDENCY : (*a.* lazy, *b.* thermometer, *c.* stinginess, *d.* independent)

93. (*a.* hit, *b.* die, *c.* invest, *d.* sprout) : BURGEON :: ENTREAT : IMPLORE

94. DEARTH : PAUCITY :: SCARCITY : (*a.* plethora, *b.* shortage, *c.* necessity, *d.* commodity)

95. DELFT : (*a.* glass, *b.* pottery, *c.* stoneware, *d.* silver) :: LIMOGES : CHINA

96. IAMB : RETURN :: TROCHEE : (*a.* stable, *b.* arrive, *c.* defend, *d.* eternal)

97. AUTOCHTHONOUS : (*a.* foreign, *b.* native, *c.* self-governing, *d.* dependent) :: LETTER : EPISTLE

98. (*a.* bells, *b.* horn, *c.* magpies, *d.* toads) : TINTINNABULATION :: GEESE : HONK

99. ELF : FLEE :: TON : (*a.* note, *b.* pound, *c.* dwarf, *d.* find)

100. CODA : (*a.* novel, *b.* musical composition, *c.* sculpture, *d.* ceramic jar) :: LANDING : FLIGHT

Answer Key for Practice Test 9

1. *c*	11. *a*	21. *a*	31. *b*	41. *b*	51. *c*	61. *c*	71. *d*	81. *c*	91. *d*
2. *a*	12. *d*	22. *a*	32. *d*	42. *c*	52. *d*	62. *c*	72. *a*	82. *b*	92. *c*
3. *d*	13. *b*	23. *d*	33. *d*	43. *b*	53. *c*	63. *d*	73. *c*	83. *b*	93. *d*
4. *c*	14. *b*	24. *c*	34. *d*	44. *a*	54. *a*	64. *c*	74. *a*	84. *d*	94. *b*
5. *a*	15. *a*	25. *c*	35. *a*	45. *d*	55. *b*	65. *a*	75. *b*	85. *a*	95. *b*
6. *b*	16. *c*	26. *a*	36. *a*	46. *d*	56. *d*	66. *b*	76. *d*	86. *c*	96. *a*
7. *b*	17. *b*	27. *d*	37. *a*	47. *a*	57. *c*	67. *c*	77. *c*	87. *d*	97. *b*
8. *c*	18. *b*	28. *d*	38. *b*	48. *b*	58. *b*	68. *a*	78. *d*	88. *d*	98. *a*
9. *b*	19. *a*	29. *b*	39. *c*	49. *d*	59. *a*	69. *b*	79. *b*	89. *d*	99. *a*
10. *c*	20. *d*	30. *d*	40. *a*	50. *c*	60. *b*	70. a	80. *a*	90. *b*	100. *b*

Explanation of Answers for Practice Test 9

1. POSTMAN : LETTER :: (*a.* surgeon, *b.* orthopedist, ***c.* obstetrician**, *d.* podiatrist) : BABY

   (c) A postman delivers a letter; an obstetrician delivers a baby.
   General Information—Description

2. CHLOROPHYLL : GREEN :: HEMOGLOBIN : (***a.* red**, *b.* black, *c.* green, *d.* blue)

   (a) Chlorophyll is a green substance; hemoglobin is a red substance.
   Natural Science—Description

3. HAPPY : (*a.* sad, *b.* gay, *c.* indifferent, ***d.* ecstatic**) :: BRIGHT : BRILLIANT

   (d) A person who is extremely happy is ecstatic; a person who is extremely bright is brilliant.
   Vocabulary—Description

4. PENCIL : PEN :: (*a.* wood, *b.* ballpoint, ***c.* graphite**, *d.* boron) : INK

   (c) The writing substance in a pencil is usually graphite; the writing substance in a pen is usually ink.
   General Information—Description

5. ONE BIRD : HAND :: TWO BIRDS : (***a.* bush**, *b.* foot, *c.* nest, *d.* head)

   (a) A familiar proverb states, "A bird in the hand is worth two in the bush."
   General Information—Completion

6. SILVER : TARNISH :: IRON : (*a.* oxidation, ***b.* rust**, *c.* magnet, *d.* tin)

   (b) When silver oxidizes, the result is called tarnish; when iron oxidizes, the result is called rust.
   General Information—Description

7. BUTTERFLY : CATERPILLAR :: (*a.* amphibian, ***b.* frog**, *c.* salamander, *d.* larva) : TADPOLE

   (b) A caterpillar is the larval form of a butterfly; a tadpole is the larval form of a frog.
   Natural Science—Description

8. GREEN : (*a.* cowardice, *b.* viciousness, ***c.* envy**, *d.* delight) :: PURPLE : RAGE

   (c) Green and purple are colors commonly used to denote emotional states. A person is said to be green with envy or purple with rage.
   General Information—Completion

9. JUDAS : JESUS :: (*a.* Augustus, ***b.* Brutus**, *c.* Lucius, *d.* Antony) : JULIUS CAESAR

(b) Judas betrayed Jesus; Brutus betrayed Julius Caesar.
Humanities—Description

10. JOLLY ROGER : (*a.* communists, *b.* fascists, ***c.* pirates**, *d.* anarchists) :: UNION JACK : UNITED KINGDOM

(c) The Jolly Roger was the emblem of pirates, while the Union Jack is the emblem of the United Kingdom.
General Information—Description

11. DIALECTIC : HEGEL :: DIALECTICAL MATERIALISM : (***a.* Marx**, *b.* Fichte, *c.* Schelling, *d.* Kant)

(a) Hegel developed the philosophical notion of the dialectic, while Marx developed the philosophical notion of dialectical materialism.
Humanities—Description

12. (*a.* screen, *b.* camera, *c.* projector, ***d.* frame**) : MOVIE FILM :: LINK : CHAIN

(d) A movie film is composed of successive frames, while a chain is composed of successive links.
General Information—Part/Whole

13. PROLOGUE : (*a.* decalogue, ***b.* epilogue**, *c.* preface, *d.* forward) :: APPETIZER : DESSERT

(b) A prologue introduces a book, and an epilogue closes it; an appetizer introduces a meal, and a dessert closes it.
Humanities—Class

14. HAMMERSTEIN : (*a.* Sondheim, ***b.* Rodgers**, *c.* Gilbert, *d.* Herman) :: LERNER : LOEWE

(b) Hammerstein and Rodgers created Broadway musicals, with Hammerstein writing the lyrics and Rodgers composing the music; Lerner and Loewe also created Broadway musicals, with Lerner writing the lyrics and Loewe composing the music.
Humanities—Class

15. (***a.* dumb**, *b.* stupid, *c.* loquacious, *d.* brilliant) : MUTE :: SMART : INTELLIGENT

(a) *Dumb* and *mute* are synonyms, as are *smart* and *intelligent.*
Vocabulary—Similarity/Contrast

16. ARCHIVES : (*a.* munitions, *b.* tombs, ***c.* documents**, *d.* animals) :: PANTRY : KITCHEN UTENSILS

(c) Documents are stored in archives, while kitchen utensils are stored in a pantry.
General Information—Description

17. DUNCAN : MACBETH :: MACBETH : (*a.* Lady Macbeth, ***b.* Macduff**, *c.* Polonius, *d.* Claudius)

(b) In Shakespeare's play *Macbeth*, Macbeth kills Duncan and Macduff kills Macbeth.
Humanities—Description

18. V : X :: D : (*a.* I, ***b.* M**, *c.* D, *d.* C)

(b) The terms of the analogy are Roman numerals; 10 is equal to twice 5, and 1000 is equal to twice 500.
Mathematics—Equality/Negation

19. JACK SPRAT'S WIFE : LEAN :: VEGETARIAN : (***a.* meat**, *b.* fat, *c.* vegetables, *d.* roots)

(a) Jack Sprat's wife would eat no lean, according to the nursery rhyme; a vegetarian will eat no meat.
General Information—Description

20. (*a.* politics, *b.* law, *c.* music, ***d.* medicine**) : HIPPOCRATES :: HISTORY : HERODOTUS

(d) Hippocrates is often referred to as the Father of Medicine, while Herodotus is known as the Father of History.
Humanities—Description

21. (***a.* Russia**, *b.* China, *c.* Japan, *d.* Hungary) : BALALAIKA :: SCOTLAND : BAGPIPES

(a) The balalaika is a Russian musical instrument; the bagpipes are a Scottish musical instrument.
Humanities—Description

22. TAILPIPE : EXHAUST :: RADIUM : (***a.* beta rays**, *b.* strontium, *c.* cosmic rays, *d.* lead)

(a) A tailpipe emits exhaust; radium emits beta rays.
Natural Science—Description

23. ARGUS : 100 :: CYCLOPS : (*a.* 1000, *b.* 10, *c.* 5, ***d.* 1**)

(d) According to legend, Argus had 100 eyes, while Cyclops had just 1.
Humanities—Description

24. CANNON : BIG BERTHA :: (*a.* battleship, *b.* bazooka, ***c.* bell**, *d.* church steeple) : BIG BEN

(c) Big Bertha is the name of a cannon; Big Ben is the name of a bell.
General Information—Class

25. (*a.* pretty, *b.* pretentious, ***c.* proud**, *d.* portly) : PEACOCK :: SILLY : GOOSE

(c) People are often likened either to a peacock or to a goose. One may be proud as a peacock, or silly as a goose.
General Information—Completion

26. HYPOCRITICAL : INSINCERE :: HYPERCRITICAL : (***a.* overcritical**, *b.* sincere, *c.* oversincere, *d.* critical)

(**a**) *Hypocritical* and *insincere* are synonyms, as are *hypercritical* and *overcritical*.
Vocabulary—Similarity/Contrast

27. (*a.* cross, *b.* aisle, *c.* refectory, ***d.* nave**) : TRANSEPT :: VERTICAL : HORIZONTAL

    (**d**) In a cross-shaped church, the nave and the transept are perpendicular to each other, as are any objects that are vertical and horizontal with respect to each other.
    Humanities—Similarity/Contrast

28. MNEMONIC : (*a.* nymph, *b.* elf, *c.* anger, ***d.* knock**) :: PNEUMATIC : GNOME

    (**d**) *Mnemonic*, *pneumatic*, *gnome*, and *knock* each has a silent consonant preceding the initial voiced consonant, ***n***.
    Nonsemantic

29. FAITH : JOB :: (*a.* wisdom, ***b.* age**, *c.* wickedness, *d.* courage) : METHUSELAH

    (**b**) In the Bible, Job distinguished himself by his great faith in God, while Methuselah distinguished himself by the great age to which he lived (969 years).
    Humanities—Description

30. MRS. GRUNDY : NARROW-MINDED :: POLLYANNA : (*a.* witty, *b.* dull, *c.* pessimistic, ***d.* optimistic**)

    (**d**) Mrs. Grundy is a literary character known for her narrow-mindedness. Pollyanna is a literary character known for her optimism.
    Humanities—Description

31. MIDNIGHT SUN : (*a.* Russia, ***b.* Norway**, *c.* China, *d.* South Pole) :: RISING SUN : JAPAN

    (**b**) Norway is the Land of the Midnight Sun, while Japan is the Land of the Rising Sun.
    General Information—Description

32. RED-BLOODED : VIGOROUS :: BLUE-BLOODED : (*a.* cowardly, *b.* sickly, *c.* prudish, ***d.* aristocratic**)

    (**d**) A vigorous person is sometimes referred to as red-blooded, while an aristocratic person is sometimes referred to as blue-blooded.
    Vocabulary—Similarity/Contrast

33. (*a.* battle, *b.* artillery, *c.* ammunition, ***d.* armory**) : WEAPONS :: CLOSET : CLOTHING

    (**d**) An armory is used to store weapons; a closet is used to store clothing.
    General Information—Description

34. CHARACTERISTIC : DEFINING :: USUALLY : (*a.* never, *b.* sometimes, *c.* rarely, ***d.* always**)

    (d) A characteristic feature is one usually possessed by an object, while a defining feature is one always possessed by an object.
    General Information—Description

35. OBVIATE : (***a.* make unnecessary**, *b.* make necessary, *c.* make obvious, *d.* make obscure) :: EXPUNGE : DELETE

    (a) To obviate is to make unnecessary; to expunge is to delete.
    Vocabulary—Similarity/Contrast

36. BROBDINGNAGIAN : GIGANTIC :: (***a.* Lilliputian**, *b.* Houyhnhnm, *c.* Vespasian, *d.* Yahoo) :: TINY

    (a) In the novel *Gulliver's Travels*, the Brobdingnagians are gigantic people, while the Lilliputians are tiny ones.
    Humanities—Description

37. RUSSIA : (***a.* tsar**, *b.* king, *c.* emperor, *d.* autarch) :: FRANCE : KING

    (a) Russia was formerly ruled by a tsar, France by a king.
    Social Science—Description

38. MINOTAUR : BULL :: CENTAUR : (*a.* cow, ***b.* horse**, *c.* pig, *d.* goat)

    (b) The minotaur, according to mythology, was part bull and part man; the centaur was part horse and part man.
    Humanities—Description

39. INTEGRAL : (*a.* acceleration, *b.* length, ***c.* area**, *d.* velocity) :: DERIVATIVE : SLOPE

    (c) In calculus, an integral can be computed to determine area, while a derivative can be calculated to determine slope.
    Mathematics—Description

40. GUSTATORY : (***a.* taste**, *b.* touch, *c.* sight, *d.* smell) :: AUDITORY : HEARING

    (a) *Gustatory* refers to taste, *auditory* to hearing.
    Natural Science—Description

41. OCTOPI : OCTOPUSES :: (*a.* cannona, ***b.* cannon**, *c.* cannones, *d.* cannonade) : CANNONS

    (b) *Octopi* and *octopuses* are both plural forms of the word *octopus*; *cannon* and *cannons* are both plural forms of the word *cannon.*
    Humanities—Similarity/Contrast

42. CRIME : WAR :: PUNISHMENT : (*a.* Destruction, *b.* Treaty, ***c.* Peace**, *d.* Retribution)

(c) *Crime and Punishment* is a novel by the Russian author Dostoevski. *War and Peace* is a novel by the Russian author Tolstoy.
Humanities—Completion

43. SUPPLY : DEMAND :: RATE : (*a.* distance, ***b.* time**, *c.* velocity, *d.* price)

(b) Supply and demand are inversely related, as are rate and time.
Mathematics—Equality/Negation

44. ICONOCLAST : (***a.* religious images**, *b.* autocracy, *c.* democratic ideals, *d.* anarchy) :: NIHILIST : SOCIAL ORDER

(a) The goal of an iconoclast is to destroy religious images; the goal of a nihilist is to destroy social order.
Vocabulary—Description

45. QUIXOTIC : CERVANTES :: FAUSTIAN : (*a.* Hegel, *b.* Faust, *c.* Schiller, ***d.* Goethe**)

(d) The word *quixotic* is derived from the name of a literary character, Don Quixote, who is the subject of a work by Cervantes; the word *faustian* is derived from the name of a character, Faust, who is the subject of a work by Goethe.
Humanities—Description

46. EXPEL : STUDENT :: (*a.* expire, *b.* expunge, *c.* expropriate, ***d.* exorcise**) : SPIRIT

(d) A student is expelled from school; a spirit is exorcised from the body.
Vocabulary—Description

47. (***a.* Julian**, *b.* Augustan, *c.* Caesarian, *d.* Publican) : GREGORIAN :: NEWTONIAN : EINSTEINIAN

(a) The Julian calendar was replaced by the Gregorian calendar; Newtonian physics was replaced by Einsteinian physics.
Humanities—Description

48. (*a.* Koch, ***b.* Pasteur**, *c.* Lister, *d.* Sabin) : RABIES :: SALK : POLIO

(b) Pasteur developed an antirabies vaccine; Salk developed an antipolio vaccine.
Natural Science—Description

49. MINNEAPOLIS : ST. PAUL :: (*a.* Uncle, *b.* Rabbit, *c.* Abelard, ***d.* Romulus**) : REMUS

(d) Minneapolis and St. Paul are twin cities. Romulus and Remus, according to legend, were twin brothers.
Humanities—Class

50. POSSE : SHERIFF :: SQUIRE : (*a.* queen, *b.* bourgeoisie, ***c.* knight**, *d.* vassal)

(c) A posse assists a sheriff; a squire assisted a knight.
General Information—Description

51. UNTOUCHABLE : (*a.* Hindu, *b.* Vishnu, ***c.* Brahman**, *d.* Krishna) :: FLOOR : CEILING

    (c) In former times, an untouchable was a member of the lowest Indian caste, while a Brahman was a member of the highest one. A floor is the lowest part of a room, while a ceiling is the highest part.
    General Information—Similarity/Contrast

52. PENTAGON : DECAGON :: RECTANGLE : (*a.* square, *b.* pentagon, *c.* heptagon, ***d.* octagon**)

    (d) A decagon has twice as many sides as a pentagon; an octagon has twice as many sides as a rectangle.
    Mathematics—Equality/Negation

53. TOWARD : IN THE DIRECTION OF :: UNTOWARD : (*a.* at the location of, *b.* away from, ***c.* unseemly**, *d.* unsafe)

    (c) *Toward* means in the direction of. *Untoward* means unseemly.
    Vocabulary Similarity/Contrast

54. EXOGAMY : OUTBREEDING :: (***a.* endogamy**, *b.* inogamy, *c.* anogamy, *d.* onogamy) : INBREEDING

    (a) *Exogamy* refers to outbreeding, while *endogamy* refers to inbreeding.
    Natural Science—Description

55. GRAND : (*a.* pauvre, ***b.* petit**, *c.* standard, *d.* legal) :: INDICT : CONVICT

    (b) A grand jury has the power to indict an individual for a crime, while a petit jury has the power to convict him or her of it.
    Social Science—Description

56. CHROMATIC : PASTEL :: ACHROMATIC : (*a.* oil, *b.* tempera, *c.* chiasma, ***d.* chiaroscuro**)

    (d) Pastel is a chromatic form of artwork, while chiaroscuro is an achromatic form.
    Humanities—Description

57. EQUATOR : LATITUDE :: (*a.* North Pole, *b.* apogee, ***c.* Greenwich**, *d.* meridian) : LONGITUDE

    (c) The equator is at 0° latitude; Greenwich is at 0° longitude.
    General Information—Description

58. ROMEO : JULIET :: PYRAMUS : (*a.* Chloe, ***b.* Thisbe**, *c.* Helen, *d.* Daphne)

    (b) Romeo and Juliet were lovers, as were Pyramus and Thisbe.
    Humanities—Class

59. PETROLEUM : GASOLINE :: BAUXITE : (***a.* aluminum**, *b.* tin, *c.* lead, *d.* fool's gold)

(**a**) Petroleum is the raw material used to make gasoline, while bauxite is the raw material from which aluminum is obtained.
Natural Science—Description

60. 0 : ADDITION :: (*a.* 0, ***b.* 1**, *c.* –1, *d.* ∞) : MULTIPLICATION

(**b**) Zero is the identity element for addition—any number plus 0 equals that number. One is the identity element for multiplication—any number times 1 equals that number.
Mathematics—Description

61. GALAHAD : (*a.* Beatrice, *b.* Round Table, ***c.* Holy Grail**, *d.* True Cross) :: JASON : GOLDEN FLEECE

(**c**) According to legend, Galahad succeeded in his quest for the Holy Grail, while Jason succeeded in his quest for the Golden Fleece.
Humanities—Description

62. RED HERRING : (*a.* lie, *b.* peccadillo, ***c.* diversion**, *d.* secret plot) :: BLUE RIBBON : FIRST PRIZE

(**c**) A red herring is a diversion. A blue ribbon is a first prize.
Vocabulary—Description

63. WATERMARK : EARMARK :: (*a.* crops, *b.* tide, *c.* silver, ***d.* paper**) : ANIMAL

(**d**) Paper is sometimes identified by a watermark; an animal is sometimes identified by an earmark.
General Information—Description

64. ETHER : STARS :: PHLOGISTON : (*a.* earth, *b.* metal, ***c.* fire**, *d.* water)

(**c**) In medieval times, it was believed that the stars were composed of a substance called ether, and that fire was composed of a substance called phlogiston.
Natural Science—Description

65. PARTY : (***a.* revel**, *b.* fight, *c.* meeting, *d.* dance) :: SWINE : BOAR

(**a**) A revel is a wild party. A boar is a form of wild swine.
General Information—Description

66. RHODE ISLAND : ALASKA :: MERCURY : (*a.* Earth, ***b.* Jupiter**, *c.* Saturn, *d.* Uranus)

(**b**) Rhode Island is the smallest state, Alaska the largest. Mercury is the smallest planet (in our solar system), Jupiter the largest.
Natural Science—Class

67. MERETRICIOUS : (*a.* egregious, *b.* excellent, ***c.* gaudy**, *d.* plain) :: APEX : SUMMIT

(**c**) *Meretricious* and *gaudy* are synonyms, as are *apex* and *summit.*
Vocabulary—Similarity/Contrast

68. ANTONY : CLEOPATRA :: (***a.* Lancelot**, *b.* Arthur, *c.* Merlin, *d.* Gawain) : GUINEVERE

    (a) Cleopatra was the mistress of Antony; Guinevere was the mistress of Lancelot.
    Humanities—Class

69. MERITOCRACY : MERIT :: PLUTOCRACY : (*a.* wisdom, ***b.* money**, *c.* power, *d.* physical prowess)

    (b) A meritocracy is rule by those demonstrating merit; a plutocracy is rule by the wealthy.
    Social Science—Description

70. INTREPID : (***a.* cowardly**, *b.* bold, *c.* voluble, *d.* taciturn) :: AGILE : CLUMSY

    (a) *Intrepid* and *cowardly* are antonyms, as are *agile* and *clumsy.*
    Vocabulary—Similarity/Contrast

71. (a. Mars, *b.* Saturn, *c.* Jupiter, ***d.* Mercury**) : HERMES :: VENUS : APHRODITE

    (d) Mercury is the Roman name, and Hermes the Greek name, for the messenger of the gods. Venus is the Roman name, and Aphrodite the Greek name, for the goddess of beauty.
    Humanities—Similarity/Contrast

72. COMPLEMENTARY ANGLES : 90° :: COMPLEMENTARY COLORS : (***a.* white**, *b.* black, *c.* violet, *d.* red)

    (a) Complementary angles sum to 90°; complementary colors sum to white.
    Natural Science—Description

73. (*a.* Jefferson, b. Adams, ***c.* Hamilton**, *d.* Madison) : BURR :: LINCOLN : BOOTH

    (c) Aaron Burr killed Alexander Hamilton, while John Wilkes Booth killed Abraham Lincoln.
    Humanities—Description

74. PUFFIN : (***a.* bird**, *b.* reptile, *c.* mammal, *d.* amphibian) :: STURGEON : FISH

    (a) A puffin is a kind of bird; a sturgeon is a kind of fish.
    General Information—Description

75. BRONZE : (*a.* aluminum, ***b.* tin**, *c.* gold, *d.* silver) :: BRASS : ZINC

    (b) Bronze is a combination of copper and tin, while brass is a combination of copper and zinc.
    Natural Science—Description

76. G MAJOR : (*a.* B minor, *b.* C minor, *c.* D minor, ***d.* E minor**) :: C MAJOR : A MINOR

(d) The keys of G major and E minor both have one sharp, while the keys of C major and A minor have none.
Humanities—Description

77. (*a.* cow, *b.* jackal, ***c.* wolf**, *d.* rabbit) : LUPINE :: DOG : CANINE

(c) To be lupine is to be wolflike; to be canine is to be doglike.
Vocabulary—Description

78. (*a.* one, *b.* few, *c.* ten, ***d.* all**) : ISOCRACY :: ONE : AUTOCRACY

(d) An isocracy is rule by all; an autocracy is rule by one.
Social Science—Description

79. LOG 10 : LOG 100 :: LOG 100 : (*a.* log 1,000, ***b.* log 10,000**, *c.* log 100,000, *d.* log 1,000,000)

(b) Log 100 is twice as great as log 10 (2 : 1). Log 10,000 is twice as great as log 100 (4 : 2).
Mathematics—Class

80. HAPPINESS : SHANGRI-LA :: (***a.* wealth**, *b.* happiness, *c.* gods, *d.* freedom) : EL DORADO

(a) Shangri-La is an imaginary land of great happiness; El Dorado is an imaginary land of great wealth.
General Information—Description

81. DRACONIAN : (*a.* cowardly, *b.* bold, ***c.* cruel**, *d.* kindly) :: STENTORIAN : LOUD

(c) A draconian person is cruel; a stentorian person is loud.
Vocabulary—Description

82. MANSION : HOUSE :: TOME : (*a.* boat, ***b.* book**, *c.* desk, *d.* church)

(b) A mansion is a large house. A tome is a large book.
Vocabulary—Description

83. NEUTRAL : 7 :: (*a.* alkaline, ***b.* acidic**, *c* hydrated, *d.* oxidized) : 1

(b) On the pH scale, 7 is neutral and 1 is acidic.
Natural Science—Description

84. PERUSE : SKIM :: REPEL : (*a.* gloss, *b.* bowdlerize, *c.* drive back, ***d.* attract**)

(d) *Peruse* and *skim* are antonyms, as are *repel* and *attract.*
Vocabulary—Similarity/Contrast

85. NUCLEOLUS : NUCLEUS :: SET : (***a.* superset**, *b.* set, *c.* subset, *d.* disjoint set)

(a) In a cell, the nucleolus is contained in the nucleus. Similarly, a set is contained in a superset.
Natural Science—Part/Whole

86. HORSEBACK RIDING : EQUITATION :: (*a.* giving birth, *b.* skydiving, ***c.* swimming**, *d.* dancing) : NATATION

(**c**) Equitation is the art of horseback riding; natation is the art of swimming.
General Information—Description

87. WHIGS : TORIES :: JACOBINS : (*a.* Fascists, *b.* Laborites, *c.* Roundheads, ***d.* Girondists**)

(**d**) During the American Revolution, the Whigs represented a radical faction and the Tories a more conservative one. During the French Revolution, the Jacobins represented a radical faction and the Girondists a more conservative one.
Humanities—Class

88. PRIME : (*a.* God, *b.* destiny, *c.* factum, ***d.* mover**) :: FIRST : CAUSE

(**d**) In Aristotelian philosophy, the prime mover was a first cause (of all movement).
Humanities—Completion

89. FRANC : FRANCE :: (*a.* lira, *b.* mark, *c.* guilder, ***d.* franc**) : SWITZERLAND

(**d**) The franc is the unit of currency in both France and Switzerland (although the two francs are not equivalent).
General Information—Description

90. (*a.* Jungfrau, ***b.* Blanc**, *c.* Matterhorn, *d.* Olympus) : ALPS :: EVEREST : HIMALAYAS

(**b**) Mont Blanc is the highest peak in the Alps; Mount Everest is the highest peak in the Himalayas.
General Information—Description

91. MELANCHOLY : (*a.* blue bile, *b.* green bile, *c.* red bile, ***d.* black bile**) :: CHOLER : YELLOW BILE

(**d**) According to the physiology of days gone by, melancholy is black bile, while choler is yellow bile.
Natural Science—Similarity/Contrast

92. ORAL : ANAL :: DEPENDENCY : (*a.* lazinesss, *b.* thermometer, ***c.* stinginess**, *d.* independence)

(**c**) In psychodynamic theory, dependency is an oral trait and stinginess an anal trait.
Social Science—Description

93. (*a.* hit, *b.* die, *c.* invest, ***d.* sprout**) : BURGEON :: ENTREAT : IMPLORE

(**d**) *Sprout* and *burgeon* are synonyms, as are *entreat* and *implore.*
Vocabulary—Similarity/Contrast

94. DEARTH : PAUCITY :: SCARCITY : (*a.* plethora, ***b.* shortage**, *c.* necessity, *d.* commodity)

(b) *Dearth* and *paucity* are synonyms, as are *scarcity* and *shortage.* (All four words are synonymous.)
Vocabulary—Similarity/Contrast

95. DELFT : (*a.* glass, ***b.* pottery**, *c.* stoneware, *d.* silver) :: LIMOGES : CHINA

(b) Delft is known for its beautiful painted pottery; Limoges is known for its beautiful painted china.
General Information—Description

96. IAMB : RETURN :: TROCHEE : (***a.* stable**, *b.* arrive, *c.* defend, *d.* eternal)

(a) *Return* is pronounced as an iamb; *stable* is pronounced as a trochee.
Humanities—Class

97. AUTOCHTHONOUS : (*a.* foreign, ***b.* native**, *c.* self-governing, *d.* dependent) :: LETTER : EPISTLE

(b) *Autochthonous* and *native* are synonyms, as are *letter* and *epistle.*
Vocabulary—Similarity/Contrast

98. (***a.* bells**, *b.* horn, *c.* magpies, *d.* toads) : TINTINNABULATION :: GEESE : HONK

(a) Tintinnabulation is a sound made by bells; honk is a sound made by geese.
Vocabulary—Description

99. ELF : FLEE :: TON : (***a.* note**, *b.* pound, *c.* dwarf, *d.* find)

(a) *Flee* is *elf* spelled backwards, but with an added *e* at the end. *Note* is *ton* spelled backwards, also with an added *e* at the end.
Nonsemantic

100. CODA : (*a.* novel, ***b.* musical composition**, *c.* sculpture, *d.* ceramic jar) :: LANDING : FLIGHT

(b) A coda concludes a musical composition; a landing concludes a flight.
Humanities—Description

Item Classification Chart

Practice Test 9 — CONTENT	RELATIONSHIP						
	Similarity/ Contrast	Description	Class	Completion	Part/ Whole	Equality/ Negation	Nonsemantic
Vocabulary	15, 26, 32, 35, 53, 67, 70, 84, 93, 94, 97	3, 44, 46, 62, 77, 81, 82, 98					
General Information	51	1, 4, 6, 10, 16, 19, 31, 33, 34, 50, 57, 63, 65, 74, 80, 86, 89, 90, 95	24	5, 8, 25	12		
Humanities	27, 41, 71	9, 11, 17, 20, 21, 23, 29, 30, 36, 38, 45, 47, 56, 61, 73, 76, 100	13, 14, 49, 58, 68, 87, 96	42, 88			
Social Science		37, 55, 69, 78, 92					
Natural Science	91	2, 7, 22, 40, 48, 54, 59, 64, 72, 75, 83	66		85		
Mathematics		39, 60	79			18, 43, 52	
Nonsemantic							28, 99

Miller Analogies Test PRACTICE TEST 10

Directions: In each of the following questions, you will find three initial terms and, in parentheses, four answer options designated *a*, *b*, *c*, and *d*. You are to select from the four answer options the one that best completes the analogy with the three initial terms. To record your answers, use the answer sheet at the back of the book.

Time: *50 minutes*

1. PEN : INK :: PENCIL : (*a*. limestone, *b*. graphite, *c*. talc, *d*. gypsum)
2. (*a*. probably, *b*. possibly, *c*. virtually, *d*. certainly) : 1 :: MAYBE : .5
3. HORRIFIC : HORROR :: SOPORIFIC : (*a*. joy, *b*. boredom, *c*. sleep, *d*. stupidity)
4. A/B : B/A :: (*a*. 1/15, *b*. 1/3, *c*. 2/3, *d*. 3/2) : 1.5
5. UNINTERRUPTED : (*a*. discrete, *b*. repeated, *c*. endless, *d*. likely) :: CONTINUOUS : CONTINUAL
6. PTOLEMY : EARTH :: COPERNICUS : (*a*. moon, *b*. sun, *c*. Jupiter, *d*. universe)
7. (*a*. sculptor, *b*. painter, *c*. poet, *d*. architect) : VENUS DE MILO :: AUTHOR : THE SCARLET LETTER
8. QUICK : RABBIT :: (*a*. sleepy, *b*. wise, *c*. hungry, *d*. angry) : OWL
9. PATRICIDE : (*a*. brother, *b*. sister, *c*. king, *d*. father) :: MATRICIDE : MOTHER
10. AMA : DOCTORS :: ABA : (*a*. athletes, *b*. miners, *c*. lawyers, *d*. historians)
11. BRENDA : (*a*. Starr, *b*. Morgenstern, *c*. Jones, *d*. Balfour) :: DICK : TRACY
12. MADISON : WAR OF 1812 :: (*a*. F. Roosevelt, *b*. Truman, *c*. Eisenhower, *d*. Kennedy) : KOREAN WAR
13. BULLET : (*a*. noose, *b*. head, *c*. force, *d*. blade) :: GUN : GUILLOTINE
14. (*a* ·, *b*. ÷, *c*. **, *d*. undefined) : MULTIPLICATION :: + : ADDITION
15. PSYCHOLOGY : MIND :: PHYCOLOGY : (*a*. herbivores, *b*. carnivores, *c*. algae, *d*. cacti)

16. (*a.* Third Estate, *b.* House, *c.* Parliament, *d.* Commons) : LOWER :: LORDS : UPPER

17. BACTERIA : (*a.* bacteria, *b.* bacterium, *c.* bacterius, *d.* bacterion) :: MANY : ONE

18. SCURVY : VITAMIN C :: KWASHIORKOR : (*a.* vitamin A, *b.* vitamin B_{12}, *c.* protein, *d.* niacin)

19. CONVERSE : CONTRAPOSITIVE :: (*a.* B → A, *b.* A → B, *c.* not B → A, *d.* not A → B) : NOT B → NOT A

20. (*a.* New York, *b.* New Mexico, *c.* Missouri, *d.* Michigan) : LAKE :: MISSISSIPPI : RIVER

21. 0 PERCENT : (*a.* pressure, *b.* wind chill, *c.* THI, *d.* humidity) :: ABSOLUTE 0 : TEMPERATURE

22. OBTUSE : ACUTE :: (*a.* 0, *b.* 100, *c.* 180, *d.* 270) : 45

23. AB : AWAY :: (*a.* a, *b.* contra, *c.* ex, *d.* ad) : WITHOUT

24. UNCLE : (*a.* paternal, *b.* avuncular, *c.* uncial, *d.* uncinate) :: BROTHER : FRATERNAL

25. (*a.* women, *b.* marriage, *c.* falsehood, *d.* enlightenment) : MISOLOGY :: NOVELTY : MISONEISM

26. LIE : (*a.* lie, *b.* lay, *c.* laid, *d.* lain) :: LAY : LAID

27. HELTER : SKELTER :: HIGGLEDY : (*a.* niggledy, *b.* piggledy, *c.* spiggledy, *d.* wiggledy)

28. SPOOL : LOOPS :: (*a.* water, *b.* pools, *c.* dinghy, *d.* tools) : SLOOP

29. RILL : (*a.* stream, *b.* lake, *c.* ocean, *d.* lagoon) : NOVELLA : NOVEL

30. SONATA : SONATINA :: CONCERTO : (*a.* concertino, *b.* concertina, *c.* concert, *d.* concerto grosso)

31. NEW JERSEY : 8:00 :: OREGON : (*a.* 5 :00, *b.* 6 :00, *c.* 9 :00, *d.* 10 :00)

32. LINCOLN : 1 :: JEFFERSON : (*a.* 3, *b.* 5, *c.* 10, *d.* 25)

33. PLINY THE ELDER : (*a.* Carthaginian, *b.* Athenian, *c.* Milanese, *d.* Roman) : : THUCYDIDES : GREEK

34. (*a.* Uruguay, *b.* Argentina, *c.* Paraguay, *d.* Guatemala) : CENTRAL :: BRAZIL : SOUTH

35. ETHER : GENERAL :: NOVOCAINE : (*a.* specific, *b.* particulate, *c.* local, *d.* toxic)

36. D'ARTAGNAN : (*a.* Hugo *b.* Mauriac, *c.* Dumas, *d.* Balzac) :: GATSBY : FITZGERALD

37. ARMY : LAND :: (*a.* Marines, *b.* Navy, *c.* CIA, *d.* Secret Service) : AMPHIBIOUS

38. TWO : (*a.* hydrogen, *b.* uranium, *c.* americium, *d.* deuterium) :: THREE : TRITIUM

39. YORK : N.Y. :: ORLEANS : (*a.* N.O., *b.* La., *c.* Fr., *d.* Miss.)

40. (*a.* Copeland, *b.* Mendelssohn, *c.* Shostakovich, *d.* Bach) : 19th :: MOZART : 18th

41. MENELAUS : (*a.* Agamemnon, *b.* Priam, *c.* Achilles, *d.* Sparticus) :: HECTOR : PARIS

42. MAJORITY : MINORITY :: (*a.* Bolshevik, *b.* Maoist, *c.* Marxist, *d.* Trotskyite) : MENSHEVIK

43. FEIGN : FINE :: (*a.* right, *b.* writ, *c.* rate, *d.* rat) : WRITE

44. FATUOUS : (*a.* bright, *b.* prodigal, *c.* contemptuous, *d.* foolish) :: FASTIDIOUS : HARD TO PLEASE

45. (*a.* Ayer, *b.* Peirce, *c.* Santayana, *d.* Russell) : PRAGMATIST :: SARTRE : EXISTENTIALIST

46. ADDITIVE : (*a.* blue, *b.* red, *c.* green, *d.* white) :: SUBTRACTIVE : YELLOW

47. PROTON : NUCLEON :: MUON : (*a.* meson, *b.* electron, *c.* pion, *d.* positron)

48. BOARD : (*a.* fifteen, *b.* checkers, *c.* bridge, *d.* thirty-six) :: DECK : TWENTY-ONE

49. C# : Db :: B# : (*a.* Cb, *b.* Bb, *c.* C, *d.* Db)

50. SEVER : PERSEVERANCE :: CUT : (*a.* perseveration, *b.* perspective, *c.* pertinence, *d.* persistence)

51. FREUD : (*a.* Skinner, *b.* Allport, *c.* Murray, *d.* Erikson) :: KOHLBERG : PIAGET

52. (*a.* ellipsoid, *b.* semicircle, *c.* rhombus, *d.* angle) : PROTRACTOR :: RECTANGLE : RULER

53. BIPOLARITY : MONOLOGUE :: (*a.* dicotyledon, *b.* stamen, *c.* deciduous, *d.* pistil) : UNION

54. (*a.* patent medicine, *b.* adage, *c.* theory, *d.* heretic) : APOTHEGM :: DEXTERITY : ADROITNESS

55. FROM : TO :: (*a.* artery, *b.* ventricle, *c.* atrium, *d.* carotid) : JUGULAR

56. SOUSA : (*a.* waltzes, *b.* symphonies, *c.* marches, *d.* hymns) :: VERDI : OPERAS

57. INVOCATION : (*a.* benediction, *b.* recessional, *c.* prayer, *d.* vesper) :: START : FINISH

58. SASKATCHEWAN : REGINA :: (*a.* Quebec, *b.* Alberta, *c.* Ontario, *d.* Manitoba) : TORONTO

59. (*a.* obvious, *b.* latent, *c.* proximate, *d.* apposite) : MANIFEST :: COVERT : OVERT

60. DIRGE : REQUIEM :: GRIEF : (*a.* thanksgiving, *b.* mourning, *c.* penitence, *d.* joy)

61. (*a.* metropolitan, *b.* synod, *c.* district, *d.* diocese) : BISHOP :: PARISH : PRIEST

62. CONSONANT : VOWEL :: COMPOSITE : (*a.* prime, *b.* irrational, *c.* integer, *d.* zero)

63. IMPLODE : (*a.* explode, *b.* beseech, *c.* implicate, *d.* burst inward) :: IMPLY : HINT AT

64. EARTH : SUN :: PLANET : (*a.* heavenly body, *b.* sol, *c.* star, *d.* nova)

65. OCTOPUS : (*a.* six, *b.* eight, *c.* ten, *d.* twelve) :: PERSON : TWO

66. QUARTER : DOLLAR :: (*a.* season, *b.* day, *c.* month, *d.* decade) : YEAR

67. CAPTAIN : (*a.* admiral, *b.* ensign, *c.* commodore, *d.* midshipman) :: CORPORAL : SERGEANT

68. DAVID : VAN DYCK :: FRENCH : (*a.* Italian, *b.* German, *c.* Flemish, *d.* British)

69. (*a.* poulet, *b.* glacé, *c.* citron, *d.* entrecote) : SWEET :: CAFÉ : BITTER

70. WAIVE : WAVE :: (*a.* relinquish, *b.* relegate, *c.* remand, *d.* redress) : UNDULATE

71. WORK : (*a.* joule, *b.* ohm, *c.* ampere, *d.* coulomb) :: POTENTIAL DIFFERENCE : VOLT

72. PHILOLOGY : LANGUAGES :: MYCOLOGY : (*a.* flowering plants, *b.* ferns, *c.* weeds, *d.* fungi)

73. DEPENDENT : INDEPENDENT :: (*a.* autochthonous, *b.* canonical, *c.* anaclitic, *d.* irrecusable) : SELF-RELIANT

74. CX : (*a.* CXV, *b.* CL, *c.* CLX, *d.* CC) :: LV : LXXV

75. CAMEL : RHINOCEROS :: HUMP : (*a.* armor, *b.* snout, *c.* horn, *d.* hide)

76. ONTOLOGY : (*a.* being, *b.* metaphysics, *c.* growth, *d.* knowledge) :: DEONTOLOGY : ETHICS

77. (*a.* leucocytes, *b.* platelets, *c.* hormones, *d.* erythrocytes) : ANEMIA :: INSULIN : DIABETES

78. CALVIN : COOLIDGE :: (*a.* Alexander, *b.* Franklin, *c.* William, *d.* Robert) : PIERCE

79. PONTIUS PILATE : JESUS :: CREON : (*a.* Orestes, *b.* Oedipus, *c.* Antigone, *d.* Electra)

80. (*a.* bellicose, *b.* periphrastic, *c.* altruistic, *d.* nihilistic) : AGGRESSION :: IRENIC : PEACE

81. FIRST : LAST :: GENESIS : (*a.* Exodus, *b.* Deuteronomy, *c.* Leviticus, *d.* Numbers)

82. πr^2 : $2\pi r$ :: AREA : (*a.* diameter, *b.* circumference, *c.* perimeter, *d.* volume)

83. BUCKINGHAM PALACE : XANADU :: ELIZABETH II : (*a.* Genghis Khan, *b.* Charles V, *c.* Citizen Kane, *d.* Donald Trump)

84. MONOGYNY : (*a.* life, *b.* religion, *c.* child, *d.* wife) :: MONOTHEISM : GOD

85. ESPRESSO : BLACK :: ORANGE PEKOE : (*a.* green, *b.* white, *c.* black, *d.* red)

86. DIANA : (*a.* Artemis, *b.* Minerva, *c.* Aphrodite, *d.* Hera) :: JUPITER : ZEUS

87. (*a.* B_b major, *b.* E_b major, *c.* F major, *d.* A major) : C MINOR :: G MAJOR : E MINOR

88. MAN : NAME :: (*a.* rig, *b.* appellation, *c.* maiden, *d.* woman) : GIRL

89. MANON LESCAUT : (*a.* wise, *b.* arrogant, *c.* promiscuous, *d.* wicked) :: TOM SAWYER : ADVENTUROUS

90. (*a.* Bull Moose, *b.* Whig, *c.* Socialist, *d.* Know-Nothing) : DEBS :: DEMOCRAT : STEVENSON

91. FIRST : CLERGY :: FOURTH : (*a.* nobles, *b.* commoners, *c.* children, *d.* journalists)

92. AMETHYST : GARNET :: PURPLE : (*a.* red, *b.* green, *c.* transparent, *d.* blue)

93. (*a.* loquacious, *b.* refractory, *c.* ostentatious, *d.* timid) : GARRULOUS :: AUDACIOUS : BOLD

94. FOUR : APRIL FOOL'S DAY :: (*a.* one, *b.* two, *c.* five, *d.* ten) : MAY DAY

95. STEEPLE : CHURCH :: (*a.* minaret, *b.* muezzin, *c.* imam, *d.* arch) : MOSQUE

96. VANILLA : (*a.* bean, *b.* Sussex, *c.* hasty, *d.* Brazil) :: RICE : YORKSHIRE

97. (*a.* Saint-Saëns, *b.* Strindberg, *c.* Suleiman, *d.* Serkin) : PLAYS :: FROST : POEMS

98. THERMO : HEAT :: ISO : (*a.* cold, *b.* pressure, *c.* humidity, *d.* same)

99. (*a.* Scotch, *b.* vermouth, *c.* gin, *d.* bourbon) : TOM COLLINS :: VODKA : BLOODY MARY

100. BELLEEK : (*a.* Scotland, *b.* Ireland, *c.* Holland, *d.* Belgium) :: LIMOGES : FRANCE

Answer Key for Practice Test 10

1. *b*	11. *a*	21. *d*	31. *a*	41. *a*	51. *d*	61. *d*	71. *a*	81. *b*	91. *d*
2. *d*	12. *b*	22. *b*	32. *b*	42. *a*	52. *b*	62. *a*	72. *d*	82. *b*	92. *a*
3. *c*	13. *d*	23. *a*	33. *d*	43. *c*	53. *a*	63. *d*	73. *c*	83. *c*	93. *a*
4. *c*	14. *a*	24. *b*	34. *d*	44. *d*	54. *b*	64. *c*	74. *b*	84. *d*	94. *c*
5. *b*	15. *c*	25. *d*	35. *c*	45. *b*	55. *d*	65. *b*	75. *c*	85. *c*	95. *a*
6. *b*	16. *d*	26. *b*	36. *c*	46. *c*	56. *c*	66. *a*	76. *a*	86. *a*	96. *c*
7. *a*	17. *b*	27. *b*	37. *a*	47. *a*	57. *a*	67. *c*	77. *d*	87. *b*	97. *b*
8. *b*	18. *c*	28. *b*	38. *d*	48. *b*	58. *c*	68. *c*	78. *b*	88. *a*	98. *d*
9. *d*	19. *a*	29. *a*	39. *b*	49. *c*	59. *b*	69. *b*	79. *c*	89. *c*	99. *c*
10. *c*	20. *d*	30. *a*	40. *b*	50. *d*	60. *b*	70. *a*	80. *a*	90. *c*	100. *b*

Explanation of Answers for Practice Test 10

1. PEN : INK :: PENCIL : (*a.* limestone, ***b.* graphite**, *c.* talc, *d.* gypsum)

   (b) A pen writes with ink; a pencil writes with graphite.
   General Information—Description

2. (*a.* probably, *b.* possibly, *c.* virtually, ***d.* certainly**) : 1 :: MAYBE : .5

   (d) Something that is certainly true has probability 1 of occurrence; something that is maybe true can have probability .5 of occurrence.
   General Information—Description

3. HORRIFIC : HORROR :: SOPORIFIC : (*a.* joy, *b.* boredom, ***c.* sleep**, *d.* stupidity)

   (c) Something horrific causes horror; something soporific causes sleep.
   Vocabulary—Description

4. A/B : B/A :: (*a.* 1/15, *b.* 1/3, ***c.* 2/3**, *d.* 3/2) : 1.5

   (c) $B/A = 1/(A/B)$; $1.5 = 1/(2/3)$.
   Mathematics—Equality/Negation

5. UNINTERRUPTED : (*a.* discrete, ***b.* repeated**, *c.* endless, *d.* likely) :: CONTINUOUS : CONTINUAL

   (b) Something that is uninterrupted is continuous; something that is repeated is continual.
   Vocabulary—Similarity/Contrast

6. PTOLEMY : EARTH :: COPERNICUS : (*a.* moon, ***b.* sun**, *c.* Jupiter, *d.* universe)

   (b) Ptolemy believed that the earth is at the center of the planetary system; Copernicus believed that the sun is at the center.
   Natural Science—Description

7. (***a.* sculptor**, *b.* painter, *c.* poet, *d.* architect) : VENUS DE MILO :: AUTHOR : THE SCARLET LETTER

   (a) Venus de Milo was created by a sculptor, *The Scarlet Letter* by an author.
   Humanities—Description

8. QUICK : RABBIT :: (*a.* sleepy, ***b.* wise**, *c.* hungry, *d.* angry) : OWL

   (b) A rabbit is reputed to be quick; an owl is reputed to be wise.
   General Information—Description

9. PATRICIDE : (*a.* brother, *b.* sister, *c.* king, ***d.* father**) :: MATRICIDE : MOTHER

(**d**) Patricide is the murder of one's father; matricide is the murder of one's mother.
Vocabulary—Description

10. AMA : DOCTORS :: ABA : (*a.* athletes, *b.* miners, ***c.* lawyers**, *d.* historians)

(**c**) The AMA (American Medical Association) is an association of doctors; the ABA (American Bar Association) is an association of lawyers.
General Information—Description

11. BRENDA : (***a.* Starr**, *b.* Morgenstern, *c.* Jones, *d.* Balfour) :: DICK : TRACY

(**a**) Brenda Starr and Dick Tracy are well-known comic-strip characters.
General Information—Completion

12. MADISON : WAR OF 1812 :: (*a.* F. Roosevelt, ***b.* Truman**, *c.* Eisenhower, *d.* Kennedy) : KOREAN WAR

(**b**) Madison was president during the War of 1812; Truman was president during the Korean War.
Humanities—Description

13. BULLET : (*a.* noose, *b.* head, *c.* force, ***d.* blade**) :: GUN : GUILLOTINE

(**d**) A gun kills by a bullet; a guillotine kills by a blade.
General Information—Description

14. (***a.*** · *b.* ÷, *c.* **, *d.* undefined) : MULTIPLICATION :: + : ADDITION

(**a**) A raised dot (·) can be used to signify multiplication; a plus sign (+) can be used to signify addition.
Mathematics—Description

15. PSYCHOLOGY : MIND :: PHYCOLOGY : (*a.* herbivores, *b.* carnivores, ***c.* algae**, *d.* cacti)

(**c**) Psychology is the science of the mind; phycology is the science of algae.
Natural Science—Description

16. (*a.* Third Estate, *b.* House, *c.* Parliament, ***d.* Commons**) : LOWER :: LORDS : UPPER

(**d**) The House of Commons is the lower house, and the House of Lords the upper house, of the British Parliament.
General Information—Description

17. BACTERIA : (*a.* bacteria, ***b.* bacterium**, *c.* bacterius, *d.* bacterion) :: MANY : ONE

(**b**) One refers to many bacteria (plural) or one bacterium (singular).
Vocabulary—Description

18. SCURVY : VITAMIN C :: KWASHIORKOR : (*a.* vitamin A, *b.* vitamin B_{12}, ***c.* protein**, *d.* niacin)

(c) Scurvy is caused by a deficiency of vitamin C; kwashiorkor is caused by a deficiency of protein.
Natural Science—Description

19. CONVERSE : CONTRAPOSITIVE :: (***a.*** **B → A**, *b.* A → B, *c.* not B → A, *d.* not A → B) : (NOT B → NOT A)

(a) The converse of *A* → *B* is *B* → *A*; the contrapositive of *A* → *B* is (not *B* → not *A*).
Humanities—Description

20. (*a.* New York, *b.* New Mexico, *c.* Missouri, ***d.*** **Michigan**) : LAKE :: MISSISSIPPI : RIVER

(d) Lake Michigan and the Mississippi River are bodies of water.
General Information—Completion

21. 0 PERCENT : (*a.* pressure, *b.* wind chill, *c.* THI, ***d.*** **humidity**) :: ABSOLUTE 0 : TEMPERATURE

(d) 0 percent is the minimum possible humidity; absolute 0 is the minimum possible temperature.
General Information—Description

22. OBTUSE : ACUTE :: (*a.* 0, ***b.*** **100**, *c.* 180, *d.* 270) : 45

(b) A 100° angle is obtuse; a 45° angle is acute.
Mathematics—Description

23. AB : AWAY :: (***a.*** **a**, *b.* contra, *c.* ex, *d.* ad) : WITHOUT

(a) The prefix *ab-* means *away*; the prefix *a-* means *without.*
Vocabulary—Similarity/Contrast

24. UNCLE : (*a.* paternal, ***b.*** **avuncular**, *c.* uncial, *d.* uncinate) :: BROTHER : FRATERNAL

(b) Someone who is avuncular is like an uncle; someone who is fraternal is like a brother.
Vocabulary—Description

25. (*a.* women, *b.* marriage, *c.* falsehood, ***d.*** **enlightenment**) : MISOLOGY :: NOVELTY : MISONEISM

(d) Misology is hatred of enlightenment; misoneism is hatred of novelty.
Vocabulary—Description

26. LIE : (*a.* lie, ***b.*** **lay**, *c.* laid, *d.* lain) :: LAY : LAID

(b) The past tense of *lie* is *lay* (or, in another meaning of *lie, lied*, but this is not an option); the past tense of *lay* is *laid.*
General Information—Class

27. HELTER : SKELTER :: HIGGLEDY : (*a.* niggledy, ***b.*** **piggledy**, *c.* spiggledy, *d.* wiggledy)

(b) *Helter-skelter* and *higgledy-piggledy* are synonyms.
Vocabulary—Completion

28. SPOOL : LOOPS :: (*a.* water, ***b.* pools**, *c.* dinghy, *d.* tools) : SLOOP

(b) *Spool* spelled backward is *loops; pools* spelled backward is *sloop*.
Nonsemantic

29. RILL : (***a.* stream**, *b.* lake, *c.* ocean, *d.* lagoon) : NOVELLA : NOVEL

(a) A rill is a small stream; a novella is a small novel.
Vocabulary—Description

30. SONATA : SONATINA :: CONCERTO : (***a.* concertino**, *b.* concertina, *c.* concert, *d.* concerto grosso)

(a) A sonatina is a small sonata; a concertino is a small concerto.
Humanities—Description

31. NEW JERSEY : 8:00 :: OREGON : (***a.* 5 :00**, *b.* 6:00, *c.* 9:00, *d.* 10:00)

(a) When it is 8:00 in New Jersey, it is 5:00 in Oregon.
General Information—Description

32. LINCOLN : 1 :: JEFFERSON : (*a.* 3, ***b.* 5**, *c.* 10, *d.* 25)

(b) The head of Lincoln appears on a 1-cent piece; the head of Jefferson appears on a 5-cent piece.
General Information—Description

33. PLINY THE ELDER : (*a.* Carthaginian, *b.* Athenian, *c.* Milanese, ***d.* Roman**) :: THUCYDIDES : GREEK

(d) Pliny the Elder was Roman; Thucydides, Greek.
Humanities—Description

34. (*a.* Uruguay, *b.* Argentina, *c.* Paraguay, ***d.* Guatemala**) : CENTRAL :: BRAZIL : SOUTH

(d) Guatemala is in Central America, Brazil in South America.
General Information—Part/Whole

35. ETHER : GENERAL :: NOVOCAINE : (*a.* specific, *b.* particulate, ***c.* local**, *d.* toxic)

(c) Ether is a general anesthetic, novocaine a local anesthetic.
General Information—Description

36. D'ARTAGNAN : (*a.* Hugo *b.* Mauriac, ***c.* Dumas**, *d.* Balzac) :: GATSBY : FITZGERALD

(c) D'Artagnan was a character created by Dumas in *The Three Musketeers*; Gatsby was a character created by Fitzgerald in *The Great Gatsby*.
Humanities—Description

37. ARMY : LAND :: (***a.* Marines**, *b.* Navy, *c.* CIA, *d.* Secret Service) : AMPHIBIOUS

    (a) The Army is intended to engage primarily in land warfare; the Marines are intended to engage primarily in amphibious warfare.
    General Information—Description

38. TWO : (*a.* hydrogen, *b.* uranium, *c.* americium, ***d.* deuterium**) :: THREE : TRITIUM

    (d) Deuterium is an isotope of hydrogen with an atomic weight of 2; tritium is an isotope of hydrogen with an atomic weight of 3.
    Natural Science—Description

39. YORK : N.Y. :: ORLEANS : (*a.* N.O., ***b.* La.**, *c.* Fr., *d.* Miss.)

    (b) (New) York (the city) is in the state of New York (N.Y.); (New) Orleans is in the state of Louisiana (La.).
    General Information—Part/Whole

40. (*a.* Copeland, ***b.* Mendelssohn**, *c.* Shostakovich, *d.* Bach) : 19th :: MOZART : 18th

    (b) Mendelssohn was a 19th century composer, Mozart, an 18th century composer.
    Humanities—Completion

41. MENELAUS : (***a.* Agamemnon**, *b.* Priam, *c.* Achilles, *d.* Sparticus) :: HECTOR : PARIS

    (a) Menelaus and Agamemnon were brothers, as were Hector and Paris.
    Humanities—Class

42. MAJORITY : MINORITY :: (***a.* Bolshevik**, *b.* Maoist, *c.* Marxist, *d.* Trotskyite) : MENSHEVIK

    (a) In Revolutionary Russia, the Bolsheviks were the majority, or greater (*bolshe*), party, and the Mensheviks were the minority, or smaller (*menshe*), party.
    Humanities—Description

43. FEIGN : FINE :: (*a.* right, *b.* writ, ***c.* rate**, *d.* rat) : WRITE

    (c) The pronounced vowel sounds are the same in *feign* and *rate*, and in *fine* and *write*.
    Nonsemantic

44. FATUOUS : (*a.* bright, *b.* prodigal, *c.* contemptuous, ***d.* foolish**) :: FASTIDIOUS : HARD TO PLEASE

    (d) *Fatuous* and *foolish* are synonyms, as are *fastidious* and *hard to please.*
    Vocabulary—Similarity/Contrast

45. (*a.* Ayer, ***b.* Peirce**, *c.* Santayana, *d.* Russell) : PRAGMATIST :: SARTRE : EXISTENTIALIST

(b) Peirce was a major philosopher in the pragmatist movement; Sartre was a major philosopher in the existentialist movement.
Humanities—Description

46. ADDITIVE : (*a.* blue, *b.* red, ***c.* green**, *d.* white) :: SUBTRACTIVE : YELLOW

(c) Green is an additive (but not a subtractive) primary color in light; yellow is a subtractive (but not an additive) primary color.
General Information—Description

47. PROTON : NUCLEON :: MUON : (***a.* meson**, *b.* electron, *c.* pion, *d.* positron)

(a) A proton is a nucleon; a muon is a meson.
Natural Science—Class

48. BOARD : (*a.* fifteen, ***b.* checkers**, *c.* bridge, *d.* thirty-six) :: DECK : TWENTY-ONE

(b) Checkers is played with a board, twenty-one with a deck.
General Information—Description

49. C# : Db :: B# : (*a.* Cb, *b.* Bb, ***c.* C**, *d.* Db)

(c) C# and D_b are played instrumentally as the same note, as are B# and C.
Humanities—Similarity/Contrast

50. SEVER : PERSEVERANCE :: CUT : (*a.* perseveration, *b.* perspective, *c.* pertinence, ***d.* persistence**)

(d) *Sever* and *cut* are synonyms, as are *perseverance* and *persistence.*
Vocabulary—Similarity/Contrast

51. FREUD : (*a.* Skinner, *b.* Allport, *c.* Murray, ***d.* Erikson**) :: KOHLBERG : PIAGET

(d) Freud, Erikson, Kohlberg, and Piaget are all prominent psychological theorists postulating stages of development.
Social Science—Class

52. (*a.* ellipsoid, ***b.* semicircle**, *c.* rhombus, *d.* angle) : PROTRACTOR :: RECTANGLE : RULER

(b) A protractor is usually in the shape of a semicircle. A ruler is usually in the shape of a rectangle.
Mathematics—Description

53. BIPOLARITY : MONOLOGUE :: (***a.* dicotyledon**, *b.* stamen, *c.* deciduous, *d.* pistil) : UNION

(a) *Bipolarity* and *dicotyledon* refer to two of something; *monologue* and *union* refer to one of something.
Vocabulary—Equality/Negation

54. (*a.* patent medicine, ***b.* adage**, *c.* theory, *d.* heretic) : APOTHEGM :: DEXTERITY : ADROITNESS

(b) *Adage* and *apothegm* are synonyms, as are *dexterity* and *adroitness.*
Vocabulary—Similarity/Contrast

55. FROM : TO :: (*a.* artery, *b.* ventricle, *c.* atrium, ***d.* carotid**) : JUGULAR

(d) The carotid is an artery carrying blood away from the heart; the jugular is a vein carrying blood to the heart.
Natural Science—Description

56. SOUSA : (*a.* waltzes, *b.* symphonies, ***c.* marches**, *d.* hymns) :: VERDI : OPERAS

(c) Sousa composed primarily marches; Verdi composed primarily operas.
Humanities—Description

57. INVOCATION : (***a.* benediction**, *b.* recessional, *c.* prayer, *d.* vesper) :: START : FINISH

(a) An invocation starts a religious service; a benediction finishes it.
General Information—Description

58. SASKATCHEWAN : REGINA :: (*a.* Quebec, *b.* Alberta, ***c.* Ontario**, *d.* Manitoba) : TORONTO

(c) The capital of the Canadian province of Saskatchewan is Regina; the capital of Ontario is Toronto.
General Information—Description

59. (*a.* obvious, ***b.* latent**, *c.* proximate, *d.* apposite) : MANIFEST :: COVERT : OVERT

(b) *Latent* and *manifest* are antonyms, as are *covert* and *overt.*
Vocabulary—Similarity/Contrast

60. DIRGE : REQUIEM :: GRIEF : (*a.* thanksgiving, ***b.* mourning**, *c.* penitence, *d.* joy)

(b) A dirge and a requiem both express grief and mourning.
Vocabulary—Description

61. (*a.* metropolitan, *b.* synod, *c.* district, ***d.* diocese**) : BISHOP :: PARISH : PRIEST

(d) A diocese is under the jurisdiction of a bishop; a parish is under the jurisdiction of a priest.
General Information—Description

62. CONSONANT : VOWEL :: COMPOSITE : (*a.* prime, *b.* irrational, *c.* integer, ***d.* zero**)

(d) All letters are either consonants or vowels; all numbers are either composite or prime.
Mathematics—Class

63. IMPLODE : (*a.* explode, *b.* beseech, *c.* implicate, ***d.* burst inward**) :: IMPLY : HINT AT

(d) To implode is to burst inward; to imply is to hint at.
Vocabulary—Similarity/Contrast

64. EARTH : SUN :: PLANET : (*a.* heavenly body, *b.* sol, ***c.* star**, *d.* nova)

(c) The earth is a planet; the sun is a star.
General Information—Class

65. OCTOPUS : (*a.* six, ***b.* eight**, *c.* ten, *d.* twelve) :: PERSON : TWO

(b) An octopus has eight arms; a person has two arms.
General Information—Description

66. QUARTER : DOLLAR :: (***a.* season**, *b.* day, *c.* month, *d.* decade) : YEAR

(a) There are four quarters in a dollar, and four seasons in a year.
General Information—Equality/Negation

67. CAPTAIN : (*a.* admiral, *b.* ensign, ***c.* commodore**, *d.* midshipman) :: CORPORAL : SERGEANT

(c) In the Navy, a captain is immediately below a commodore in rank; in the Army, a corporal is immediately below a sergeant in rank.
General Information—Description

68. DAVID : VAN DYCK :: FRENCH : (*a.* Italian, *b.* German, ***c.* Flemish**, *d.* British)

(c) David was a French painter; Van Dyck was a Flemish painter.
Humanities—Description

69. (*a.* poulet, ***b.* glacé**, *c.* citron, *d.* entrecote) : SWEET :: CAFÉ : BITTER

(b) Glacé (ice cream) is sweet; café (coffee) is bitter.
General Information—Description

70. WAIVE : WAVE :: (***a.* relinquish**, *b.* relegate, *c.* remand, *d.* redress) : UNDULATE

(a) To waive is to relinquish; to wave is to undulate.
Vocabulary—Similarity/Contrast

71. WORK : (***a.* joule**, *b.* ohm, *c.* ampere, *d.* coulomb) :: POTENTIAL DIFFERENCE : VOLT

(a) A joule is a unit of work; a volt is a measure of potential difference.
Natural Science—Description

72. PHILOLOGY : LANGUAGES :: MYCOLOGY : (*a.* flowering plants, *b.* ferns, *c.* weeds, ***d.* fungi**)

(d) Philology is the study of languages; mycology is the study of fungi.
Natural Science—Description

73. DEPENDENT : INDEPENDENT :: (*a.* autochthonous, *b.* canonical, ***c.* anaclitic**, *d.* irrecusable) : SELF-RELIANT

    (**c**) *Dependent* and *anaclitic* are synonyms, as are *independent* and *self-reliant.*
    Vocabulary—Similarity/Contrast

74. CX : (*a.* CXV, ***b.* CL**, *c.* CLX, *d.* CC) :: LV : LXXV

    (**b**) The terms of the analogy are Roman numerals expressing the ratio 110 : 150 :: 55 : 75.
    Mathematics—Equality/Negation

75. CAMEL : RHINOCEROS :: HUMP : (*a.* armor, *b.* snout, ***c.* horn**, *d.* hide)

    (**c**) A camel may have one hump or two; a rhinoceros may have one horn or two.
    General Information—Description

76. ONTOLOGY : (***a.* being**, *b.* metaphysics, *c.* growth, *d.* knowledge) :: DEONTOLOGY : ETHICS

    (**a**) Ontology is the study of being; deontology is the study of ethics.
    Humanities—Description

77. (*a.* leucocytes, *b.* platelets, *c.* hormones, ***d.* erythrocytes**) : ANEMIA :: INSULIN : DIABETES

    (**d**) Anemia is characterized by a shortage of erythrocytes, diabetes by a shortage of insulin.
    Natural Science—Description

78. CALVIN : COOLIDGE :: (*a.* Alexander, ***b.* Franklin**, *c.* William, *d.* Robert) : PIERCE

    (**b**) Calvin Coolidge and Franklin Pierce were both presidents of the United States.
    General Information—Completion

79. PONTIUS PILATE : JESUS :: CREON : (*a.* Orestes, *b.* Oedipus, ***c.* Antigone**, *d.* Electra)

    (**c**) Pontius Pilate sentenced Jesus to death, Creon sentenced Antigone to death.
    Humanities—Description

80. (***a.* bellicose**, *b.* periphrastic, *c.* altruistic, *d.* nihilistic) : AGGRESSION :: IRENIC : PEACE

    (**a**) Someone who is bellicose fosters aggression; someone who is irenic fosters peace.
    Vocabulary—Description

81. FIRST : LAST :: GENESIS : (*a.* Exodus, ***b.* Deuteronomy**, *c.* Leviticus, *d.* Numbers)

(b) Genesis is the first book of the Torah; Deuteronomy, the last book.
Humanities—Description

82. $\pi r^2 : 2\pi r$ :: AREA : (*a.* diameter, ***b.* circumference**, *c.* perimeter, *d.* volume)

(b) πr^2 is the formula for the area of a circle; $2\pi r$ is the formula for the circumference of a circle.
Mathematics—Equality/Negation

83. BUCKINGHAM PALACE : XANADU :: ELIZABETH II : (*a.* Genghis Khan, *b.* Charles V, ***c.* Citizen Kane**, *d.* Donald Trump)

(c) Buckingham Palace is the abode of Elizabeth II; Xanadu was the abode of Citizen Kane (a fictitious character fashioned after William Randolph Hearst).
General Information—Description

84. MONOGYNY : (*a.* life, *b.* religion, *c.* child, ***d.* wife**) :: MONOTHEISM : GOD

(d) Monogyny is belief in one wife; monotheism is belief in one God.
Vocabulary—Description

85. ESPRESSO : BLACK :: ORANGE PEKOE : (*a.* green, *b.* white, ***c.* black**, *d.* red)

(c) Espresso (coffee) is black in color; orange pekoe (tea) is also black in color.
General Information—Description

86. DIANA : (***a.* Artemis**, *b.* Minerva, *c.* Aphrodite, *d.* Hera) :: JUPITER : ZEUS

(a) Diana and Artemis are the Roman and Greek names, respectively, for the goddess of the moon and of hunting; Jupiter and Zeus are the Roman and Greek names, respectively, for the king of the gods.
Humanities—Similarity/Contrast

87. (*a.* B_b major, ***b.* E_b major**, *c.* F major, *d.* A major) : C MINOR :: G MAJOR : E MINOR

(b) The keys of E_b major and C minor both have three flats; the keys of G major and E minor both have one sharp.
Humanities—Similarity/Contrast

88. MAN : NAME :: (***a.* rig**, *b.* appellation, *c.* maiden, *d.* woman) : GIRL

(a) The letters in *man* form the first three letters in *name* reversed; the letters in *rig* form the first three letters in *girl* reversed.
Nonsemantic

89. MANON LESCAUT : (*a.* wise, *b.* arrogant, ***c.* promiscuous**, *d.* wicked) :: TOM SAWYER : ADVENTUROUS

(c) Manon Lescaut is a promiscuous literary character; Tom Sawyer is an adventurous one.
Humanities—Description

90. (*a.* Bull Moose, *b.* Whig, ***c.* Socialist**, *d.* Know-Nothing) : DEBS :: DEMOCRAT : STEVENSON

(c) Eugene Debs was an unsuccessful Socialist candidate for president; Adlai Stevenson was an unsuccessful Democratic candidate for president.
Humanities—Description

91. FIRST : CLERGY :: FOURTH : (*a.* nobles, *b.* commoners, *c.* children, ***d.* journalists**)

(d) The clergy formed the First Estate; journalists form what is sometimes called the Fourth Estate.
Vocabulary—Description

92. AMETHYST : GARNET :: PURPLE : (***a.* red**, *b.* green, *c.* transparent, *d.* blue)

(a) An amethyst is purple; a garnet is red.
General Information—Description

93. (***a.* loquacious**, *b.* refractory, *c.* ostentatious, *d.* timid) : GARRULOUS :: AUDACIOUS : BOLD

(a) *Loquacious* and *garrulous* have similar meanings, as do *audacious* and *bold.*
Vocabulary—Similarity/Contrast

94. FOUR : APRIL FOOL'S DAY :: (*a.* one, *b.* two, ***c.* five**, *d.* ten) : MAY DAY

(c) April Fool's Day is the first day of the fourth month; May Day is the first day of the fifth month.
General Information—Description

95. STEEPLE : CHURCH :: (***a.* minaret**, *b.* muezzin, *c.* imam, *d.* arch) : MOSQUE

(a) A steeple protrudes from the top of a church; a minaret protrudes from the top of a mosque.
General Information—Description

96. VANILLA : (*a.* bean, *b.* Sussex, ***c.* hasty**, *d.* Brazil) :: RICE : YORKSHIRE

(c) Four types of pudding are vanilla pudding, hasty pudding, rice pudding, and Yorkshire pudding.
General Information—Class

97. (*a.* Saint-Saëns, ***b.* Strindberg**, *c.* Suleiman, *d.* Serkin) : PLAYS :: FROST : POEMS

(b) Strindberg wrote plays; Frost wrote poems.
Humanities—Description

98. THERMO : HEAT :: ISO : (*a.* cold, *b.* pressure, *c.* humidity, ***d.* same**)

(d) *Thermo-* is a prefix meaning *heat*; *iso-* is a prefix meaning *same.*
Vocabulary—Similarity/Contrast

99. (*a.* Scotch, *b.* vermouth, ***c.* gin**, *d.* bourbon) : TOM COLLINS :: VODKA : BLOODY MARY

(c) A Tom Collins is a mixed drink containing gin; a Bloody Mary is a mixed drink containing vodka.
General Information—Description

100. BELLEEK : (*a.* Scotland, ***b.* Ireland**, *c.* Holland, *d.* Belgium) :: LIMOGES : FRANCE

(b) Belleek is a town in Ireland (and also a generic name for a type of porcelain). Limoges is a town in France (and also a generic name for a type of china).
General Information—Description

Item Classification Chart

Practice Test 10	RELATIONSHIP						
CONTENT	Similarity/ Contrast	Description	Class	Completion	Part/ Whole	Equality/ Negation	Nonsemantic
Vocabulary	5, 23, 44, 50, 54, 59, 63, 70, 73, 93, 98	3, 9, 17, 24, 25, 29, 60, 80, 84, 91		27		53	
General Information		1, 2, 8, 10, 13, 16, 21, 31, 32, 35, 37, 46, 48, 57, 58, 61, 65, 67, 69, 75, 83, 85, 92, 94, 95, 99, 100	26, 64, 96	11, 20, 78	34, 39	66	
Humanities	49, 86, 87	7, 12, 19, 30, 33, 36, 42, 45, 56, 68, 76, 79, 81, 89, 90, 97	41	40			
Social Science			51				
Natural Science		6, 15, 18, 38, 55, 71, 72, 77	47				
Mathematics		14, 22, 52	62			4, 74, 82	
Nonsemantic							28, 43, 88

Part Five Review for the *Miller Analogies Test*

What This Review Contains

As stated earlier in this book, the *MAT* is a test of vocabulary and general information as well as specific information in diverse areas. It is not possible to review the content of all the subjects that may be included in an *MAT* exam. The reviews provided in this chapter are intended as brief refreshers. They may help you to recall important names, events, and terms in different areas of study. If you think that you are weak in any one or several fields of study, we suggest that you consult *Barron's New Student's Concise Encyclopedia* and references in particular subjects.

Vocabulary

The vocabulary list below consists of words often used in graduate tests. For some entries, synonyms, antonyms, or other related words are provided as an added help in handling analogy questions.

abdicate to denounce; to discard; to abandon
aberration something not typical; a deviation
abhorrence repugnance; detestation
abjure to renounce upon oath
abnegation self-denial
abrogate to break, as a treaty or law
abscond to depart secretly; to hide (oneself)
absolve to set free from an obligation or the consequences of guilt
abstain to refrain deliberately from an action or practice, usu. as a form of self-denial
abstemious sparing or moderate, especially in eating or drinking (antonym: **gluttonous**)
abstruse hard to understand or grasp; esoteric
abut to border on; to terminate at the boundary or point of contact
abysmal immeasurable; bottomless
accolade an award or honor; high praise
acquiesce to agree silently; to accept tacitly
acrophobia the fear of heights
acumen keenness

adamant unyielding; stubborn
addle to throw into confusion; to confound
adjure to command solemnly; to advise earnestly; to beg
adroit showing skill, cleverness, or resourcefulness
adulation excessive praise
adumbrate to intimate or foreshadow; to obscure
aestivate (estivate) to spend the summer in an inactive state
agglomeration a collection in a mass, heap, or cluster; aggrandizement
agoraphobia the fear of open spaces
alacrity liveliness or eagerness; readiness (antonym: **lassitude**)
allegory a symbolic expression or description
allusion an indirect reference to something else; a hint
alms charity; something given to the poor (usu. refers to small change)
alpinism mountain climbing
altruistic unselfish; concerned with the welfare of others
ambergris a product of sperm whales used in the manufacture of perfume
amphora an ancient two-handled Greek jar
anathema a ban or curse; a denunciation accompanied by excommunication
andiron a metal support used for holding logs in a hearth
androphobia the fear of men
anneal to toughen or to strengthen
anodyne a pain reliever
anomaly an aberration; a deviation; an irregularity
antipathy firm dislike; hatred (antonym: **sympathy**)
antiseptic free from germs, exceptionally clean
antithesis the direct opposite
aphelion the point in a planet's orbit that is farthest from the sun
apocalyptic of, or relating to, a revelation or discovery
apocryphal of doubtful authenticity; spurious
apogee the point in a satellite's orbit that is farthest from the center of the earth
aquiline hooked; like an eagle
arachnophobia the fear of spiders
archon the chief magistrate in ancient Athens; any ruler
arid dull; unimaginative; extremely dry
arrogate to claim or seize without justification; to usurp
artifice cleverness; ingenuity
assiduous diligent
assuage to ease the intensity of; to appease; to pacify (antonym: **exacerbate**)
astraphobia the fear of lightning
atrophy a wasting away; degeneration
attenuate to lessen in amount, force, or value; to weaken
austral southern (antonym: **boreal**)
axiom a self-evident rule or truth; a widely accepted saying
azure sky blue
baleful menacing; harmful
balmy soothing; mild
banal trite; commonplace
bellicose inclined to start wars or fights (antonym: **pacific**)
beneficent beneficial (antonym: **deleterious**)
benign gracious; favorable; not threatening to health (antonym: **malignant**)

bibliophile one who loves books
biennial occurring every two years
bifurcate divided in two branches; forked
blighted withered or rotten; destroyed; frustrated
blithe happy; merry; cheerful
bombastic pompous; overblown; turgid
boreal northern (antonym: **austral**)
boycott to engage in a concerted refusal to have dealings with (a person, store, organization) as a sign of disapproval [derived from Charles C. Boycott, an English land agent who was ostracized in Ireland because of his refusal to lower rents]
broach to make known for the first time; to open up (a subject) for discussion
bromidic lacking originality; trite
brontophobia the fear of thunder
brook to bear or tolerate; to put up with
brusque abrupt or short in manner or speech
buccal pertaining to the cheeks or side of the mouth
bucolic pastoral; relating to rural life
buffoon a clown or ludicrous figure; someone who amuses with jokes or tricks
bulbous rotund; round like a bulb
bumptious aggressive and assertive in an offensive way (antonym: **shy; self-effacing**)
buoyant (1) having the ability to float; (2) cheerful; gay
burnish to make shiny or lustrous; to polish
burnoose a hooded Arabic cloak
  cassock a loose robe worn by priests
cabal group united to plot, esp. the overthrow of authority
cache (1) a hiding place; (2) something hidden in a secure place
cacophony a harsh-sounding mixture of words, voices, or sounds
caduceus the emblem of the medical profession (a staff with intertwined snakes and wings at the top)
cajole to persuade a reluctant person to do something; to coax
caliber the diameter of the bore of a gun
  gauge the size of a shotgun; measure of the interior diameter of the barrel
calumny a lie told to damage another's reputation; slander
candid frank
canonical orthodox; authoritative
capitulate to cease resisting; to surrender (often after negotiations)
capricious unpredictable; governed by a whim
captious critical; fault-finding
carp to complain
cashmere a fine wool from a cashmere goat [derived from Kashmir, India]
catharsis purification of emotions, esp. through art
  bathos sentimentalism; overdone pathos; triteness; anticlimax
  pathos something that evokes pity, compassion, or sorrow
catholic universal (antonym: **provincial; parochial**)
caustic acrid; biting
cavil to raise trivial objections; to nitpick
cerulean resembling the blue of the sky
chaff waste material from the threshing of wheat
  dross waste material from molten metal

slag scoria; refuse from the melting of metals or reduction of ore
tailings waste material from the preparation of ores or grains
chartreuse yellow-green
chastise to criticize harshly; to castigate
chauvinism excessive or blind patriotism [derived from Nicholas Chauvin, a character in a French play]
chicanery trickery; artful deception
chimerical fantastically visionary; wildly fanciful
choleric easily angered or irritated
Cimmerian (1) *adj.* shrouded in gloom and darkness; (2) *n.* a mythical people described by Homer as dwelling in gloom
stygian (1) dark and gloomy; (2) relating to the Styx (in Greek mythology, the river of the underworld)
circumlocution an indirect expression; wordy or evasive language
circumspect considering all options; cautious
clandestine surreptitious; secret
claustrophobia the fear of closed places
clemency an act of leniency; mercy
cloy to satiate
glut to oversupply; to satiate
coalesce to grow together; to unite into a whole
coda a passage that concludes a musical or literary work
cogent pertinent; compelling; convincing
cognizant perceptive; observant
colloquial of or relating to conversation; characteristic of informal speech
collusion a secret agreement, esp. for an illegal purpose
compulsion an impulse to perform an irrational act
phobia an inexplicable fear of something
conjoin to join or act together
contentious argumentative; quarrelsome
contumacious rebellious; stubbornly disobedient; renegade
conundrum a puzzle; a riddle
cooper a maker of casks or barrels
corroborate to confirm; to back up with evidence
cowl (1) a hood; (2) a cover for an engine
croupier a collector and payer of bets at a casino
culinary having to do with the kitchen or cooking
cynophobia the fear of dogs
cynosure the center of interest
dauntless fearless
debacle a violent breakdown; a sudden overthrow
debauchery wild living; corruption by sensuality
debilitate to weaken (antonym: **invigorate**)
debonair suave; courteous; sophisticated
deciduous falling off or shedding at a certain season; ephemeral; not permanent
declaim to make a bombastic speech
decorous proper; in good taste; correct
defalcate to embezzle; to abscond with money
deleterious harmful (antonym: **beneficial; salubrious; salutary**)
delineate to describe; to portray; to sketch
deliquesce to melt away or dissolve; to become soft, esp. with age
delusion a deception; a false psychotic belief regarding oneself or others

demur to object; to take exception
denim a durable, twilled, usually cotton fabric woven with white filling thread [derived from *serge de Nime* (Nîmes, France)]
denouement the unfolding or outcome of a series of events
denounce to express strong disapproval, esp. publicly
depraved morally corrupt or evil
deprecate to play down; to belittle
depredate to lay waste; to plunder
desiccate to dry out
despot a ruler with absolute power
desultory lacking plan, regularity, or purpose; random
dexterous mentally skillful; artful; clever
dialectic logical argumentation
diametric completely opposed; at opposite extremes
diaphanous sheer; extremely delicate
diatribe a bitter denunciation (antonym: **panegyric**)
dichotomy division, esp. into two contradictory groups
didactic intended to teach, moralize, or preach
diffident shy; lacking in self-confidence
dilatory tending to cause delay (antonym: **expeditious**)
dilettante one who is involved in a variety of things, none of them seriously; dabbler
diminution a decrease; a lessening
dint a force; a power
disavow to deny
discomfit to confuse, to deject; to frustrate; to deceive
discourse to converse; to discuss formally
disingenuous lacking in candor
disinterested unbiased
dissemble to feign or pretend
dissenter one who goes against an opinion; nonconformist
dissuade to persuade someone not to do something
djellabah a loose-fitting gown worn in North Africa (see also **burnoose**)
doctrinaire dogmatic
doggerel comic, loose verse
dolt a stupid person
doughty fearless; valiant
draconian severe (as a code of laws); cruel
dray a vehicle used to haul goods
  teamster a person who drives a truck as an occupation
ductile malleable
dunce a dull-witted or stupid person [derived from John Duns Scotus, whose writings were ridiculed in the 16th century]
duplicity concealment of one's true intentions by misleading words or actions; deception
ebullient lively; enthusiastic; boiling up
eclectic selecting from many sources what seems to be the best; catholic
ecumenical (1) having to do with a body of churches; (2) worldwide or general in extent or application
edification instruction; improvement; enlightenment
efface to make indistinct by wearing away; to erase or remove
effervescent lively; bubbly (antonym: **effete**)

effete exhausted; worn-out (antonym: **effervescent)**
effluvium a disagreeable or noxious vapor; escaping gas
effusive overflowing; very demonstrative
egregious conspicuously bad; flagrant
egress (1) *n.* exit; (2) *v.* to go out from
elan dash; vigorous spirit
elegy a lament for the dead
elucidate to shed light upon; to make clear
emanate to send out; to emit
eminent prominent; famous; standing above others in some quality or position
endue to provide; to endow
enervate to exhaust, weaken, or unnerve (antonym: **invigorate)**
engender to bring into being; to produce
enigma a baffling situation; something that is hard to explain or solve
ephemeral lasting a short time; transient
epiphany a sudden, and often divine, enlightenment or realization
epitome a typical or ideal example
equivocal ambiguous; deliberately confusing; able to be interpreted in more than one way
erratic unpredictable; wandering; arbitrary (antonym: **static; stable**)
eschew to avoid; to shun
euphemism (1) the substitution of a positive expression for something that may be interpreted as negative or distasteful; (2) the expression that is substituted
evanescent fleeting; hardly visible; ephemeral
exacerbate to make more violent or more severe (antonym: **assuage; appease**)
exculpate to exonerate; to clear of guilt or blame
exigent urgent; requiring prompt action; taxing
expedite to speed up; to hasten
explicate to explain
expunge to strike out; to obliterate or erase
facetious humorous; not serious
factitious artificial; sham (antonym: **authentic**)
fagoting a type of embroidery
fallacious erroneous; deceiving; misleading
fallible capable of making a mistake or error
fastidious hard to please; fickle
fatuous silly; inane
fealty allegiance
feasible practical; workable
feckless worthless; feeble
fecund fruitful; fertile
fervid very hot; intense in feeling or emotion; impassioned
fetid having an offensive odor
vapid flat; uninteresting; insipid
fetish (1) a charm; a talisman; an amulet; an object thought to deflect evil or bring luck; (2) a fixation; an object of obsessive desire; a preoccupation
fiduciary a trustee
fitful irregular; spasmodic
flaccid limp; flabby (antonym: **resilient)**
flag to weaken; to slow down

flagon a flask with a handle and lid
tureen a casserole or bowl usually used to serve soup
foible a minor flaw or shortcoming in character; a weakness
foment to instigate, incite, or arouse
foray (1) *v.* to ravage for spoils; to pillage; (2) *n.* sudden, sometimes brief, invasion
forbear an ancestor or forefather
fortuitous happening by chance; unplanned
fractious unruly; quarrelsome
franchise the right to vote; a special privilege granted to a few; the right to market certain goods in a particular region
fraught laden; charged
frenetic frantic; frenzied
froward habitually disobedient; not willing to compromise
frugal economical; thrifty; sparing
fuchsia vivid reddish purple
fugacious disappearing after a short time; short-lived; evanescent
fulminate to denounce; to send forth invectives; to explode
fulsome (1) abundant; copious; (2) morally offensive; disgusting
furtive sly; shifty
gainsay to deny; to contradict
galvanize (1) to stimulate or excite; (2) to coat with zinc
gamut the entire range
garner to collect; to accumulate
garrote to strangle and rob
garrulous wordy; extremely talkative; gabby (antonym: **taciturn**)
gauche lacking social grace; crude; awkward
gaunt excessively thin; lean
gelding a castrated male horse
genre an artistic category or type
genuflect to go down on one's knee; to kneel, usu. in obedience or respect
germane closely related; relevant; fitting
glabrous smooth; referring to a surface without hair or projections
hirsute roughly hairy
goad to urge, egg on, or incite to do something (antonym: **curb**)
gorgon one of three snake-haired sisters whose glance turned the beholder into stone
gourmand one who eats and drinks excessively; glutton
gratuitous not required by the circumstances; unwarranted; unnecessary
gregarious liking companionship; sociable
griffin a mythical animal having the head and wings of an eagle and the body and legs of a lion
chimera (1) a fire-breathing monster with the head of a lion, the body of a goat, and the tail of a serpent; (2) illusion or mental fabrication.
minotaur a monster, half man and half bull, confined in a labyrinth
guffaw a loud, boisterous burst of laughter
guile deceitful cunning; cleverness
gulch a deep pit; a ravine
hackneyed overused; trite; commonplace
haiku a type of unrhymed Japanese poem consisting of three lines
halcyon peaceful; tranquil
harangue a ranting speech without much real meaning

harbinger someone or something that foreshadows what is to come
Hellene a native or inhabitant of Greece
heretic one who goes against an established religion or belief; nonconformist
hermeneutics the study of principles of interpretation (e.g., of the Bible)
hermetic sealed off from external influence; airtight; abstruse or occult
herpetophobia the fear of snakes
hiatus a gap or interruption in time or in a continuum
hibernate to spend the winter in a dormant, inactive state
hierarchy a graded or ranked classification determined on the basis of age, economic status, or class
hirsute hairy (antonym: **glabrous**)
hoary gray or white with age
homily an inspirational discourse; a sermon
homogeneous of uniform structure or composition
homophobia the fear of homosexuals
homophones words that sound alike but have different meanings
homonyms homophones; also, words that are spelled the same but have different meanings (e.g., *cleave, quail, bear*)
hone to sharpen
hyaline transparent or almost so; glassy
hybrid anything that is the product of at least two different sources
hydroponics cultivation of plants in liquid nutrients
hyperbole an exaggeration
hypertrophy an exaggerated increase or complexity
hypocritical pretending to have qualities or virtues that are not possessed; dissembling
hypothetical based on conjecture; conditional
empirical based on expertise, observation, or experimental evidence
iconoclast one who destroys religious images or attacks established beliefs
vandal one who destroys property
idyllic carefree and lighthearted; peaceful
igneous referring to rock formed from molten magma; volcanic
metamorphic referring to rock formed from sedimentary rock and changed through pressure or heat
ignominious infamous; despicable
imbue to permeate or influence
imminent about to happen (usu. referring to something threatening)
immiscible incapable of being mixed
immutable not susceptible to change
impassive apathetic; expressionless
impecunious having little or no money
impermeable impervious; not permitting passage through
impolitic unwise; injudicious
imprecate to curse
improvident not providing for the future; careless
prescient having foresight or foreknowledge of the future
impugn to attack, esp. as false or lacking integrity
inanition a loss of vitality from lack of food and water
incarnadine blood red
inchoate beginning; insipient; only imperfectly formed
incipient just beginning; in the early stages; commencing
incisive keen; direct; decisive

incommodious troublesome; inconvenient
incongruous not like the others in a group; out of place; incompatible
incontrovertible unquestionable; indisputable
incorrigible unruly; delinquent
inculcate to teach and impress by repetition
indemnify (1) to secure against loss; (2) to compensate for hurt or loss
indigenous having originated naturally in a particular environment
indigent impoverished
induction (1) an initiation into military service; (2) reasoning from parts to whole
ordination an initiation into religious service
ineluctable inescapable; inevitable
inimical hostile; unfriendly (antonym: **amicable**)
iniquitous vicious; wicked
innuendo a veiled allusion; insinuation
insurgent a person who revolts against established authority
intractable hard to manage; unruly; obstinate
intransigent stubborn; uncompromising
intrepid fearless (antonym: **timorous**)
inure to accustom to accept something undesirable; to habituate
invective insulting or abusive language
invidious offensive; envious; obnoxious
irascible easily angered; choleric; malevolent
jalousie a type of blind or shutter having adjustable slats or louvers and usu. made of glass
jargon specialized terminology of a certain group; a lingo
jejune immature; juvenile
jenny a female donkey
jettison to sacrifice cargo to lighten a ship or vehicle
jetty a projection or structure extending into a body of water
jezebel a shameless, brazen woman
jocose humorous; witty
jocular habitually happy or cheerful
jocund gay; cheerful
judicious wise; sagacious; prudent
junk (1) trash; something that is not worth saving; (2) a type of Chinese ship
junta a political group or committee, esp. after a revolution
juxtapose to place right next to something
kaleidoscope (1) a succession of changing patterns or scenes; (2) a changing pattern or scene
kindle to activate or inspire; to arouse
kindred (1) *n.* relatives; kinship; (2) *adj.* similar in nature; like
kinetic related to motion
knave a sly, deceitful man or boy
kudos praise; compliments
labyrinth a place full of intricate passageways; something extremely complex or intricate
laconic concise (antonym: **verbose; redundant)**
lambent flickering; softly bright or radiant, as a candle
lampoon harsh, satirical writing, usu. attacking an individual
lascivious lewd; lustful; wanton
lassitude fatigue; weariness (antonym: **alacrity**)

laudable worthy of praise
lethargic slow moving; sluggish
levity lightness; lack of seriousness; frivolity
libertine a person who is not restrained by convention or morality
licentious lacking moral restraints, esp. sexual ones; lustful
ligneous woodlike
limpid clear and simple in style; transparent; serene and untroubled
  lucid clear; sane; translucent; luminous
  pellucid reflecting light evenly; easy to understand
litigate to try in court; to contest in law
littoral relating to the shore or coastal region
loggia a roofed, open gallery, like a porch
loquacious talkative
lucre monetary gain; profit
ludicrous laughable; ridiculous
lugubrious gloomy; sorrowful
lurid (1) gruesome; shocking; (2) ghastly pale
magenta deep purplish red
malefactor an evil-doer; a criminal
malfeasance wrongdoing; official misconduct
malignant evil; injurious; tending to produce death (antonym: **benign**)
mandatory necessary; obligatory
marred injured; blemished; damaged
martinet a strict disciplinarian
masticate to chew
maudlin foolishly sentimental or morose
maverick a rebel; a nonconformist
megalomaniac one who exhibits delusions of omnipotence or grandeur
mercurial quickly changing; inconstant
meretricious attractive only on the surface; superficial; pretentious
meticulous extremely concerned with details; well organized
miasma a depleting or corrupting influence or atmosphere
millenium a thousand years
miscreant a heretic; a villain; one who commits illegal acts
misogynistic characterized by hatred of women
mitigate to soften; to lessen the severity of
moot questionable; debatable
mordant biting in manner or style; incisive
motility movement
munificent lavish; generous; liberal
nadir (1) the lowest point; (2) a point in the sky opposite the zenith
naiad a water nymph
napery table linens
necromancy magic; witchcraft
  chiromancy palmistry
necrophobia the fear of death
necropolis a cemetery
nefarious wicked; vile
nexus a connection or link
niggardly stingy
noisome offensive; harmful

nomenclature a standardized system of symbols for a particular subject, usu. art or science
nonfeasance failure to perform an act that should have been completed
notorious widely and unfavorably known
nuance a subtle distinction, variation, or quality
nugatory inconsequential; trifling
nullify to void legally; to make of no consequence
numismatist one who studies and collects coins and tokens
nuncupative not written; oral
nyctophobia the fear of darkness
obdurate persistent; unyielding
obfuscate to confuse (antonym: **clarify**)
objurgate to denounce harshly; to declaim; to castigate
obliterate to destroy completely; to cause to disappear
obloquy (1) abusive language; (2) bad repute
obscurant tending to make obscure
obsequious obedient; subservient
sycophant a servile, self-seeking flatterer
obtrude to force, usu. oneself or one's ideas on another without request
ocher earthy yellow or red
ochlophobia the fear of crowds
officious meddling; interfering
olfactory relating to the sense of smell
oligarchy form of government in which control is placed in the hands of a few, esp. associated with corruption
omnipotent all-powerful
omnipresent being all places at once
omniscient knowing everything
omnivore one who eats both animals and vegetables
onomatopoeia the use of words whose sounds convey their meanings (e.g., *buzz, hiss*)
ontogeny the development of an organism
onus a burden; an obligation
ophidiophobia the fear of snakes
opprobrium disgrace due to a shameful act
opus a major work, esp. a set of musical compositions
ornithophobia the fear of birds
oscillate to swing back and forth; to vary
osmosis diffusion through a membrane
ossify to become hard as a bone
ostentatious showy; pretentious
oviparous producing eggs that hatch outside the maternal body
palindrome a word, sentence, or number that reads the same backward and forward (e.g., *mom*)
palliate to cover up with excuses; to extenuate
panegyric high praise; a tribute; an encomium (antonym: **diatribe**)
paradigm an example; a pattern; an archetype
paradox (1) something true that appears to be false; (2) something false that appears to be logical
pariah an outcast
parry (1) to ward off; (2) to escape by dodging

parsimony the quality of being careful with money; thrift (antonym: **extravagance**)
partisan one who is committed to a particular person, cause, or idea
parvenu one recently risen to an unaccustomed position and not yet possessing the requisite dignity or characteristics; upstart
paucity a small amount; a scarcity
pecuniary having to do with money
pedantic characterized by an ostentatious display of learning
pedometer an instrument used to measure the distance walked
penultimate next to last
peremptory precluding a right of action, delay, or debate; admitting of no contradiction
perfidious faithless; disloyal; treacherous
peripatetic wandering; itinerant
peruse to read carefully; to study
pervade to spread throughout
petulant ill-tempered; irritable; fractious
philatelist one who studies and collects stamps
  -phile a love of or affinity for (e.g., *philogyny*: love of women)
  -phobe a fear of or aversion to
philistine (1) characterized by material rather than spiritual or artistic values; (2) narrow-minded or uninformed with respect to a specific topic area
piscatorial of or relating to fish
platen (1) a roller on a typewriter; (2) a flat plate
platitude the state of being dull, banal, or trite
plethora a superfluity; an excess
plumb *n.* a lead weight used to find the true vertical; (2) *v.* to measure the depth of; to fathom
polemic strong argument in refutation of another; disputation; practice of engaging in controversy
poltroon a coward
potlatch (1) a ceremonial feast, with gifts, of northwest coast Indians; (2) a festival or celebration
precipitous steep
precocious exhibiting maturity at an early age
prescience the anticipation of upcoming events; foresight
  prevaricate to deviate from the truth; to lie
probity honesty; uprightness; rectitude
profusion a great amount; an abundance
prognosticate to forecast; to prophesy
propinquity closeness; proximity
proxy a person authorized to act for another (e.g., to vote corporate stock)
pseudonym a fictitious or pen name
  surname (1) a family name; (2) an added name or nickname
puce dark red
puerile childish; juvenile
pundit an expert; an authority; a critic; a savant
purloin to steal
purview a range of authority, competence, or responsibility; scope
pusillanimous cowardly; fearful
Pyrrhic usu. referring to a victory won at excessively high cost
quaff to drink heartily

quagmire a bog; a difficult or entrapping situation; a predicament
qualm (1) a sudden onset of illness, esp. of nausea; (2) a feeling of unease about a point of conscience
quandary a state of confusion or doubt
quell to suppress
querulous complaining; whining
quintessence the essence of something in its most concentrated form; the purest representative from a certain category
quisling a traitor [derived from Vidkum Quisling, a Norwegian who collaborated with the Nazis during World War II]
quittance a release from debt or obligation
quixotic foolishly impractical and idealistic; capricious
quizzical (1) eccentric; odd; (2) inquisitive; questioning
quondam former; sometime
quorum the minimum number of a group that must be present to conduct business legally
quotidian daily
rancorous with ill-will; with enmity (antonym: **benevolent**)
raze to demolish completely; to destroy
recalcitrant obstinately defiant of authority; resistant
recidivism repeated relapse, as in tendency to repeat criminal activity
reciprocal (1) mutual; shared; common; (2) inversely related
recondite obscure; concealed; incomprehensible; esoteric
recumbent lying down; leaning; resting
recusant marked by refusal to obey authority
redolent having a pleasing scent; fragrant
refurbish to freshen or make new; to renovate
relegate to assign to a place of insignificance; to banish
relume to light or light again; to rekindle; to reestablish
remonstrate to object; to protest
reprehend to voice disapproval of
reprobate a villain; an immoral person
repugnant distasteful; abhorrent; obnoxious (antonym: **congenial**)
rescind to take away; to remove
resilient able to recover easily from hardship or misfortune; flexible
revile to use abusive speech; to rail; to scold
ribald rude or offensive; indecent
risible capable of laughing or provoking laughter
rookery a breeding place among rocks for mammals (e.g., seals) or birds
roseate overoptimistic; cheerful
rotund round; plump; chubby
ruminate to reflect on something; to ponder
saboteur one who willfully hinders, through destruction or obstruction, industrial production or a nation's war effort
  fifth column supporters of an enemy that engage in sabotage within defense lines or national boundaries
sagacious wise; astute; perspicacious
salubrious healthy; promoting well-being; salutary (antonym: **deleterious**)
sanctimonious (1) devout; holy; (2) hypocritically devout or holy
sanction to authorize or approve
sanguine hopeful
sardonic disdainful; sarcastic

satiric using ridicule or sarcasm to convey criticism; lampooning
saturnine gloomy; sullen; morose
savant one with detailed knowledge in a specialized field
  prodigy highly talented child
  virtuoso one who is highly skilled in the practice of an art, esp. music
scintilla a minute trace or jot; an iota
  tittle a particle
sectarian of or relating to a sect or a smaller group within a larger group that adopts only certain beliefs; narrow-minded
sequester (1) to set apart from others; to segregate; (2) to confiscate
sidereal related to the stars; astral
sophomoric (literally "wise fool") believing one's level of knowledge and maturity to be higher than it actually is
soporific marked by, or causing, sleepiness or lethargy; drowsy
sordid wretched; vile; foul
spelunker one who studies and explores caves as a hobby
splenetic hot-tempered; easily angered
spurious false; forged; counterfeit
staid sedate; serious; grave
sterile unimaginative; unfruitful; bare (antonym: **fecund; fertile**)
stolid dull; unemotional; immovable
stoma, stomata a minute opening in outside surface of a plant (e.g., a leaf) for the passage of gases
striated referring to muscle with alternate light and dark bands, as opposed to smooth muscle
strident loud; harsh; grating
superfluous more than necessary; extra
surmise to imagine; to make inferences based on insufficient evidence
surreptitious secret; covert (antonym: **brazen; overt**)
sybaritic voluptuous; sensual
sycophant servile flatterer; parasite
synthesis the combination of parts to form a whole, or of thesis and antithesis to form a higher truth
tacit unspoken; implied (antonym: **explicit**)
taciturn silent; having little inclination to talk (antonym: **garrulous**)
tactile perceptible by touch; tangible
tangential touching only the edge; marginally relevant
tangerine a deep orange to almost scarlet mandarin orange [derived from Tangiers, Morocco]
tawdry appearing gaudy or cheap
temerity audacity; effrontery; boldness (antonym: **caution**)
temporal referring to time, as opposed to eternity; secular
tenet a doctrine upheld by members of an organization
tepid moderately warm; lukewarm
termagant a shrew; a nagging woman, as Xanthippe (Socrates' wife); a virago; an ogress; a harpy
terrestrial having to do with the earth
terse (1) polished; refined; (2) short and to the point; concise
therapeutic used in the treatment of diseases or disorders; curative
timbre the quality of a sound or tone, distinctive of a particular voice or instrument
timorous fearful; timid (antonym: **intrepid**)

tirade a long, intemperate speech; diatribe
torpid dormant; lacking energy; lethargic; apathetic; dull
vapid lacking vitality; flat; uninteresting
torque (1) *n*. a twisting or turning force; (2) *v*. to cause to rotate or twist
torrid oppressively hot
tort a civil wrong for which the injured party is entitled to compensation
tractable docile; malleable; obedient (antonym: **unruly**)
transient lasting only a short time; changing; ephemeral; transitory
trenchant (1) caustic; penetrating; (2) separate; distinct
triskaidekaphobia the fear of the number 13
truculent cruel; brutal; belligerent
turbid muddy
turpitude baseness; corruption; depravity
umbrage (1) a feeling of offense or annoyance; (2) a shadow; a hint; a suspicion
unctuous oily; smug; suave
undulate to move in wavelike motions; to fluctuate
unduly excessively
unequivocal clear; obvious; certain
ungainly hard to handle; unwieldy; clumsy
ungulate hooflike; referring to hoofed animals
urbane polished; polite or finished in manner
utopian referring to paradise or an impossible ideal
uxoricide the murder of one's wife
vacillate to waver; to fluctuate; to oscillate
vacuous stupid; lacking intelligence
vagrancy the state of being homeless (legally, a misdemeanor)
vapid insipid; spiritless
venal corruptible
venerate to honor
venial forgivable
verbose wordy (antonym: **laconic**)
viable (1) capable of living; (2) able to stand or develop independently
vicarious experienced through another medium; experienced through imaginary participation in the events of another's life
vilify to slander; to verbally abuse; to defame
virago a loud, overbearing woman; a termagant
viscous thick; having a gummy consistency
vitriolic caustic; biting
viviparous producing living young, as most mammals, some reptiles, and a few fishes
volatile easily aroused; explosive
volition choice or decision; will
voracious ravenous; gluttonous; insatiable
vulpine foxlike; crafty
wan pale; sickly
wanton flirtatious; lascivious
whet to stimulate; to incite; to make more intense, esp. an appetite
wizened shrunken and wrinkled with age
wright a worker, esp. in wood; used in combination with another word (e.g., *wheelwright*, *playwright*)
wroth intensely angry; incensed

xanthic yellowish
xenophobia the fear of strangers
yean to give birth, used of sheep or goats
yore time long past
yowl to cry out loudly; to wail
zealot one who is enthusiastic, sometimes fanatical, about a cause
zenith (1) the highest point ; (2) the highest point reached by a celestial body (antonym: **nadir**)

Special Collective Nouns

bed of roses
bevy of beauties
cache of jewels
clew of worms
clutch of eggs
coven of witches
covey of quails
drift of swans
gaggle of geese
kindle of kittens
leap of leopards
litter of puppies
lock of hair
muster of peacocks
parcel of penguins
pod or **gam** of whales
pride of lions
rafter of turkeys
shoal or **school** of fish
string of pearls
swarm of bees
walk of snails

-ology Words

The suffix *-ology* means the study of or the science of. The root of the word gives you the key to the field of study. The suffix *ist* added to the name of the field of study refers to someone who works in that area. For example, the root *herpe* means reptile. Herpetology is the study of reptiles, and a herpetologist is one who studies snakes.

In the following definitions, "the study of" or "the science of" is understood.

alalogy algae
anthropology human beings—their distributions, origins, classifications, physical characteristics, environmental and social relations, and cultures
archaeology remains of past human life and activities
axiology values and value judgments (e.g., in ethics)
bacteriology bacteria
biology living organisms and vital processes
cosmology nature, origin, structure, and space-time relationships of the universe
cryptology codes and ciphers
cytology cell and its functions
deontology ethics

enology wines and wine making
entomology insects
epistemology the nature, grounds, and limits of knowledge
eschatology end of the world
ethology animal behavior under natural conditions
etiology causes of phenomena
geology earth and its history
gerontology aging and the problems of the aged
hagiology saints and other revered persons
herpetology reptiles and amphibians
histology living tissue
homology similarity in structure (thought to be due to common origin)
horology measurement of time
ichthyology fishes
kinesiology principles of mechanics and anatomy in relation to human movement
limnology fresh waters
mammalogy mammals
morphology structures and forms of plants and animals; word formation in a language
mycology fungi
numismatology coins
oncology tumors
ontology nature and relations of being
ophthalmology structure, function, and diseases of the eye
ornithology birds
paleontology fossils
parasitology parasites and parasitism
pathology diseases
philology language, speech, linguistics, and literature
physiology functions and activities of living organisms
primatology primates, especially other than recent humans
radiology use of radiant energy (X rays, radium, etc.) in the diagnosis and treatment of disease
taxonomy classification of living organisms
teleology final causes or purpose in nature
thanatology death and dying
toxicology poisons, their effects, and the problems involved
urology urinary system
virology structure and function of viruses
zoology animals

Word Demons

Some words are frequently misused because they sound alike, are spelled almost the same, or are very close in meaning. The following is a list of such words. You should be familiar with the correct spelling, meaning, and use of each word.

adapt to change or adjust
When she moved to the foreign country, she had to adapt to new customs.
adept skilled
He was adept in all aspects of carpentry.
adopt to accept or embrace, to accept formally
The couple hope to adopt several children.
The council voted to adopt the new amendment.

adverse unfavorable, unfriendly, opposing
She overcame several adverse conditions to win the race.
averse opposed
The councilwoman was averse to the new proposal.

advice suggestion
The best advice I can give you is to read as much as you can.
advise to counsel, to give suggestions
We advise you to start studying for the test as soon as possible.

affect influence, be of importance to, produce an effect on
The rain will affect the picnic plans.
affect to make a pretense of, to fake, to feign
She affects a British accent.
effect result, consequence; to bring about, to produce
The farmers felt the effect of the drought.
The drought effected a major change in the farmers' life.

affront insult, offense
His comment was an affront to the speaker.
confront to face
He will confront the student with the evidence.

allusion reference to
The author uses several allusions to Greek mythology in his story.
illusion unreal image
She has the illusion that I like jazz; I don't.

apprise to let know, to inform
The judge will apprise the jury of the pertinent statutes.
appraise to estimate the value of
The painting was appraised at two million dollars.

chronic constant, long-lasting
Parking is a chronic problem in the inner city.
acute short-lived, perhaps severe
He had acute appendicitis.

coherent intelligible, meaningful, logical
The newscaster gave a coherent report of the accident.
inherent innate, essential, intrinsic
Freedom of speech is an inherent part of the Bill of Rights.

complacent contented
The students were complacent about their grades.
complaisant willing, obliging
All day long the complaisant horse pulled the vegetable cart.

complement to complete, to go well with
Two angles complement each other when they add up to 180 degrees.
Cranberries complement a turkey dinner.
compliment a remark of courtesy or respect, praise
I'd like to compliment you on the excellent job that you did.

continual repeated, happening often
His continual absence from classes resulted in his suspension.
continuous uninterrupted, ceaseless
The continuous hum of the machine gave her a headache.

credible believable, plausible
The child's story simply was not credible.
creditable worthy of credit or praise, commendable
The teacher did a creditable job in preparing the students for the test.
credulous ready to believe, gullible, easily convinced
The credulous woman accepted the neighbor's story without question.

denote to refer to explicitly
The word *black* denotes the characteristic of an object that reflects no color.
connote to suggest
The word *black* has been taken to connote wickedness or evil.

depredation sack, plunder, robbing
The effects of the Huns' depredation of the villages were obvious.
deprecation disapproval, disparagement
The deprecation of the new exhibit hall by all of the townspeople was disheartening to the architect.

detract to take away from, to diminish
The cracked sidewalks detract from the appearance of the house.
distract to divert, to turn away from
The student was unable to concentrate because the loud noises from the street distracted him.

discreet prudent, careful, tactful
The attorney was discreet in his questioning of the young girl.
discrete separate, distinct, separate
The party was composed of two discrete groups—the progressives and the conservatives.

disinterested impartial, having nothing to gain
The chairperson was completely disinterested in the outcome of the committee vote.
uninterested not interested in, unconcerned, incurious
The boy was completedly uninterested in the subjects he had to study.

elicit to draw out
She questioned him for an hour but was unable to elicit any information.
illicit unlawful, illegal
The police will crack down on all illicit parking.

eminent prominent, illustrious, preeminent
Gandhi was an eminent statesman.
imminent close at hand, impending
The jury's verdict is imminent.
immanent inherent, innate, intrinsic
Psychologists are studying behavior patterns to determine which are immanent and which are acquired.

farther to a greater distance
The runway was only one-half mile farther than the site of the plane crash.
further more, additionally (in time or degree)
The council will discuss the budget further in the next meeting.

fewer smaller in number
There are fewer students in school now than 10 years ago.
less more limited in amount
Inflation is less now than in the late 1970s.

flammable combustible, able to burn
inflammable combustible, able to burn
You must be careful when storing flammable material.
(The antonym of *flammable* and *inflammable* is *unflammable*.)

flout to scorn, to treat with disdain
Her unconventional dress flouted the guests' sensibilities.
flaunt to show off, to exhibit
The boy flaunted his new scout badge.

homogeneous of the same kind, uniform, unmixed, similar in structure
It was a homogeneous class, all the students having basically the same socioeconomic and educational background.
The classes were homogeneously grouped according to abilities.
heterogeneous mixed or varied in composition
The class was heterogeneous, with students from different economic and educational backgrounds.
The crowd outside the theater was a heterogeneous group of students and townspeople.

imply to hint, to suggest, to indicate
The teacher's frown implied that the girl's answer was wrong.
infer to conclude from known facts or premises
From the evidence presented, the judge inferred that the defendant was guilty.

ingenious clever
The ingenious monkey figured out how to reach the bananas by constructing a platform.
ingenuous frank, artless, naive
The ingenuous child told his grandmother that he didn't like her dress.

ludicrous ridiculous
Italian western movies may seem ludicrous to an American.
lugubrious gloomy
The music was lugubrious, suitable for a funeral.

perquisite privilege that comes with a job
Members of Congress receive mailing privileges as a perquisite.
prerequisite necessity, something required beforehand
Mathematics is a prerequisite for most physics courses.

precipitate to bring on, to hasten, to quicken
The Great Depression precipitated the rise of fascism in Germany.
precipitous steep
Prices during the inflation period rose precipitously.

persecute to harass, to badger, to victimize
The Puritans came to America after they were persecuted for their religious beliefs.
prosecute to put on trial, to indict, to bring legal action against
The state will prosecute him for drug trafficking.

perspective viewpoint
From the perspective of the Native American, land is sacred.
prospective future, expected
The prospective merger of the two companies caused a flurry of activity on the stock market.

precede to go in front of
An incubation period usually precedes the onset of the disease.
proceed to go ahead
After you reach the center of town, proceed three more blocks to the hotel.

prescribe to order or advise (as in medicine)
The physician will prescribe a drug to combat the infection.
proscribe to condemn, to disapprove, to outlaw
During the Middle Ages, the Catholic Church proscribed certain books by scientists.

supplement to add to something
He will supplement his regular school work with night and summer courses.
supplant to replace, to usurp the place of
Robots will supplant workers in some factories.

venal capable of being bribed, corrupt
The judge was accused of being venal and accepting large sums of money.

venial forgivable
His continual tardiness was often annoying but venial.

Selected Foreign Words and Phrases Used in English

addenda a list of additions (Latin)
ad hoc for a particular purpose (Latin)
agent provocateur one who incites another person or an organization (French)
alfresco outdoors (Italian)
alter ego a second self; a trusted friend (Latin)
amour-propre self-esteem (French)
au courant informed of the latest (French)
bête noire a strongly detested person or thing (French)
bon vivant an epicure; a lover of good living (French)
bravura a display of spirit and dash (Italian)
causus belli a pretext or reason that justifies or allegedly justifies an attack of war (Latin)
caveat emptor let the buyer beware (Latin)
chef d'oeuvre chief work; masterpiece (French)
comme il faut as it ought to be; proper (French)
contretemps an inopportune or embarrassing situation (French)
corpus delicti the evidence necessary to prove that a crime has been committed (Latin)
coup de grâce a final, decisive blow or event (French)
cul-de-sac a dead end (French)
de facto actual (Latin)
de jure technically (Latin)
de rigueur necessary, obligatory (French)
dernier cri the last word; the newest fashion (French)
déshabillé undressed or partially undressed (French)
enfant terrible a bad child; one whose behavior is embarrassing (French)
errata a list of errors (Latin)
ex cathedra by virtue of one's position or office (Latin)
idée fixe an idea that dominates one's mind, especially for a long time (French)
in extenso at full length (Latin)
in extremis near death (Latin)
ingenue the stage role of an ingenuous girl; a naive girl (French)
in loco parentis in the place of a parent; acting as a guardian (Latin)
in re in reference to (Latin)
insouciance indifference; lack of concern (French)
in vacuo in a vacuum (Latin)
junta group (usually military) that assumes leadership after a coup or overthrow of a government (Spanish)
laissez-faire a policy of free trade or noninterference (French)

mélange a mixture or medley, often of incongruous elements (French)
ménage a household (French)
mirabilis dictu wonderful to relate (Latin)
modus operandi a method of procedure, working, or operating (Latin)
ne plus ultra the highest point that can be attained; the acme (Latin)
noblesse oblige nobility obligates; the behavior and graciousness of the nobility (French)
nolo contendere no contest; legally, not contesting a charge against one, but without pleading guilty (Latin)
nom de plume a pen name (French)
non sequitur something that does not logically follow (Latin)
nuance a subtle distinction (French)
pax vobiscum peace be with you; peace (Latin)
persona non grata an unacceptable or unwelcome person (Latin)
pièce de resistance the main course or dish; the most valuable object (French)
presto rapidly, quickly (Italian)
prima facie on the face of; at first view (Latin)
pro bono publico for the public good (Latin)
pro forma done as a matter of form (Latin)
pro rata proportionally according to a factor (Latin)
pro tempore (pro tem) for the time being; temporarily (Latin)
punctilio a fine point; a minute detail of conduct (Italian)
quid pro quo something given or received for something else; substitute (Latin)
raison d'être reason for being (French)
rapprochement establishing a cordial relationship; developing mutual understanding (French)
rara avis an unusual specimen (Latin)
rendezvous an appointment for two or more people to meet at a particular place (French)
riposte a retort; a retaliatory verbal sally (French)
safari a trip or journey (Swahili)
salaam peace (as a salutation) (Arabic)
sanctum sanctorum the holy of holies; the office of an awesome person (Latin)
sang froid cold blood; self-possession, composure (French)
sine qua non indispensable (Latin)
soupçon suspicion; a little bit or trace, as in a recipe (French)
sui genera one of a kind (Latin)
tour de force a feat of strength, skill, or ingenuity (French)
vendetta a blood feud (Italian)
vis-à-vis face to face with; in relation to; as compared with (French)
zeitgeist the spirit of the times (German)

Alphabets and Their Characteristics

Alphabet	Characteristics/Comments
Cyrillic	Slavic and Russian languages
Cuneiform	Ancient Egyptian iconographic writing
Heiroglyphic	Ancient Egyptian ideographic writing
Devanagari	Indian writing with syllabic features
Greek	Ancient or modern; Greek alphabet
Hebrew	written right to left, no vowels
Arabic	written right to left, no vowels
Roman	used in Romance languages and English
ogham	Old Irish, 5th and 6th century, notches
rune	Germanic, from 3rd to 13th centuries

Geography

It is not possible to provide a review of basic geography here. Since questions involving name changes of countries and cities have appeared on some *MAT* exams, a table of such changes is given below.

Current Name	Previous Names
Angola	Portuguese West Africa
Bangladesh	East Pakistan
Belize	British Honduras
Cambodia	French Indo-China
Chad	French Equatorial Africa
Ethiopia	Abyssinia
Ghana	Gold Coast
Guyana	British Guiana
Ho Chi Minh City	Saigon
Indonesia	Netherlands East Indies
Iran	Persia
Iraq	Mesopotamia, Babylon, Assyria
Istanbul	Constantinople
Laos	French Indo-China

Current Name	Previous Names
Madagascar	Malagasy
Namibia	South West Africa
Niger	French West Africa
Petrograd	Leningrad, Petrograd
Santo Domingo	Trujillo
Sri Lanka	Ceylon
Surinam	Dutch Guiana
Thailand	Siam
Volgograd	Stalingrad; Tsaritsyn
Zaire	Congo
Zambia	Northern Rhodesia
Zimbabwe	Rhodesia

History

MAT analogies may include the names of people, events, wars, treaties, conferences, and documents important in U.S. and world history. The following may serve as a quick review.

Explorers

Amundsen (Norwegian) was first to reach South Pole and to fly over North Pole
Balboa (Spanish) Pacific Ocean
Cabot (English) explored North America
Coronado (Spanish) mythical city of Cibola, SW region of the U.S.
Cortes (Spanish) Mexico, Aztec nation
Cartier (French) St. Lawrence river region
De Soto (Spanish) Cuba, Florida, SE region of U.S.
Diaz (Portuguese) Cape of Good Hope
Drake (British) circumnavigated the globe; helped defeat Spanish Armada
Hudson (British) Hudson River, Hudson Bay area
Peary (American) North Pole (disputed claim; prior claim of Fred Cook)
Pizarro (Spanish) Peru, Inca empire
Raleigh, Sir Walter (British) eastern coast of U.S.
Scott, Robert (British) Antartica, South Pole (prior claim of Amundsen)

Inventors

Daimler first high-speed internal-combustion engine
Diesel first internal-combustion engine using fuel oil instead of gasoline
Edison light bulb, phonograph

Franklin lightning rod
Gutenberg movable type, printing press
Marconi wireless radio
Montgolfier hot-air balloon
Stephenson first steam locomotive
Whitney interchangeable parts, cotton gin

Liberators or Unifiers

Bismarck Germany
Bolivar Venezuela, Peru, Bolivia
Garibaldi Italy
San Martin Peru, Chile (march across the Andes)
O'Higgins Chile

Major Wars

Knowledge of the most important events and treaties associated with major wars will help in taking the *MAT.* Below is a list of some major items that may be found in analogies.

The American Revolution
first battles—Lexington and Concord
major battles—Bunker Hill, Fort Ticonderoga, Saratoga, Valley Forge
Declaration of Independence—declared that colonies were free from England, 1776
Continental Congress—federal legislature of the 13 colonies under the Articles of Confederation
Constitution—replaced Articles of Confederation in 1789
end of war—surrender of British General Cornwallis to George Washington at Yorktown; treaty recognizing the United States as a separate nation signed in Paris

American Civil War
start of war—Harper's Ferry
first battles—Fort Sumter and Bull Run (both Confederate victories)
major battles—Antietam, Fredericksburg, Gettysburg, Shiloh (the Union named battles after towns; the Confederates named battles after streams), Sherman's March to the Sea, Vicksburg (great victory for Grant)
end of war—surrender of General Lee to General Grant at Appomatox

French Revolution
start of war—storming of the Bastille
important events/documents—Declaration of the Rights of Man and Citizen (Preamble to the Constitution), 1791; Reign of Terror, which ended 9 Thermidor (July 27, 1794) with the execution of Robespierre; coup d'etat of 18 Brumaire (November 9–10, 1799) whereby Napoleon I becomes consul
end of war—treaty of Amiens, France

Russian Civil War
conflicting sides—Bolsheviks (majority) vs. Mensheviks (minority)
leaders of opposing sides—Lenin and Trotsky (Reds) vs. Kerensky and Plekanov (Whites)

World War I
start of war—assassination of Archduke Ferdinand; sinking of *Lusitania* (British ship with American passengers) by the Germans led to U.S. entry into the war
major battles—Ypres, Marne, Verdun, Somme offensive
characteristics—trench warfare, use of poison gas
end of war—Treaty of Versailles; attempt to divide nations on basis of national self-determination; establishment of the League of Nations

World War II
major events—Munich Pact, policy of appeasement, associated with British Prime Minister Chamberlain
start of war—blitzkrieg over Poland; sinking of *Arizona* and other ships at Pearl Harbor attack in Honolulu led to U.S. declaration of war against Japan and Germany
major battles—Dunkirk, Ardennes, Alamein (North Africa), Stalingrad
characteristics—tank warfare, blitzkrieg, use of massive bombing by air force; development of atomic weapons
end of war—Japan surrenders unconditionally at Potsdam Conference

Other Conferences and Peace Treaties

Ghent, Belgium—end of War of 1812
Panmunjon, Korea—end of Korean War
Potsdam (German) Conference—meeting of Truman, Churchill (replaced by Atlee), and Stalin during World War II
Reykjavik Conference—Reagan-Gorbachev summit meeting
Vienna, Congress of—end of Napoleonic Wars
Yalta Conference—meeting of Roosevelt, Churchill, and Stalin during World War ll

Social Sciences

The following brief list of people and movements in the social sciences is intended as a quick review only.

Adler Austrian psychiatrist; inferiority complex
Binet and Simon French psychologists; development of IQ tests
Dewey American educator/philosopher; pragmatism
empiricism or logical positivism Russell, Wittgenstein, G.E. Moore
Erikson American psychologist; stage theory of development
Freud Austrian psychiatrist; sexual drive, Oedipus complex

Gall German anatomist/physiologist; study of nervous system and brain, founded pseudoscience of phrenology
Galton English scientist; belief in heredity as predeterminant force, IQ tests
Gestalt Wertheimer, Kohler, Koffka
Harlow American psychologist; importance of attachment for baby monkeys
Horney American psychiatrist; importance of social and cultural influences on behavior
Hume Scottish philosopher; use of induction
James American philosopher; pragmatism, functionalism
Jung Swiss psychiatrist; self-realization
Kant German philosopher; proposed categorical imperative
Kohlberg American psychologist; moral stages of development
Kohler German-American psychologist; Gestaltist, worked with chimps
Leibnitz German philosopher/mathematician; use of deduction
Mill English philosopher; used principle of utility
Pavlov Russian physiologist/psychologist; conditioning of reflexes, worked with dogs
Peirce American philosopher; pragmatist
Piaget Swiss psychologist; stage theory of intellectual development
Skinner American psychologist; behaviorist; studied effects of reinforcement on behavior; worked with rats, pigeons (Skinner box)
Thorndike American educator/psychologist; intelligence, IQ tests, worked with cats
Titchener American psychologist; structuralist
Watson American psychologist; behaviorist

Art and Architecture

Use the following list of the most important artists and architects and schools and movements in art history as a quick review. The names of artists associated with the movement or school and the works of particular artists are given in parentheses.

Important Artists, Architects, and Schools/Movements

abstract art art form that assumes that artistic values reside in form and color and are independent of the subject of the art or painting
abstract expressionism 1940s-to-1950s American art movement stressing spontaneous, nonrepresentational creation with emphasis on the paint itself; first truly American school of art (Pollock)
art deco 1920s-to-1930s art movement stressing highly decorative art, utilizing geometric, streamlined forms inspired by industrial design (Chrysler Building in New York City)
art nouveau 1895-to-1905 "new art" movement characterized by motifs of highly stylized flowing plants, curving lines, and fluent forms
ashcan school early 20th century school of American realist painters who abandoned idealized subjects for more sordid aspects of urban life

Audubon early 19th century American artist and illustrator known for his color engravings of birds (*Birds in America*)

Barbizon school mid-19th century group of landscape artists who rejected the classical and romantic to portray nature as they perceived it; forerunner of impressionism (Rousseau)

baroque late 16th-to-early 18th century movement, developed in Italy, that stressed grand theatrical effects and elaborate ornamentation (Palace of Versailles)

Bauhaus most famous school of architecture and design of modern times; founded in Germany in 1919; austere, geometric style (founder: Gropius; teachers: Klee and Kandinsky)

beaux arts architectural style, popular from 1890 to 1920, using formal and classical techniques

Bosch early 16th century painter considered perhaps the greatest master of fantasy ever (*Garden of Earthly Delights*)

Botticelli 15th century Italian Renaissance artist (*The Birth of Venus, St. Sebastian*)

Brancusi 19th century Romanian sculptor known for highly simplified archetypical human and animal forms (*The Kiss, Bird in Space*)

Bruegel (the Elder) 16th century Flemish painter known for peasant scenes and large landscapes; sometimes known as "Peasant Bruegel" (*Hunters in the Snow, The Harvesters*)

Byzantine art Eastern (Greek) art of the 5th to 15th centuries, characterized by Oriental motifs, formal design, and free use of gilding

Caldecott 19th century English illustrator known for his illustrations of children's books; the prestigious Caldecott Award is given annually for excellence in children's book illustration

Calder 20th century American sculptor and abstract painter best known for mobiles and stabiles (nonmoving sculptures) (*Lobster Trap and Fish Tail, Spiral*)

Cellini 16th century Florentine sculptor, goldsmith, and designer of coins and medals (*Perseus* bronze, gold saltcellar)

Cézanne 19th century French painter, often considered the forerunner of many 20th century art movements; romantic, impressionist, classical, and naturalistic influences are all condensed in his work (*Grande Baigneuses, Se Portrait, The Black Clock, Card Players*)

Chagall 20th century French painter of Russian-Jewish origin, forerunner of surrealism (*The Juggler, The Green Violinist*)

chiaroscuro the balance of light and shadow in a picture; used to describe works that are predominantly dark, like those of Rembrandt

classicism art attributed to ancient Greece and Rome, characterized by discipline, harmony, objectivity, and reason

cloisonné a process of enameling in which a design is displayed in strips of metal on a china or metal background, making channels, or cloisons, to hol the enamel colors

Cole 19th century American landscape painter; member of the Hudson River school of painting

collage a picture built up wholly or partly from pieces of paper, cloth, or othe material stuck on canvas or other surface; (early cubists, dadaists, Matisse)

Constable 19th century English landscape painter (*The Holy Wain*)

constructivism movement, since the 1920s, principally in Russia, involving the creation of three-dimensional art, using iron, glass, plastic, and other materials to express technological society (Calder's mobiles)

Copley 18th century American portrait painter

cubism 1907-to-1915 art movement, mainly French, characterized by fragmentation of reality; used geometric forms in nature as a departure from representational art; a reaction to impressionism (Picasso)

Currier and Ives 19th century American lithographers known for prints depicting American life

dada 1915-to-1923 international antiart movement reflecting cynicism by producing bizarre works that represented the absurd (*Mona Lisa with a Mustache*)

Dali 20th century Spanish painter, considered one of the foremost surrealists (*Premonition of the Civil War, Christ of St. John of the Cross, Persistence of Memory)*

Daumier 19th century French lithographer, cartoonist, and social satirist (*The Print Collector, The People of Justice)*

Degas late 19th–early 20th century French painter (*Study of a Dancer, Woman on Horseback*)

de Kooning 20th century Dutch abstract painter known for distorted shapes and tragic expressions *(Woman, I)*

Delacroix 19th century French painter of the Romantic period (*Liberty at the Barricades*)

Donatello 15th century Florentine sculptor; one of the founders of Italian Renaissance sculpture (*David, St. George Slaying the Dragon*)

Dürer late 15th–early 16th century German artist known for his woodcuts and engravings (*His Mother,* a charcoal drawing; *Adam and Eve*, an engraving; and *The Apocalypse,* a series of woodcuts)

engraving a method of multiplying prints. See also, **relief**, **intaglio**, and **lithography**.

Ernst 20th century German-born French artist, a leading surrealist and one of the founders of dada; known for his "reveries" (*Europe After the Rain, Mundus est Fabula*)

expressionism 20th century art in which the expression of the artist takes precedence over rational and faithful rendering of the subject matter; stress on emotions and inner visions (van Gogh, El Greco)

fauvism work of early 20th-century impressionists, characterized by strident color and distortion; first artistic revolution of the 20th century (Matisse, Roualt)

Fayum portrait realistic form of portraiture found on shrouds and mummy cases from the 1st to 4th centuries

fresco wall painting; painting on wet plaster

frieze middle section of a building, where relief sculpture was often executed

Fuller 20th century American avant-garde architect famous for his geodesic domes

futurism 1910 Italian art movement that stressed motion and sought to glorify the machine by painting and sculpting multitudes of moving parts

Gainsborough 18th century English painter of landscapes and portraits (*Blue Boy*)

gargoyle in Gothic architecture, a bizarre creature whose open mouth was used as a gutter to carry water away from the walls

Gauguin 19th century French painter best known for his depiction of simple life in Tahiti (*Indian Ocean Maiden*)

glazing a process of applying a transparent layer of oil paint over a solid one so that the color of the first layer is greatly modified

Gothic 12th-to-16th century style of architecture typical of northern Europe (cathedrals with elaborate architecture and stained glass panels)

Goya late 18th–early 19th century Spanish painter and printmaker (*Majas on a Balcony*)

Greco, El 16th century Spanish painter *(The Annunciation, The Burial of the Count of Orgaz)*

Hogarth 18th century English artist (*Signing the Marriage Contract*)

Holbein (the Younger) 16th century German Renaissance painter *(Dance of Death, Dead Christ)*

holograph an image in three dimensions created by a laser passing through a photographic film or plate without a camera

Homer late 19th century American painter and illustrator; Civil War illustrations

Hopper 20th century American artist known for bleak, surreal scenes depicting city life and the ennui of workers

Hudson River school mid-19th century American school of landscape painting known for its romantic scenes glorifying nature

impasto thick application of pigment to canvas

impressionism late 19th century French school that stressed visual impression; first of the modern art movements (Monet, Renoir, Degas)

intaglio engraving on stone to achieve a concave effect; opposite of cameo

Johns 20th century American pop artist known for blown-up images (*Flags, Targets*)

Kandinsky late 19th–early 20th century Russian-born German artist, one of the founders of the abstract movement; known for kinetic lines

kinetic art art that moves through magnets, motorized parts, etc.

Klee late 19th–early 20th century Swiss painter and etcher known for his whimsical works that sought to portray reality through its inner nature (*Inventions, Senecio*)

Leonardo da Vinci late 15th–early 16th century Italian artist and scientist; most versatile genius of the Renaissance (fresco: *The Last Supper*; paintings: *Mona Lisa*; notebook drawings of human anatomy)

lithography method of printing that uses wax and ink on hard plates

luminism American art movement associated with impressionism, concerned with the effect of light

Maillol late 19th–early 20th century French painter and sculptor (*The Three Graces, Seated Woman*)

Manet 19th century French painter who contributed much to the development of impressionism, although he himself was not a member of the group (*The Fifer, Guitarist*)

mannerism 1520s-to-1590s school of art and architecture characterized by the exotic and confusing and the distortion of the human form (El Greco, Vassari)

Matisse late 19th–early 20th century French artist known for his still-life subjects; a member of the fauve group and influenced by impressionism (*Jazz: Icarus, Fruits and Flowers*)

Michelangelo late 15th–early 16th century Italian sculptor, painter, architect, and poet who embodied the Renaissance (*Pieta, David, Madonna and Child,* ceiling of the Sistine Chapel)

Mies van der Rohe 20th century German-American architect known for clean-line skyscrapers of glass and metal and for steel-framed furniture (Barcelona chair)

minimal art contemporary art movement that rejects emotional expression and stresses restraint, understatement, and precision

Miró 20th century Spanish surrealist painter known for depicting fantasies (*Dutch Interior, Woman and Bird in the Moonlight*)

mobile a kinetic sculpture consisting of shapes cut from different materials and hung at different levels (Calder)

modern art art, since the 1850s, that has extricated itself from subject matter and stresses form

Modigliani late 19th–early 20th century Italian sculptor and painter known for his sad, elongated faces (*Seated Nude, The Brown Haired Girl*)

Mondrian late 19th–early 20th century Dutch abstract painter known for his geometric shapes (*Composition with Red, Yellow and Blue)*

Monet late 19th–early 20th century French painter, a leader of impressionism; known for seeing nature with an "objective eye" (*Water Lily* paintings)

montage sticking one layer over another, especially photographs applied to an unusual background; associated with cubists

Moore 20th century British sculptor known for large-scale abstract works and "truth to materials" doctrine (*Family Group*)

Moses (Grandma) late 19th–early 20th century American painter known for her simple depictions of New England life and landscapes

Murillo 17th century Spanish painter (*Immaculate Conception, Beggar Boy*)

Nast 19th century American illustrator and cartoonist known for his depictions of Tweed ring and Tammany Hall

naturalism late 19th century art movement that tried to depict humans and society true to life and in precise detail

neoclassicism 1790s-to-1830s rejection of rococo and a return to classical style; characterized by restraint and balance

O'Keeffe 20th century American painter known for her large New Mexican landscapes

op art 1960s American art movement derived from popular culture and commercial art, with art culled from everyday life (Warhol)

pastiche piece of art created in the style of a particular artist or movement but not faked, as in forgery

Picasso 20th century Spanish painter, sculptor, and printmaker considered one of the foremost artists of the 20th century. After his "Blue period" paintings of despairing people and his "Rose period" circus paintings, he turned to cubism and still later to surrealism and collage (*Guernica, Three Musicians, Artists*).

pointillism 1880s art form in which tiny dots of paint, when viewed from a distance, take on the shape of objects (Seurat)

Pollock 20th century American painter of the abstract expressionist school known for his large canvases (later cut up) that aim to create subconscious reality

Raphael early 16th century Italian painter who, along with Leonardo da Vinci and Michelangelo, is considered a creator of the Renaissance (*Transfiguration, St. Michael, Saint George and the Dragon*)

realism art form that attempts to search for the squalid and depressing with a style of strict attention to detail

relief sculpture that is not free standing; in having a background, the sculpture resembles a painting

Rembrandt 17th century Dutch painter who is best known for his portraits but who also did landscapes, Biblical subjects, and etchings (*Self Portrait with Sprouting Beard, Night Watch, The Anatomy Lesson of Dr. Nicolaes Tulp*)

Remington 19th century American painter, illustrator, and sculptor known for his romantic scenes of the American Old West

Renoir late 19th–early 20th century French painter; a founder of impressionism (*Moulin de la Galette, Les Grandes baigneuses*)

Reynolds 18th century British portrait painter

rococo 1730s-to-1780s style of European art that glorified asymmetrical ornamentation on paneling, porcelain, and jewelry to display a love of gaiety and elegance

Rodin late 19th–early 20th century French sculptor, the most famous sculptor of the late 19th century (*The Thinker, The Kiss*)

romanticism a current throughout art history that stresses the importance of fantasy and the imagination over reason and order

Rothko 20th century Russian-born American abstract expressionist painter known for his canvases of irregular shapes and bands of color

Rouault late 19th–early 20th century French expressionist painter (*The Apprentice, Christian Nocturne, The Holy Face*)

Rousseau 19th century French painter, one of the foremost primitive artists of the modern age (*The Sleeping Gypsy, The Dream*)

Rubens late 16th–early 17th century Flemish baroque painter, the most famous artist of northern Europe in his day (*The Judgment of Paris, Portrait of Helene Fourment, The Descent from the Cross*)

Sargent late 19th–early 20th century American portrait painter (*Lady Hamilton*)

serial art the repetition, possibly with slight variation, of a particular image in a work of art (Warhol)

serigraphy a type of silk screen painting

Seurat 19th century French artist who introduced pointillism (*Sunday Afternoon on the Island of La Grande Jatte*)

sfumato painting technique in which one tone is blended into another without an abrupt outline

still life the depiction of inanimate objects

surrealism art form, since 1924, that seeks to reveal psychological reality behind appearances; subject matter stresses dreams, fantasies, and the subconscious (Magritte, Dali, Miró)

symbolism 1885 movement in art that sought to depict the world through the visionary eye of dreams and illusions

Titian 16th century Italian artist, one of the greatest masters of the Renaissance (*Assumption, Venus of Urbino, Venus and Adonis*)

Toulouse-Lautrec 19th century French artist influenced by the impressionists (*Jane Avril, The Moulin Rouge*)

triptych three panels, usually arranged or joined by hinges so that the two wings can be folded over to cover the larger central panel

Turner late 18th–early 19th century British landscape artist (*Fighting Téméraire*

Utrillo late 19th–early 20 century French painter (*Sacré Coeur*)

van Dyck 17th century Flemish painter *(Charles I of England in Hunting Dress, Portrait of Charles V)*

van Eyck 15th century Flemish painter known for his perfection of the oil medium

van Gogh 19th century Dutch postimpressionist painter (*The Sunflowers, Starry Night, Self-Portrait)*

Velasquez 17th century Spanish painter (*The Maids of Honor, Pope Innocent X)*

Vermeer 17th century Dutch painter known for his domestic scenes (*Woman With a Water Jug, The Lacemaker*)

vignette decoration, often of leaves, adorning the first letter of a chapter or book section

Vuillard late 19th–early 20th century French postimpressionist painter (*Under the Trees*)

Warhol 20th century American pop artist (*Ten-Foot Flowers*)

Whistler 19th century American painter and etcher (*Whistler's Mother)*

Wood 20th century American regionalist painter famous for midwestern American themes (*American Gothic*)

Wren late 17th–early 18th century English architect known for his reconstruction of St. Paul's Cathedral and other parts of London

Wright 20th century American architect known for "organic architecture" (Taliesin West, Guggenheim Museum in New York City)

Wyeth, Andrew 20th century American painter known for his depictions of Chadds Ford, Pennsylvania, and Maine fishing village subjects (*Ground Hog Day)*

Famous Art Museums in the World

Guggenheim	New York
Hagia Sophia	Istanbul
Hermitage	Leningrad
Louvre	Paris
Metropolitan	New York
Pergamon	Berlin
Prado	Madrid
Rijks	Amsterdam
Tate	London
Tretyakov	Moscow
Uffizi	Florence

Literary Forms and Figures

The following is a list of many important writers and literary terms. The works of particular authors are given in parentheses.

Aeschylus earlist Greek dramatist (*Prometheus Bound, The Oresteia*)

allegory a narrative poem or prose work in which persons, events, and objects represent or stand for something else, frequently abstract ideas

alliteration the repetition of consonant sounds in two or more neighboring words or syllables

assonance the close repetition of similar vowel sounds

Aristophanes Greek playwright, master of Old Comedy (*Lysistrata, The Frogs*)

Austen English novelist (*Pride and Prejudice, Emma)*

Baldwin American author (*Go Tell It on the Mountain)*

Balzac French novelist (*The Human Comedy, Cousin Bette, Pere Goriot)*

Baudelaire French symbolist writer (*The Flowers of Evil)*

Beat Movement American writers of the 1950s who expressed their feelings of alienation from society (Kerouac, Ginsberg, Ferlinghetti*)*

Bellow American novelist (*Seize the Day, Herzog*)

Beyle, Marie-Henri (pseudonym **Stendhal**) one of the leading 19th century French novelists, famous for the psychological and political insight of his works (*The Red and the Black, The Charterhouse of Parma*)

bildungsroman a novel, usually autobiographical, that covers the principal subject's life from adolescence to maturity

Blair, Eric (pseudonym **George Orwell**) British novelist (*Animal Farm, 1984)*

Blake visionary English poet, engraver, and artist; early Romantic (*Songs of Innocence, Songs of Experience, The Marriage of Heaven and Hell*)

blank verse poetry in which each line must have 10 syllables and a specific rhythm (iambic pentameter); the lines are unrhymed

free verse a verse form without regular meter (Whitman's *Leaves of Grass* is written in free verse)

Boswell wrote famous biography of Samuel Johnson

Brontë sisters English authors (Charlotte, *Jane Eyre;* Emily, *Wuthering Heights*)

Browning, Elizabeth Barrett English poet, married to Robert Browning (*Sonnets from the Portuguese*)

Browning, Robert English poet, married to Elizabeth Barrett Browning, known for dramatic monologues (*My Last Duchess*)

Bryant American nature poet ("Thanatopsis")

Bunyan 17th century English writer of religious allegories (*Pilgrim's Progress*)

Byron English Romantic poet (*Childe Harold's Pilgrimage, Don Juan*)

Camus French existentialist writer (*The Stranger)*

canto a major division of a long poem

Cather American author, wrote about 1880s pioneering life in the Midwest (*O Pioneers!, My Antonia*)

Cervantes Spanish writer (*Don Quixote de la Mancha)*

Chaucer 14th century English author, often called the Father of English Poetry (*The Canterbury Tales*)

Chekhov Russian writer, best known for his plays (*The Cherry Orchard, The Three Sisters*)

Christie English mystery writer; created the famous detective Hercule Poirot

classicism literature characterized by balance, restraint, unity, and proportion; epitomized by Virgil, Pope, Homer

Clemens, Samuel (pseudonym **Mark Twain**) American author (*Tom Sawyer, Huckleberry Finn, A Connecticut Yankee in King Arthur's Court)*

Coleridge English Romantic poet; with Wordsworth, published *Lyrical Ballads*, which inaugurated the romantic movement in England (*The Rime of the Ancient Mariner*, "Kubla Khan," "Christabel")

Cooper 18th century American novelist who wrote about the American frontier (*Leather-Stocking Tales*, which includes *The Last of the Mohicans* and *The Deerslayer*)

couplet two successive rhyming lines of poetry, usually having the same meter

Dante (13th–early 14th century) considered the greatest Italian poet (*The Divine Comedy*, an allegory in verse consisting of 100 cantos)

deconstructionism contemporary literary criticism

Defoe early English novelist (*Robinson Crusoe, Moll Flanders*)

Dickens English novelist (*David Copperfield, A Tale of Two Cities, Oliver Twist, Nicholas Nickleby, A Christmas Carol*)

Dickinson one of the great American poets of the 19th century ("Because I Could Not Stop for Death")

Donne considered the greatest English metaphysical poet ("The Flea," "Death Be Not Proud")

Dos Passos American author, best known for his trilogy *U.S.A.* about the first 30 years of 20th century America

Dostoyevsky Russian novelist (*Crime and Punishment, The Brothers Karamazov, The Idiot*)

Doyle English author, creator of Sherlock Holmes and his aide, Watson

Dreiser American novelist associated with naturalist movement (*Sister Carrie, An American Tragedy*)

Dumas French novelist and dramatist (*The Three Musketeers, The Count of Monte Cristo*)

Eliot, George see **Mary Ann Evans**

Eliot, T. S. 20th century English (American born) poet, dramatist, and critic (*Prufrock and Other Observations, The Waste Land, Murder in the Cathedral*)

Emerson American poet and essayist; central figure in American transcendentalism

epistolary novel a novel in which the story is carried forward entirely through letters from one or more persons (Richardson's *Pamela*)

epithalamion or **epithalamium** a song or poem written to celebrate marriage

Euripides Greek tragic dramatist (*Medea*)

Evans, Mary Ann (pseudonym **George Eliot**) English novelist (*Middlemarch, The Mill on the Floss, Silas Marner*)

existentialism school of thought based on belief that people have free will and are therefore completely responsible for their actions (Sartre, Camus)

Faulkner 20th century American novelist; wrote about the South; known for his use of stream of consciousness (*The Sound and the Fury, As I Lay Dying, Absalom, Absalom!*)

Fielding early English novelist (*Tom Jones, Joseph Andrews*)

Fitzgerald considered the literary spokesperson for America's "Jazz Age" [the "Lost Generation"] (*This Side of Paradise, The Great Gatsby*)

Flaubert French novelist (*Madame Bovary*)

Frost most popular 20th century American poet ("Stopping by Woods on a Snowy Evening," "Mending Wall," "After Apple-Picking")

Gardener American writer, author of Perry Mason mysteries

genre a type or classification of literary work (e.g., tragedy, comedy, epic, satire, lyric, novel, essay, biography)

Goethe German poet, playwright, and novelist (*Faust,* a verse play in which the character Mephistopheles is the devil; *The Sorrows of Young Werther*, an epistolary novel)

Golding 20th century English author (*Lord of the Flies*)

Gray early English Romantic poet ("Elegy Written in a Country Churchyard")

haiku form of verse or poetry made up of 3 unrhymed lines containing 5, 7, and 5 syllables, respectively

sonnet 14-line poem with rigidly prescribed rhyme scheme

Hardy the last of England's great Victorian novelists (*Mayor of Casterbridge, Tess of the D'Urbervilles, Jude the Obscure, Far from the Madding Crowd, The Return of the Native*)

Hawthorne 19th century American author who set many of his stories against the somber background of Puritan New England (*The Scarlet Letter,* in which Hester Pryne is the adulteress, Arthur Dimmesdale the adulterer, and Roger Chillingworth the husband; *The House of the Seven Gables*)

Hemingway American author, noted for his crisp, economical, highly charged prose style and his ideals of courage, endurance, and honor (*A Farewell to Arms, For Whom the Bell Tolls, The Old Man and the Sea*)

Hersey American novelist, known for his works about World War II (*A Bell for Adano*)

Hesse German author (*Siddhartha, Steppenwolf, Narcissus and Goldmund, Magister Ludi*)

Homer the earliest Greek writer whose works have survived; his two major epics, *The Iliad* and *The Odyssey*, are both about events connected with the Trojan War

hubris excessive pride leading to the downfall of the hero in a tragic drama

Hugo French novelist (*The Hunchback of Notre Dame, Les Misérables*)

Huxley English novelist and critic (*Brave New World*)

hyperbole bold overstatement or extravagant exaggeration of fact, used for either serious or comic effect

Ibsen Norwegian playwright; considered the father of modern realistic drama (*A Doll's House, Hedda Gabler*)

irony a literary device in which the meaning stated is contrary to the one intended

James American author, known for his subtle psychological character studies (*The Turn of the Screw, The Ambassadors, Daisy Miller, Washington Square, The Portrait of a Lady*)

Johnson 18th century English writer, noted for Boswell's famous biography of him, as well as for his *Dictionary of the English Language, The Lives of the English Poets*, and *Rasselas*

Joyce Irish author, noted for use of interior monologue and stream of consciousness (*Ulysses, Portrait of the Artist as a Young Man, The Dubliners, Finnegan's Wake*)

Keats English Romantic poet ("Endymion," "Ode to a Nightingale," "Ode on a Grecian Urn," "La Belle Dame sans Merci")

kitsch a German word that literally means "trash" and frequently is applied to a work of poor quality that appeals to low-brow tastes

Lamb English essayist

lampoon in prose or poetry, a vicious character sketch or satire of a person

Lawrence English novelist, poet, and short-story writer (*Sons and Lovers, Lady Chatterley's Lover*)

Lewis early 20th century American novelist and social critic (*Main Street, Babbitt, Arrowsmith, Elmer Gantry*)

London American novelist and short-story writer, whose works deal romantically with elemental struggles for survival (*Call of the Wild*)

Longfellow most popular American poet of the 19th century (*Evangeline, Hiawatha*)

lost generation term coined by Gertrude Stein, originally referring to the many young American writers who gathered in Paris after World War I (Hemingway, Fitzgerald)

Mailer contemporary American novelist, essayist, and journalist (*The Naked and the Dead*)

Mann American (German-born) author (*Death in Venice, The Magic Mountain*)

Marlowe 16th century English poet and dramatist; he was the first to use blank verse on the stage, influenced Shakespeare (*Dr. Faustus, The Jew of Malta*)

Melville 19th century American novelist (*Moby Dick,* in which Ismael narrates the story of Captain Ahab's search for a white whale; *Billy Budd; Typee*)

Mencken the most influential American critic of the 1920s and early '30s

Miller, Arthur contemporary American dramatist (*Death of a Salesman, The Crucible, The Misfits*)

Miller, Henry 20th century American author (*Tropic of Cancer, Tropic of Capricorn*)

Milne English author, creator of *Winnie-the-Pooh*

Milton 17th century English poet (*Paradise Lost, Paradise Regained, Samson Agonistes*, all three written when he was blind)

Molière (stage name of **Jean Baptiste Poquelin**) the greatest French writer of comedy (*Tartuffe, The Misanthrope*)

motif the recurrence of a theme, word pattern, or character in a literary work

Nabokov American author (*Lolita, Invitation to a Beheading*)

naturalism a type of realistic fiction that developed in France, America, and England in the late 19th and early 20th centuries. It presupposes that human beings are like puppets, controlled completely by external and internal forces.

realism the idea that people have a measure of free will

octave a poetic stanza with eight lines

sestet a poetic stanza with six lines

ode a sustained lyric poem with a noble theme and intellectual tone

O'Neill one of the greatest American playwrights (*The Emperor Jones, Desire Under the Elms, Ah! Wilderness, The Iceman Cometh, Long Day's Journey Into Night*)

onomatopoeia a word whose sound is descriptive of its sense of meaning

Orwell see **Eric Blair**

Ovid Roman poet (*Metamorphoses, The Art of Love*)

oxymoron an expression that employs two opposing terms; for example, "benign neglect"

parable a story told to illustrate a moral truth or lesson

parody a humorous literary work that ridicules a serious work by imitating and exaggerating its style

personification a figure of speech that gives human forms and characteristics to abstractions, objects, animals, etc.

Petrarch 14th century Italian poet and scholar, known for his love poems and his discovery of classical authors (*Canzoniere [Book of Songs]*, a collection of 400 of his poems, most of them about a woman named Laura)

Poe 19th century American poet, critic, and short-story writer; the father of modern mystery and detective fiction ("The Murders in the Rue Morgue," "The Fall of the House of Usher," "The Raven")

Pope the greatest English poet of the early 1700s, brilliant satirist (*The Rape of the Lock, An Essay on Criticism, An Essay on Man*)

potboiler an inferior literary work written solely to provide the author with money

Pound American poet and critic, one of the most influential poets and controversial figures of the 20th century (*Cantos*)

Proust French author (*The Remembrance of Things Past*, the story of his life told as an allegorical search for truth)

Pushkin Russia's most celebrated poet; also wrote plays and other prose (*Eugene Onegin, The Bronze Horseman*)

Racine 17th century French classicist writer of tragic drama (*Phaedra, Andromache*)

roman à clef a novel based on real persons and events

romantic movement 19th century literary movement that began in England; contrasts with classicism; emphasizes passion rather than reason, and imagination and inspiration rather than logic (Blake, Wordsworth, Coleridge, Shelley, Keats, Byron)

Sandburg major 20th century American poet, also an historian and a biographer (*Abraham Lincoln*, "The Fog," "Chicago")

satire a type of literary work that uses sarcasm, wit, and irony to ridicule and expose the follies of mankind (*The Rape of the Lock, Gulliver's Travels*)

Scott late 18th–early 19th century Scottish novelist and poet; inventor of the historical novel (*The Lady of the Lake, Waverly, Ivanhoe*)

Shakespeare the towering figure in English literature, considered both the greatest dramatist and the greatest poet

Shaw English (Irish-born) author of satirical plays (*Pygmalion*, used as basis for *My Fair Lady; Man and Superman; Saint Joan*)

Shelley early 19th century English Romantic poet (*Prometheus Unbound, Adonais, Ode to the West Wind*)

simile figure of speech in which a comparison between two distinctly different things is indicated by the word *like* or *as* ("O my love is like a red, red rose")
metaphor figure of speech in which a statement of identity instead of comparison is made ("O my love is a red, red rose")

sonnet a poem of 14 iambic pentameter lines and a rigidly prescribed rhyme scheme; two types: Italian or Petrarchan, and English or Shakespearean

Sophocles Greek dramatist (*Oedipus the King, Antigone*)

Spenser great Elizabethan poet (*The Faerie Queene*)

Stein American author, central figure in a circle of outstanding artist and writer expatriots in Paris (*The Autobiography of Alice B. Toklas*)

Steinbeck 20th century American author, known for his powerful novels about agricultural workers (*The Grapes of Wrath, Of Mice and Men, East of Eden*)

Stendhal see **Marie-Henri Beyle**

Stevenson 19th century Scottish novelist, essayist, and poet; known for his adventure stories (*Treasure Island, Kidnapped, A Child's Garden of Verses*)

stream of consciousness literary style, employed especially by Joyce and Faulkner, that presents the inner thoughts of a character in an uneven, endless stream that simulates the character's consciousness

Swift late 17th–18th century English author, great satirist (*Gulliver's Travels,* "A Modest Proposal")

Thoreau American philosopher and writer; renowned for having lived the doctrines of transcendentalism ("Civil Disobedience," *Walden*)

Tolkien English author (*The Hobbit, The Lord of the Rings*)

Tolstoy 19th century Russian author, one of the world's greatest novelists (*War and Peace, Anna Karenina*)

transcendentalism school of thought based on belief in the essential unity of all creation, the innate goodness of human beings, and the supremacy of insight over logic and experience for the revelation of the deepest truths (Thoreau, Emerson)

Twain see **Samuel Clemens**

Updike contemporary American author (*Rabbit* series)

Vergil or **Virgil** greatest Roman poet; wrote the *Aeneid*, the epic that tells of the founding of Rome and describes the adventures of Aeneas, the legendary Trojan hero who founded the city

Victorian Age refers to 19th century England; typified by optimism and conservative ideals

Voltaire 18th century French author (*Candide*)

Walker, Alice 20th century American author (*The Color Purple*)

Whitman one of the great American poets; his poems sing the praise of America and democracy (*Leaves of Grass*, "O Captain! My Captain!" a poem on Lincoln's death)

Wilde late 19th century Irish playwright, poet, and novelist; attacked Victorian narrow-mindedness and complacency (*The Picture of Dorian Gray, The Importance of Being Earnest*)

Wilder American novelist and playwright (*The Bridge of San Luis Rey, Our Town, Matchmaker*, which was the basis for the Broadway musical *Hello, Dolly*)

Williams considered the greatest American playwright (*The Glass Menagerie, A Streetcar Named Desire, Cat on a Hot Tin Roof*)

Wolfe American author, known for his autobiographical novels (*Look Homeward, Angel; You Can't Go Home Again*)

Woolf English novelist and critic; with her husband Leonard, provided a center for the Bloomsbury Group, an informal group of famous intellectuals (*Mrs. Dalloway, To the Lighthouse*)

Wordsworth English romantic poet (*Lyrical Ballads, The Prelude*)

Wright 20th century American author, known for his description of black life in America (*Native Son, Black Boy*, his autobiography)

Yeats Irish poet and dramatist, considered by many the greatest poet of his time; led the Irish Literary Revival; his love for Maud Gonne, a beautiful Irish nationalist leader, influenced many of his plays and love lyrics

Zola leader of the French naturalistic school, which deemphasized the role of free will in human life (*Nana; J'accuse*, which helped win a new trial for Alfred Dreyfus)

Music

Use the following list of the most important composers and music terms as a quick review. The works of particular composers are given in parentheses.

adagio slow; a slow movement; slower than andante, faster than largo
allegro lively; rather fast, but not as fast as presto
alto a high adult male voice, employing falsetto; a lower female voice
andante at moderate speed, between allegro and adagio
aria air; song, especially a complex one in an opera or oratorio ("Batti, Batti" from Mozart's opera *Don Giovanni*)
arpeggio chord (e.g., on a piano) performed spread out
Bach late 17th–early 18th century German composer of baroque style; organ music and cantatas (*Brandenburg Concertos; St. Matthew Passion*)
bagatelle short, light piece, often for piano (Beethoven)
ballad old song, often a folk song, that tells a story, with the music repeated for each verse (Wagner's *The Flying Dutchman*)
ballet form of dancing, of Italian origin, that usually uses orchestra music, full stage decoration (*The Sleeping Beauty, Giselle, The Nutcracker*)
baroque 1600-to-1750 style of music (Monteverdi, Bach)
Bartók 20th century Hungarian composer who developed Hungarian national musical style; known for dissonant, atonal sounds (*Bluebeard's Castle*)
bass lowest male voice; the lower regions of musical pitch
Beethoven late 18th–early 19th century German composer, considered one of the greatest composers of all time (9 symphonies, including *Eroica, Pastoral*, the *Ninth* or *Choral*; piano concerto *Emperor*; opera *Fidelio*)
Berlioz 19th century French composer (*Fantastic Symphony*)
bolero Spanish dance
Borodin 19th century Russian composer (opera *Prince Igor*)
Bernstein 20th century American conductor and composer (*The Age of Anxiety* symphony; *West Side Story* musical)
Brahms 19th century German composer and pianist known for his symphonies, piano concertos, and chamber music (*First, Second, Third, Fourth symphonies*; song *Lullaby*)
Brandenburg Concertos six works by J.S. Bach for varying instrumental combinations
Bruckner 19th century Austrian composer and organist known for his symphonies
buffo (buffa) comic bass, as in an opera
cadence a progression of chords giving an effect of closing a sentence
cantata an extended choral work, with or without solo voices, and usually with orchestral accompaniment
Casals 20th century Spanish cellist
chamber music music intended for a room as distinct from a large hall or theater
chanson type of song popular in 14th-to-16th century France
Chopin 19th century Polish composer known for his piano works
chorale a type of traditional German hymn-tune for congregational use; an instrumental piece based on a chorale

chord a blending of two or more notes

classicism 1770s-to-1830s period; opposed to romanticism and folk or popular music (Haydn, Mozart, and Beethoven)

coda section of movement added as a rounding off rather than a structural necessity

coloratura agile, florid style of vocal music

concerto work making contrasted use of solo instruments and orchestra, generally in 3 movements (Beethoven, Mozart)

contralto lowest female singing range

Copland 20th century American composer and pianist (opera *The Tender Land, Music for the Theater,* many film scores)

counterpart simultaneous combination of 2 or more melodies to make musical sense

crescendo music that gradually becomes louder

Debussy late 19th–early 20th century French impressionist-style composer (opera *Pelleas and Melisande, The Afternoon of a Faun, La Mer*)

diminuendo music that slowly becomes softer

Dvorák 19th century Czech (Bohemian) composer known for his symphonies (*From the New World*)

étude an instrumental piece written to demonstrate the facility of the performer

fortissimo music played very loudly

fugue a musical composition in which one or two themes are repeated by different interweaving voices (Bach)

Gershwin 20th century American pianist and composer of popular music (*Rhapsody in Blue, An American in Paris*)

Grieg 19th century Norwegian composer and pianist (music for *Peer Gynt*)

Handel late 17th–early 18th century German baroque composer (oratorio *Messiah*, opera *Rinaldo*)

Haydn 18th century Austrian composer (symphonies *The Surprise* and *The Clock*, oratorios *The Creation* and *The Seasons*)

interval distance between 2 notes insofar as one is higher or lower than the other

Kodaly late 19th–20th century Hungarian composer; edited Hungarian folk songs (with Bartók) (*Psalmas Hungaricus*, opera *Háry Janos*)

largo slow

lento slow

libretto text of an opera or oratorio

liederkranz song-cycle (Schumann's *Liederkreis*)

Liszt 19th century Hungarian romantic-style pianist and composer (*Dante Sonata, The Preludes*)

madrigal 16th–17th century composition for several voices

Mahler late 19th–early 20th century Austrian composer and conductor (*Symphony of a Thousand*)

Mendelssohn 19th century German composer and conductor (operetta *Son and Stranger*, *Scottish* symphony, *Elijah*, overture to *Midsummer Night's Dream*)

Menotti 20th century Italian-American composer of opera (*Amahl and the Night Visitors*)

Milhaud 20th century French composer (operas *David* and *Christopher Columbus*, ballets *Jeux de printemps* and *Creation of the World*)

Monteverdi late 16th–early 17th century Italian composer (opera *La favola d'Orfeo)*

Mozart 18th century Austrian composer, mainly of operas and piano concertos (*Don Giovanni, The Marriage of Figaro, The Magic Flute, Cosi Fan Tutte*)

Mussorgsky 19th century Russian composer (operas *Boris Godunov, Pictures at an Exhibition, Night on Bald Mountain*)

nocturne melancholy composition for one or more instruments

opera drama in which all or most characters sing and music constitutes a principal element

opera buffa comic opera

oratorio religious composition for orchestra, chorus, and soloists

Orff 20th century German composer and conductor (operas: *Oedipus the Tyrant*, incidental music and choral works, *Songs of Catullus, Carmina Burana*)

Pachelbel 17th century German organist and composer of keyboard music

Paganini late 18th–early 19th century Italian violinist and composer (*Bell Rondo, The Carnival of Venice*)

presto fast

Prokofiev 20th century Russian composer and pianist (*Peter and the Wolf*)

Puccini late 19th–early 20th century Italian composer (operas *Madame Butterfly, La Bohème, Tosca*)

Rachmaninov late 19th–early 20th century Russian composer and pianist (*Rhapsody on a Theme of Paganini, The Isle of the Dead*)

Rameau 18th century French composer and organist (*Castor et Pollux*)

quartet four musical instruments played together

Ravel late 19th–early 20th century French composer (*Bolero, Gaspard de la Nuit, Spanish Rhapsody*)

Rodgers 20th century American composer of light music; worked with writers Hart and Hammerstein (*The Sound of Music, A Connecticut Yankee, Oklahoma!*)

rondo form of composition in which one section recurs intermittently

Rossini 19th century Italian composer (operas *The Barber of Seville, Othello, William Tell*)

Rubinstein 20th century Polish-born American pianist

Scarlatti late 17th–early 18th century Italian composer, chiefly of opera

Schönberg 20th century Austrian-American composer (*Ode to Napoleon*, opera *Moses and Aaron*)

Schubert, Franz 19th century Austrian composer (*Impromptus, Moments Musicaux*)

Schumann, Robert 19th century German composer and pianist

Scriabin late 19th–early 20th century Russian composer and pianist (*Divine Poem*)

Segovia 20th century Spanish classical guitarist

Shostakovich 20th century Russian composer (*Leningrad* symphony, opera *The Golden Age*, ballet *Songs of the Forests*)

Sibelius late 19th–early 20th century Finnish composer (*Finlandia*)

Smetana 19th century Czech composer and pianist (opera *The Bartered Bride*)

sonata instrumental musical composition usually of 3 or 4 movements (sonatina–short sonata)

soprano highest female voice

Sousa late 19th–early 20th century American band conductor and composer of marches (*Stars and Stripes Forever*)
Stern 20th century Russian-born American violinist
Stradivari family of renowned violin makers
Strauss, Johann 19th century Austrian violinist, conductor, and composer of waltzes (*The Blue Danube, Tales from the Vienna Woods*)
Strauss, Richard late 19th–early 20th century German composer and conductor (*Symphonic Poem*, operas *Salome, Elektra*)
Stravinsky 20th century Russian-born composer, pianist, and conductor (ballets *The Firebird, Petrushka*, and *The Rite of Spring*, opera *The Rake's Progress*)
symphony grand orchestral work in 4 movements
Tchaikovsky 19th century Russian composer (*Pathéthique* symphony, ballets *Swan Lake, The Sleeping Beauty, The Nutcracker*)
tenor highest normal male voice (apart from alto, which uses falsetto)
Verdi 19th century Italian composer (operas *Rigoletto, il Trovatore, Don Carlos, Falstaff, Aïda, Requiem*)
Vivaldi late 17th–early 18th century Italian violinist and composer (*The Four Seasons*)
Wagner 19th century German composer and conductor known for cycles of opera and use of leitmotif (operas *The Flying Dutchman, Tristan and Isolde, The Ring des Nibelungen*)
Weber late 18th–early 19th century German composer, conductor, and pianist (operas *Der Freischütz, Oberon*)
Weil 20th century German-born American composer (opera *The Threepenny Opera*)

Science

Detailed knowledge of the sciences is not required for the *MAT*. What is necessary is a general familiarity with the major people, theories, and terms of science. It is impossible to review biology, physics, chemistry, geology and the other sciences here. Below are a list of major scientists, a table of animal names that include vocabulary that may appear in an analogy, a brief explanation of classification terms, and a geologic time scale chart.

Important Scientists

Bequerel (French) discovered radioactivity
Copernicus (Polish) founded modern astronomy, declared that sun is center of solar system
Curie, Marie and **Pierre** (French) discovered radium, polonium
Darwin (English) natural selection, theory of evolution
Einstein (German) theory of relativity
Fermi (Italian-American) radioactivity, chain reactions, H-bomb
Fleming (British) discovered penicillin
Galen (ancient Greek) physician, studied personality
Galileo (Italian) astronomer and physicist, laws of gravity

Gauss (German) mathematician and astronomer, invented electric telegraph
Herschel (British) astronomer
Hippocrates (ancient Greek) physician, father of medicine (oath)
Jenner (British) physician, cowpox vaccine
Linnaeus (Swedish) devised system of classifying living organisms
Lister (British) surgeon, promoted antiseptic methods
Lamarck (French) naturalist, theory of inheritance of acquired characteristics
Lysenko (Soviet) geneticist, follower of Lamarck, led to demise of Soviet biology
Mendel (Austrian) botanist, transmission of characteristics in plants (genetics)
Pasteur (French) chemist, germ theory, use of heat to destroy bacteria
Ptolemy (Egyptian) astronomer, geocentric theory of solar system
Rutherford (British) physicist, radioactivity
Sabin (American) developed oral vaccine against polio
Salk (American) developed first vaccine against polio
Watson and **Crick** (British) biophysicists, discovered structure of DNA molecule (double helix)

Animal Names

Animal	Male	Female	Offspring	Adjective Form
bear			cub	ursine
cattle	bull steer (castrated)	cow	calf	bovine
chicken	rooster capon (castrated)	hen	chick	
deer	buck	doe	fawn	cervine
fox		vixen	cub	vulpine
goat		nanny	kid	
hog	boar	sow	shoat	
horse	gelding (castrated)	mare	foal, colt (m.) filly (f.)	equine
lion		lioness	cub	leonine
pig	boar	sow	piglet	porcine
sheep		ewe	lamb	ovine
swan	cob		cygnet	

Taxonomy

Taxonomy is the science of classifying living organisms. Each living organism is given a scientific name—for example, *Homo sapiens* for human beings—that consists of a genus name—in our example, *Homo*—and a species name—*sapiens*. Organisms are also grouped into larger taxa (singular, taxon) based on similarities in structure and evolutionary relationships. The following table lists the major taxonomic groups, briefly describes each, and provides an example.

Classification Group	Definition	Example
kingdom	largest classification unit; most scientists agree on a basic 5-kingdom system	Animalia
phylum	major division of a kingdom	Chordata
class	division of a phylum	Vertebrata
order	division of a class; contains one or more related families	Primates
family	division of an order; contains one or more related genera; members often show obvious similarities	Hominidae
genus	division of a family; contains one or more closely related species; part of scientific name (written with initial capital letter and italicized)	*Homo*
species	basic unit of classification; a group of organisms that can mate and produce offspring; second word of scientific name; always lower case and italicized	*sapiens*

Geologic Time Scale

Era	Periods	Life Forms
Azoic era	(earliest period after formation of the earth)	
Precambrian time:		
Archeozoic era		
Proterozoic era		spores, marine algae
Paleozoic era	Cambrian period	
	Ordovician	fishes
	Silurian	
	Devonian	amphibians
	Carboniferous	insects, reptiles, gymnosperm
	Permian	ferns
Mesozoic	Triassic	first dinosaurs
	Jurassic	reptiles dominant, first birds, mammals
	Cretacious	dinosaurs climax, disappear; flowering plants

Era	Periods	Life Forms
Cenozoic	Tertiary	
	Paleocene, Eocene, Oligocene, Miocene, Pliocene Epochs	earliest placental mammals modern mammals
	Quaternary	humankind
	Pleistocene epoch	(glacial)
	Holocene epoch	

Mythology

Adonis Greek god of male beauty
Aphrodite Greek goddess of love, beauty, and fertility. Roman counterpart: Venus; Norse counterpart: Freya
Apollo one of the twin children of Zeus (the other twin is Artemis); Greek god of prophecy, medicine, and music. Norse counterpart: Frey
Ares Greek god of war; son of Zeus and Hera. Roman counterpart: Mars
Artemis one of the twin children of Zeus (the other twin is Apollo); Greek goddess of the moon, woods, forest, animals, and the hunt. Roman counterpart: Diana
Asgard home of the Norse gods
Athena Greek goddess of wisdom, cities, and handicrafts; "sprung full-blown from the head of Zeus." Roman counterpart: Minerva
Balder Norse god of the sun. Greek counterpart: Helios
Ceres Roman god of grain. Greek counterpart: Demeter
Cronus and **Rhea** Greek gods; parents of the gods. Roman counterparts: Saturn and Ops
Demeter Greek goddess of harvest and fertility. Roman counterpart: Ceres
Diana Roman goddess of the moon, forest, animals, and the hunt. Greek counterpart: Artemis
Dionysus Greek god of wine and joy, son of Zeus. Roman counterpart: Bacchus
Frey Norse god; twin brother of Freyja. Greek counterpart: Apollo
Freyja Norse goddess; twin of Frey; goddess of love and fertility. Greek counterpart: Aphrodite
Frigga Norse goddess of heavens, love, and household; wife of Odin
Hades Greek ruler of the dead and god of the underworld. Roman counterpart: Pluto
Helios Greek sun god. Roman counterpart: Sol; Norse counterpart: Balder
Hera Greek goddess; sister and wife of Zeus and queen of the gods. Roman counterpart: Juno; Norse counterpart: Frigga
Hermes Greek messenger of the gods; symbol is caduceus. Roman counterpart: Mercury
Ishtar Babylonian goddess of love and war. Greek counterpart: Aphrodite

Juno Roman goddess; wife and sister of Jupiter. Greek counterpart: Hera; Norse counterpart: Frigga

Jupiter Roman king of the gods. Greek counterpart: Zeus; Norse counterpart: Odin

Mercury Roman messenger and god of commerce. Greek counterpart: Hermes

Minerva Roman goddess of wisdom, cities, and handicrafts; like Greek Athena, said to have sprung fullblown from king of the gods. Greek counterpart: Athena

Neptune Roman sea god. Greek counterpart: Poseidon; Norse counterpart: Njord

Njord Norse god of the sea. Greek counterpart: Poseidon; Roman counterpart: Neptune

Odin Norse king of the gods. Greek counterpart: Zeus; Roman counterpart: Jupiter

Olympus Home of the Greek gods

Pluto Roman ruler of the underworld. Greek counterpart: Hades

Poseidon Greek god of the sea; symbol is a trident. Roman counterpart: Neptune; Norse counterpart: Njord

Saturn and **Ops** Roman gods; parents of the gods. Greek counterparts: Cronus and Rhea

Thor Norse god of thunder

Valhalla Norse hall of heroes

Venus Roman goddess of love, good fortune, and vegetation. Greek counterpart: Aphrodite; Norse counterpart: Freyja

Zeus Greek king of the gods. Roman counterpart: Jupiter; Norse counterpart: Odin

Part Six The *Miller Analogies Test*

History of the *MAT*

The *MAT* was developed for use at the University of Minnesota, where it was first administered in 1926. At that time, its use was restricted to this university. However, the test received a great deal of attention from psychologists and educators, and it was subsequently made more widely available on a restricted basis. Today, it may be administered only at licensed centers, and distribution of the test booklets is carefully regulated. New forms of the test have been issued periodically over the years, each of which has test items of equal average difficulty and of similar content.

What the *MAT* Measures

Recognition of Relationships

According to the *Miller Analogies Test Manual* (1970), the "*Miller Analogies Test (MAT)* was developed to measure scholastic aptitude at the graduate school level. . . . The test items require the recognition of relationships rather than the display of enormous erudition [p. 3]."

As is often the case with standardized tests, theory is rosier than practice. While there is no question but that the "recognition of relationships" is required, its importance relative to that of plain (and some not so plain) knowledge (or "enormous erudition," if you prefer) is probably overstated in the Manual.

Vocabulary

Meer, Stein, and Geertsma (1955) investigated the relationship of *MAT* scores to scores on each subtest of the *Wechsler-Bellevue Intelligence Scale* (Wechsler, 1944), a former version of what has been among the most popular and highly respected intelligence tests (yes, some people actually do respect such things). These authors found by far the strongest relationship between scores on the *MAT* and scores on the Vocabulary subtest of the Wechsler-Bellevue. The second strongest relationship was with scores on the Information subtest. The correlation between scores on the *MAT* and those on the verbal reasoning (Similarities) subtest of the Wechsler-Bellevue was not statistically significant!

Although this study was conducted on a restricted population, and therefore must be interpreted with caution, it points out something you will soon discover on your own: Vocabulary and, to a lesser extent, general information play an important role in determining *MAT* scores. No matter how good you are at reasoning, you first have to recognize and comprehend the concepts with which you are supposed to reason. You will probably find some (if not many) items on which your difficulty does not involve reasoning with the concepts, but of understanding them in the first place.

In one respect, all of this is not as bad as it sounds. Numerous studies have found that vocabulary is the best single predictor both of general intelligence and of performance in a fairly wide variety of tasks. This fact will probably be of more comfort to those who view themselves as walking dictionaries (or even better, walking encyclopedias) than to those whose vocabularies haven't kept up with their razor-sharp reasoning abilities.

Acculturation What, then, does the *MAT* measure, if not pure verbal reasoning ability (whatever that is)? One word can probably describe this factor as well as a lot: *acculturation*. The test measures the extent to which an individual has become acculturated to the concepts of Western (and particularly white middle-class American) civilization, and to the language in which they are expressed. This statement has several implications:

1. Participants in other cultures will generally be at a disadvantage in taking the test. Although *no* test is genuinely culture-free, some are more culture-laden than others. The *MAT* is about as heavily culture-laden as any.
2. As stated above, reasoning ability is not sufficient for a high score, although it is necessary. Knowledge of sophisticated concepts is prerequisite for reasoning ability to come into play.
3. The *MAT* will be a good predictor of future performance to the extent that performance is dependent upon the comprehension and utilization of cultural concepts.

Just how good a predictor is the *MAT*? Let's take up that question now.

Success of the *MAT* as a Measuring Instrument

Many studies have looked at how well the *MAT* predicts graduate school performance. A much smaller number have looked at the test as a predictor of success in occupational settings. Since the number of such studies is limited, we shall be concerned only with research of the former kind.

A review of the literature on the validity of the *MAT* (how well it measures what it is supposed to measure) safely permits one uninformative generalization about the usefulness of the *MAT* in various types of situations: About the only way to find out how valid the *MAT* will be in a given situation is to try it and find out. There are no stunning and clear-cut patterns in the results, perhaps in part because what one school calls basket weaving another calls textile engineering. While situational generalizations are not possible, however, more global statements can be made.

Validity *On the average*, the *MAT* accounts for slightly more than 5% of the variance in various types of graduate school performance. In the large majority of studies, it accounts for more than 1%, but less than 15%, of this variance. This means that the *MAT* generally affords a low level of predictive accuracy to those who use it.

The best predictive scholastic aptitude tests account for up to 20% or even 25% of the variance in school performance, so that on this basis the *MAT* does not rank with the best tests as a predictor. However, these "best tests" tend to be predictors of high school and sometimes undergraduate grades. At this level, straightforward verbal ability tends to be as good a predictor as anything else. In graduate school, however, professors look for such exotic traits as creativity in designing experiments (in science) and level of rapport achieved with patients (in medicine). Even straightforward course work requires more complex combinations of abilities than are usually needed in high school and undergraduate programs. As a result, graduate school performance is harder to predict in part because all students who go on to graduate school tend to be high in ability, so there is not so much range in performance to predict!

It may surprise you to learn that, on the whole, the *MAT* is about as good a predictor of graduate school performance as any other test around, and that even undergraduate grades usually provide only a little better prediction. The simple fact is that *nothing* provides consistently good prediction of performance in graduate-level programs, and educators resort to the *MAT* and similar tests on the assumption that some prediction is better than none at all. This is true as long as the test results are not misused. If the test scores are considered in conjunction with various other sources of information, if they are interpreted as indicating a range rather than a specific level of ability, and if the limitations on their validity are fully appreciated, then they can be somewhat helpful in spite of their usually low predictive power. If the scores are misused, usually by their being overinterpreted, then they certainly illustrate an application of the maxim that "A little knowledge is a dangerous thing." Fortunately, gross misinterpretation is becoming increasingly rare as educators become more sophisticated in the use of standardized tests.

Now that you have become aware of some limitations surrounding *MAT* and other test scores, you won't feel it necessary to hide in a dark corner if your test score isn't what you'd hoped for, and you won't sell autographs (not quite yet, anyway) if your score is much better than you'd imagined possible. Your score can give you and others who interpret it properly some guidance as to how you might perform in graduate work or employment. Many other factors—motivation, study habits, intellectual curiosity, personal sense of well-being, and the like, as well as abilities not tapped by the *MAT*—will also enter into your future success in whatever program you enter.

Stability of *MAT* Scores

As the preceding section states, scores on a given form of the *MAT* usually account for only 1% to 15% of the variance in diverse criteria of performance in graduate school. However, there is something for which such scores usually account for 85% to 90% of the variance, and that is scores on another form of the *MAT*. There you have it. Scores on one form of the *MAT* are excellent predictors of scores on another form of the *MAT*. But you should realize just what this tidbit means. It means that, when a group of people take the test twice (a different form each time), their ranks within the group will probably not change much. However, even if their *ranks* in relation to each other remain stable, their scores may not. Most people gain around 5 points on a second administration. Does this mean you should take the test twice? Probably not. First, you will have capitalized on much of this *practice effect* by reading this book and working at the practice tests it contains. Second, educators and administrators using the test realize that people tend to gain in score from one testing to the next, and they are therefore likely to discount small gains. Large gains, however, are another story, and often indicate that for one reason or another, one of the scores is not representative of the candidate's true ability. In such cases, the higher score almost always counts as much as or more than the lower score. For this reason, if you feel reasonably confident that you were at some sort of disadvantage during the first administration, you may want to consider taking the test again. However, such retesting will be a waste of time and money unless the disadvantage was genuine. You should remember that, even if your score was not quite what you'd hoped for, it is only one of many factors considered in making most admissions, financial aid, and employment decisions.

What *MAT* Scores Mean

Your score on the *MAT* will be reported to you as a *raw score*—you are informed of the number of questions you answered correctly, which may range anywhere from zero to one hundred. Before learning what the score means, you should learn what it does *not* mean.

The first thing for you to do is to rid yourself of any preconceptions you may have about percentage scores. A frequent one is that 90–100% = A, 80–89% = B, 70–79% = C, 60–69% = D, and anything below that is failing. Unfortunately, some *MAT* preparation books foster rather than dispel such erroneous notions. For example, one such book provides five practice tests, and suggests that a score of 475 (95%) is excellent, 425 (85%) is good, 350 (70%) is passing, and anything less is failing. Forget it! These standards may or may not be appropriate for the practice tests in that particular book, but they have no conceivable relation to the *MAT.*

In the first place, there is no such thing as a failing score on the *MAT*. Although a very few institutions may establish cut-off scores (a practice of dubious merit), almost none rely on the *MAT* to the exclusion of other sources of information. Such total reliance would be irresponsible and counterproductive. Second, what is an excellent score in one program may be just average in another, and quite low in a third. *MAT* scores simply cannot be interpreted in absolute terms. They can be interpreted only in relation to those of other individuals applying to programs similar or identical to your own.

Because raw scores are virtually uninterpretable taken by themselves, the test publisher provides percentile equivalents for various groups of individuals who have taken the *MAT.* What is a percentile equivalent? It is the number of people out of 100 whose scores your own score exceeds. Thus, if your score places you in the 56th percentile, this means that your score was higher than those of 56% of the people who were in the particular reference group for which the percentiles were computed. In general terms, the middle score in a group is the 50th percentile, and the highest score is the 100th percentile.

How do raw scores on the *MAT* run when converted to percentile form? To give you an idea, an *Examinee's Report* (1988) gives the following raw score equivalents for the 25th, 50th, and 75th percentiles for applicants to graduate school:

		Percentile	
Proposed Graduate Major	**25**	**50**	**75**
psychology	41	54	66
education	34	47	60
natural sciences	35	50	64
social sciences	37	48	63
humanities	40	53	66
social work	38	50	62
nursing	39	50	61

These *norms* should make clear to you both the overall difficulty of the *MAT* (the scores are out of a maximum possible score of 100) and the importance of viewing raw scores relative to those of an appropriate norm group. Needless to say, norms vary widely not only from one subject area to another, but also from one institution to another.

Estimating Your *MAT* Score

Many students applying for admission and financial aid find themselves required to take one or more aptitude tests other than the *MAT*. One of the most frequently taken tests of this type is the *Graduate Record Examination* (*GRE*). A few studies have examined the relationship between scores on the two aptitude tests. The degree of relationship varies from study to study, but on the average the *MAT* accounts for about 50% of the variance in the *GRE* Verbal test. The degree of association with the Mathematics section of the *GRE* is invariably lower.

The degree of overlap between the *GRE* Verbal and the *MAT* is clearly not so high that one can reasonably say that the two tests measure the same thing. The two certainly measure similar abilities. Cureton and Scott (1967) studied scores of individuals on both tests, and developed a conversion formula that enables one to predict scores on one test from scores on the other. Thus, if you have taken the *GRE* Verbal, you can estimate what your *MAT* score will be; if you have taken the *MAT*, you can estimate your *GRE* Verbal score. The conversions can be accomplished through the following two equations, which are mathematically equivalent:

$$\text{MAT} = \frac{\text{GRE}-\text{V}}{6} - 36$$

$$\text{GRE-V} = 6(\text{MAT}) + 216$$

To predict your *MAT* score, divide your *GRE* Verbal score by 6 and subtract 36 points. To predict your *GRE* Verbal score, multiply your *MAT* score by 6 and add 216 points.

Should you choose to enter the uncertain world of the prediction game by using either of the above formulas, you must keep two points in mind. First, the two tests are *not* identical. These equations provide only *rough* estimates, and you shouldn't be surprised if the predictions are off. Second, the equations don't work well for *GRE* Verbal scores over 770, or *MAT* scores above 90. However, if either of your scores is at these levels, converting scores should be the last thing you have to worry about.

A Word of Caution

A final word of caution is in order with regard to the prediction of your *MAT* score. Obviously, one way to make this prediction is to average your scores on the practice tests in this book, but such a procedure is risky. Items on actual editions of the *MAT* are pretested by giving them as experimental items to large numbers of individuals who take the *MAT*. Only experimental items that precisely match older items are used on new forms of the test. The various forms of the *MAT* are thus referred to as *equated.*

Since the *MAT* is a restricted test, it was of course not possible to equate the practice tests in this book to actual *MAT* forms, and hence estimates of *MAT* scores obtained by averaging scores on these practice tests will be imprecise. Experience indicates that scores on the practice tests tend to run slightly lower than actual *MAT* scores. You might therefore look at your scores on these tests as conservative estimates of what you can expect your *MAT* score to be. Of course, in some cases, individuals may do worse on the actual test; the prediction game, as you know by now, is a very uncertain one. The important thing, however, is not that you go into the test knowing what your score will be (you'll find out just a few days after you take the test), but that you go in knowing that you will get a score that reflects your intellectual ability and not an inability to take tests. After working through this book, you can be confident that you will do your very best on the actual test.

A Note to Be Reread When You Get Your Score

If you did well, congratulations. You have good reason to be proud of yourself. The *MAT* is one of the most difficult ability tests around, and a high score is a genuine accomplishment.

If you didn't do as well as you'd hoped, don't despair. Follow the simple steps below:

STEP 1: Look back and observe how well the *MAT* predicts (or, rather, doesn't predict) graduate school performance. It's not that the *MAT* is worse than other similar tests. It's just that all of these tests don't predict that well. You should be feeling a little better already.

STEP 2: Ask your friendly local librarian for a copy of the January 1973, issue of *The American Psychologist*, and check out the article by David McClelland, "Testing for Competence Rather Than for 'Intelligence.' " McClelland's main point is simple. While aptitude tests provide some (but not much) prediction of performance in school, their ability to predict success in life (as measured by virtually any criterion except test scores and grades) is practically zero. So keep your test score in perspective. In the long run, it isn't that important.

References

Ace, M. E., & R. W. Dawis. (1973). Item structure as a determinant of item difficulty in verbal analogies. *Educational and Psychological Measurement, 33,* 143–149.

Bransford, J., & R. Stein. (1993). *The IDEAL Problem Solver: A Guide for Improving Thinking, Learning, and Creativity* (2nd ed.). New York: W. H. Freeman.

Cureton, E. E., & T. B. Scott. (1967). Equivalent scores for the Graduate Record Verbal and Miller Analogies Test. *Educational and Psychological Measurement, 27,* 611–615.

Examinee's report. *Miller Analogies Test.* (1988). San Antonio: The Psychological Corporation.

McClelland, D. C. (1973). Testing for competence rather than for "intelligence." *The American Psychologist, 28,* 1–14.

Meer, B., M. I. Stein, & R. Geertsma. (1955). An analysis of the Miller Analogies Test for a scientific population. *The American Psychologist, 10,* 33–34.

Miller Analogies Test Information Bulletin. (1986). San Antonio: The Psychological Corporation.

Miller, G. (1951). *Language and Communication*. New York: McGraw-Hill.

Preparing for the Miller Analogies Test. (1988). San Antonio: The Psychological Corporation.

Sternberg, R. J. (1977) Component processes in analogical reasoning. *Psychological Review, 84,* 353–378.

Sternberg, R. J. (1977). *Intelligence, Information Processing, and Analogical Reasoning. The Componential Analysis of Human Abilities.* Hillsdale, N. J.: Lawrence Erlbaum Associates.

Sternberg, R. J. (1986). *Intelligence Applied.* San Diego: Harcourt, Brace, Jovanovich.

Sternberg, R. J. (1988). *The Triarchic Mind.* New York: Viking-Penguin.

Sternberg, R. J. & R. K. Wagner. (1993). The g-ocentric view of intelligence and job performance is wrong. *Current Directions in Psychological Research, 2 (1),* 1–4.

Wechsler, D. (1944). *Measurement of Adult Intelligence.* Baltimore: Williams and Wilkins.

Willner, A. (1964). An experimental analysis of analogical reasoning. *Psychological Reports, 15,* 479–494.

Part Seven What Does It Mean to Be Intelligent?

Two boys are walking in a forest. They are quite different. The first boy's teachers think that he is smart, his parents think that he is smart, and, as a result, he thinks that he is smart. He has good test scores, good grades, and other good paper credentials that will get him far in his scholastic life.

Few people consider the second boy smart. His test scores are nothing great, his grades aren't so good, and his other paper credentials are, in general, marginal. At best, people would call him shrewd or street smart.

As the two boys walk through the forest, they encounter a problem, namely, a huge, furious, hungry-looking grizzly bear. It is charging straight at them.

The first boy, calculating that the grizzly bear will overtake them in 17.3 seconds, panics. In this state, he looks at the second boy, who is calmly taking off his hiking boots and putting on his jogging shoes.

The first boy says to the second boy, "You must be crazy. There is no way we are going to outrun that grizzly bear!"

The second boy replies, "That's true. But all I have to do is outrun you!"

In the preceding story, both boys are smart, but they are smart in different ways. This part of the book is about different ways of being smart and about different ways of using the smarts we have. All tests, including the *MAT*, measure only a small part of intelligence. Many people with modest test scores are nevertheless highly intelligent.

Styles of Intelligence

People can be smart in at least three major ways, and one of the tragedies of our system of education is that only one of them is typically valued on tests and in the classroom. Yet no way is any better than either of the others, and, ironically, the style of intelligence that schools most readily recognize as smart may well be less useful to many students in their adult lives.

The styles of intelligence that students can bring into their classrooms and into their lives include the following three (Sternberg, 1988):

1. The analytic style

Alice (a real student, but with her name changed) was the teacher's dream. She scored high on tests, wrote excellent papers, performed well in class, and in general, did everything that a teacher would expect a bright student to do. As a result, Alice was always considered to be at or near the top of her class. Her high test scores were accepted as a valid indicant of her ability to do outstanding work throughout her academic career. Yet by the time Alice was finished with graduate school, she was performing at a very modest level. About 70 to 80% of her classmates were doing better.

The question that naturally arises is, What went wrong? The answer, quite simply, is that, while Alice was excellent at remembering and analyzing other people's ideas, she was not very good at coming up with original concepts. Consequently, she faltered in advanced schooling, where (as in life) it is necessary to come up with ideas of one's own.

If we think about schooling as preparation for the world of work, we need to be concerned about whether schooling requires and develops creative thinking because, for Alice to stay competitive in most jobs, it will be necessary for her to come up with her own ideas.

In science, for example, real endeavor is not comparable to getting A's that represent nothing more than the ability to memorize facts in a book or to solve ready-made problems at the ends of chapters. The practice of science requires the ability to come up with creative, significant ideas that make a difference to the field and, ultimately, to the world.

People who generate important scientific ideas are not necessarily those who are the best at memorizing facts or solving textbooks problems. Indeed, they may be people who don't particularly like to do these things and who therefore do not show themselves at their best in school settings.

The same dynamic applies in other occupations. Consider writing or art. It is one thing to succeed in writing good essays when told what to write about, or to draw nice pictures when told what the pictures should show. It is quite another thing to come up with one's own ideas for stories or pictures. For example, outside my daughter's classroom, I once observed roughly two dozen pictures of children's houses. They were nice pictures of houses, but it was clear that the teacher had told the students what to draw—it did not seem likely that 24 kids had independently decided to draw pictures of houses. In the real world of art or writing, though, someone is not always there to tell the artist or writer what his or her creation should deal with. Indeed, creative writers and artists are, almost by definition, people who come up with their own imaginative ideas.

The problem with the current situation is, of course, that telling students what to do is often unrealistic with respect to what they will be required to do later. Educators need to stop formulating problems for students and instead urge them to formulate problems for themselves.

One could argue that most students will not become scientists or writers or artists, but the situation is no different in a very pragmatic occupation like business. Many of the executives interviewed during our studies of practical intelligence complain that one can hire a top-level graduate of a business school and get someone who may be good at analyzing textbook cases, but is unable to come up with innovative ideas for new business products or services, rearrangements that create more shelf space, or ways to stay competitive with similar industries in other countries.

The point, of course, is that there are large gaps between the kind of performance needed for success in a business setting and the kind of performance needed for success in schools, even schools that are supposed to be quite practical in training students for the world of business. Thus we often end up with adults who are unable to do what is expected of them.

The same problem even afflicts education itself. It is one thing to get A's in education courses and quite another to succeed when called upon to be innovative in a classroom setting. I know from experience just how challenging classroom situations can be. For example, several years ago I was giving a lecture at the University of Puerto Rico, and I found myself confronting a serious classroom management problem, namely, the professors of education in the audience just weren't listening. For whatever reasons, they had decided to tune out, and they were walking around the room and in and out of the room, and generally not being very attentive.

I tried the standard, uncreative techniques one learns in the course of training to be a teacher. I tried lowering my voice in the hope that these professors would then lower their voices so that they would be able to hear me. Of course, I was assuming that they wanted to hear me, an assumption that proved false. Instead, they appeared to be grateful that I had lowered my voice so that they could hear themselves better. I then tried asking them to be quiet, but that didn't work, either. Finally, after I had given up, a woman in the audience shot up and said something in rapid-fire Spanish. After that, you could have heard a pin drop, and the audience remained silent for the rest of the session.

What did she say? She had capitalized on her understanding that Puerto Rico is a shame culture, not a guilt culture. My attempts to make the audience feel guilty of bad manners might have worked in the mainland United States, but were ineffective in Puerto Rico. In contrast, the woman pointed out to the audience that, if they continued to be noisy, I would leave with a poor impression of the University of Puerto Rico. I would then report this bad impression to others. She said that the audience had no right to convey a bad impression and thereby to cast shame on the university. This appeal was effective in achieving the behavioral change that I had unsuccessfully sought.

Why is it that students whom we consider to be bright tend to be bright like Alice? In other words, why are they so often test-smart, but not necessarily smart in other ways?

I think that children are not born to be smart in this limited way, but that we make them so. Our system of education, in essence, creates Alices by continually reinforcing or rewarding students for being test-smart. Indeed, the main lesson that students learn is that it pays to be smart like Alice.

One indication that schools mold students into Alices comes from Joe Glick's study of the Kpelle tribe. Glick asked adult members of the tribe to sort terms into categories. For example, they might be asked to sort for names of fruits (apple, orange, grapefruit) or names of vegetables (celery, lettuce, broccoli) or names of vehicles (bus, boat, car). Glick found that the Kpelles sorted functionally. For example, they would sort "apple" with "eat" and "car" with "gas" because people eat apples and cars use gas.

In our culture, only young children sort functionally. The Kpelle's functional kind of sorting behavior is considered stupid when it is done by an adult. Older children and adults are expected to sort taxonomically (putting fruits together) or hierarchically (putting the word *fruit* over the names of different fruits and then perhaps putting the word *food* over the whole lot).

Glick tried, without initial success, to get the Kpelle to sort in other ways. When he was about to conclude that they simply didn't have the mental ability to do things any differently, he decided as a last resort to ask them how a stupid person would do the task. At this point, they sorted taxonomically, and with no trouble at all. Why would the Kpelle consider taxonomic sorting stupid? The answer is that the Kpelle do not grow up in our educational system and—even more important—do not take our tests. In everyday life, we tend to think functionally. We think of eating apples or using gas in cars. We learn to think taxonomically in school, but for the most part this kind of thinking remains limited to artificial settings. A problem arises, therefore, when advanced students or career aspirants have to start thinking in ways that they have not been conditioned in school to think, that is, when they need to start turning out their own ideas rather than reciting back or analyzing ideas that other people have had.

Because these kinds of skills have not been actively encouraged or selected for, students tend not to develop them. In this respect, then, our schools essentially mislead and misprepare students by developing and rewarding a set of skills that will be important in later life, but much less important than they are in school.

2. The creative-synthetic style

A student whom I shall call Barbara (not her real name) exhibits a second style of intelligence. Barbara's grades were good, although by no means spectacular. Her undergraduate teachers thought that she was terrific, despite the fact that her scores on standardized tests were very weak.

When Barbara applied to our graduate program in psychology, she was rejected by an almost unanimous vote. In fact, I was the only person who voted to admit her. Even though Barbara had included a portfolio of her work, which demonstrated a high degree of competence, most of the admissions people decided on the basis of her test scores. In other words, they had more confidence in fallible and often weak predictors of creative work than they did in the work itself. We often see this odd situation in education today. The predictor of the performance has become more important than the performance itself!

Why has this apparently illogical situation come to be? Why do we pay more attention to predictors than to performance? And, in general, why do we pay so much attention to results on tests of IQ and related abilities?

I believe that, to achieve a more balanced perspective on testing, we need to understand why we rely upon test scores so heavily. In my opinion there are at least five reasons why test scores tend to be overused.

The first is the *quantitative pseudoprecision reason*. By that I mean that we overuse quantitative data because they appear to be so precise. We see numbers and assume that they have a lot to tell us. In fact, we know from research that people will use numbers in making decisions even if they are told that the numbers are irrelevant to the decision that they have to make. It seems likely, then, that if people believe that test scores are at least somewhat relevant, they will give these figures great weight in making decisions.

The problem is that these numbers are actually of only very limited validity, no matter how exact they seem to be. We need to recognize that the tests we have are quite limited in what their results can predict, notwithstanding appearances to the contrary.

A second reason that we overuse quantitative data is what I call the *culpability reason*, a fear of being blamed for not having used available numbers. Why should a person be criticized for not using numbers?

Suppose that a person making an admissions decision goes with the numbers, and the person predicted to succeed does not subsequently succeed. Who is to blame? In practice, we tend to blame the testing company, the school from which the student came, or practically anybody except the person who made the admissions decision. That person can't be blamed, having decided on the basis of paper credentials. Thus, he or she made a safe decision.

Suppose, on the other hand, that this person had admitted someone like Barbara, someone with doubtful paper credentials. What happens if that student flounders? Then the admitting official is in a position of potential culpability.

Critics can go back, look at the test scores, and conclude that the person who should be blamed for the mistake is the person who made the decision to admit a poor prospect. After all, anyone could have looked at the paper credentials and seen that the student wouldn't succeed!

So to admit a student with marginal scores is to put oneself on the line. If that student doesn't succeed—and in any category of students there will be some who don't—the reviewing official's reputation is jeopardized. People may even wonder why a person who can't make such a simple selection or placement decision is doing that job.

The third reason is the *similarity reason*. Obviously, the people making the admissions decisions must, at some time, have gained admission themselves. In other words, their test scores were high enough to get them into whatever kind of program they are now making decisions about. We tend to view people who are like ourselves as smart. Since the people now making admissions decisions once had decent test scores themselves, it is natural for them to favor applicants with pretty high scores. Thus the system perpetuates itself as people continually choose others like themselves, and the result is that we keep getting more Alices and fewer Barbaras.

I call the fourth reason the *publication reason*. Because test scores are published, a lot has come to hinge on them. For example, in my home state of Connecticut, the statewide mastery test scores appear to be a major determinant of property values.

How has this happened? Simple. The local newspapers report test scores district by district. When people read the newspapers, they take test scores as proxies for the quality of schooling in a particular locale. They become reluctant to pay high prices for real estate in areas with lower test scores; and conversely, because they want the best for their children, they will pay more for real estate in areas that have schools with higher test scores.

With private schools, colleges, and universities, the situation is very similar. The reputations of institutions of higher education hinge in part on the perceived quality of their students, and the perceived quality is higher if the test scores are higher. Again, the result is a self-perpetuating system that creates a strong incentive to keep scores high, even though they are very narrow measures of accountability.

My fifth and final reason for our overreliance on quantified data is one I refer to as the *rain-dance reason*. Here's the idea. Suppose that I go to a place, find it attractive, and would like to tour around. Typically, though, I find that I don't have the time—I must go in and out almost immediately. A year later, I decide that I want to return, and the question is, How can I get myself invited back? I know that my former hosts won't reinvite me to hear my talks on thinking because I've already given those.

Now suppose further that the place is a nice town in the Southwest of the United States, or perhaps in Israel or any other place with a really dry climate. I just tell the people there that, for a specified fee, I can make it rain, and that, if I don't, I will give them double their money back. How can they turn me down? They invite me to visit and make it rain. I go, and the next morning I do a rain dance. After I do the dance, I spend the rest of the day touring. Of course, it may not rain after I do the dance. Probably it won't. In fact, probably everyone doubts that my doing a rain dance will produce rain. That night, my hosts will ask for double their money back.

I say that they must be kidding—in a severe drought zone, they can't expect a single rain dance to make it rain. Sometimes two, three, four, or more applications of the rain dance are needed before it rains. Accordingly, I continue to do the rain dance each morning and tour the rest of the day. Eventually, of course, it rains. I thank the local residents for their hospitality (and my fee) and go home.

The point of this story is that superstitions persist by virtue of the great difficulty encountered in refuting them. Indeed, superstitions are, by their nature, almost undebunkable. People have believed in rain dances for thousands of years precisely because, if someone dances long enough, it will eventually rain.

None of us, of course, think that we have superstitions. We have *beliefs*. Nonetheless, it is easy to see that we are all subject to superstitions. One only has to observe people waiting for an elevator. Even after the call button has been pressed, people will continue to press the button. The expectation is the more one presses the button, the sooner the elevator will come—a belief, of course, that is false.

There's a similar sort of superstition at work in education. We often believe that people with test scores below a certain point cannot successfully do the work in a given program or institution. Because of this belief, we do not give them the chance to do the work. As a result, we can go on believing year after year that people with scores below that point cannot do the work because we never encounter people with lower scores who are doing the work. We have set up a system that precludes evidence that might contradict our beliefs.

I know from experience that this rain dance problem is not merely hypothetical. As a student in elementary school, I was beset by test anxiety and thus did very poorly on intelligence tests. The psychologist would come into the room to administer the test, and I would panic, with the predictable result. Consequently, during the first three years of elementary school, my teachers did not believe that I was capable of producing very good work. As someone who is eager to please, I gave them exactly what they expected: mediocre work. They were happy that my work was what they expected, and I was happy, more or less, that they were happy.

In fourth grade, I happened to have a teacher who believed that I was capable of doing better. I wanted to please this teacher, too, so I did better. But the irony is that I could have continued going through school doing mediocre work had it not been for that one teacher who believed in me.

I have heard other people tell similar stories that reveal an error we make over and over again. We create our own self-fulfilling prophecies (it will rain if I dance; students with low test scores aren't capable of certain work), and then when the prophecies come true, we conclude that our reasoning must have been correct. Often, however, nothing could be farther from the truth.

For instance, I hired Barbara as a research associate because I believed that she showed much better potential than the test scores indicated. And I was not disappointed. Her work as a research associate was highly creative and innovative. Two years later, she was admitted as the top pick into our program. But do you suppose that Barbara's case changed the system? Not one iota. If anything people's reaction was to regard Barbara as an odd exception to a sound rule. We need to open up our thinking and reappraise our educational superstitions if we are ever to change the way our educational system functions.

3. The practical style.

Celia (not her real name), when she applied, had grades that were good but not great, test scores that were good but not great, and letters of recommendation that were good but not great. In fact, just about everything in her application seemed to be good but not great. Naturally, we admitted Celia because every program needs people who are good but not great. Indeed, in our program, her work proved to be exactly what we would have predicted: good but not great—so we figured we had hit it on that one.

But what a surprise Celia gave us when it came to getting a job! Everyone wanted to hire Celia! That raised an intriguing question: Why would someone who lacked Alice's analytic ability and Barbara's creative ability do so spectacularly well in the job market?

The answer was actually very simple. Celia was something like the second boy in my opening bear-in-the-forest story. She had an abundance of practical intelligence, or simple common sense. She could go into an environment, figure out what she needed to do to thrive there, and then do it.

For example, Celia knew how to interview effectively, how to interact well with other students, and how to get her work done. She also was aware of what kinds of things do and don't work. In other words, she was street smart in an academic setting. She knew something that is true, though seldom acknowledged: that in school, as well as life, one needs a certain amount of practical smartness in order to adapt to the environment.

Whereas almost everyone would accept Alice as smart, and many people would regard Barbara as smart (albeit in her own way), few people would think of Celia as smart. They might concede that she has common sense, but would not see that as part of intelligence. They might even say that she is manipulative and reject the idea that being manipulative is an element of intelligence.

Not so. The kind of practical intelligence that Celia exhibits is every bit as important as Alice's analytic or Barbara's synthetic intelligence. The reason is that different situations call for different kinds of intelligence. Furthermore, if we value only one kind of intelligence in school, we will seriously underestimate a lot of students. We will peg them as much less intelligent than they really are.

This tendency to undervalue certain forms of intelligence became apparent in our own research in California. We compared conceptions of intelligence among parents of different ethnic groups. We found that the more parents emphasize social competence skills in their conception of intelligence, the less bright their own children look according to standard cognitive tests used in schools. In other words, the mismatch between what the parents emphasized in their environment and what the schools required in their environment resulted in kids who might be quite competent in the home and community setting, but who would be judged as intellectually lacking in the school.

Along a similar line of inquiry, Shirley Heath compared the language behavior of children in three communities:

- Trackton, a lower social class black community
- Roadville, a lower social class white community
- Gateway, a middle social class white community

Heath found that the children from Trackton performed quite a bit worse than those from Roadville or Gateway as soon as all the children started school, but that the idea of how smart children are in school may be largely dependent on the match between parental and school conceptions of intelligence. The children in Trackton, therefore, might actually have been no less intelligent than the children in Roadville or Gateway.

For example, parents in Trackton were found to emphasize the importance of nonverbal communication. To communicate successfully in Trackton, it was necessary to be very adept at nonverbal cues, both with respect to understanding them and with respect to transmitting them. In Roadville and Gateway, on the other hand, more emphasis was placed on verbal skills, an emphasis that was a better match to the demands of the school. As a result, children from Roadville and Gateway appeared smarter than children from Trackton but may not actually have been smarter. Once again, the middle class (especially the white middle class) benefited from the match between school values and home and community values.

It is quite plausible to argue that white middle-class culture undervalues the importance of nonverbal communication. For example, many boring teachers or professors can go on being boring year after year precisely because they ignore the nonverbal communication of the audience. None of the students has the courage to risk an F by *telling* the teachers or professors that they are boring. If these educators were to pay attention to nonverbal cues, however, they might well realize their failure to command attention and might even do something about it.

Sensitivity to nonverbal communication can be a key to success in an interview setting also. Information as to how well an interview is going is almost exclusively nonverbal. Interviewers know that they are not supposed to reveal their feelings about the person being interviewed. At times, there may be nothing they would rather say than, "Please leave now. I know that we have another 25 minutes left in the interview, but we both know that you are wasting my time and I am wasting yours." The interviewer may feel that way, but certainly can't say so. Nevertheless, the interviewer's feelings are likely to leak out nonverbally. If the applicant is sensitive to the nonverbal communication, he or she at least has a chance of changing the way the interview is going.

In short, the ways of Trackton have something to teach us all. A child from Roadville or Gateway would look as stupid in Trackton as a child from Trackton would look in Roadville or Gateway. We need to acknowledge the multiple styles of intelligence.

It is interesting as well to compare Roadville to Gateway. When the children from these two communities start school, they look roughly comparable. Within a few years, however, the white middle-class children from Gateway are doing better than the white lower-class children from Roadville. What happened? Do the Roadville children have some kind of "inherited cumulative deficit," as some would have us believe? I believe that the explanation is a lot simpler: that the views about the nature of education and intelligence that are commonly held in Roadville render the children there less smart *appearing* in school.

For example, parents in Roadville are more likely to believe that their role as teachers stops when their children start school; at that point, parents stop intervening in their children's education. Gateway parents, on the other hand, continue to intervene, to the advantage of their children.

Moreover, parents from Roadville emphasize memory in their concept of intelligence, whereas Gateway parents emphasize reasoning. As the years go by and reasoning becomes more important, the children from Gateway become progressively more advantaged.

Even in adulthood, there is evidence that many people possess contextual intelligence that is quite different from IQ-like intelligence. For example, our work on the practical intelligence of managers shows no significant degree of statistical association between practical and academic intelligence. Steve Ceci's work on bettors at a race track found results that were consistent with ours. Ceci determined that the average IQ in a group of successful bettors was approximately 97, or slightly below average. Along the same lines, Jean Lave showed that women shoppers who could easily compute mentally the better value between two products were hardly able to do the same operations when they were presented in paper-and-pencil format.

In sum, context matters. We cannot consider intelligence in isolation from context. To do so may lead to seriously erroneous conclusions about children's capacity to learn. All the investigations described above suggest that practical intelligence matters, but unfortunately it is not what our tests measure, nor is it sufficiently emphasized in schools. Educators need to begin to consider not only the intelligence of Alice, but also that of Barbara and Celia.

Of course, although people usually have a preferred style of intelligence, they do not use only one style exclusively. In everyone, there is some combination of analytic, creative, and practical intelligence. We need to foster *all* these aspects of intelligence, not to favor just one. In addition, we need to recognize that people who are really smart in their lives are those who figure out (a) what it is they are good at, (b) what it is they are not good at, and (c) what they can do to make the most of their strengths while remediating or compensating for their weaknesses.

In other words, the most functionally intelligent people are not necessarily the ones with the greatest degree of intelligence in any of its three styles. Being smart in the real world means making the most of what one has, not conforming to any preset stereotypical pattern of what others may consider smart. It is this view of intelligence and of styles of intelligence that we need to adopt in order to obtain the most from our students and ourselves. Being academically smart, like Alice, is important in school and even, to an extent, in later life; but there is more to intelligence than what tests such as the *MAT* measure!

Styles of Thought

Just as people have different styles of intelligence, so they have different styles of applying their intellect. These thinking styles, or ways of deploying intelligence, must be understood in order for people to benefit fully from instruction. Although there are many different styles of thought, I will describe just three (Sternberg, 1988). These thinking styles will be exemplified by three college friends.

The friends—Alex, Bob, and Cyril (the names have been changed)—looked remarkably similar in intellect when they entered college. All had high *Scholastic Aptitude Test* scores and very high academic averages. Their patterns of intellectual strengths and weaknesses were apparently similar; all were more verbal than quantitative: good reasoners, but rather weak in spatial relations. Thus, in terms of standard theories of intelligence, the three roommates looked very much alike.

Three Specific Thinking Styles

Today, all three friends are successful in their jobs, and all have achieved national recognition for their work. Thus, whatever differences may exist among the three cannot be attributed to motivational differences. Yet, beyond the intellectual and motivational similarities of the three roommates lie some salient differences that have profoundly affected the lives of Alex, Bob, and Cyril. Each prefers one of three different thinking styles:

1. The executive style
Alex, a lawyer, could be characterized (and would characterize himself) as fairly conventional, rule-bound, and comfortable with details and structure. An excellent implementer, he does well at what others tell him to do, as a lawyer must. Alex has commented that, to him, intellectual perfection would be a technically flawless, loophole-free contract or other legal document that would absolutely bind any signatories to its terms. In a nutshell, Alex is an *executor of systems*. He figures systems out and functions within them extremely well, as shown by his present status as a partner in a major national law firm.

Alex's traits are compared with Bob's and Cyril's in Table 1.

TABLE 1. Comparison of Traits Varying with Styles of Thought

	Style		
Trait	**Executive**	**Legislative**	**Judicial**
attitude toward rules	like to follow rules	like to create their own rules	like to evaluate rules
preferred approach for getting tasks done	like to choose from existing ways to get tasks done	like coming up with their own ways to get tasks done	like to judge existing structures
type of problems preferred	ones that are prestructured of prefabricated	ones that are unstructured, not prefabricated	ones that call for analysis evaluation of existing things or ideas
attitude toward content and structure	like to fill in content within existing structures	like to create structure as well as content	like to judge both structure and content
preferred activities	predefined ones like algebraic word problems, applying rules to already structured engineering problems, enforcing rules, teaching lessons based on others' ideas and on enforcing rules	creative, constructive, planning-based ones like writing papers, designing projects, or creating new business or educational structures	judgment-related ones like writing critiques, giving opinions, judging people and their work, evaluating programs
some preferred occupations	lawyer, police officer, builder (of others' designs), surgeon, soldier, proselytizer (of others' systems), and manager (lower echelon)	writer, artist, scientist, investment banker, policy maker, and architect	judge, critic, program evaluator, admissions officer, grant or contract monitor, systems analyst, and consultant

2. The legislative style

Bob, a university professor, is quite different stylistically from Alex. He is fairly unconventional; unlike Alex, he dislikes following or even dealing with other people's rules and has relatively few rules of his own. In fact, although he has some basic principles that he views as invariants, he tends not to take rules very seriously but rather to view them as conveniences that are meant to be changed or even broken as situations require. Bob dislikes details and is generally comfortable working within a structure only if it is his own. He does certain things well, but usually only if they are things he wants to do, rather than what someone else wants him to do. Bob's idea of intellectual perfection would be the generation of a great idea and a compelling demonstration that the idea is correct, or at least useful. In brief, Bob is a *creator of systems.* The fairly well-known psychological theories that he has designed reflect his interest in system creation.

3. The judicial style

Cyril, a psychotherapist, is like Bob but unlike Alex in being fairly unconventional. Like Bob, he dislikes others' rules; but, unlike Bob, he has a number of his own. Cyril tends to be indifferent to details, but he likes working within certain structures; they need not be of his own devising, but they have to be ones that he has approved as correct and suitable. Cyril's idea of intellectual perfection would be a difficult but correct psychological diagnosis, followed by an optimal psychotherapeutic intervention. All in all, Cyril is a *judge of systems.* His enthusiasm—perhaps passion—for judging was apparent early in his career; as a college student, he constructed a test (we called it "the Cyril Test") to give to others (especially to dates), thereby to judge the suitability of their values and standards. Cyril was also editor of the college course critique, a role that required the evaluation of all undergraduate courses at the university.

General Issues Regarding Thinking Styles

Having introduced the concept of thinking styles in a fairly concrete way, we can proceed to some general issues that include but also go beyond questions of executive, legislative, and judicial functions.

First, it is important to keep in mind that a person does not have one exclusive style. Rather, people tend to specialize, and some people specialize more than others. For example, one individual may be strongly legislative and weakly executive and judicial, whereas another may be just about equally balanced among the three functions. Thus, people differ not only in their direction of specialization, but also in their degree of specialization.

This point leads to a practical implication. Because at some point in life, people encounter problems involving all three kinds of functions, at least some balance is desirable so that a person will not become hopelessly bogged down on problems that do not correspond to his or her preferred mode or modes of specialization. People may also need to use one style in the service of another; for instance, a primarily legislative type may have to use the judicial function to further legislative ends.

A second observation is that, although it is important for people to develop all three stylistic functions, the issue of fit between persons and problems should not be sidestepped. People will gravitate toward problems that can be solved according to their preferred styles of thought. Judges like to judge (judicial style); novelists like to imagine fictional worlds (legislative style); police officers like to uphold existing laws (executive style).

Third, the proclivity toward one or more styles must be distinguished from actual ability to implement the preferred styles. It seems likely that most people will prefer styles that capitalize upon their strengths, but there is no logical or psychological reason why preferences and abilities will always correspond optimally. All of us know people who, for example, should have chosen another occupation. Some people may prefer styles that are not as well suited to their abilities as are others, so in measuring styles it is important to assess both the predilection toward a particular style and the ability to implement that style.

Fourth, the match between people's styles and preferred tasks applies especially to jobs, for although styles of thought are independent of level of intelligence in general, they probably are not independent of the level of intelligence within a particular domain. As a result, two people with equal levels and profiles of intelligence may perform differently in a job not because of innate intelligence or motivational differences, but because of thinking-style differences. For example, the legislative individual who is a brilliant scientist might look considerably duller in a field such as entry-level business management, which emphasizes executive skills. Thus, it is important to fit not only level and style of intelligence to jobs, but level and style of thinking as well.

A fifth observation is that two subsets of the same career can sometimes call for different styles. For example, despite the fact that professors of comparative literature or history and professors of biology or psychology are all professors, the demands of their jobs are quite different. A comparative literature or history professor needs to be more judicial, because he or she essentially establishes a reputation on the basis of analytic (judgmental) skills. In contrast, the scientist must demonstrate skill in generating theories or experiments (such skill is legislative in nature). Of course, neither kind of job is unidimensional. Scientists must judge their own ideas and those of others. Literary theorists must build as well as critique systems. Still, the emphases in their work are clearly different. What is sad, I believe, is that sometimes a person whose preferred style matches his or her job (e.g., executive style in lower level management) is promoted for that match, and then is placed in a job that mismatches the preferred style (e.g., executive style in upper level management, where a more legislative or judicial style is needed). Conversely, people whose styles might be a good match at the upper levels of their work may never have a chance to demonstrate their competence if they are derailed because their styles do not match the lower levels.

Sixth, in work, school, or personal life, certain stylistic combinations probably work better than others, and some friction can be expected among people with different styles. Legislators may find executives boring and uninspiring. Executives may find legislators impractical. Both types may chafe at the remarks of judges, who often seem to be excessively critical. (Perhaps it is not a coincidence that Cyril, the psychotherapist and judicial type, is still unmarried. Perhaps it is equally uncoincidental that the two people in a legislative-executive couple sometimes find it difficult to communicate with each other about what each values in life.)

Because any subject can be taught in a way that is compatible with any style, students will gravitate to learning activities that are compatible with their preferred styles, just as teachers will tend to teach in ways that are compatible with their own styles.

This principle leads to another important implication: *Both students and teachers tend to exploit their preferred styles, which may or may not match.* It is natural for people to seek activities that match their preferred thinking styles. People will be more motivated to perform such activities and often will be better at them. Furthermore, the same activity that engages one student may bore another—not necessarily because the latter student is uninterested in the content, but because the style of the activity does not match his or her preference.

When a student rejects an activity because it does not match his or her thinking style, teachers often mistake the refusal for boredom with the subject matter. To prevent such errors and capitalize on opportunities for student learning, it is important for teachers to be aware of their students' preferred styles.

Most important, when a mismatch exists between the preferred style of the teacher and that of a particular student, the student may frequently seem bored, simply because teachers tend to teach, create assignments, and develop tests in ways that reflect their own preferred thinking styles. We are all susceptible to this bias. Indeed, I consciously broadened my own teaching once I realized that I was slanting my classroom presentations, assignments, and tests in a direction that benefited students with my preferred legislative style, but that unfairly penalized students with executive or judicial bents.

A Final Observation

Ultimately, the intellectually effective individual is the one who figures out what his or her strengths and weaknesses are, and then also sees how to capitalize on the strengths while compensating for or remediating the weaknesses. This person makes the most of him- or herself, and that is precisely what makes a person truly intelligent. To be smart and effective in your life, you don't need high test scores.

Answer Sheet — Pretest

1. Ⓐ Ⓑ Ⓒ Ⓓ
2. Ⓐ Ⓑ Ⓒ Ⓓ
3. Ⓐ Ⓑ Ⓒ Ⓓ
4. Ⓐ Ⓑ Ⓒ Ⓓ
5. Ⓐ Ⓑ Ⓒ Ⓓ
6. Ⓐ Ⓑ Ⓒ Ⓓ
7. Ⓐ Ⓑ Ⓒ Ⓓ
8. Ⓐ Ⓑ Ⓒ Ⓓ
9. Ⓐ Ⓑ Ⓒ Ⓓ
10. Ⓐ Ⓑ Ⓒ Ⓓ
11. Ⓐ Ⓑ Ⓒ Ⓓ
12. Ⓐ Ⓑ Ⓒ Ⓓ
13. Ⓐ Ⓑ Ⓒ Ⓓ
14. Ⓐ Ⓑ Ⓒ Ⓓ
15. Ⓐ Ⓑ Ⓒ Ⓓ
16. Ⓐ Ⓑ Ⓒ Ⓓ
17. Ⓐ Ⓑ Ⓒ Ⓓ
18. Ⓐ Ⓑ Ⓒ Ⓓ
19. Ⓐ Ⓑ Ⓒ Ⓓ
20. Ⓐ Ⓑ Ⓒ Ⓓ
21. Ⓐ Ⓑ Ⓒ Ⓓ
22. Ⓐ Ⓑ Ⓒ Ⓓ
23. Ⓐ Ⓑ Ⓒ Ⓓ
24. Ⓐ Ⓑ Ⓒ Ⓓ
25. Ⓐ Ⓑ Ⓒ Ⓓ
26. Ⓐ Ⓑ Ⓒ Ⓓ
27. Ⓐ Ⓑ Ⓒ Ⓓ
28. Ⓐ Ⓑ Ⓒ Ⓓ
29. Ⓐ Ⓑ Ⓒ Ⓓ
30. Ⓐ Ⓑ Ⓒ Ⓓ
31. Ⓐ Ⓑ Ⓒ Ⓓ
32. Ⓐ Ⓑ Ⓒ Ⓓ
33. Ⓐ Ⓑ Ⓒ Ⓓ
34. Ⓐ Ⓑ Ⓒ Ⓓ
35. Ⓐ Ⓑ Ⓒ Ⓓ
36. Ⓐ Ⓑ Ⓒ Ⓓ
37. Ⓐ Ⓑ Ⓒ Ⓓ
38. Ⓐ Ⓑ Ⓒ Ⓓ
39. Ⓐ Ⓑ Ⓒ Ⓓ
40. Ⓐ Ⓑ Ⓒ Ⓓ
41. Ⓐ Ⓑ Ⓒ Ⓓ
42. Ⓐ Ⓑ Ⓒ Ⓓ
43. Ⓐ Ⓑ Ⓒ Ⓓ
44. Ⓐ Ⓑ Ⓒ Ⓓ
45. Ⓐ Ⓑ Ⓒ Ⓓ
46. Ⓐ Ⓑ Ⓒ Ⓓ
47. Ⓐ Ⓑ Ⓒ Ⓓ
48. Ⓐ Ⓑ Ⓒ Ⓓ
49. Ⓐ Ⓑ Ⓒ Ⓓ
50. Ⓐ Ⓑ Ⓒ Ⓓ
51. Ⓐ Ⓑ Ⓒ Ⓓ
52. Ⓐ Ⓑ Ⓒ Ⓓ
53. Ⓐ Ⓑ Ⓒ Ⓓ
54. Ⓐ Ⓑ Ⓒ Ⓓ
55. Ⓐ Ⓑ Ⓒ Ⓓ
56. Ⓐ Ⓑ Ⓒ Ⓓ
57. Ⓐ Ⓑ Ⓒ Ⓓ
58. Ⓐ Ⓑ Ⓒ Ⓓ
59. Ⓐ Ⓑ Ⓒ Ⓓ
60. Ⓐ Ⓑ Ⓒ Ⓓ
61. Ⓐ Ⓑ Ⓒ Ⓓ
62. Ⓐ Ⓑ Ⓒ Ⓓ
63. Ⓐ Ⓑ Ⓒ Ⓓ
64. Ⓐ Ⓑ Ⓒ Ⓓ
65. Ⓐ Ⓑ Ⓒ Ⓓ
66. Ⓐ Ⓑ Ⓒ Ⓓ
67. Ⓐ Ⓑ Ⓒ Ⓓ
68. Ⓐ Ⓑ Ⓒ Ⓓ
69. Ⓐ Ⓑ Ⓒ Ⓓ
70. Ⓐ Ⓑ Ⓒ Ⓓ
71. Ⓐ Ⓑ Ⓒ Ⓓ
72. Ⓐ Ⓑ Ⓒ Ⓓ
73. Ⓐ Ⓑ Ⓒ Ⓓ
74. Ⓐ Ⓑ Ⓒ Ⓓ
75. Ⓐ Ⓑ Ⓒ Ⓓ
76. Ⓐ Ⓑ Ⓒ Ⓓ
77. Ⓐ Ⓑ Ⓒ Ⓓ
78. Ⓐ Ⓑ Ⓒ Ⓓ
79. Ⓐ Ⓑ Ⓒ Ⓓ
80. Ⓐ Ⓑ Ⓒ Ⓓ
81. Ⓐ Ⓑ Ⓒ Ⓓ
82. Ⓐ Ⓑ Ⓒ Ⓓ
83. Ⓐ Ⓑ Ⓒ Ⓓ
84. Ⓐ Ⓑ Ⓒ Ⓓ
85. Ⓐ Ⓑ Ⓒ Ⓓ
86. Ⓐ Ⓑ Ⓒ Ⓓ
87. Ⓐ Ⓑ Ⓒ Ⓓ
88. Ⓐ Ⓑ Ⓒ Ⓓ
89. Ⓐ Ⓑ Ⓒ Ⓓ
90. Ⓐ Ⓑ Ⓒ Ⓓ
91. Ⓐ Ⓑ Ⓒ Ⓓ
92. Ⓐ Ⓑ Ⓒ Ⓓ
93. Ⓐ Ⓑ Ⓒ Ⓓ
94. Ⓐ Ⓑ Ⓒ Ⓓ
95. Ⓐ Ⓑ Ⓒ Ⓓ
96. Ⓐ Ⓑ Ⓒ Ⓓ
97. Ⓐ Ⓑ Ⓒ Ⓓ
98. Ⓐ Ⓑ Ⓒ Ⓓ
99. Ⓐ Ⓑ Ⓒ Ⓓ
100. Ⓐ Ⓑ Ⓒ Ⓓ

Answer Sheet — Practice Test 1

1. Ⓐ Ⓑ Ⓒ Ⓓ	26. Ⓐ Ⓑ Ⓒ Ⓓ	51. Ⓐ Ⓑ Ⓒ Ⓓ	76. Ⓐ Ⓑ Ⓒ Ⓓ
2. Ⓐ Ⓑ Ⓒ Ⓓ	27. Ⓐ Ⓑ Ⓒ Ⓓ	52. Ⓐ Ⓑ Ⓒ Ⓓ	77. Ⓐ Ⓑ Ⓒ Ⓓ
3. Ⓐ Ⓑ Ⓒ Ⓓ	28. Ⓐ Ⓑ Ⓒ Ⓓ	53. Ⓐ Ⓑ Ⓒ Ⓓ	78. Ⓐ Ⓑ Ⓒ Ⓓ
4. Ⓐ Ⓑ Ⓒ Ⓓ	29. Ⓐ Ⓑ Ⓒ Ⓓ	54. Ⓐ Ⓑ Ⓒ Ⓓ	79. Ⓐ Ⓑ Ⓒ Ⓓ
5. Ⓐ Ⓑ Ⓒ Ⓓ	30. Ⓐ Ⓑ Ⓒ Ⓓ	55. Ⓐ Ⓑ Ⓒ Ⓓ	80. Ⓐ Ⓑ Ⓒ Ⓓ
6. Ⓐ Ⓑ Ⓒ Ⓓ	31. Ⓐ Ⓑ Ⓒ Ⓓ	56. Ⓐ Ⓑ Ⓒ Ⓓ	81. Ⓐ Ⓑ Ⓒ Ⓓ
7. Ⓐ Ⓑ Ⓒ Ⓓ	32. Ⓐ Ⓑ Ⓒ Ⓓ	57. Ⓐ Ⓑ Ⓒ Ⓓ	82. Ⓐ Ⓑ Ⓒ Ⓓ
8. Ⓐ Ⓑ Ⓒ Ⓓ	33. Ⓐ Ⓑ Ⓒ Ⓓ	58. Ⓐ Ⓑ Ⓒ Ⓓ	83. Ⓐ Ⓑ Ⓒ Ⓓ
9. Ⓐ Ⓑ Ⓒ Ⓓ	34. Ⓐ Ⓑ Ⓒ Ⓓ	59. Ⓐ Ⓑ Ⓒ Ⓓ	84. Ⓐ Ⓑ Ⓒ Ⓓ
10. Ⓐ Ⓑ Ⓒ Ⓓ	35. Ⓐ Ⓑ Ⓒ Ⓓ	60. Ⓐ Ⓑ Ⓒ Ⓓ	85. Ⓐ Ⓑ Ⓒ Ⓓ
11. Ⓐ Ⓑ Ⓒ Ⓓ	36. Ⓐ Ⓑ Ⓒ Ⓓ	61. Ⓐ Ⓑ Ⓒ Ⓓ	86. Ⓐ Ⓑ Ⓒ Ⓓ
12. Ⓐ Ⓑ Ⓒ Ⓓ	37. Ⓐ Ⓑ Ⓒ Ⓓ	62. Ⓐ Ⓑ Ⓒ Ⓓ	87. Ⓐ Ⓑ Ⓒ Ⓓ
13. Ⓐ Ⓑ Ⓒ Ⓓ	38. Ⓐ Ⓑ Ⓒ Ⓓ	63. Ⓐ Ⓑ Ⓒ Ⓓ	88. Ⓐ Ⓑ Ⓒ Ⓓ
14. Ⓐ Ⓑ Ⓒ Ⓓ	39. Ⓐ Ⓑ Ⓒ Ⓓ	64. Ⓐ Ⓑ Ⓒ Ⓓ	89. Ⓐ Ⓑ Ⓒ Ⓓ
15. Ⓐ Ⓑ Ⓒ Ⓓ	40. Ⓐ Ⓑ Ⓒ Ⓓ	65. Ⓐ Ⓑ Ⓒ Ⓓ	90. Ⓐ Ⓑ Ⓒ Ⓓ
16. Ⓐ Ⓑ Ⓒ Ⓓ	41. Ⓐ Ⓑ Ⓒ Ⓓ	66. Ⓐ Ⓑ Ⓒ Ⓓ	91. Ⓐ Ⓑ Ⓒ Ⓓ
17. Ⓐ Ⓑ Ⓒ Ⓓ	42. Ⓐ Ⓑ Ⓒ Ⓓ	67. Ⓐ Ⓑ Ⓒ Ⓓ	92. Ⓐ Ⓑ Ⓒ Ⓓ
18. Ⓐ Ⓑ Ⓒ Ⓓ	43. Ⓐ Ⓑ Ⓒ Ⓓ	68. Ⓐ Ⓑ Ⓒ Ⓓ	93. Ⓐ Ⓑ Ⓒ Ⓓ
19. Ⓐ Ⓑ Ⓒ Ⓓ	44. Ⓐ Ⓑ Ⓒ Ⓓ	69. Ⓐ Ⓑ Ⓒ Ⓓ	94. Ⓐ Ⓑ Ⓒ Ⓓ
20. Ⓐ Ⓑ Ⓒ Ⓓ	45. Ⓐ Ⓑ Ⓒ Ⓓ	70. Ⓐ Ⓑ Ⓒ Ⓓ	95. Ⓐ Ⓑ Ⓒ Ⓓ
21. Ⓐ Ⓑ Ⓒ Ⓓ	46. Ⓐ Ⓑ Ⓒ Ⓓ	71. Ⓐ Ⓑ Ⓒ Ⓓ	96. Ⓐ Ⓑ Ⓒ Ⓓ
22. Ⓐ Ⓑ Ⓒ Ⓓ	47. Ⓐ Ⓑ Ⓒ Ⓓ	72. Ⓐ Ⓑ Ⓒ Ⓓ	97. Ⓐ Ⓑ Ⓒ Ⓓ
23. Ⓐ Ⓑ Ⓒ Ⓓ	48. Ⓐ Ⓑ Ⓒ Ⓓ	73. Ⓐ Ⓑ Ⓒ Ⓓ	98. Ⓐ Ⓑ Ⓒ Ⓓ
24. Ⓐ Ⓑ Ⓒ Ⓓ	49. Ⓐ Ⓑ Ⓒ Ⓓ	74. Ⓐ Ⓑ Ⓒ Ⓓ	99. Ⓐ Ⓑ Ⓒ Ⓓ
25. Ⓐ Ⓑ Ⓒ Ⓓ	50. Ⓐ Ⓑ Ⓒ Ⓓ	75. Ⓐ Ⓑ Ⓒ Ⓓ	100. Ⓐ Ⓑ Ⓒ Ⓓ

Answer Sheet — Practice Test 2

1. Ⓐ Ⓑ Ⓒ Ⓓ
2. Ⓐ Ⓑ Ⓒ Ⓓ
3. Ⓐ Ⓑ Ⓒ Ⓓ
4. Ⓐ Ⓑ Ⓒ Ⓓ
5. Ⓐ Ⓑ Ⓒ Ⓓ
6. Ⓐ Ⓑ Ⓒ Ⓓ
7. Ⓐ Ⓑ Ⓒ Ⓓ
8. Ⓐ Ⓑ Ⓒ Ⓓ
9. Ⓐ Ⓑ Ⓒ Ⓓ
10. Ⓐ Ⓑ Ⓒ Ⓓ
11. Ⓐ Ⓑ Ⓒ Ⓓ
12. Ⓐ Ⓑ Ⓒ Ⓓ
13. Ⓐ Ⓑ Ⓒ Ⓓ
14. Ⓐ Ⓑ Ⓒ Ⓓ
15. Ⓐ Ⓑ Ⓒ Ⓓ
16. Ⓐ Ⓑ Ⓒ Ⓓ
17. Ⓐ Ⓑ Ⓒ Ⓓ
18. Ⓐ Ⓑ Ⓒ Ⓓ
19. Ⓐ Ⓑ Ⓒ Ⓓ
20. Ⓐ Ⓑ Ⓒ Ⓓ
21. Ⓐ Ⓑ Ⓒ Ⓓ
22. Ⓐ Ⓑ Ⓒ Ⓓ
23. Ⓐ Ⓑ Ⓒ Ⓓ
24. Ⓐ Ⓑ Ⓒ Ⓓ
25. Ⓐ Ⓑ Ⓒ Ⓓ
26. Ⓐ Ⓑ Ⓒ Ⓓ
27. Ⓐ Ⓑ Ⓒ Ⓓ
28. Ⓐ Ⓑ Ⓒ Ⓓ
29. Ⓐ Ⓑ Ⓒ Ⓓ
30. Ⓐ Ⓑ Ⓒ Ⓓ
31. Ⓐ Ⓑ Ⓒ Ⓓ
32. Ⓐ Ⓑ Ⓒ Ⓓ
33. Ⓐ Ⓑ Ⓒ Ⓓ
34. Ⓐ Ⓑ Ⓒ Ⓓ
35. Ⓐ Ⓑ Ⓒ Ⓓ
36. Ⓐ Ⓑ Ⓒ Ⓓ
37. Ⓐ Ⓑ Ⓒ Ⓓ
38. Ⓐ Ⓑ Ⓒ Ⓓ
39. Ⓐ Ⓑ Ⓒ Ⓓ
40. Ⓐ Ⓑ Ⓒ Ⓓ
41. Ⓐ Ⓑ Ⓒ Ⓓ
42. Ⓐ Ⓑ Ⓒ Ⓓ
43. Ⓐ Ⓑ Ⓒ Ⓓ
44. Ⓐ Ⓑ Ⓒ Ⓓ
45. Ⓐ Ⓑ Ⓒ Ⓓ
46. Ⓐ Ⓑ Ⓒ Ⓓ
47. Ⓐ Ⓑ Ⓒ Ⓓ
48. Ⓐ Ⓑ Ⓒ Ⓓ
49. Ⓐ Ⓑ Ⓒ Ⓓ
50. Ⓐ Ⓑ Ⓒ Ⓓ
51. Ⓐ Ⓑ Ⓒ Ⓓ
52. Ⓐ Ⓑ Ⓒ Ⓓ
53. Ⓐ Ⓑ Ⓒ Ⓓ
54. Ⓐ Ⓑ Ⓒ Ⓓ
55. Ⓐ Ⓑ Ⓒ Ⓓ
56. Ⓐ Ⓑ Ⓒ Ⓓ
57. Ⓐ Ⓑ Ⓒ Ⓓ
58. Ⓐ Ⓑ Ⓒ Ⓓ
59. Ⓐ Ⓑ Ⓒ Ⓓ
60. Ⓐ Ⓑ Ⓒ Ⓓ
61. Ⓐ Ⓑ Ⓒ Ⓓ
62. Ⓐ Ⓑ Ⓒ Ⓓ
63. Ⓐ Ⓑ Ⓒ Ⓓ
64. Ⓐ Ⓑ Ⓒ Ⓓ
65. Ⓐ Ⓑ Ⓒ Ⓓ
66. Ⓐ Ⓑ Ⓒ Ⓓ
67. Ⓐ Ⓑ Ⓒ Ⓓ
68. Ⓐ Ⓑ Ⓒ Ⓓ
69. Ⓐ Ⓑ Ⓒ Ⓓ
70. Ⓐ Ⓑ Ⓒ Ⓓ
71. Ⓐ Ⓑ Ⓒ Ⓓ
72. Ⓐ Ⓑ Ⓒ Ⓓ
73. Ⓐ Ⓑ Ⓒ Ⓓ
74. Ⓐ Ⓑ Ⓒ Ⓓ
75. Ⓐ Ⓑ Ⓒ Ⓓ
76. Ⓐ Ⓑ Ⓒ Ⓓ
77. Ⓐ Ⓑ Ⓒ Ⓓ
78. Ⓐ Ⓑ Ⓒ Ⓓ
79. Ⓐ Ⓑ Ⓒ Ⓓ
80. Ⓐ Ⓑ Ⓒ Ⓓ
81. Ⓐ Ⓑ Ⓒ Ⓓ
82. Ⓐ Ⓑ Ⓒ Ⓓ
83. Ⓐ Ⓑ Ⓒ Ⓓ
84. Ⓐ Ⓑ Ⓒ Ⓓ
85. Ⓐ Ⓑ Ⓒ Ⓓ
86. Ⓐ Ⓑ Ⓒ Ⓓ
87. Ⓐ Ⓑ Ⓒ Ⓓ
88. Ⓐ Ⓑ Ⓒ Ⓓ
89. Ⓐ Ⓑ Ⓒ Ⓓ
90. Ⓐ Ⓑ Ⓒ Ⓓ
91. Ⓐ Ⓑ Ⓒ Ⓓ
92. Ⓐ Ⓑ Ⓒ Ⓓ
93. Ⓐ Ⓑ Ⓒ Ⓓ
94. Ⓐ Ⓑ Ⓒ Ⓓ
95. Ⓐ Ⓑ Ⓒ Ⓓ
96. Ⓐ Ⓑ Ⓒ Ⓓ
97. Ⓐ Ⓑ Ⓒ Ⓓ
98. Ⓐ Ⓑ Ⓒ Ⓓ
99. Ⓐ Ⓑ Ⓒ Ⓓ
100. Ⓐ Ⓑ Ⓒ Ⓓ

Answer Sheet — Practice Test 3

1. Ⓐ Ⓑ Ⓒ Ⓓ
2. Ⓐ Ⓑ Ⓒ Ⓓ
3. Ⓐ Ⓑ Ⓒ Ⓓ
4. Ⓐ Ⓑ Ⓒ Ⓓ
5. Ⓐ Ⓑ Ⓒ Ⓓ
6. Ⓐ Ⓑ Ⓒ Ⓓ
7. Ⓐ Ⓑ Ⓒ Ⓓ
8. Ⓐ Ⓑ Ⓒ Ⓓ
9. Ⓐ Ⓑ Ⓒ Ⓓ
10. Ⓐ Ⓑ Ⓒ Ⓓ
11. Ⓐ Ⓑ Ⓒ Ⓓ
12. Ⓐ Ⓑ Ⓒ Ⓓ
13. Ⓐ Ⓑ Ⓒ Ⓓ
14. Ⓐ Ⓑ Ⓒ Ⓓ
15. Ⓐ Ⓑ Ⓒ Ⓓ
16. Ⓐ Ⓑ Ⓒ Ⓓ
17. Ⓐ Ⓑ Ⓒ Ⓓ
18. Ⓐ Ⓑ Ⓒ Ⓓ
19. Ⓐ Ⓑ Ⓒ Ⓓ
20. Ⓐ Ⓑ Ⓒ Ⓓ
21. Ⓐ Ⓑ Ⓒ Ⓓ
22. Ⓐ Ⓑ Ⓒ Ⓓ
23. Ⓐ Ⓑ Ⓒ Ⓓ
24. Ⓐ Ⓑ Ⓒ Ⓓ
25. Ⓐ Ⓑ Ⓒ Ⓓ
26. Ⓐ Ⓑ Ⓒ Ⓓ
27. Ⓐ Ⓑ Ⓒ Ⓓ
28. Ⓐ Ⓑ Ⓒ Ⓓ
29. Ⓐ Ⓑ Ⓒ Ⓓ
30. Ⓐ Ⓑ Ⓒ Ⓓ
31. Ⓐ Ⓑ Ⓒ Ⓓ
32. Ⓐ Ⓑ Ⓒ Ⓓ
33. Ⓐ Ⓑ Ⓒ Ⓓ
34. Ⓐ Ⓑ Ⓒ Ⓓ
35. Ⓐ Ⓑ Ⓒ Ⓓ
36. Ⓐ Ⓑ Ⓒ Ⓓ
37. Ⓐ Ⓑ Ⓒ Ⓓ
38. Ⓐ Ⓑ Ⓒ Ⓓ
39. Ⓐ Ⓑ Ⓒ Ⓓ
40. Ⓐ Ⓑ Ⓒ Ⓓ
41. Ⓐ Ⓑ Ⓒ Ⓓ
42. Ⓐ Ⓑ Ⓒ Ⓓ
43. Ⓐ Ⓑ Ⓒ Ⓓ
44. Ⓐ Ⓑ Ⓒ Ⓓ
45. Ⓐ Ⓑ Ⓒ Ⓓ
46. Ⓐ Ⓑ Ⓒ Ⓓ
47. Ⓐ Ⓑ Ⓒ Ⓓ
48. Ⓐ Ⓑ Ⓒ Ⓓ
49. Ⓐ Ⓑ Ⓒ Ⓓ
50. Ⓐ Ⓑ Ⓒ Ⓓ
51. Ⓐ Ⓑ Ⓒ Ⓓ
52. Ⓐ Ⓑ Ⓒ Ⓓ
53. Ⓐ Ⓑ Ⓒ Ⓓ
54. Ⓐ Ⓑ Ⓒ Ⓓ
55. Ⓐ Ⓑ Ⓒ Ⓓ
56. Ⓐ Ⓑ Ⓒ Ⓓ
57. Ⓐ Ⓑ Ⓒ Ⓓ
58. Ⓐ Ⓑ Ⓒ Ⓓ
59. Ⓐ Ⓑ Ⓒ Ⓓ
60. Ⓐ Ⓑ Ⓒ Ⓓ
61. Ⓐ Ⓑ Ⓒ Ⓓ
62. Ⓐ Ⓑ Ⓒ Ⓓ
63. Ⓐ Ⓑ Ⓒ Ⓓ
64. Ⓐ Ⓑ Ⓒ Ⓓ
65. Ⓐ Ⓑ Ⓒ Ⓓ
66. Ⓐ Ⓑ Ⓒ Ⓓ
67. Ⓐ Ⓑ Ⓒ Ⓓ
68. Ⓐ Ⓑ Ⓒ Ⓓ
69. Ⓐ Ⓑ Ⓒ Ⓓ
70. Ⓐ Ⓑ Ⓒ Ⓓ
71. Ⓐ Ⓑ Ⓒ Ⓓ
72. Ⓐ Ⓑ Ⓒ Ⓓ
73. Ⓐ Ⓑ Ⓒ Ⓓ
74. Ⓐ Ⓑ Ⓒ Ⓓ
75. Ⓐ Ⓑ Ⓒ Ⓓ
76. Ⓐ Ⓑ Ⓒ Ⓓ
77. Ⓐ Ⓑ Ⓒ Ⓓ
78. Ⓐ Ⓑ Ⓒ Ⓓ
79. Ⓐ Ⓑ Ⓒ Ⓓ
80. Ⓐ Ⓑ Ⓒ Ⓓ
81. Ⓐ Ⓑ Ⓒ Ⓓ
82. Ⓐ Ⓑ Ⓒ Ⓓ
83. Ⓐ Ⓑ Ⓒ Ⓓ
84. Ⓐ Ⓑ Ⓒ Ⓓ
85. Ⓐ Ⓑ Ⓒ Ⓓ
86. Ⓐ Ⓑ Ⓒ Ⓓ
87. Ⓐ Ⓑ Ⓒ Ⓓ
88. Ⓐ Ⓑ Ⓒ Ⓓ
89. Ⓐ Ⓑ Ⓒ Ⓓ
90. Ⓐ Ⓑ Ⓒ Ⓓ
91. Ⓐ Ⓑ Ⓒ Ⓓ
92. Ⓐ Ⓑ Ⓒ Ⓓ
93. Ⓐ Ⓑ Ⓒ Ⓓ
94. Ⓐ Ⓑ Ⓒ Ⓓ
95. Ⓐ Ⓑ Ⓒ Ⓓ
96. Ⓐ Ⓑ Ⓒ Ⓓ
97. Ⓐ Ⓑ Ⓒ Ⓓ
98. Ⓐ Ⓑ Ⓒ Ⓓ
99. Ⓐ Ⓑ Ⓒ Ⓓ
100. Ⓐ Ⓑ Ⓒ Ⓓ

Answer Sheet — Practice Test 4

1. Ⓐ Ⓑ Ⓒ Ⓓ
2. Ⓐ Ⓑ Ⓒ Ⓓ
3. Ⓐ Ⓑ Ⓒ Ⓓ
4. Ⓐ Ⓑ Ⓒ Ⓓ
5. Ⓐ Ⓑ Ⓒ Ⓓ
6. Ⓐ Ⓑ Ⓒ Ⓓ
7. Ⓐ Ⓑ Ⓒ Ⓓ
8. Ⓐ Ⓑ Ⓒ Ⓓ
9. Ⓐ Ⓑ Ⓒ Ⓓ
10. Ⓐ Ⓑ Ⓒ Ⓓ
11. Ⓐ Ⓑ Ⓒ Ⓓ
12. Ⓐ Ⓑ Ⓒ Ⓓ
13. Ⓐ Ⓑ Ⓒ Ⓓ
14. Ⓐ Ⓑ Ⓒ Ⓓ
15. Ⓐ Ⓑ Ⓒ Ⓓ
16. Ⓐ Ⓑ Ⓒ Ⓓ
17. Ⓐ Ⓑ Ⓒ Ⓓ
18. Ⓐ Ⓑ Ⓒ Ⓓ
19. Ⓐ Ⓑ Ⓒ Ⓓ
20. Ⓐ Ⓑ Ⓒ Ⓓ
21. Ⓐ Ⓑ Ⓒ Ⓓ
22. Ⓐ Ⓑ Ⓒ Ⓓ
23. Ⓐ Ⓑ Ⓒ Ⓓ
24. Ⓐ Ⓑ Ⓒ Ⓓ
25. Ⓐ Ⓑ Ⓒ Ⓓ
26. Ⓐ Ⓑ Ⓒ Ⓓ
27. Ⓐ Ⓑ Ⓒ Ⓓ
28. Ⓐ Ⓑ Ⓒ Ⓓ
29. Ⓐ Ⓑ Ⓒ Ⓓ
30. Ⓐ Ⓑ Ⓒ Ⓓ
31. Ⓐ Ⓑ Ⓒ Ⓓ
32. Ⓐ Ⓑ Ⓒ Ⓓ
33. Ⓐ Ⓑ Ⓒ Ⓓ
34. Ⓐ Ⓑ Ⓒ Ⓓ
35. Ⓐ Ⓑ Ⓒ Ⓓ
36. Ⓐ Ⓑ Ⓒ Ⓓ
37. Ⓐ Ⓑ Ⓒ Ⓓ
38. Ⓐ Ⓑ Ⓒ Ⓓ
39. Ⓐ Ⓑ Ⓒ Ⓓ
40. Ⓐ Ⓑ Ⓒ Ⓓ
41. Ⓐ Ⓑ Ⓒ Ⓓ
42. Ⓐ Ⓑ Ⓒ Ⓓ
43. Ⓐ Ⓑ Ⓒ Ⓓ
44. Ⓐ Ⓑ Ⓒ Ⓓ
45. Ⓐ Ⓑ Ⓒ Ⓓ
46. Ⓐ Ⓑ Ⓒ Ⓓ
47. Ⓐ Ⓑ Ⓒ Ⓓ
48. Ⓐ Ⓑ Ⓒ Ⓓ
49. Ⓐ Ⓑ Ⓒ Ⓓ
50. Ⓐ Ⓑ Ⓒ Ⓓ
51. Ⓐ Ⓑ Ⓒ Ⓓ
52. Ⓐ Ⓑ Ⓒ Ⓓ
53. Ⓐ Ⓑ Ⓒ Ⓓ
54. Ⓐ Ⓑ Ⓒ Ⓓ
55. Ⓐ Ⓑ Ⓒ Ⓓ
56. Ⓐ Ⓑ Ⓒ Ⓓ
57. Ⓐ Ⓑ Ⓒ Ⓓ
58. Ⓐ Ⓑ Ⓒ Ⓓ
59. Ⓐ Ⓑ Ⓒ Ⓓ
60. Ⓐ Ⓑ Ⓒ Ⓓ
61. Ⓐ Ⓑ Ⓒ Ⓓ
62. Ⓐ Ⓑ Ⓒ Ⓓ
63. Ⓐ Ⓑ Ⓒ Ⓓ
64. Ⓐ Ⓑ Ⓒ Ⓓ
65. Ⓐ Ⓑ Ⓒ Ⓓ
66. Ⓐ Ⓑ Ⓒ Ⓓ
67. Ⓐ Ⓑ Ⓒ Ⓓ
68. Ⓐ Ⓑ Ⓒ Ⓓ
69. Ⓐ Ⓑ Ⓒ Ⓓ
70. Ⓐ Ⓑ Ⓒ Ⓓ
71. Ⓐ Ⓑ Ⓒ Ⓓ
72. Ⓐ Ⓑ Ⓒ Ⓓ
73. Ⓐ Ⓑ Ⓒ Ⓓ
74. Ⓐ Ⓑ Ⓒ Ⓓ
75. Ⓐ Ⓑ Ⓒ Ⓓ
76. Ⓐ Ⓑ Ⓒ Ⓓ
77. Ⓐ Ⓑ Ⓒ Ⓓ
78. Ⓐ Ⓑ Ⓒ Ⓓ
79. Ⓐ Ⓑ Ⓒ Ⓓ
80. Ⓐ Ⓑ Ⓒ Ⓓ
81. Ⓐ Ⓑ Ⓒ Ⓓ
82. Ⓐ Ⓑ Ⓒ Ⓓ
83. Ⓐ Ⓑ Ⓒ Ⓓ
84. Ⓐ Ⓑ Ⓒ Ⓓ
85. Ⓐ Ⓑ Ⓒ Ⓓ
86. Ⓐ Ⓑ Ⓒ Ⓓ
87. Ⓐ Ⓑ Ⓒ Ⓓ
88. Ⓐ Ⓑ Ⓒ Ⓓ
89. Ⓐ Ⓑ Ⓒ Ⓓ
90. Ⓐ Ⓑ Ⓒ Ⓓ
91. Ⓐ Ⓑ Ⓒ Ⓓ
92. Ⓐ Ⓑ Ⓒ Ⓓ
93. Ⓐ Ⓑ Ⓒ Ⓓ
94. Ⓐ Ⓑ Ⓒ Ⓓ
95. Ⓐ Ⓑ Ⓒ Ⓓ
96. Ⓐ Ⓑ Ⓒ Ⓓ
97. Ⓐ Ⓑ Ⓒ Ⓓ
98. Ⓐ Ⓑ Ⓒ Ⓓ
99. Ⓐ Ⓑ Ⓒ Ⓓ
100. Ⓐ Ⓑ Ⓒ Ⓓ

Answer Sheet — Practice Test 5

1. (A) (B) (C) (D)
2. (A) (B) (C) (D)
3. (A) (B) (C) (D)
4. (A) (B) (C) (D)
5. (A) (B) (C) (D)
6. (A) (B) (C) (D)
7. (A) (B) (C) (D)
8. (A) (B) (C) (D)
9. (A) (B) (C) (D)
10. (A) (B) (C) (D)
11. (A) (B) (C) (D)
12. (A) (B) (C) (D)
13. (A) (B) (C) (D)
14. (A) (B) (C) (D)
15. (A) (B) (C) (D)
16. (A) (B) (C) (D)
17. (A) (B) (C) (D)
18. (A) (B) (C) (D)
19. (A) (B) (C) (D)
20. (A) (B) (C) (D)
21. (A) (B) (C) (D)
22. (A) (B) (C) (D)
23. (A) (B) (C) (D)
24. (A) (B) (C) (D)
25. (A) (B) (C) (D)
26. (A) (B) (C) (D)
27. (A) (B) (C) (D)
28. (A) (B) (C) (D)
29. (A) (B) (C) (D)
30. (A) (B) (C) (D)
31. (A) (B) (C) (D)
32. (A) (B) (C) (D)
33. (A) (B) (C) (D)
34. (A) (B) (C) (D)
35. (A) (B) (C) (D)
36. (A) (B) (C) (D)
37. (A) (B) (C) (D)
38. (A) (B) (C) (D)
39. (A) (B) (C) (D)
40. (A) (B) (C) (D)
41. (A) (B) (C) (D)
42. (A) (B) (C) (D)
43. (A) (B) (C) (D)
44. (A) (B) (C) (D)
45. (A) (B) (C) (D)
46. (A) (B) (C) (D)
47. (A) (B) (C) (D)
48. (A) (B) (C) (D)
49. (A) (B) (C) (D)
50. (A) (B) (C) (D)
51. (A) (B) (C) (D)
52. (A) (B) (C) (D)
53. (A) (B) (C) (D)
54. (A) (B) (C) (D)
55. (A) (B) (C) (D)
56. (A) (B) (C) (D)
57. (A) (B) (C) (D)
58. (A) (B) (C) (D)
59. (A) (B) (C) (D)
60. (A) (B) (C) (D)
61. (A) (B) (C) (D)
62. (A) (B) (C) (D)
63. (A) (B) (C) (D)
64. (A) (B) (C) (D)
65. (A) (B) (C) (D)
66. (A) (B) (C) (D)
67. (A) (B) (C) (D)
68. (A) (B) (C) (D)
69. (A) (B) (C) (D)
70. (A) (B) (C) (D)
71. (A) (B) (C) (D)
72. (A) (B) (C) (D)
73. (A) (B) (C) (D)
74. (A) (B) (C) (D)
75. (A) (B) (C) (D)
76. (A) (B) (C) (D)
77. (A) (B) (C) (D)
78. (A) (B) (C) (D)
79. (A) (B) (C) (D)
80. (A) (B) (C) (D)
81. (A) (B) (C) (D)
82. (A) (B) (C) (D)
83. (A) (B) (C) (D)
84. (A) (B) (C) (D)
85. (A) (B) (C) (D)
86. (A) (B) (C) (D)
87. (A) (B) (C) (D)
88. (A) (B) (C) (D)
89. (A) (B) (C) (D)
90. (A) (B) (C) (D)
91. (A) (B) (C) (D)
92. (A) (B) (C) (D)
93. (A) (B) (C) (D)
94. (A) (B) (C) (D)
95. (A) (B) (C) (D)
96. (A) (B) (C) (D)
97. (A) (B) (C) (D)
98. (A) (B) (C) (D)
99. (A) (B) (C) (D)
100. (A) (B) (C) (D)

Answer Sheet — Practice Test 6

1. Ⓐ Ⓑ Ⓒ Ⓓ	26. Ⓐ Ⓑ Ⓒ Ⓓ	51. Ⓐ Ⓑ Ⓒ Ⓓ	76. Ⓐ Ⓑ Ⓒ Ⓓ
2. Ⓐ Ⓑ Ⓒ Ⓓ	27. Ⓐ Ⓑ Ⓒ Ⓓ	52. Ⓐ Ⓑ Ⓒ Ⓓ	77. Ⓐ Ⓑ Ⓒ Ⓓ
3. Ⓐ Ⓑ Ⓒ Ⓓ	28. Ⓐ Ⓑ Ⓒ Ⓓ	53. Ⓐ Ⓑ Ⓒ Ⓓ	78. Ⓐ Ⓑ Ⓒ Ⓓ
4. Ⓐ Ⓑ Ⓒ Ⓓ	29. Ⓐ Ⓑ Ⓒ Ⓓ	54. Ⓐ Ⓑ Ⓒ Ⓓ	79. Ⓐ Ⓑ Ⓒ Ⓓ
5. Ⓐ Ⓑ Ⓒ Ⓓ	30. Ⓐ Ⓑ Ⓒ Ⓓ	55. Ⓐ Ⓑ Ⓒ Ⓓ	80. Ⓐ Ⓑ Ⓒ Ⓓ
6. Ⓐ Ⓑ Ⓒ Ⓓ	31. Ⓐ Ⓑ Ⓒ Ⓓ	56. Ⓐ Ⓑ Ⓒ Ⓓ	81. Ⓐ Ⓑ Ⓒ Ⓓ
7. Ⓐ Ⓑ Ⓒ Ⓓ	32. Ⓐ Ⓑ Ⓒ Ⓓ	57. Ⓐ Ⓑ Ⓒ Ⓓ	82. Ⓐ Ⓑ Ⓒ Ⓓ
8. Ⓐ Ⓑ Ⓒ Ⓓ	33. Ⓐ Ⓑ Ⓒ Ⓓ	58. Ⓐ Ⓑ Ⓒ Ⓓ	83. Ⓐ Ⓑ Ⓒ Ⓓ
9. Ⓐ Ⓑ Ⓒ Ⓓ	34. Ⓐ Ⓑ Ⓒ Ⓓ	59. Ⓐ Ⓑ Ⓒ Ⓓ	84. Ⓐ Ⓑ Ⓒ Ⓓ
10. Ⓐ Ⓑ Ⓒ Ⓓ	35. Ⓐ Ⓑ Ⓒ Ⓓ	60. Ⓐ Ⓑ Ⓒ Ⓓ	85. Ⓐ Ⓑ Ⓒ Ⓓ
11. Ⓐ Ⓑ Ⓒ Ⓓ	36. Ⓐ Ⓑ Ⓒ Ⓓ	61. Ⓐ Ⓑ Ⓒ Ⓓ	86. Ⓐ Ⓑ Ⓒ Ⓓ
12. Ⓐ Ⓑ Ⓒ Ⓓ	37. Ⓐ Ⓑ Ⓒ Ⓓ	62. Ⓐ Ⓑ Ⓒ Ⓓ	87. Ⓐ Ⓑ Ⓒ Ⓓ
13. Ⓐ Ⓑ Ⓒ Ⓓ	38. Ⓐ Ⓑ Ⓒ Ⓓ	63. Ⓐ Ⓑ Ⓒ Ⓓ	88. Ⓐ Ⓑ Ⓒ Ⓓ
14. Ⓐ Ⓑ Ⓒ Ⓓ	39. Ⓐ Ⓑ Ⓒ Ⓓ	64. Ⓐ Ⓑ Ⓒ Ⓓ	89. Ⓐ Ⓑ Ⓒ Ⓓ
15. Ⓐ Ⓑ Ⓒ Ⓓ	40. Ⓐ Ⓑ Ⓒ Ⓓ	65. Ⓐ Ⓑ Ⓒ Ⓓ	90. Ⓐ Ⓑ Ⓒ Ⓓ
16. Ⓐ Ⓑ Ⓒ Ⓓ	41. Ⓐ Ⓑ Ⓒ Ⓓ	66. Ⓐ Ⓑ Ⓒ Ⓓ	91. Ⓐ Ⓑ Ⓒ Ⓓ
17. Ⓐ Ⓑ Ⓒ Ⓓ	42. Ⓐ Ⓑ Ⓒ Ⓓ	67. Ⓐ Ⓑ Ⓒ Ⓓ	92. Ⓐ Ⓑ Ⓒ Ⓓ
18. Ⓐ Ⓑ Ⓒ Ⓓ	43. Ⓐ Ⓑ Ⓒ Ⓓ	68. Ⓐ Ⓑ Ⓒ Ⓓ	93. Ⓐ Ⓑ Ⓒ Ⓓ
19. Ⓐ Ⓑ Ⓒ Ⓓ	44. Ⓐ Ⓑ Ⓒ Ⓓ	69. Ⓐ Ⓑ Ⓒ Ⓓ	94. Ⓐ Ⓑ Ⓒ Ⓓ
20. Ⓐ Ⓑ Ⓒ Ⓓ	45. Ⓐ Ⓑ Ⓒ Ⓓ	70. Ⓐ Ⓑ Ⓒ Ⓓ	95. Ⓐ Ⓑ Ⓒ Ⓓ
21. Ⓐ Ⓑ Ⓒ Ⓓ	46. Ⓐ Ⓑ Ⓒ Ⓓ	71. Ⓐ Ⓑ Ⓒ Ⓓ	96. Ⓐ Ⓑ Ⓒ Ⓓ
22. Ⓐ Ⓑ Ⓒ Ⓓ	47. Ⓐ Ⓑ Ⓒ Ⓓ	72. Ⓐ Ⓑ Ⓒ Ⓓ	97. Ⓐ Ⓑ Ⓒ Ⓓ
23. Ⓐ Ⓑ Ⓒ Ⓓ	48. Ⓐ Ⓑ Ⓒ Ⓓ	73. Ⓐ Ⓑ Ⓒ Ⓓ	98. Ⓐ Ⓑ Ⓒ Ⓓ
24. Ⓐ Ⓑ Ⓒ Ⓓ	49. Ⓐ Ⓑ Ⓒ Ⓓ	74. Ⓐ Ⓑ Ⓒ Ⓓ	99. Ⓐ Ⓑ Ⓒ Ⓓ
25. Ⓐ Ⓑ Ⓒ Ⓓ	50. Ⓐ Ⓑ Ⓒ Ⓓ	75. Ⓐ Ⓑ Ⓒ Ⓓ	100. Ⓐ Ⓑ Ⓒ Ⓓ

Answer Sheet — Practice Test 7

1. Ⓐ Ⓑ Ⓒ Ⓓ	26. Ⓐ Ⓑ Ⓒ Ⓓ	51. Ⓐ Ⓑ Ⓒ Ⓓ	76. Ⓐ Ⓑ Ⓒ Ⓓ
2. Ⓐ Ⓑ Ⓒ Ⓓ	27. Ⓐ Ⓑ Ⓒ Ⓓ	52. Ⓐ Ⓑ Ⓒ Ⓓ	77. Ⓐ Ⓑ Ⓒ Ⓓ
3. Ⓐ Ⓑ Ⓒ Ⓓ	28. Ⓐ Ⓑ Ⓒ Ⓓ	53. Ⓐ Ⓑ Ⓒ Ⓓ	78. Ⓐ Ⓑ Ⓒ Ⓓ
4. Ⓐ Ⓑ Ⓒ Ⓓ	29. Ⓐ Ⓑ Ⓒ Ⓓ	54. Ⓐ Ⓑ Ⓒ Ⓓ	79. Ⓐ Ⓑ Ⓒ Ⓓ
5. Ⓐ Ⓑ Ⓒ Ⓓ	30. Ⓐ Ⓑ Ⓒ Ⓓ	55. Ⓐ Ⓑ Ⓒ Ⓓ	80. Ⓐ Ⓑ Ⓒ Ⓓ
6. Ⓐ Ⓑ Ⓒ Ⓓ	31. Ⓐ Ⓑ Ⓒ Ⓓ	56. Ⓐ Ⓑ Ⓒ Ⓓ	81. Ⓐ Ⓑ Ⓒ Ⓓ
7. Ⓐ Ⓑ Ⓒ Ⓓ	32. Ⓐ Ⓑ Ⓒ Ⓓ	57. Ⓐ Ⓑ Ⓒ Ⓓ	82. Ⓐ Ⓑ Ⓒ Ⓓ
8. Ⓐ Ⓑ Ⓒ Ⓓ	33. Ⓐ Ⓑ Ⓒ Ⓓ	58. Ⓐ Ⓑ Ⓒ Ⓓ	83. Ⓐ Ⓑ Ⓒ Ⓓ
9. Ⓐ Ⓑ Ⓒ Ⓓ	34. Ⓐ Ⓑ Ⓒ Ⓓ	59. Ⓐ Ⓑ Ⓒ Ⓓ	84. Ⓐ Ⓑ Ⓒ Ⓓ
10. Ⓐ Ⓑ Ⓒ Ⓓ	35. Ⓐ Ⓑ Ⓒ Ⓓ	60. Ⓐ Ⓑ Ⓒ Ⓓ	85. Ⓐ Ⓑ Ⓒ Ⓓ
11. Ⓐ Ⓑ Ⓒ Ⓓ	36. Ⓐ Ⓑ Ⓒ Ⓓ	61. Ⓐ Ⓑ Ⓒ Ⓓ	86. Ⓐ Ⓑ Ⓒ Ⓓ
12. Ⓐ Ⓑ Ⓒ Ⓓ	37. Ⓐ Ⓑ Ⓒ Ⓓ	62. Ⓐ Ⓑ Ⓒ Ⓓ	87. Ⓐ Ⓑ Ⓒ Ⓓ
13. Ⓐ Ⓑ Ⓒ Ⓓ	38. Ⓐ Ⓑ Ⓒ Ⓓ	63. Ⓐ Ⓑ Ⓒ Ⓓ	88. Ⓐ Ⓑ Ⓒ Ⓓ
14. Ⓐ Ⓑ Ⓒ Ⓓ	39. Ⓐ Ⓑ Ⓒ Ⓓ	64. Ⓐ Ⓑ Ⓒ Ⓓ	89. Ⓐ Ⓑ Ⓒ Ⓓ
15. Ⓐ Ⓑ Ⓒ Ⓓ	40. Ⓐ Ⓑ Ⓒ Ⓓ	65. Ⓐ Ⓑ Ⓒ Ⓓ	90. Ⓐ Ⓑ Ⓒ Ⓓ
16. Ⓐ Ⓑ Ⓒ Ⓓ	41. Ⓐ Ⓑ Ⓒ Ⓓ	66. Ⓐ Ⓑ Ⓒ Ⓓ	91. Ⓐ Ⓑ Ⓒ Ⓓ
17. Ⓐ Ⓑ Ⓒ Ⓓ	42. Ⓐ Ⓑ Ⓒ Ⓓ	67. Ⓐ Ⓑ Ⓒ Ⓓ	92. Ⓐ Ⓑ Ⓒ Ⓓ
18. Ⓐ Ⓑ Ⓒ Ⓓ	43. Ⓐ Ⓑ Ⓒ Ⓓ	68. Ⓐ Ⓑ Ⓒ Ⓓ	93. Ⓐ Ⓑ Ⓒ Ⓓ
19. Ⓐ Ⓑ Ⓒ Ⓓ	44. Ⓐ Ⓑ Ⓒ Ⓓ	69. Ⓐ Ⓑ Ⓒ Ⓓ	94. Ⓐ Ⓑ Ⓒ Ⓓ
20. Ⓐ Ⓑ Ⓒ Ⓓ	45. Ⓐ Ⓑ Ⓒ Ⓓ	70. Ⓐ Ⓑ Ⓒ Ⓓ	95. Ⓐ Ⓑ Ⓒ Ⓓ
21. Ⓐ Ⓑ Ⓒ Ⓓ	46. Ⓐ Ⓑ Ⓒ Ⓓ	71. Ⓐ Ⓑ Ⓒ Ⓓ	96. Ⓐ Ⓑ Ⓒ Ⓓ
22. Ⓐ Ⓑ Ⓒ Ⓓ	47. Ⓐ Ⓑ Ⓒ Ⓓ	72. Ⓐ Ⓑ Ⓒ Ⓓ	97. Ⓐ Ⓑ Ⓒ Ⓓ
23. Ⓐ Ⓑ Ⓒ Ⓓ	48. Ⓐ Ⓑ Ⓒ Ⓓ	73. Ⓐ Ⓑ Ⓒ Ⓓ	98. Ⓐ Ⓑ Ⓒ Ⓓ
24. Ⓐ Ⓑ Ⓒ Ⓓ	49. Ⓐ Ⓑ Ⓒ Ⓓ	74. Ⓐ Ⓑ Ⓒ Ⓓ	99. Ⓐ Ⓑ Ⓒ Ⓓ
25. Ⓐ Ⓑ Ⓒ Ⓓ	50. Ⓐ Ⓑ Ⓒ Ⓓ	75. Ⓐ Ⓑ Ⓒ Ⓓ	100. Ⓐ Ⓑ Ⓒ Ⓓ

Answer Sheet — Practice Test 8

1. Ⓐ Ⓑ Ⓒ Ⓓ
2. Ⓐ Ⓑ Ⓒ Ⓓ
3. Ⓐ Ⓑ Ⓒ Ⓓ
4. Ⓐ Ⓑ Ⓒ Ⓓ
5. Ⓐ Ⓑ Ⓒ Ⓓ
6. Ⓐ Ⓑ Ⓒ Ⓓ
7. Ⓐ Ⓑ Ⓒ Ⓓ
8. Ⓐ Ⓑ Ⓒ Ⓓ
9. Ⓐ Ⓑ Ⓒ Ⓓ
10. Ⓐ Ⓑ Ⓒ Ⓓ
11. Ⓐ Ⓑ Ⓒ Ⓓ
12. Ⓐ Ⓑ Ⓒ Ⓓ
13. Ⓐ Ⓑ Ⓒ Ⓓ
14. Ⓐ Ⓑ Ⓒ Ⓓ
15. Ⓐ Ⓑ Ⓒ Ⓓ
16. Ⓐ Ⓑ Ⓒ Ⓓ
17. Ⓐ Ⓑ Ⓒ Ⓓ
18. Ⓐ Ⓑ Ⓒ Ⓓ
19. Ⓐ Ⓑ Ⓒ Ⓓ
20. Ⓐ Ⓑ Ⓒ Ⓓ
21. Ⓐ Ⓑ Ⓒ Ⓓ
22. Ⓐ Ⓑ Ⓒ Ⓓ
23. Ⓐ Ⓑ Ⓒ Ⓓ
24. Ⓐ Ⓑ Ⓒ Ⓓ
25. Ⓐ Ⓑ Ⓒ Ⓓ
26. Ⓐ Ⓑ Ⓒ Ⓓ
27. Ⓐ Ⓑ Ⓒ Ⓓ
28. Ⓐ Ⓑ Ⓒ Ⓓ
29. Ⓐ Ⓑ Ⓒ Ⓓ
30. Ⓐ Ⓑ Ⓒ Ⓓ
31. Ⓐ Ⓑ Ⓒ Ⓓ
32. Ⓐ Ⓑ Ⓒ Ⓓ
33. Ⓐ Ⓑ Ⓒ Ⓓ
34. Ⓐ Ⓑ Ⓒ Ⓓ
35. Ⓐ Ⓑ Ⓒ Ⓓ
36. Ⓐ Ⓑ Ⓒ Ⓓ
37. Ⓐ Ⓑ Ⓒ Ⓓ
38. Ⓐ Ⓑ Ⓒ Ⓓ
39. Ⓐ Ⓑ Ⓒ Ⓓ
40. Ⓐ Ⓑ Ⓒ Ⓓ
41. Ⓐ Ⓑ Ⓒ Ⓓ
42. Ⓐ Ⓑ Ⓒ Ⓓ
43. Ⓐ Ⓑ Ⓒ Ⓓ
44. Ⓐ Ⓑ Ⓒ Ⓓ
45. Ⓐ Ⓑ Ⓒ Ⓓ
46. Ⓐ Ⓑ Ⓒ Ⓓ
47. Ⓐ Ⓑ Ⓒ Ⓓ
48. Ⓐ Ⓑ Ⓒ Ⓓ
49. Ⓐ Ⓑ Ⓒ Ⓓ
50. Ⓐ Ⓑ Ⓒ Ⓓ
51. Ⓐ Ⓑ Ⓒ Ⓓ
52. Ⓐ Ⓑ Ⓒ Ⓓ
53. Ⓐ Ⓑ Ⓒ Ⓓ
54. Ⓐ Ⓑ Ⓒ Ⓓ
55. Ⓐ Ⓑ Ⓒ Ⓓ
56. Ⓐ Ⓑ Ⓒ Ⓓ
57. Ⓐ Ⓑ Ⓒ Ⓓ
58. Ⓐ Ⓑ Ⓒ Ⓓ
59. Ⓐ Ⓑ Ⓒ Ⓓ
60. Ⓐ Ⓑ Ⓒ Ⓓ
61. Ⓐ Ⓑ Ⓒ Ⓓ
62. Ⓐ Ⓑ Ⓒ Ⓓ
63. Ⓐ Ⓑ Ⓒ Ⓓ
64. Ⓐ Ⓑ Ⓒ Ⓓ
65. Ⓐ Ⓑ Ⓒ Ⓓ
66. Ⓐ Ⓑ Ⓒ Ⓓ
67. Ⓐ Ⓑ Ⓒ Ⓓ
68. Ⓐ Ⓑ Ⓒ Ⓓ
69. Ⓐ Ⓑ Ⓒ Ⓓ
70. Ⓐ Ⓑ Ⓒ Ⓓ
71. Ⓐ Ⓑ Ⓒ Ⓓ
72. Ⓐ Ⓑ Ⓒ Ⓓ
73. Ⓐ Ⓑ Ⓒ Ⓓ
74. Ⓐ Ⓑ Ⓒ Ⓓ
75. Ⓐ Ⓑ Ⓒ Ⓓ
76. Ⓐ Ⓑ Ⓒ Ⓓ
77. Ⓐ Ⓑ Ⓒ Ⓓ
78. Ⓐ Ⓑ Ⓒ Ⓓ
79. Ⓐ Ⓑ Ⓒ Ⓓ
80. Ⓐ Ⓑ Ⓒ Ⓓ
81. Ⓐ Ⓑ Ⓒ Ⓓ
82. Ⓐ Ⓑ Ⓒ Ⓓ
83. Ⓐ Ⓑ Ⓒ Ⓓ
84. Ⓐ Ⓑ Ⓒ Ⓓ
85. Ⓐ Ⓑ Ⓒ Ⓓ
86. Ⓐ Ⓑ Ⓒ Ⓓ
87. Ⓐ Ⓑ Ⓒ Ⓓ
88. Ⓐ Ⓑ Ⓒ Ⓓ
89. Ⓐ Ⓑ Ⓒ Ⓓ
90. Ⓐ Ⓑ Ⓒ Ⓓ
91. Ⓐ Ⓑ Ⓒ Ⓓ
92. Ⓐ Ⓑ Ⓒ Ⓓ
93. Ⓐ Ⓑ Ⓒ Ⓓ
94. Ⓐ Ⓑ Ⓒ Ⓓ
95. Ⓐ Ⓑ Ⓒ Ⓓ
96. Ⓐ Ⓑ Ⓒ Ⓓ
97. Ⓐ Ⓑ Ⓒ Ⓓ
98. Ⓐ Ⓑ Ⓒ Ⓓ
99. Ⓐ Ⓑ Ⓒ Ⓓ
100. Ⓐ Ⓑ Ⓒ Ⓓ

Answer Sheet — Practice Test 9

1. Ⓐ Ⓑ Ⓒ Ⓓ
2. Ⓐ Ⓑ Ⓒ Ⓓ
3. Ⓐ Ⓑ Ⓒ Ⓓ
4. Ⓐ Ⓑ Ⓒ Ⓓ
5. Ⓐ Ⓑ Ⓒ Ⓓ
6. Ⓐ Ⓑ Ⓒ Ⓓ
7. Ⓐ Ⓑ Ⓒ Ⓓ
8. Ⓐ Ⓑ Ⓒ Ⓓ
9. Ⓐ Ⓑ Ⓒ Ⓓ
10. Ⓐ Ⓑ Ⓒ Ⓓ
11. Ⓐ Ⓑ Ⓒ Ⓓ
12. Ⓐ Ⓑ Ⓒ Ⓓ
13. Ⓐ Ⓑ Ⓒ Ⓓ
14. Ⓐ Ⓑ Ⓒ Ⓓ
15. Ⓐ Ⓑ Ⓒ Ⓓ
16. Ⓐ Ⓑ Ⓒ Ⓓ
17. Ⓐ Ⓑ Ⓒ Ⓓ
18. Ⓐ Ⓑ Ⓒ Ⓓ
19. Ⓐ Ⓑ Ⓒ Ⓓ
20. Ⓐ Ⓑ Ⓒ Ⓓ
21. Ⓐ Ⓑ Ⓒ Ⓓ
22. Ⓐ Ⓑ Ⓒ Ⓓ
23. Ⓐ Ⓑ Ⓒ Ⓓ
24. Ⓐ Ⓑ Ⓒ Ⓓ
25. Ⓐ Ⓑ Ⓒ Ⓓ
26. Ⓐ Ⓑ Ⓒ Ⓓ
27. Ⓐ Ⓑ Ⓒ Ⓓ
28. Ⓐ Ⓑ Ⓒ Ⓓ
29. Ⓐ Ⓑ Ⓒ Ⓓ
30. Ⓐ Ⓑ Ⓒ Ⓓ
31. Ⓐ Ⓑ Ⓒ Ⓓ
32. Ⓐ Ⓑ Ⓒ Ⓓ
33. Ⓐ Ⓑ Ⓒ Ⓓ
34. Ⓐ Ⓑ Ⓒ Ⓓ
35. Ⓐ Ⓑ Ⓒ Ⓓ
36. Ⓐ Ⓑ Ⓒ Ⓓ
37. Ⓐ Ⓑ Ⓒ Ⓓ
38. Ⓐ Ⓑ Ⓒ Ⓓ
39. Ⓐ Ⓑ Ⓒ Ⓓ
40. Ⓐ Ⓑ Ⓒ Ⓓ
41. Ⓐ Ⓑ Ⓒ Ⓓ
42. Ⓐ Ⓑ Ⓒ Ⓓ
43. Ⓐ Ⓑ Ⓒ Ⓓ
44. Ⓐ Ⓑ Ⓒ Ⓓ
45. Ⓐ Ⓑ Ⓒ Ⓓ
46. Ⓐ Ⓑ Ⓒ Ⓓ
47. Ⓐ Ⓑ Ⓒ Ⓓ
48. Ⓐ Ⓑ Ⓒ Ⓓ
49. Ⓐ Ⓑ Ⓒ Ⓓ
50. Ⓐ Ⓑ Ⓒ Ⓓ
51. Ⓐ Ⓑ Ⓒ Ⓓ
52. Ⓐ Ⓑ Ⓒ Ⓓ
53. Ⓐ Ⓑ Ⓒ Ⓓ
54. Ⓐ Ⓑ Ⓒ Ⓓ
55. Ⓐ Ⓑ Ⓒ Ⓓ
56. Ⓐ Ⓑ Ⓒ Ⓓ
57. Ⓐ Ⓑ Ⓒ Ⓓ
58. Ⓐ Ⓑ Ⓒ Ⓓ
59. Ⓐ Ⓑ Ⓒ Ⓓ
60. Ⓐ Ⓑ Ⓒ Ⓓ
61. Ⓐ Ⓑ Ⓒ Ⓓ
62. Ⓐ Ⓑ Ⓒ Ⓓ
63. Ⓐ Ⓑ Ⓒ Ⓓ
64. Ⓐ Ⓑ Ⓒ Ⓓ
65. Ⓐ Ⓑ Ⓒ Ⓓ
66. Ⓐ Ⓑ Ⓒ Ⓓ
67. Ⓐ Ⓑ Ⓒ Ⓓ
68. Ⓐ Ⓑ Ⓒ Ⓓ
69. Ⓐ Ⓑ Ⓒ Ⓓ
70. Ⓐ Ⓑ Ⓒ Ⓓ
71. Ⓐ Ⓑ Ⓒ Ⓓ
72. Ⓐ Ⓑ Ⓒ Ⓓ
73. Ⓐ Ⓑ Ⓒ Ⓓ
74. Ⓐ Ⓑ Ⓒ Ⓓ
75. Ⓐ Ⓑ Ⓒ Ⓓ
76. Ⓐ Ⓑ Ⓒ Ⓓ
77. Ⓐ Ⓑ Ⓒ Ⓓ
78. Ⓐ Ⓑ Ⓒ Ⓓ
79. Ⓐ Ⓑ Ⓒ Ⓓ
80. Ⓐ Ⓑ Ⓒ Ⓓ
81. Ⓐ Ⓑ Ⓒ Ⓓ
82. Ⓐ Ⓑ Ⓒ Ⓓ
83. Ⓐ Ⓑ Ⓒ Ⓓ
84. Ⓐ Ⓑ Ⓒ Ⓓ
85. Ⓐ Ⓑ Ⓒ Ⓓ
86. Ⓐ Ⓑ Ⓒ Ⓓ
87. Ⓐ Ⓑ Ⓒ Ⓓ
88. Ⓐ Ⓑ Ⓒ Ⓓ
89. Ⓐ Ⓑ Ⓒ Ⓓ
90. Ⓐ Ⓑ Ⓒ Ⓓ
91. Ⓐ Ⓑ Ⓒ Ⓓ
92. Ⓐ Ⓑ Ⓒ Ⓓ
93. Ⓐ Ⓑ Ⓒ Ⓓ
94. Ⓐ Ⓑ Ⓒ Ⓓ
95. Ⓐ Ⓑ Ⓒ Ⓓ
96. Ⓐ Ⓑ Ⓒ Ⓓ
97. Ⓐ Ⓑ Ⓒ Ⓓ
98. Ⓐ Ⓑ Ⓒ Ⓓ
99. Ⓐ Ⓑ Ⓒ Ⓓ
100. Ⓐ Ⓑ Ⓒ Ⓓ

Answer Sheet — Practice Test 10

1. Ⓐ Ⓑ Ⓒ Ⓓ	26. Ⓐ Ⓑ Ⓒ Ⓓ	51. Ⓐ Ⓑ Ⓒ Ⓓ	76. Ⓐ Ⓑ Ⓒ Ⓓ
2. Ⓐ Ⓑ Ⓒ Ⓓ	27. Ⓐ Ⓑ Ⓒ Ⓓ	52. Ⓐ Ⓑ Ⓒ Ⓓ	77. Ⓐ Ⓑ Ⓒ Ⓓ
3. Ⓐ Ⓑ Ⓒ Ⓓ	28. Ⓐ Ⓑ Ⓒ Ⓓ	53. Ⓐ Ⓑ Ⓒ Ⓓ	78. Ⓐ Ⓑ Ⓒ Ⓓ
4. Ⓐ Ⓑ Ⓒ Ⓓ	29. Ⓐ Ⓑ Ⓒ Ⓓ	54. Ⓐ Ⓑ Ⓒ Ⓓ	79. Ⓐ Ⓑ Ⓒ Ⓓ
5. Ⓐ Ⓑ Ⓒ Ⓓ	30. Ⓐ Ⓑ Ⓒ Ⓓ	55. Ⓐ Ⓑ Ⓒ Ⓓ	80. Ⓐ Ⓑ Ⓒ Ⓓ
6. Ⓐ Ⓑ Ⓒ Ⓓ	31. Ⓐ Ⓑ Ⓒ Ⓓ	56. Ⓐ Ⓑ Ⓒ Ⓓ	81. Ⓐ Ⓑ Ⓒ Ⓓ
7. Ⓐ Ⓑ Ⓒ Ⓓ	32. Ⓐ Ⓑ Ⓒ Ⓓ	57. Ⓐ Ⓑ Ⓒ Ⓓ	82. Ⓐ Ⓑ Ⓒ Ⓓ
8. Ⓐ Ⓑ Ⓒ Ⓓ	33. Ⓐ Ⓑ Ⓒ Ⓓ	58. Ⓐ Ⓑ Ⓒ Ⓓ	83. Ⓐ Ⓑ Ⓒ Ⓓ
9. Ⓐ Ⓑ Ⓒ Ⓓ	34. Ⓐ Ⓑ Ⓒ Ⓓ	59. Ⓐ Ⓑ Ⓒ Ⓓ	84. Ⓐ Ⓑ Ⓒ Ⓓ
10. Ⓐ Ⓑ Ⓒ Ⓓ	35. Ⓐ Ⓑ Ⓒ Ⓓ	60. Ⓐ Ⓑ Ⓒ Ⓓ	85. Ⓐ Ⓑ Ⓒ Ⓓ
11. Ⓐ Ⓑ Ⓒ Ⓓ	36. Ⓐ Ⓑ Ⓒ Ⓓ	61. Ⓐ Ⓑ Ⓒ Ⓓ	86. Ⓐ Ⓑ Ⓒ Ⓓ
12. Ⓐ Ⓑ Ⓒ Ⓓ	37. Ⓐ Ⓑ Ⓒ Ⓓ	62. Ⓐ Ⓑ Ⓒ Ⓓ	87. Ⓐ Ⓑ Ⓒ Ⓓ
13. Ⓐ Ⓑ Ⓒ Ⓓ	38. Ⓐ Ⓑ Ⓒ Ⓓ	63. Ⓐ Ⓑ Ⓒ Ⓓ	88. Ⓐ Ⓑ Ⓒ Ⓓ
14. Ⓐ Ⓑ Ⓒ Ⓓ	39. Ⓐ Ⓑ Ⓒ Ⓓ	64. Ⓐ Ⓑ Ⓒ Ⓓ	89. Ⓐ Ⓑ Ⓒ Ⓓ
15. Ⓐ Ⓑ Ⓒ Ⓓ	40. Ⓐ Ⓑ Ⓒ Ⓓ	65. Ⓐ Ⓑ Ⓒ Ⓓ	90. Ⓐ Ⓑ Ⓒ Ⓓ
16. Ⓐ Ⓑ Ⓒ Ⓓ	41. Ⓐ Ⓑ Ⓒ Ⓓ	66. Ⓐ Ⓑ Ⓒ Ⓓ	91. Ⓐ Ⓑ Ⓒ Ⓓ
17. Ⓐ Ⓑ Ⓒ Ⓓ	42. Ⓐ Ⓑ Ⓒ Ⓓ	67. Ⓐ Ⓑ Ⓒ Ⓓ	92. Ⓐ Ⓑ Ⓒ Ⓓ
18. Ⓐ Ⓑ Ⓒ Ⓓ	43. Ⓐ Ⓑ Ⓒ Ⓓ	68. Ⓐ Ⓑ Ⓒ Ⓓ	93. Ⓐ Ⓑ Ⓒ Ⓓ
19. Ⓐ Ⓑ Ⓒ Ⓓ	44. Ⓐ Ⓑ Ⓒ Ⓓ	69. Ⓐ Ⓑ Ⓒ Ⓓ	94. Ⓐ Ⓑ Ⓒ Ⓓ
20. Ⓐ Ⓑ Ⓒ Ⓓ	45. Ⓐ Ⓑ Ⓒ Ⓓ	70. Ⓐ Ⓑ Ⓒ Ⓓ	95. Ⓐ Ⓑ Ⓒ Ⓓ
21. Ⓐ Ⓑ Ⓒ Ⓓ	46. Ⓐ Ⓑ Ⓒ Ⓓ	71. Ⓐ Ⓑ Ⓒ Ⓓ	96. Ⓐ Ⓑ Ⓒ Ⓓ
22. Ⓐ Ⓑ Ⓒ Ⓓ	47. Ⓐ Ⓑ Ⓒ Ⓓ	72. Ⓐ Ⓑ Ⓒ Ⓓ	97. Ⓐ Ⓑ Ⓒ Ⓓ
23. Ⓐ Ⓑ Ⓒ Ⓓ	48. Ⓐ Ⓑ Ⓒ Ⓓ	73. Ⓐ Ⓑ Ⓒ Ⓓ	98. Ⓐ Ⓑ Ⓒ Ⓓ
24. Ⓐ Ⓑ Ⓒ Ⓓ	49. Ⓐ Ⓑ Ⓒ Ⓓ	74. Ⓐ Ⓑ Ⓒ Ⓓ	99. Ⓐ Ⓑ Ⓒ Ⓓ
25. Ⓐ Ⓑ Ⓒ Ⓓ	50. Ⓐ Ⓑ Ⓒ Ⓓ	75. Ⓐ Ⓑ Ⓒ Ⓓ	100. Ⓐ Ⓑ Ⓒ Ⓓ